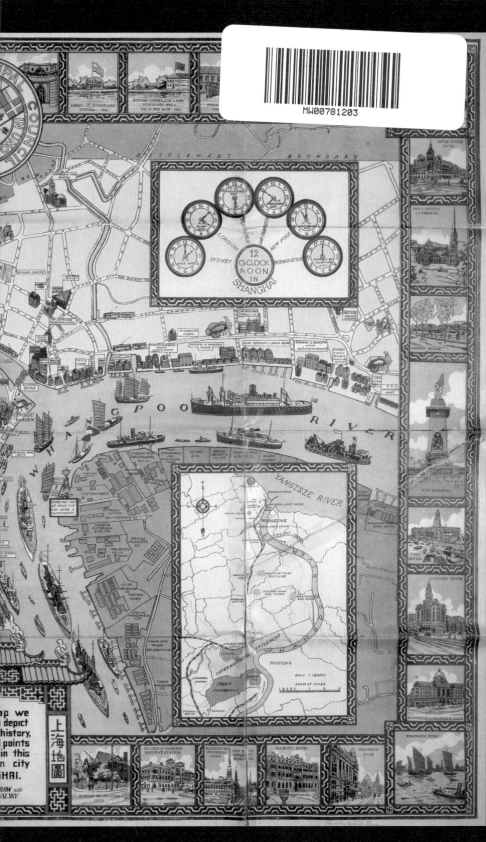

Carl Crow -
A Tough Old China Hand

Hong Kong University Press thanks Xu Bing for writing the Press's name in his Square Word Calligraphy for the covers of its books. For further information, see p. iv.

"Look at the means which a man employs, consider his motives, observe his pleasures. A man simply cannot conceal himself."

Confucius

"Life itself. Nothing more intensely living can be imagined."

Aldous Huxley on Shanghai in 1926

"Never let the truth get in the way of a good story."

Anonymous

For Lisa (Xu Ni)

Carl Crow -
A Tough Old China Hand

*The Life, Times, and Adventures of
an American in Shanghai*

Paul French

香港大學出版社
HONG KONG UNIVERSITY PRESS

Hong Kong University Press
14/F Hing Wai Centre
7 Tin Wan Praya Road
Aberdeen
Hong Kong

First published 2006
Reprinted 2007

ISBN-13: 978-962-209-802-2
ISBN-10: 962-209-802-9

British Library Cataloguing-in-Publication Data
A catalogue record for this book is available from the British Library.

Secure On-line Ordering
http://www.hkupress.org

Printed and bound by Pre-Press Limited, Hong Kong, China.

Hong Kong University Press is honoured that Xu Bing, whose art
explores the complex themes of language across cultures, has written
the Press's name in his Square Word Calligraphy. This signals our
commitment to cross-cultural thinking and the distinctive nature of
our English-language books published in China.

"At first glance, Square Word Calligraphy appears to be nothing more
unusual than Chinese characters, but in fact it is a new way of rendering
English words in the format of a square so they resemble Chinese
characters. Chinese viewers expect to be able to read Square Word
Calligraphy but cannot. Western viewers, however are surprised to find
they can read it. Delight erupts when meaning is unexpectedly revealed."
— Britta Erickson, *The Art of Xu Bing*

Contents

Names and Spelling

To avoid confusing readers, as far as possible Chinese names for places in this book are rendered in pinyin for the sake of clarity and consistency. Any other method is too problematic. Crow himself switched spellings throughout his writings, confusing matters further. As the writer, and one time Shanghailander, Emily Hahn once commented when tackling the question of rendering Chinese into English, "This writer has done her best but knows it is not good enough, and meekly bends her head before the inevitable storm."

Chinese names are used with the family name indicated first followed by their patronymic, as is standard in China, e.g. Soong Ching-ling, Soong Mei-ling and Soong Ai-ling all being members of the Soong family. Some exceptions include those that are spelled in various ways but are well known to readers, such as Sun Yat-sen (rather than Sun Zhongshan). Where they were commonly used, the English names adopted by Chinese are included and where people may be better or alternatively known by other names these are included as endnotes.

Money

All figures quoted in the text are as quoted at the time.

Like many Shanghailanders at the time, Carl Crow used the Mexican dollar, for many years the currency most frequently used by foreigners and sometimes referred to as the Dollar Mex. According to Crow, the eagle-headed Mexican dollar was introduced "To avoid carrying around five to ten pound lumps of silver [*taels*] as spending money, ... and it remains the standard currency of most ports ... Local foreign banks issue paper notes payable in Mexican dollars and prices at hotels and stores are quoted in them." The value of the Dollar Mex varied from slightly more than a US silver dollar to about 50 percent of the US dollar's value. At the same time, Chinese silver *taels* and other denominations also circulated, including US dollars, British pounds and Indian rupees, among others. *Tael* is originally a word from Malay pidgin that came to mean one ounce of Chinese silver.

Acknowledgments

In the late 1990s I was the co-author of a guide to Asian consumers called *One Billion Shoppers*. The title was primarily designed to grab the attention of book browsers but was also a sideways tribute to Carl Crow whose *Four Hundred Million Customers* had been a major inspiration despite its being 60 years old. Crow's writing about China still appeared fresh despite the tumultuous Chinese half-century that had passed in the interim. During the writing of this book, many people told me they had read and been inspired by Crow over the years and wanted to know more about China, Shanghai and, in particular, Carl. They are the real reason for this book.

However, some people must be mentioned by name. My partner at Access Asia and occasional co-author Matthew Crabbe was supportive and giving of his time. In Shanghai Tess Johnston and Lynn Pan, two of the city's most thorough chroniclers, were obvious first stops and both were helpful and encouraging from the start. Likewise Patrick Cranley at the Shanghai Historic House Association was an early adopter of my Crow project and gave me a platform to try to resurrect Crow to modern day Shanghailanders, as did Michelle Garnaut and Tina Kanagaratnam at M-on-the-Bund; Tania Matthews and Linda Hoenig of the Shanghai Ex-Patriate Association; Anne-Cecile Noique; and the Shanghai Foreign Correspondents' Club.

Robin Bordie and Andy Rothman enthusiastically pitched in with help when I was stuck on how to find the time and resources to access Crow's archive far away from Shanghai in Missouri. Robin was kind enough to persuade her father John Bordie to visit the archive to help work out what the author Nicholas Shakespeare once described as "seeking from the dead what they did not reveal in life." John was a tenacious master at patching together fragments of information. Dennis George Crow, Carl's great-nephew, was also immediately helpful and shed light on many areas of his esteemed ancestor's life and times as well as being generous with family records and his superb collection of photographs of old China (www.dennisgeorgecrow.com). Without John and Dennis's efforts, this book would have been simply impossible.

Clinton Dines, Peter Gordon, John Van Fleet, Mark O'Neill, Joe Studwell and Chris Torrens were also all friends who urged me to get on and finish the book and helped me progress in various ways. Tani E. Barlow at the University of Washington and Ellen Johnston Laing of the University of Michigan were both extremely helpful in understanding Carl Crow's adventures in the advertising business. Thanks are also due to Colin Day and his team at the Hong Kong University Press for adopting this project so wholeheartedly and making many helpful criticisms along the way.

The Carl Crow archive at the University of Missouri turned out to be a treasure trove. In Missouri, thanks must go to William Stoltz of the Western Historical Manuscript Collection at the University of Missouri and Laurel Boeckman of the State Historical Society of Missouri. Also Michael Heist at Princeton University Library's Department of Rare Books and Special Collections filled several gaps for me. The US Department of Justice and the Federal Bureau of Investigation should also be thanked for supplying a range of documents on Crow under the Freedom of Information/Privacy Acts.

Yet again, Lisa (Xu Ni) was ever patient with the whole project despite the inevitable late dinners, lost weekends and obsessive behavior on the author's part.

Illustration Credits

The photographs on pages 2, 8 and 76 as well as the illustration on page 176 are courtesy of Dennis George Crow. The photograph on page 29 is used by permission of the State Historical Society of Missouri, Columbia, Missouri. The photographs on pages 117 and 122 are from the John Benjamin Powell Papers, 1910–1952 courtesy of the Western Historical Manuscript Collection–Columbia, Missouri. The photograph on page 224 is from the Carl Crow Papers, 1913–1945 courtesy of the Western Historical Manuscript Collection–Columbia, Missouri. The advertisement reproduced on page 97 is reproduced through the courtesy of Professor Tani E. Barlow, whose research on the emergence of the "sexy modern girl icon" in the Shanghai advertising markets of the 1920s and 1930s is forthcoming. The illustrations on pages 18 and 106 are from the author's collection as is the map that forms the endpaper.

The cartoon illustrations in this book are by the White Russian Shanghai cartoonist Sapajou – Georgii Avksentievich Sapojnikoff. The illustrations used are from Carl Crow's *Four Hundred Million Customers* (Harper & Brothers, New York, 1937); D. De Martel & L. De Hoyer, *Silhouettes of Peking* (China Booksellers Ltd, Peking, 1926); and Shamus A'Rabbitt's *Ballads of the East* (A. R. Hager, Shanghai, 1937).

INTRODUCTION

A Quarter Century in China

Strange Odors of Camphor Wood and Hot Peanut Oil

When Carl Crow stepped onto the shore of Shanghai's Bund in the summer of 1911, he stepped into a China that was on the cusp of a period of massive upheaval and change. Shanghai was also a city on the verge of becoming the most modern and Westernized city in Asia. As a guidebook to the city claimed:

> High hats and low necks; long tails and short knickers; inebriates and slumming puritans. Wine, women and song. Whoopee! The throb of the jungle tom-tom; the symphony of lust; the music of a hundred orchestras; the shuffling of feet; the rhythm of abandon; the hot smoke of desire under the floodlights; it's all fun.[1]

In August 1911 Shanghai was not quite yet the Paris of the East, the Whore of Asia or the Capital of the Tycoons. All that was to come later. When Crow arrived, Shanghai was a small settlement largely dominated by the British and their merchant trading firms. It was clustered along the banks of the Huang Pu

River and governed by the strange system of extraterritoriality that put foreigners beyond the reach of Chinese justice and subject to penalties only from their own courts and judges. The Shanghai Municipal Council (SMC) represented the 14 powers with an interest in the city and ran the International Settlement. Despite the SMC's motto, *Omnia Juncta in Uno* ("All Joined in One"), in reality the Council was dominated by the British in 1911. The French maintained their concession separately. At most, the International Settlement and Frenchtown covered 12 square miles with the Chinese-administered portion of the city covering a further eight. Shanghai was emerging as a modern metropolis and the dominant trading city of the Far East but the jazz, the art deco skyscrapers, the famous nightlife, the booming economy and even the majestic Bund that became so recognizable internationally in the 1930s were not yet in place.

Carl Crow came to Shanghai to help establish a new newspaper in the city but ended up staying a quarter of a century before being forced to leave as the Japanese launched their attack on Shanghai in 1937. Unlike most foreigners arriving in Shanghai at the time, he didn't come to build empire or out of any particular interest in China; he came as a young American keen to make his fortune, his name and a success of himself. He was willing to admit that when he first moved to China he found the "huge masses of humanity" somewhat terrifying yet strangely fascinating. He noted:

The Shanghai Bund 1913. When Crow arrived the Bund was still developing. The grand edifices that were to define the Shanghai waterfront were still to come.

I will never forget the first stroll I ever took in a Chinese city. It was the second day of my arrival in Shanghai and I started out alone to explore the place, wandering about on an aimless route. Soon I found myself on a crowded street with no English signs and no white faces – there was no one who even remotely resembled the people with whom I had lived from the time of my birth. It was a July day and many of the small tradesmen were sitting in front of their shops stripped to the waist, comfortably fanning their fat stomachs. Everywhere I looked there were people, people, people – strange people – all of whom seemed to be converging on me. The air was full of strange odors of camphor wood and hot peanut oil.[2]

Thirty years later, when he had returned to America, Crow was to remark that the smells of camphor and peanut oil would make him homesick for Shanghai, but in 1911 he had had his first encounter with China and the strange language, smells and street cries had all seemed overwhelmingly foreign. At that time, Crow was just another Shanghai sojourner, not yet an Old China Hand, and he didn't aim to be one; rather, he was worried about getting lost and never finding his hotel again. Crow also had to admit that in 1911 memories of the murderous Boxer Rebellion of 1900 were still quite fresh in the minds of foreigners arriving in China and he was not a little nervous at the adventure he had embarked upon.

Like other Americans before him and even more that followed, Crow arrived with the idea that China would be both a fascinating place to live in and somewhere to make money. The voyage to China had not been overly eventful. Westbound passages across the Pacific to Shanghai were usually regarded as rather dismal as most of the passengers were returning from home leave to jobs they didn't much care for on the China coast. He remembered that the ship stewards referred to the westbound voyage from the US as "bringing back the empties", while the eastbound voyage from China to the US was a far livelier affair with men and women embarking on home leave and feeling rich with the boat hosting "... many parties of the kind that used to be called 'carousals'."[3] The crew preferred the eastward voyage, as the tips were better too.

Still, Crow got an early taste of what brought the ambitious, the curious and the desperate to Shanghai in those early years. Onboard he had met a Canadian of about the same age who had already been successful in running a chain of restaurants in Calgary which catered for the poor and was convinced that China was where a string of cheap restaurants could really make a fortune. Crow was later to write that many came with unrealistic dreams. It seems this fellow passenger was Crow's first encounter with the species as his plans failed due to his overestimating the potential market and he ended up penniless and reduced to dealing opium to survive. As the ship slipped into the headwaters of the mighty Yangtze and ploughed up the muddy brown Huang Pu towards the Bund, he couldn't help wondering whether he too was embarking on an unrealistic dream of success in the Far East.

An Outbreak of Measles

Shanghai (which, rather unromantically, means "by the sea") was the major port of the Orient at a time when Hong Kong and Singapore remained somewhat drab and dreary backwaters. Young clerks sent out from England to the Far East dreaded a Hong Kong posting and were relieved if they were assigned to Shanghai. Hong Kong was a naval base and known for its pestilential climate; and Singapore was a steaming hot port with few attractions. Shanghai was different. Already the city's fame was starting to spread around the world as, alternatively, the Paris of the East or the Whore of the Orient depending on your viewpoint and tastes. In 1911 Shanghai was still a young and growing city. Until the early 1800s it had been no more than a small village 17 miles from the Yangtze River estuary. It was a flat, largely barren area prone to flooding. However, its strategic position afforded it the opportunity of commanding all trade entering the gateway of the Yangtze that flowed through China all the way to Sichuan and on to Tibet and offered the prospect of opening up the massive interior of China to foreign trade.

Opium and foreigners were crucial to Shanghai's emergence as a world city – Crow called them an "outbreak of measles." The First Opium War of 1839 changed the fortunes of the village of Shanghai forever. After the modern, well-equipped British Royal Navy made short work of the ancient battleships of the Qing dynasty, the various treaty ports granted to the British as part of the post-war settlement included Shanghai. Captain George Balfour arrived to take up the post of first resident British Consul with a translator, a surgeon and a clerk. Balfour selected the best location for the Royal Navy's anchorage and sited the new British Concession slightly north of the walled Chinese town. With control of Shanghai, the British had control of the Yangtze delta, the silk capital of Suzhou and the Grand Canal that linked Eastern China to Beijing. Shanghai was rapidly to become the main port of departure for Chinese goods to Europe and America, and also the major point at which goods, and people, from Europe and America flowed into China.

Before long, the British Concession was joined by an American Concession on the north side of Suzhou Creek (the two merged to become the International Settlement in 1863), while the French developed their own separate concession further along the riverfront. Americans soon started arriving in Shanghai, initially as missionaries rather than businessmen. The waterfront began to develop and take shape, eventually emerging as the raised Bund with some of the most impressive and grand buildings in the Far East. Soon Shanghai's freebooting style of capitalism attracted the business community as well as numerous criminals, drifters, swindlers, refugees – and, also, Carl Crow.

By 1911 business in Shanghai was prospering and people were doing well which was more than could be said for the Manchu-run dynasty that governed China. The city was home to approximately one million people, less than 20,000 of whom were foreigners. The Opium Wars had shown the weakness of the Chinese military, and the restless and more libertarian southern China was increasingly slipping from their control. The imperial government, controlled by the Empress Dowager Ci Xi, had stubbornly resisted any Japanese Meiji-style reforms, suppressed the merchant class and refused to adapt Western technology to strengthen China. In 1851, the Taiping Rebellion had broken out led by Hong Xiuquan, a self-proclaimed mystic who believed he was the younger brother of Jesus. Though ahead of its time in many ways, the Taiping believed in Old Testament eye-for-an-eye violence: they left 20 to 30 million Chinese dead and were only prevented from seizing Shanghai by a hastily-convened mercenary force which defended the city. The Taiping Heavenly Kingdom was never finally created and died out in 1864, but the destabilizing influence that the Taiping represented continued to plague the Qing dynasty. At the turn of the century, the forces of the Boxer Rebellion had once again threatened the foreign community and the Qing dynasty.

As Crow's ship docked in Shanghai, the omens were not good. The Yangtze had just suffered the worst flood in living memory, creating a refugee problem and threatening to ruin the entire crop of the Yangtze delta for the year. He admitted that he found the city a dirty place in these years before Shanghai's great building boom when its skyscraper hotels, mansions and the magnificent Bund were to rise. Things were to change, but the shock for the newly-arrived Crow was real. Eventually he was to see the changes wrought by the new Nationalist government and switched his opinion to pondering how a people could maintain such high standards of cleanliness in the face of such poverty and overcrowding.

Carl Crow once described himself as one of the "tough Old China Hands" that lived in Shanghai. This was probably not quite true. Between the wars, the China Hands (or, as they were then often referred to, "Orientalists") of Shanghai were more likely to be confirmed imperialists and colonialists than friends of China or Dr. Sun Yat-sen's new Nationalist government that overthrew the Qing in 1911. They were often far from tough and mostly rarely ventured outside the relative safety of Shanghai's International Settlement, protected, as they were, by the extraterritoriality laws. Crow repeatedly butted heads with the older generation of China Hands whose general belief was that the Middle Kingdom had gone to the dogs centuries before and that any new government was just a temporary aberration. The things to do, they said, were: maintain a watching brief on the leaders of the country; keep the wheels of commerce turning while preserving the rights and privileges of the Great Powers in China; and, most of all, continue to make money. During his time in China, Crow was accused of being too sympathetic to the Chinese, opposed to foreign interests, and overly anti-Japanese – and of the unforgivable sin of having "gone native". These were all meant as insults, but Crow usually decided to accept them as compliments.

But all of this was in the future. For now, Crow was a Griffin – a newcomer to the China Coast. He didn't know what to expect: whether he would be successful and make money or sail home a bankrupt; and whether he would survive and thrive or find China too much and opt to scurry back to a regular pay cheque from a provincial American newspaper. It was all for the taking and, if nothing else, Crow was determined from the start that the experience – long, short or something in between – should be fun and educational. A quarter of a century later he was convinced that making that first trip had been the best decision he ever made. He never lost his fascination with China and the Chinese, declaring in 1937 that "I am as keenly interested in them [*the Chinese*] today as I was when I was thrilled by my first ricksha ride, a quarter of a century ago."[4] Throughout his China years, Crow always stuck to his early credo – to have fun. More than 30 years after stepping ashore in China for the first time, he wrote: "It is to be hoped that manufacturers had a lot of fun out of their ventures because they didn't make much money."[5]

Crow was not typical of the foreigners who came to Shanghai in the first half of the twentieth century. He quickly developed a love of China and a sympathy for the Chinese, while most opted to stay aloof and belittle the country and its people out of a false sense of superiority. However, like all the other foreigners who lived on the China coast, Crow originally came from somewhere else.

1

From the Mid-West to the China Coast

Poor But Daring

Before he arrived in Shanghai feeling nervous, uncertain and wondering what would become of him, Crow had made his way from the wilds of Missouri to the shores of China. Even before he sailed, his gift for telling a story and the Crow family's general tendency to have kissed the Blarney Stone was already deeply embedded.

Herbert Carl Crow was born in the town of Highland, Missouri, on September 26, 1883, 79 years after Lewis and Clark had first charted the Missouri territory. He was the son of George Washington Crow, born on July 4, 1857 and Elvira Jane Sharrock-Crow who was just 19 when Carl was born. Carl's brother, Leslie Ray, was born in 1886 and his sister Lora in 1889, followed by a second sister Roma. His father, who was a country schoolteacher and occasional college lecturer, made a reasonable living. Young Herbert Carl was always known simply as "Carl." The family home was in Highland, a town in largely rural Perry County and a community too small to warrant an inclusion in the 1883 *Missouri State Gazetteer and Business Directory.*

Carl (left) and his brother Leslie Ray photographed in a Missouri photo studio shortly before he left for China.

Elvira Sharrock-Crow, Carl's mother photographed around 1940.

George Washington Crow, Carl's father photographed in the 1870s.

Crow traced his own roots back to England and Ireland. A certain James Sharrock was born in England in 1750, probably in the county of Lancashire. Sharrocks is a common name there, derived from Shorrock's Green, then a small village about four miles from the town of Blackburn and once well known for its locally-produced cheese. Thus the original Sharrock lived at or near Shorrock's Green and at some point the *o* became an *a*. That James wished to leave England and try his luck in the new world was not overly surprising. The stretch of country between Lancashire across to the west coast and Liverpool was at the center of England's industrial revolution; and while James may have been born into a small rural village, the area around him was convulsed by the shift from an agrarian economy to being a major concentration of William Blake's "dark Satanic mills." Many contemporaries of James decided that a life of enclosed drudgery and wage slavery in the new factories was not for them and opted to head for pastures new.

James died in America at 76 leaving seven surviving children, one of whom, Timothy, was 51 when his father died. Timothy married and had 10 children. His second son, also called Timothy, married and also had 10 children, one of whom was Carl's grandfather who himself went on to have eight children. James Sharrock had landed in New York and with countless others moved gradually westwards. The Sharrocks were devout and church-going Methodists who worked largely as farmers and teachers, with not a few lay preachers among them. Methodism was strong in Missouri at the time as the major protestant sect along with the Lutherans and the Baptists.

The Crows came to America through a very different route which was shrouded in more mystery and a source of much family legend. Crow believed his family had come from Ireland where an ancestor, William Crowe, had once been an official in Cromwell's administration in Dublin and had witnessed the arrival of the New Model Army in Kilkenny, the nominal capital of the Catholic Confederacy at the time, in March 1650. At some point, a member of the Crowe family disgraced himself and, forced to leave Ireland, sailed for a new life, free of shame, in America. Somewhere on the journey from Ireland to America, the *e* got lost. To Crow, the most important things about his Irish heritage were that this side of the family gave him his raven hair and slightly darker skin tone as well as his lifelong gift, one that ran in the family, of being able to tell a good story.

It certainly seems that both the Crows and the Sharrocks were independently-minded folk – somewhat reclusive, pioneer types who sought a better and freer life in America. Commenting on this generation in American history, Crow said: "… all Americans were poor and were made daring by the conviction that they were destined to become wealthy."[1] He talked of a great uncle who had moved west from Ohio to Missouri before finding the state too crowded (this being the overcrowding of Missouri in the early 1800s) and deciding to move south again to relatively deserted Eastern Texas. However, his great uncle apparently felt hemmed in when another man bought some adjacent land and built a house three miles away, forcing the highly claustrophobic Crow ancestor to relocate to West Texas where for 10 years he had no neighbour closer than 10 miles. In his wanderings around the Far East, Carl clearly inherited the pioneering gene more than the reclusive gene. He wrote that, at each stop before he moved on, his great uncle declared the place "just too damned crowded."[2]

The family never lost that trait so clearly apparent in their great uncle's desire for peace and privacy. Over the decades, they became gradually urbanized and conformed to modern society by moving into apartment buildings and houses on neatly laid-out streets, but the yearning for a sort of glorious isolation never entirely left the Crows. By the time he got to Shanghai, Carl's isolationist traits seemed not to have completely deserted him either, and later he returned to America to briefly live the life of a fruit rancher. While in China, he always talked about renting a country villa or a place in one of the hill retreats near Shanghai; and even as late as the summer of 1937, China's last peaceful summer before the war, he was considering a second home in the less crowded Chinese seaside resort town of Qingdao.

Carl was born into firm mid-western pioneer traditions. Missouri, originally part of the Louisiana Purchase, had only been admitted as a state 62 years before he was born in August 1821 as part of the Missouri Compromise. Missouri was known then as the "Gateway to the West," serving as a departure point for settlers and containing both the major travel points of the Mississippi and Missouri rivers. During the American Civil War (1861–65), Missouri was split in half with some parts adhering to the Union and others seceding with the southern states. Brother had fought brother in Missouri.

Staunch Methodism largely defined the family. Crow himself, though a regular Sunday school attendee as a child, was not later noticeably religiously observant; indeed he came to find organized religion largely silly. He came to view preachers and ministers in early America as involved in just another form of marketing – ideas and beliefs rather than products. In his 1943 history of the rise of America's commercial system, *The Great American Customer*, he likened the life of the itinerant preacher to that of the frontier peddler who toured the remote farms with a dazzling array of merchandise. However, as Crow observed, while the peddler with his new goods, gossip and news of the outside world was sure of a welcome everywhere, the itinerant preacher "… was sure of a welcome only in the homes of those of his own sect."[3] From a young age, Carl sought to escape the rural and religious confines of Highland and make his own way in the world.

He received a relatively good basic education at a variety of country schools that were strong on morality and religion, and this was reinforced by his extended and generally pious family. The bulk of his education involved learning by rote and memorizing poetry and rhymes. Crow hated all this memorizing of works, such as William Cullen Bryant's *Thanatopsis* which he could still remember 50 years later and was at the time a set text for American schoolchildren. Needless to say, as someone who would later make his living with words – either writing for newspapers, publishing books or composing advertising copy – literature and poetry appealed to him. He recalled enjoying immensely reading stories of romance and adventure in far-flung places.

The Crows were not what would have been described as desperately poor in the last decades of nineteenth century Missouri, but they were still fairly remote from the home comforts of the more sophisticated east coast. Talking later about the problems of finding suitable baths and toilets in China during his travels, he commented: "I flatter myself that I am not so hidebound as others may be, for I was born in a community where the possession of a privy was something of a social distinction, and bathtubs were unknown."[4] He recalled that the family was able to maintain a level of decency but anything that incurred extra labor was scorned. He remembered his mother and her friends discussing a man who lived in the county seat 20 miles away who was reputed to change his shirt daily. The women agreed that it must be a very "mean and selfish man who would put his wife to such an unnecessary lot of washing and ironing just to gratify a silly whim."[5]

The America that Crow was born into was one in a state of change. The country was industrializing rapidly. In 1883, the year of Carl's birth, Thomas Edison installed the first electric lighting system using overhead wires in Roselle, New Jersey; and in May of the same year, New York opened the Brooklyn Bridge to traffic after 14 years of construction. In 1883, as a reflection of the growth of industry and commerce in the country, Alabama had become the first state to enact an anti-trust law. Culturally, America was changing too as the new waves of immigration started to create a peculiarly indigenous American culture. In 1883, the first vaudeville theatre opened in Boston, Massachusetts, while Mark Twain, the bard of America's rural idyll, published his classic *Life on the Mississippi.*

Crow's father died in 1899 when Carl was just 16, after which he was forced to leave school to become a printer's apprentice. He worked as a journeyman printer jobbing across Missouri for several years, including spending the summer of 1902 as the typesetter on the *Lead Belt News* in Flat River, Missouri. Crow was the only employee as the editor/owner of the paper, Bill Lewis, wrote the day's edition while Carl typeset and printed it. He was paid 50 cents a week and allowed to sleep in the office. He was able to pick up some extra money on the side by printing leaflets for traveling preachers. In return for securing this work, he promised to attend one preacher's sermon and recalled: "I went and found no one but the preacher and the janitor, and the janitor didn't wait for the sermon. When it became apparent that no one else was coming, he preached the whole sermon to me, but he didn't take up a collection."[6]

When he was just 19, he borrowed some money and founded his own weekly newspaper. It was a success and, having sold the paper for a profit in 1906, he used the money to attend Carleton College, a private liberal arts school in Northfield, Minnesota, which had been founded in 1866 as an independent and highly selective institution. Crow then decided to continue his studies nearer home at the University of Missouri. He was able to gain admission to Carleton partly due to the fact that his father had briefly been on the college's faculty. His short time in Northfield saw him living in the then pioneer town that served a far-flung agricultural community on the banks of the Cannon River and which had only come into being in the mid-nineteenth century.

A friend who proved less than trustworthy absconded with Crow's life savings and so he ended up arriving at the University of Missouri with just $7 in his pocket. This unexpected lack of funds meant that Crow was forced to work his way through college. He used his skills as a printer to make some money and also acted as a reporter and editor for the *Columbia-Missouri Herald* newspaper, while also at times serving as a stringer for a variety of other regional American papers, including *The Chicago Tribune*, *The St. Louis Post-Dispatch*, and *The Kansas City Star*. This was basic cub reporting, while writing for the *Missourian* was essentially writing for his local newspaper as it was based in Columbia and had only been established in 1908.

Missouri University had a tradition of encouraging journalism as a formal discipline and in 1908 established the first specialized department for the training of journalists under Dean Walter Williams. From its establishment, the School was controversial, with many journalists arguing that the job of writing for newspapers couldn't be taught in an academic setting and that long apprenticeships in the field were a better training ground than a classroom. Indeed, opposition had been so strong that the Missouri State Senate had resoundingly defeated a bill in 1895 requesting that a Chair of Journalism be established and also refused permission for the University to grant degrees in journalism. It was Walter Williams, the editor of the *Columbia-Missouri Herald* and a university curator, with the support of the Missouri Press Association, who managed to change the politicians' minds and finally got the School established.

Williams soon built the School up into a center of excellence for journalistic training and became recognized as an international authority on journalism in his own right. He was appointed a Fellow of the Kahn Foundation for Foreign Travel of American Teachers in 1913 and, in 1914, traveled the world visiting newspaper plants and offices. In 1915, he became the Director of the International Press Congress in San Francisco and also the first-ever President of the grandly named Press Congress of the World. He also headed the American Association of Schools and Departments of Journalism in 1916 and wrote several books on the trade that became standard texts in most of the new journalism schools that began to appear across America following Missouri's success.[7]

Williams also traveled to the Far East on a mission for the US government, visiting Russia, China and Japan in late 1918 and early 1919, after which he returned to the US and embarked on a tour across the country lecturing about the state of development of Asia's newspaper industry.[8] Before all that, he had encouraged the young Carl to enrol as a student at the University of Missouri.

The Murder Beat, Skewered Bulls and Throat-slitting Chinese

The cash-strapped Crow didn't last long at Missouri University, leaving after less than a year and without graduating. Paid newspaper work took precedence over his studies to the extent that he quit to become a partner of Williams' in the *Columbia-Missouri Herald*. In reality, Crow had barely done anything at Missouri; his college records revealed that he only attended 12 hours of lectures, achieved no grades whatsoever and was recorded as having "left class."[9]

From Missouri Crow eventually headed south in 1909 to work on the *Fort Worth Star-Telegram*. In Fort Worth he learned to play a mean game of poker and drink hard liquor, and visited the bayous of Texas. As the police reporter, he covered many murder trials and even witnessed one fatal gun battle. Later, when working nights as the city editor of the *China Press* in Shanghai, Crow would remember his Fort Worth days with affection. When strong local news stories were lacking in Shanghai and he was wondering what to fill his front page with, Crow would wistfully daydream of his Texan sojourn and the steady and reliable stream of local homicides and robberies that guaranteed the paper no lack of good attention-grabbing local news.

He was not earning much as the *Star-Telegram's* police reporter but he was learning the profession. A series of freelance articles he wrote for some trade magazines while sitting around waiting for a crime to be committed or a jury to make a decision gave him some money and he visited Mexico on his first trip abroad. Ever on the look-out for stories he could sell to trade publications, Crow visited the isthmus of Tehuantepec where he noted the traditional native Mexican female headdress, a white veil with ribbons and lace trimming.

Crow picked up a story from a Colorado mining engineer working in Tehuantepec that the origin of this exotic headdress went back to when a French frigate had been shipwrecked off the coast en-route to Buenos Aires. The natives, after drinking all the brandy and wine aboard, were left with a consignment of children's dresses originally destined for a department store in the Argentine capital. They had no use for the dresses until one of the native women put the little bodice on her head and the skirt fell down the back. This started a new fashion that lasted until the lucky salvager of the shipwrecked packing case ran out of dresses. Afterwards a German salesman who happened upon Tehuantepec received an order for children's dresses to be worn as headdresses. The German instructed his factory in Hamburg to start manufacturing immediately for shipment to the Mexican coast. Crow repeated this apocryphal story in an article for a Chicago magazine that covered the millinery trade and bemoaned the fact that American business had been so lax in missing an opportunity right in its own backyard. A Des Moines newspaper picked up the story and ran it as an editorial, sternly warning American businessmen that this sort of commercial oversight was simply not good enough. Crow returned from holiday to discover that the traditional headdresses predated any French frigates along the Mexican coast or department stores in Argentina; and he found a cheque for $35 on his mat from the Chicago publisher with which he purchased a new suit.

He clearly enjoyed his first taste of foreign life in Mexico, noting the "golden skinned maidens who grace the dirty streets of Tehuantepec"[10] and taking in a bullfight. Though he was repulsed by the cruel slaughter of the bull and declared that he would have fled from the sight if he hadn't been the guest of some Mexican friends, eventually he stuck it out and admitted, somewhat sheepishly, that by the time the sixth bull of the day was skewered to death he was roaring approval with the rest of the crowd.

By early 1911 Crow was writing regular articles for the *Saturday Evening Post* and occasionally for *Pearson's Magazine*, generally considered a fairly conservative and dull read, as well as for *Systems and Technical World, Van Norden* and *Hamptons*. Most of these articles dealt with urbanization and changes to the rural economy, and railroad building. He wrote a series of articles on the southwest and Texas for the *Post*, covering the division of the large ranches in the west and the changing role of tenant farmers in the south.[11] The *Saturday Evening Post* was widely read in America at the time. It was an early example of the American style of newspaper, the origins of which can be traced back to 1729 when it had been founded by the 22-year-old Benjamin Franklin as the

Pennsylvania Gazette, one of just five regular publications in the American colonies. Franklin himself had created the *Gazette* after acquiring a struggling paper called, rather long-windedly, *The Universal Instructor in All Arts and Sciences and Pennsylvania Gazette*. The *Post* went from strength to strength and became known not just for its news and current affairs coverage but also later for championing the new American style of hard-boiled detective fiction alongside profiles of successful businessmen. In the first two decades of the twentieth century, the *Post* was aimed squarely at America's middle class and was published as a commercial, mass-circulation magazine that appealed to a wider audience than other journals of a slightly more highbrow type, such as *The New Yorker*, that appeared later.

As a modern publication, the *Post* could thank Cyrus H. Curtis, who had acquired the paper in 1897 and was responsible for creating its style and reputation as "America's Magazine." It showcased the best American writers, artists and illustrators of the day, including the little-known Crow and the very well-known Jack London; and it later became famous for its instantly recognizable Norman Rockwell covers. The paper's mission was to interpret America to itself and one out of every 10 Americans read it.

Pearson's Magazine was also largely seen as right-wing at this time, though after 1916, under the editorship of Frank Harris, it was to become a leading radical anti-war paper. However, for Crow, being published in the *Post* and *Pearson's* as a relatively young writer – he was still under 30 – brought kudos and a larger readership as by 1913 the *Post* had boosted its circulation to approximately two million. It also brought some extra money, which Crow, despite being promoted to the post of assistant to the publisher, needed to supplement his rather meager salary at the *Star-Telegram*.

Though he was starting to make his name, he decided not to stay in America. In 1910, Tom Millard, a fellow Missourian, contacted him by telegram following a recommendation by Walter Williams with the offer of a job on a new English language morning newspaper he was starting to be called the *China Press* in the far away International Settlement of Shanghai on the China coast. Crow admitted a slight hesitation when the job offer arrived. China was an unknown country and, when the writers of potboilers needed a stage set for atrocities, they invariably found China irresistible and had managed to give the country a sinister reputation in the popular American imagination. As he wrote later, looking back on the China he had imagined before setting out, "The result was to give the good-natured inoffensive Chinese the reputation of being throat-slitting villains. That was the mental picture I had of them when I received a telegram offering me a job in Shanghai and didn't know whether I had to travel by the Atlantic or the Pacific to get to China."[12]

After five years in Texas, and having cut his teeth as a reporter, Crow booked his passage to Shanghai in June 1911 and set out for China. The fare from San Francisco to China was relatively cheap – about half that from London to Shanghai – so Crow could comfortably afford the trip and start a new life. As he left for China, the *Star-Telegram* reported his departure by describing Crow as "Not only one of the brightest and best known newspapermen in the southwest, but one of the most popular as well."[13] The *Houston Chronicle* bade him farewell from Texas by recalling an anecdote from his time at the *Star-Telegram*:

When a cub reporter, Mr Crow had a thrilling experience with a woman named Parrot. Young and trusting, he was "doing police". In the course of his work, he was looking over the "blotter," as the book holding records of arrests is called.

Running his finger down the line he came to the simple notation: "Parrot, cause of arrest, profanity."

He scented a story, "What! Arrest a parrot for swearing?", he asked the sergeant. The policeman was a natural joker and couldn't resist the chance to "string" a cub. He told him about it in detail. The youthful reporter speeded back to the office and wrote a long story, giving house number and street. He said in the story that the parrot was arrested for using oaths and even went so far as to tell the words."

That night a very irate Mrs Parrot called up the office. She wanted to "talk to the reporter who wrote it." … and he was forced to listen to all the biting things that an angry woman can think of for several minutes.

When she finished, she said: "And I want to know your name, too, sir!" Her voice sizzled at this juncture.

"Certainly," he replied in his best Missouri dialect. "Mrs Parrot, this is Mr Crow."

"You think you are smart young fellow", she yelled, and the only other thing the offending reporter heard was the snapping of the telephone hook as she hung up her receiver."[14]

Shanghai beckoned and Crow booked his passage.

2

The China Press Man

Shanghai's Newest Newspaper

Production of the *China Press* (known as the *Ta Lu Pao* in Chinese) started in the summer of 1911, with Crow paid $300 per month and officially employed as the associate city editor with special responsibility for covering diplomatic affairs and Tom Millard as editor-in-chief. Despite this initially extensive remit and glamorous job title, in reality he was the night editor at first and was immediately responsible for making up the front page every day – a job that filled him with dread at the prospect that there would not be enough decent news. This would leave him with an empty front page and prove the pessimistic local British press corps correct in their predictions that an American-style newspaper in Shanghai was doomed to failure.

The hours were anti-social: 10 p.m. till 2 a.m. daily. Often he was forced to retire to the *China Press*'s private staff bar for a stiff drink to consider how to fill that blank front page. Sometimes stories did have to be embellished to justify their position above the fold as news from abroad was often scant. He shared the problem of filling the front page with another Millard recruit to Shanghai

The China Press *soon emerged as a major English language newspaper on the China Coast.*

and former Fort Worth newspaperman, Charles Herbert Webb, who was the managing editor. Both would sit around at night trying to keep cool by loitering near the open windows, drinking cups of cooling green tea and smoking an endless number of cigarettes.

Crow was based in ramshackle offices in a crowded building with no air-conditioning at Lane 126, 11 Szechuen Road, a block back from the Bund. He had few sources to call upon beyond a free, and rather paltry, German newswire that reflected Berlin's increasingly belligerent view of the world, and a Reuters' report which was edited in London and dispatched east, targeted mainly at the British community in India. Even this Reuters' dispatch reached Crow in a shortened form, being firstly edited in Bombay before being sent along to the further reaches of empire in Shanghai, Hong Kong, and Singapore. Despite the editing process, Crow was still faced with an unhealthy and boring selection of stories. They dealt with the minutiae of life in British India and, in particular, the commercial center of the Raj, Calcutta – salt taxes, the coming and goings of various British regiments, tribal unrest in Kashmir. All foreign news, including news from America, was by-lined from London to stress the role of the British capital as the center of the world and also to reflect the secondary status of America in world affairs. Only after America entered the First World War in 1917 was news from America by-lined from Washington or New York rather than London. Though Crow scoured the local news for tidbits, he had little luck at first and was later forced to help set up a translation agency to do the job, as well as using some of the *China Press*'s Chinese journalists as sources.

Of course, hindsight is a wonderful thing. The somewhat sedate, comfortable and profitable though slow-moving world of the far fringes of empire were about to change with the Wuchang uprising of October 1911, the imminent collapse of the Qing dynasty, the fall of the Manchus and the Nationalist revolution of 1911. However, Crow, though sensing something in the wind and believing that domestic Chinese affairs were about to become more internationally important, could not foretell the fall of a dynasty. Until it actually collapsed, he was left in a small, largely insignificant enclave. Though increasingly international, Shanghai was still effectively an outpost of the British Empire, in the shadow of India and of little interest to most readers – even those living in Shanghai.

As a newspaperman, Crow began to circulate in a British-dominated society that found his mid-western Missouri accent amusing (Crow tended to say *Warshington* as well as *afeared* instead of "afraid" and a-*fixin* rather than "getting ready") and where, as he noted, the general Anglo hacks' belief was that China was a country of "400 million guinea pigs who could live a hundred years without one of them doing anything interesting enough to get his name in the paper."[1] The British had become so bored with events and machinations within the Manchu court that they generally believed it to be an ossified institution capable of little more than collecting taxes to support the wealth of the Court of the Flowery Kingdom. Besides, as his fellow journalist the Scot Richard Wood told Crow, "Most of them [*the Manchu court*] live in Peking and telegraph tolls are high."[2]

Crow started to settle into the life of a local hack, learning to move around the city and do the day-to-day chores essential to producing a daily paper. He managed to negotiate the system at the British police court with Wood's help and also headed part way up the Yangtze to cover the tragic effects of the drastic floods of 1911. Shanghai was still relatively well ordered and lawful before the 1920s and 1930s were to see the city rival Chicago in terms of overt and blatant gangsterism as well as bloody political violence. Crow found himself once again missing the certainty of his days reporting in Fort Worth with its "regular supply of homicides."[3] During his first week in Shanghai, he had thought himself lucky when at daybreak he heard what he took to be machine-gun fire followed by rifle shots nearby. He visualized a glittering start to his China career, imagining "a bloodthirsty clash between warring tongs – of dead bodies in alleyways and the wounded staggering through the streets."[4] He piled out of bed, dressed hurriedly, grabbed his camera and ran out of his hotel towards the gunfire. When he got to the Garden Bridge that crosses Suzhou Creek at the northern end of the Bund, he realized this was the scene of the carnage. He peeked his head cautiously over the bridge hoping to get a front-page photo rather than a bullet between the eyes. However, all Crow photographed were the captains and crew of two small sampans who were setting off firecrackers, a tradition before starting work. Crow clearly had a lot to learn.

The court system at the time was determined by the extraterritoriality laws in place since the end of the Opium Wars and what the Chinese referred to as the "unequal treaties." Fourteen foreign nations, the signatories to "favored nation" agreements with China, exercised extraterritorial privileges and rights in Shanghai. In practice, this meant that American citizens in the Settlement went before the United States Court for China and sentenced prisoners were dispatched either to Manila or returned to America, while British subjects went before the British court with criminal sentences served in China or Hong Kong. Each of the other countries had its own court. The French operated their own system in Frenchtown, while Chinese residing in the International Settlement fell under the jurisdiction of the two Chinese Provisional courts, the Shanghai Special Area District Court and a "Second Branch" of the Jiangsu Province High Court, with foreign judges "assisting" Chinese judges.

Despite this cornucopia of courts, events of real newsworthiness were few and far between and the *China Press* seemed doomed to fail and reinvent itself as an American-slanted version of the British-run press. A major problem for

Crow, Millard and the *China Press* was that their contention that events in China were worthy of importance was largely unverifiable. With few reporters outside the major foreign treaty ports, rumours of warlords, court intrigue, rebellions and provincial battles were just trickles of stories that never quite managed to be printable despite their sensationalism in a local context. By the time they reached Shanghai, the stories were either too old, too embellished or just too obscure. Of course, the news was also expatriate-centered – a minor robbery of a foreigner's home in Shanghai was major news while the growing kidnappings and robberies of entire inland villages by marauding bandit gangs that had little impact on foreign Shanghai society were relegated to a few sentences, if covered at all. To most of the foreigners in Shanghai, the Chinese remained a mysterious people and China's great hinterland a distant and little known territory, and the majority of foreigners preferred things to stay that way. One night Crow saw total disaster looming when he and Webb were left discussing how to fill the front page with the latest edict from the Municipal Council's Health Department – "Eat and drink nothing that has not been boiled, cooked or otherwise sterilised." This seemed less than cutting-edge news to Crow and the morale-oozing *China Press* editorial team.

The *China Press* wanted to change the perception of Shanghai as being cut off from the daily events in a rapidly changing China. This was the period of British supremacy before the First World War when British newspapers could still seriously run a headline "Fog in English Channel – Continent Isolated." The *China Press*'s founder Tom Millard (in full, Thomas Franklin Fairfax Miller) was an American war correspondent and Sinologist who had written a number of books on Asia and who was later to found *Millard's Review of the Far East* in 1917. In 1922, he moved on to work for the Chinese government as a consultant, the *Review* having been effectively bought out and taken over by John Benjamin Powell, who was known to most people simply as "J. B." The erudite and soft-spoken Powell changed the name to the less egocentric *China Weekly Review* (though the *Review*'s holding company was always called the Millard Publishing Company) and continued to edit it until it was closed down and Powell was arrested after Japanese troops entered the foreign concessions at the end of 1941. Though he came to be one of the pre-eminent American China Hands in Shanghai, like Crow he had little or no knowledge of Shanghai prior to Millard's telegram offering him a job. Powell also hailed from rural Missouri, and had attended business school and worked on the *Quincy Whig* before enrolling at the Missouri School of Journalism. He had then worked on the *Courier Post* in Hanibal, Missouri, before returning to the School of Journalism as an instructor and then heading to Shanghai.

Millard had started the *China Press* partly with the vision that the paper should promote contact between the foreign community and the Chinese. He went so far as to install several prominent Chinese on the paper's board of directors and actively sought to promote China stories to the front pages using the adage that news about China should be treated in the same way as the big New York papers covered US news.

Crow's quick adoption of a pro-Chinese viewpoint virtually immediately after he arrived in Shanghai was undoubtedly a result of his close contact with Millard. Prior to moving to Shanghai, Crow had never really evinced any strong opinions on China, the Chinese or the Orient. His pre-China journalism had certainly tended to champion the underdog – the pioneer against the large landowner or the citizen against the rampant town planner – in a classic American position of support for the little guy. Millard, in contrast, was an established China Hand and his vocal and well thought out stance on China was a clear influence on Crow. The suave and immaculately dressed Millard, as well as the "owlish-looking" and usually bespectacled J. B. Powell, who was always seen "smoking a corncob pipe" and was heavily involved in the local "Good Roads Committee,"[5] were Western journalists in Shanghai that acted as advocates for China. Millard was reasonably academic and precise in his advocacy for China while Crow developed a more personal touch in his writing style and J. B. Powell became more political. Jonathan Mirsky, in his essay *Getting The Story In China*, quotes Peter Rand, an authority on the history of China reporting, who said of Millard, "He wanted to influence American policy ..."[6] – to be precise, influence it towards a pro-Chinese and anti-Japanese stance. The work of Crow and Millard, as well as later that of Powell, was almost universally reproduced in translated form in the Chinese press in Shanghai as progressive foreign opinion of the time.

Crow was engaged in active journalism but his skills, indeed the skills he had been hired for, were in laying up pages rather than commenting on Chinese affairs. That was to come later. As well as overseeing the final proofs of the *China Press*, Crow was also responsible for making sure the paper actually got printed. Unlike many journalists, Crow did not mind rolling up his sleeves and working alongside the Chinese printing staff to get the paper out, and he was always amazed that the typesetters, most of whom spoke or wrote no English, managed a remarkably high degree of accuracy with few spelling or punctuation errors.

His apprenticeship as a printer in Missouri had left him with an abiding interest in printing presses and gadgets, and tinkering with machinery. As the *China Press* started to sell more copies and its circulation reached 3,500 to 4,500 daily, it also started to make a profit. To cope with the increased demand, Crow bought a new press that printed from large rolls of paper rather than flat sheets.

Newspaper printing had been in the midst of a revolution when Crow arrived in Shanghai as more sophisticated methods of picture reproduction were introduced which moved on from lithography to photogravure and collotype, while the old rotary presses were being replaced with flat plate machines. The new press at the *China Press* was state of the art, matched in Shanghai only by those owned by its major paper, the *North-China Daily News*, and the textbooks-to-advertising printer, the Commercial Press. At maximum speed it could turn out 5,000 papers an hour, a sizeable amount for an English language newspaper market the size of Shanghai's between the wars. The *China Press* could publish and then use its presses for other jobs to raise further revenue.

Despite this, Crow's attempts at being a modern printer were thwarted by his concern that, if the machine was started up at full speed, the roll of newsprint would break, causing delays and lost paper. In what Crow considered a great example of American ingenuity, he devised a complicated motor that controlled the speed of the press: it allowed the press to start gradually and build up to full pelt to prevent breakages and stoppages. He was so proud of his invention that he took a group of friends out to the print shop one day to see it in action. He was immediately shocked to see the Chinese pressman start the machine at an extremely high speed with Crow's motor disarmed and useless. He soon discovered that the pressman had his foot on the driving pulley, which was an excellent and simple way of controlling the speed of the press. When the roll broke, the pressman could stop the machine far faster than any motor or switch and actually further reduced wastage and stoppage time. Crow remarked years later in the mid-1930s that the same press was still churning out the paper while his self-designed motor was lying forlornly on a shelf, still unused and gathering dust.

Yearning for Action

As an editor on the *China Press*, Crow started his extensive travels around China invariably accompanied by his portable typewriter. Traveling in China was a slow business and the accommodation provided was often pretty basic. Occasionally he would have to live for several weeks at a time in uncomfortable rooms in Chinese inns, sharing his space with bedbugs and rats. Like other travelers, he would place his bed – usually a light folding cot he had brought himself (along with a blanket to prevent having to rent an invariably flea-ridden one from the inn) – in the middle of the room with each leg of the bed immersed in a tin of kerosene to discourage fleas, centipedes and other insects. He would leave a lighted candle at the end of the bed to further discourage vermin, though this still meant that he would spend many restless nights listening to scampering rats. Sometimes the only answer was to pay a few coppers to the proprietor of the inn for the loan of the resident cat to keep the rat population at bay. And always there was the joy of the common toilet or the large covered (but not sealed) "honey bucket" that was emptied once a day.

His first major trip outside the comparative safety of Shanghai's International Settlement was up the Yangtze to cover the severe flooding that occurred in 1911. The floods left 100,000 people dead and approximately 3.8 million homeless and destitute as the mighty river flooded and created a lake 80 by 35 miles where once arable land and villages had stood.

The British-run press afforded the disaster a few lines but Millard felt more was needed, in particular an eye-witness account. Crow undertook a 600-mile round trip up river to interview starving refugees, Manchu officials and the local foreign community of up-country missionaries. Despite the scorn the British hacks had for such "local" news, Crow's eye-witness accounts attracted a significant amount of attention in Shanghai and led to the establishment of a charitable fund to aid the victims of the floods. However, those who showed an interest remained a minority, as most of Shanghai's foreign residents remained closer to events in London or the Raj than to those occurring in the provinces immediately surrounding Shanghai. For Crow, the trip was the start of a concerted attempt to report life in the interior of China to the foreign community – an attempt he stuck to diligently but which was little appreciated by most of his Shanghai readers even as his reputation as an interpreter of China back in America grew.

Other factors got in the way of reporting local news too. Shortly before the final fall of the Manchu court, Crow covered the story of the death of an old eunuch who had served the famous Manchu Empress Dowager and Dragon Queen Ci Xi (who had died in 1908 mysteriously on the same day as her son, the reigning emperor). The story moved from an interesting historical footnote to scandal when it was revealed that, after the eunuch's death, it became apparent that he had in fact never had the all-too-necessary operation to qualify him for eunuch-hood. He had lived in the Forbidden City, an environment where uncastrated men were generally not allowed, in the trust of Ci Xi; and he had been surrounded by the women of the court for decades without its being discovered that he had retained the offending appendage deemed liable to pollute the imperial blood line if ever used. Crow reported the story with relish, but the British press refused to note it, considering the whole business too scandalous and possibly too degenerate for their apparently more easily shocked British readers.

The *China Press* forged ahead in search of stories and an identity in its attempt to give Shanghai a new sort of newspaper. However, it had competition.

3
Living at the End of the Wires

Notes on Native Affairs

Like most people who arrive in China with some sort of business plan, Carl Crow had an idea to change the way things were done. His initial dream was to produce an English language newspaper in Shanghai in the American style. At that time, the American style on which Crow had been trained in the US consisted of filling the front page with what was deemed "important news," giving each story its own individual headline. This was a radical departure for the Shanghai English language press which was dominated by British-run, suburban English-style newspapers that, as Crow said, were edited "on the theory that London was the centre of the world, and other parts of the British Empire came next. After that came the interests of foreigners in China; and then the activities of Chinese or events in China that were of importance only as they affected the lives or interests of foreigners."[1]

Most news deemed important in the British press was contained in several daily columns entitled *Company Meetings*, *Shipping Notices* and *Notes on Native Affairs*. This sort of newspaper had suited the largely British expatriate population of Shanghai with their insular world of trade, amateur dramatics, sports and desire for news from back home. 1911 was a rich year for the British-controlled newspapers that had more than enough "local" news with the June Coronation of George V in London.

British culture, ways of thinking and outlooks dominated Shanghai – not least in the fact that five out of the total of nine seats on the SMC were reserved for Brits. Indeed G. E. Morrison of the *London Times* – the famed Morrison of Peking, a man completely of the British Empire and the most famous foreign correspondent in China at the time – declared in 1910 that "To me the suggestion is preposterous that British influence is waning in China. On the contrary, I think that British prestige has never been higher than at present."[2] However, by 1911 Shanghai's foreign population was changing. It was becoming decidedly less English and more varied and rich, and other newspapers such as the French language *L'Echo de Chine* were emerging to service these groups. The number of Americans, as well as other nationalities, was rising, and they demanded a more cosmopolitan, less Anglo-centric, feel to their daily paper. The latest test match cricket scores, the comings and goings of English society in India and the machinations of the British parliament were of little or no interest to a growing segment of "Shanghailanders" – as those Europeans who made Shanghai their home were dubbed.

However, in 1911 the British style was still dominant, with the *North-China Daily News*, owned by the Morriss family, and the *Shanghai Times* dominating the major English language market.[3] These, and other older newspapers, published in the British-controlled treaty ports invariably featured advertisements on the front page, rigidly compartmentalized story columns inside to induce a sense of familiarity for the reader, and a London by-line on just about all stories whether they originated from New York, Colombo, Lahore or Hong Kong. They also included lots of local information on amateur operettas, sports and society gatherings, as well as who had arrived in Shanghai on that week's boat. Though the list of arrivals invariably contained more celebrity "D" names unknown to most, they were useful to the British who followed London society and to those frustrated single males in Shanghai who hoped for the arrival of a potential wife – the so-called "Empire Women" who, unable to secure a man at home and reaching a certain age, came to the colonies in search of a husband in expatriate British society where breeding, marriage and the need for available white women was greater and expectations lower. It was a tactic that saved many a plain but respectable English lady from a dour life of spinsterhood and good works in England and many a colony-wandering Englishman from a life of bachelorhood, but it was not necessarily gripping reading for anyone else.

The life of the British in Shanghai, until the convulsions of 1911, had been comfortable, well-heeled and insular, a situation that did not really change markedly until the Japanese invasion of 1937. As the Sinologist and former Chinese Maritime Customs Service officer L. A. Lyall commented, "The British residents in Shanghai are the spoilt children of the Empire. They pay no taxes to China, except that landowners pay a very small land tax, and no taxes to England. Judges and consuls are provided for them; they are protected by the British fleet, and for several years they have had in addition a British army to defend them; and for all this expenditure the British taxpayer pays." The historian John Keay summed up Shanghai when he described the city as "empire without imperial responsibilities."[4]

The oldest foreign newspaper in China, the *North-China Daily News,* really had an unassailable position as the major English language paper in the city; indeed its influence extended beyond Shanghai to much of the British-controlled Far East. The paper had grown from the old weekly *North-China Herald,* which was still published as the weekly edition of the daily, and was read in many major capitals around the world for news of China. It focused on British interests in Asia, mostly covered local events and included a section called *Outports* featuring news from Singapore and Hong Kong as well as some reports from the Chinese interior supplied by missionaries picking up some extra income as stringers. The paper was owned by the Morriss family, British Catholics of Jewish descent. Though originally founded in 1850, H. E. Morriss had bought the paper in 1881. His sons eventually took over the daily running of the family's extensive newspaper and publishing business at their "stable and stuffy"[5] offices on the fifth floor at 17 The Bund, known locally as "The Old Lady of the Bund."[6]

H. E. Morriss died in 1918 but there were three brothers, Henry (Harry or H. E. Morriss Jr.), Gordon and Hailey who continued his business enterprises. According to Ralph Shaw, a British soldier turned journalist who worked on the paper in the 1930s, the eldest of the three brothers, Harry, had his office on the second floor of the newspaper's Bund building and controlled the company; and his brother Gordon, whose stockbroking firm, Lester, Johnson and Morriss, was situated in the Japanese bank building next door, also took a keen directorial interest in the newspaper. The third brother, however, was somewhat different. Again according to Shaw, "Hailey, alas, remained in England where he had blotted the family copy-book by a long series of sexual escapades that had taken him to court, to prison and to prominence in the *News of the World.*"[7] The Morriss family had amassed significant wealth from Mohawk's publishing empire and then Henry's bullion-broking business and eventually built the Morriss Estate, which occupied a full block in the densely-populated French Concession, and was acquired by Harry Morriss as their art deco style family compound in the 1920s.[8] The brothers were keen racehorse and dog owners

(Harry's racehorse *Manna* was the winner of the 1925 English Derby), a habit they had inherited from their father whose nickname "Mohawk" was given to him after he started naming all his racehorses with American-Indian names, such as *Shawendassie* ("South Wind") and *Minnehaha* ("Laughing Water"). This interest was a bonus for the Morriss estate, which, handily, was adjacent to the French-built dog track, the Canidrome[9] on Rue Cardinal Mercier, which opened in 1928 and could hold 50,000 spectators. The brothers were able to walk their greyhounds over conveniently to the Canidrome for races.

The only competition to the *North-China Daily News* was the *Shanghai Times*. The *Times* was owned by another Briton, E. S. Nottingham. Crow, who strongly disliked the paper's editorial line, commented that the Japanese had "practically gained control" though it was still "generally supposed to be British" by many readers. In later years the paper became an outright apologist for Japanese excesses.[10]

The English language press in Shanghai may have been British-dominated – Ralph Shaw described it as a "transplanted Fleet Street"[11] – but Crow had other ideas. The American-funded *China Press*[12] was originally started by Wu Ting-fang and Y. C. Tong (both of whom had previously worked together for the Chinese Telegraph Administration in Shanghai), as well as Crow's first mentor in Shanghai Tom "Tommie" Millard. It was to be a truly international newspaper with headlines dictated by world events and not dissimilar in layout to the *New York Herald-Tribune*. The *China Press* team's ambitions were immediately scorned by the many naysayers in the British journalistic community such as Crow's early "chum" in Shanghai, the Aberdonian Richard Wood. The heavily-accented Scot worked on a British afternoon newspaper and had already been in Shanghai for fully a year, making him vastly more experienced than the newly-berthed China virgin Crow. Wood and others viewed Shanghai through the prism of the rigid hierarchy of the British Empire and didn't believe that the treaty ports and China generated enough major news to maintain the style that the *China Press* was aiming for – despite the imminent crumbling of the Manchu dynasty and the establishment of "the father of the Chinese Republic" Sun Yat-sen's government. However, that was all in the future. According to Crow, the British press in China, to a man (and it was just about all men), foretold the early demise of the *China Press*. Crow worried that the Brits might be right but professional pride meant that he continued to argue that an American-style newspaper would and could be produced successfully in Shanghai.

The paper was officially a Chinese-American enterprise registered in Delaware, to avoid censorship as well as to hide some involvement from the Chinese government and the fact that Wu Ting-fang remained a trustee. Other investors included Charles Crane, a wealthy Chicago businessman, philanthropist and Arabist who funded the purchase of the printing press Crow was so fond of tinkering with,[13] and Benjamin Fleischer, another Missourian with a newspaper background who was based in Japan.

The Missouri University School of Journalism supplied many of the leading American journalists who worked on the China Coast.

The fact that three Missourians – Millard, Fleischer, and Crow – were involved in the Shanghai newspaper business in 1911 may have seemed a coincidence but over time the number and the power of Missourians in the Shanghai press grew and grew. This was not wholly by accident but rather due to the strong connections forged among graduates of the University of Missouri's School of Journalism, the institution which was on many occasions to provide the men (and a few women too) that staffed the end of the wires in China. This network was to serve Crow well over the years.

Corn Cobbers and Cowboy Correspondents

Along with Millard, Crow became part of the nucleus of what became known as the "Missouri News Colony" in China – known, rather uncharitably, by the British journalists in Shanghai as the "Corn Cobbers," the "Cowboy Correspondents," or the "Prize Pumpkins of Missouri." The Colony was one of the recognized groups of foreign journalists alongside the large British contingent and a smaller caucus of Australians. Crow was an influential member of the Colony: he was at the *China Press* and also the China correspondent for the United Press (UP), and he established UP's first China bureau, for which many of the Missouri News Colony were later to work.[14] Millard, the Colony's founding member, was also a native Missourian and a graduate of the University of Missouri, as well as being a good friend of Benjamin "B. W." Fleisher, another Missourian, a former Far East Correspondent for the *New York Herald-Tribune* and the founder of the *Japan Advertiser* in Yokohama in 1909.

Millard became well known internationally for his books – including *Our Eastern Question* (1916), *Conflict of Policies in Asia* (1924) and *The End of Exterritoriality in China* (1931) – all of which were influential in the US and the China-watching community at the time. He gave many of the younger Missourians and other young Americans who moved to China their first jobs, including Crow and J. B. Powell. The *China Press* remained a major employer of Americans. For example, it was the first port of call for a young Harold Issacs, the son of a New York real estate magnate who was later headhunted by the left-leaning Agnes Smedley to work on the Communist-funded *China Forum* – and was later described by the judge of the American Court in China as an "obnoxious young Bolshevik" for his book, *Tragedy of the Chinese Revolution*, that praised popular revolt. Millard was a well known man-about-town in Shanghai in 1911. He lived in the smart Astor House Hotel, and was renowned for his snappy dress and abilities on the dance floor, as well as his established liberal views. Millard had worked on the *New York Herald* as a drama critic before being sent to China as an international correspondent to cover the Boxer Rebellion. When J. B. Powell first met Millard in 1917 he described him as "... a short, slender man weighing perhaps 125 pounds and dressed so perfectly that I wondered how he would be able to sit down without wrinkling his immaculate suit."[15] Despite his conventional appearance, Millard was also known for his rigorous defence of a free press and his right to print what he considered fit. When J. B. Powell later asked him what they should print in the *China Press*, Millard replied "Anything we damn please."[16]

In part, Millard had established the *Press* to counter what he saw as the strength of British colonial opinion in Shanghai, a view that was to first attract Americans such as Crow and later leftists such as Issacs. Millard was incredibly well connected. As well as the Boxers, he had covered the Russo-Japanese War (1905), and he knew Sun Yat-sen and other leaders of the Nationalist movement, as well as F. C. Tong, Shanghai's first modern banker. His contacts with Wu Ting-fang and other Chinese involved in the founding of the *China Press* went back a long way too.

As Millard, Fleisher, and Crow had all known the Dean of Missouri University's School of Journalism, Walter Williams, an early history of the School was able to write that "Thereafter when a man was wanted for American newspaper work in the Orient the first query usually went to Dean Walter Williams."[17] Crow and J. B. Powell were handed their first trans-oceanic telegrams by Williams, both from Millard, both looking for bright Missouri graduates to go to China.

In a 1928 article in the *New York Herald-Tribune*, Millard described the Missouri News Colony as a "... chain which during the last fifteen years has brought about twenty five students of the Missouri School of Journalism to Japan and China."[18] The Colony eventually encompassed a later generation of Missouri journalists in Asia, including H. S. Jewell who worked on the *Ta Kung Pao* in Chongqing and Edgar Snow, a leftist writer who was to become famous for interviewing Mao Zedong in Yanan and writing *Red Star Over China*.

The Colony's influence was extensive. In Shanghai, Crow and Millard were at the *China Press*, while J. B. Powell arrived to provide coverage for the *Chicago Tribune* and the *Manchester Guardian*. Missourian Morris J. Harris was working for Associated Press (AP) and stayed in China till the 1940s, eventually managing to leave Japanese-occupied Shanghai on the evacuation ship the *USS Gripsholm*. Yet another Missourian, Henry Francis "Frank" Misselwitz, was with the *New York Times* as a Shanghai-based staff correspondent. Misselwitz, who was slightly younger than Crow, went on to write a well-received book on China called *The Dragon Stirs: An Intimate Sketch-book of China's Kuomintang Revolution, 1927–1929*.[19]

The Colony also had members in Beijing, including Joseph "Glen" Babb who was the chief correspondent for AP in China and a regular contributor to the *Times of India*. In addition, the Colony included a number of Chinese and Japanese students who had studied in Missouri and then returned home. Many of these young Chinese had gone to Missouri to study in the later stage of the Qing dynasty; and they were part of what Hugo de Burgh in his study *The Journalist in China: Looking to the Past for Inspiration*[20] described as those younger Chinese intellectuals who had become aligned to an intellectual movement "aimed at subjecting Confucian orthodoxy to rational scrutiny ... large numbers of Chinese went abroad to live in countries outside their world and returned wealthy and knowledgeable about lands which it was increasingly difficult to accept were barbarian, as tradition would have it."[21] Many of these young people studied medicine, engineering or military tactics but some also studied journalism and for this group the Missouri School of Journalism was a major center. With the dying days of the Qing and the rise of republicanism, journalism increasingly became an ideal career for a new breed of patriot. Shanghai was a major point of return for them after their studies. There were also jobs for them, as in 1911 it was estimated that over 500 newspapers and thousands of magazines were being published in China, as well as all the foreign papers and wire services.

Prominent among the Chinese graduates from Missouri was Hollington "Holly" K. Tong[22] who had been taught by J. B. Powell and who was covering affairs in Tianjin for a variety of American and English newspapers, as well as being the director of a local newspaper. Tong also wrote for the *China Weekly Review* and went on to become editor of the *Peking Daily News* in 1918. He was a missionary-educated Suzhou native who had studied at Columbia University in New York as well as in Missouri. In the 1930s he continued his journalism career and moved to the, by then, Chinese-owned *China Press* as the chief editorial writer and general manager after a stint working for the Chinese Ministry of Communications.

Another Missouri alumnus, Hin Wong from Honolulu (in fact the first ethnic-Chinese graduate of the School of Journalism), was well known in Guangzhou in southern China. He edited a local paper and supplied occasional pieces to the American press through AP, and he also helped Crow to research his best-selling *Handbook for China*. Other Colony members included Kan Lee who was to handle publicity for the Chinese Ministry of Finance in the Nationalist government; and the tradition carried on right up to the 1949 revolution when another Missourian David Lu (Wu Chi-wei) worked for the Central News Agency of China and also as a correspondent for the *St. Louis Post-Dispatch*.[23] Woo Kya-tang, yet another alumnus, was to become the managing editor of the *China Press* in 1940 and be targeted for "deportation" (which ultimately involved arrest and torture) by the Japanese after they invaded Shanghai in 1937. The most prominent Japanese graduate was Yoshinori "Bob" Horiguchi, who had a Japanese father and Belgian mother. He worked as a correspondent for the Japanese Domei News Agency and later moved on to be a translator and press officer for the Japanese army in Shanghai in 1937 before spending time in Washington and then, after Pearl Harbor in 1941, as Domei's European correspondent based in Vichy France. The six-foot-tall Bob married another Missouri graduate, Karen Horiguchi, and was known to be highly conflicted about Japan's actions in China and often turned to drink to try and resolve his inner conflicts.

Women were also prominent members of the Colony and their ranks included Chinese graduate Eva Chang, who edited a Chinese language women's magazine and did publicity work for the YWCA in China. Margaret Powell contributed to the *China Weekly Review* as well as arranging publicity in China for the BAT Motion Picture Studio,[24] while another Missouri graduate, Louise Blakeney Wilson, ran the women's section of the *North-China Daily News* from its grand offices on the Bund. She was later to join the editorial staff of the *Manila Bulletin* in the late 1920s.

The Colony was immensely influential in the news media in Shanghai and across China at the time. According to Millard, "all the principal news services that were sent out from Shanghai had Missouri School of Journalism men at this end [*China*] of the wires."[25] The interconnectedness of the Colony is perhaps best shown in a special edition of the *China Weekly Review* issued in October 1928 to celebrate the achievements of the Nationalist government. J. B. Powell edited the issue and mentioned both Millard and Crow on the first page for their reporting on the *China Press*. Inside were articles by a series of Colony members, including Louise Wilson on women in China, Hin Wong on the situation in southern China, Henry Misselwitz on Sun Yat-sen's mausoleum in Nanjing, along with references to the work of other Colony members.[26]

Most of the Colony arrived after Crow. In 1911 the network was small – just Millard and Crow in Shanghai and Fleischer in Japan. Crow was very much the new boy in town, but he was about to be part of a news-gathering revolution in China as the world woke up to events in the Middle Kingdom and a dynasty which had lasted for two and a half centuries collapsed. The *New York Times* China correspondent Hallett Abend, who covered much the same period and ground as Crow, wrote that "Newspaper work in those years was a continuous series of stirring adventures, wide travel, and a widening circle of acquaintance with men who were making history in the Far East."[27] Crow's period of stirring adventure and making history was about to begin.

4

The Collapse of the Qing Dynasty and Opportunities Abound

Chinese dogs always bark at a foreigner

Lit Cigarettes, Exploding Bombs and the Fall of the Manchus

In October 1911 Crow received word that a revolt against Manchu rule had occurred in the treaty port of Hankou. The local telegraph operator had been too afraid to send the report to Beijing for fear of reprisal and the court's general "shoot-the-messenger" approach to bad news. However, as the telegram had been pre-paid, it had to be sent somewhere; and so after a roundabout route, it ended up on the desk of the associate city editor of the *China Press* in Shanghai, Carl Crow. On that particular night Crow was in one of his periodic quandaries about what exactly to fill the front page with and, while willing to admit that he was yet far from an expert on the machinations between the Qing court in Beijing and its republican rivals, he needed news.

With the help of the more experienced Millard, Crow decided to run the story but with the caution of changing "revolution" to "minor revolt" in case the event turned out to be yet another premature uprising that would be put down swiftly by Beijing and fizzle out, with little follow-up except the beheading of the rebellious local officials. Though the Qing dynasty was on its last legs, this was not immediately apparent even to many experienced Sinologists such as

Millard, let alone China Griffins, or greenhorns like Crow who a couple of months before hadn't known whether he should cross the Atlantic or the Pacific to get to Shanghai. The basic thinking of most foreign observers, including those regarded as "Old China Hands," was that the Qing had survived for centuries and though periodic uprisings had occurred throughout that time the dynasty had still endured. Why should this rebellion be any different in the long run? The Hankou story was relegated to the inside pages and the day's headline was about some now long-forgotten pronouncement by the German Kaiser.

However, the Qing had been in severe trouble for over 50 years with rebellions and a growing realization that the outside world was gradually impinging on Beijing's self-imposed isolation. The few concessions made to the modern world didn't help matters. When the court gave more power to the provincial gentry it weakened the center; and when it abolished the traditional civil service examination system it lost its supportive elite. Corruption and court intrigue grew and the Treasury's coffers became increasingly depleted, not least from fighting the Taiping rebellion that lasted 14 years and left an estimated 20 to 30 million Chinese dead. After the Taiping uprising, another chance for reform had been missed when Xi Ci led a coup that ousted the reformist Emperor, her nephew, and ended with his death, probably due to poisoning ordered by her. The Boxer Rebellion in 1900 and the enthronement of the three-year-old boy-Emperor, Pu Yi, in 1909 were yet more nails in the coffin of the dynasty, along with defeats in the two Opium Wars and a disastrous war with Japan. The resultant foreign treaty ports, extraterritoriality laws and forced indemnity payments to the foreign powers caused wider discontent with the Manchu's mishandling of the country. In this environment, the sort of anti-Manchu nationalist republicanism espoused by people like Dr. Sun Yat-sen thrived.

The initial catalyst for the revolt was the accidental explosion of a bomb that occurred when a careless revolutionary dropped a lit cigarette in the workshop of some rebel conspirators in Hankou's Russian Concession on October 9. The ensuing explosion had alarmed a nervous German butcher who called the police who in turn uncovered a revolutionary plot. Seals, plans, and documents were seized which implicated members of the city's Wuchang Garrison. As police had seized their membership list, the instigators decided to act immediately to preserve themselves, having a choice between arrest, torture and probable beheading, or putting up a fight. Though they jumped the gun, their timing turned out to be excellent. Revolts tended to happen in China in the autumn after the harvest was gathered and when the majority of peasants would be amenable to partaking of a little disturbance without losing their crops. Indeed, rebellious generals who had opted for summer uprisings had found themselves disastrously bereft of peasant support in the past and consequently bereft of their heads.

The city of Hankou, whose name means "mouth of the Han River", was technically a British-controlled treaty port and had been since January 1862. Located in Hubei province, Hankou formed one of a triumvirate of cities on the Yangtze, known as the Wu-Han cities, including Wuchang and Hanyang (and now amalgamated as the city of Wuhan). Hankou itself was located approximately 600 miles from the mouth of the Yangtze. The three cities had a total population of about 1.3 million, of which foreigners comprised just 2,000. Though nominally controlled by the British, the city retained a Chinese city within its boundaries as well as Japanese, Russian, German and French Concessions on its northern bank, with what at the time was considered a fine Bund that extended along the river for two miles. Hankou had grown rapidly since the concessions had been established and growth was further spurred by the completion of the Hankou-Beijing railway in 1906 that made the city a major hub for Yangtze delta trade with northern China. The Russians had been in Hankou for a long time making and trading brick tea. By 1911 Hankou had emerged from its original position as little more than a suburb of Hanyang and had developed a separate identity and strong trade links with both Beijing and Shanghai, as well as daily passenger services to Shanghai; and during the high-water period of the summer and autumn, ocean steamers sailed directly from Hankou for Europe. However, in Crow's famous travel guide, the *Handbook for China* first published in 1913, he noted rather harshly of Hankou that "There is little here of interest to the tourist."[1]

The rebellion caused alarm as the complacency that this was just another uprising ebbed away among many of the longer-term residents of the foreign community in China. They viewed Hankou as the major competitor to Shanghai for Yangtze trade; and they saw shades of the Boxer Rebellion of a decade before that had seen foreigners lose their heads as the Manchu leaders looked on non-intervening, and eventually led to the joint nations expeditionary army taking Beijing by force and looting it in the process. Alarm reached such levels in Shanghai that many women and children were dispatched homewards to safety by boat until things calmed down. Meanwhile, along the reaches of the upper Yangtze, Manchu Bannermen were deserting to the rebels, troops that had switched sides had seized the Hankou arsenal, a powerful Manchu Viceroy was beheaded by his own security detail (who wrapped his head in a blanket and sent it to the Viceroy in a neighboring province as a warning), and more defecting Bannermen fought pitched battles with those still faithful to Beijing.

Many of the Bannermen had become increasingly unhappy with the lack of opportunity for promotion, low pay, long postings away from home and the fact that they were also acting as a police force in places where a modern constabulary did not yet exist. Being a soldier could be honorable but to be reduced largely to collecting taxes and keeping drunks of the street was frankly demeaning. It was no coincidence that the Wuchang Garrison, which mutinied on October 10,[2] a day after the catalyst of the accidentally exploding bomb, was at the heart of the 1911 revolt and had also been judged by some foreign observers to be the best disciplined and trained garrison in China. The revolt appeared to be premature but it continued to spread. By this point, Crow felt he had better raise the snowballing Hankou incident with Millard again: when Crow asked "Don't you think we had better call this thing a revolution?", Millard said "I suppose you might as well."[3]

Millard was more circumspect than the recently-arrived Crow. He had been in China longer and knew that these rebellions had a history of fizzling out pretty fast, leaving the newsmen who had started hailing the onset of a revolution looking a little silly and their newspapers with a reputation for "crying wolf."

As well as needing news, Crow had also noted that the *New York Herald's* correspondent in China, William Henry (Bill) Donald, was covering the story. At the time, the *New York Herald* was one of the American papers to maintain a full-time reporter, rather than a stringer, in China and had a reputation for international coverage. The *Herald* had been founded in 1835 and had financed Stanley's expedition to Africa to find Livingstone as well as G. W. De Long's ill-fated expedition to the Arctic in 1879. The paper had already established a European edition based in Paris and also became famous for being based at the junction of 34th Street, Broadway and Sixth Avenue in New York that eventually became known as "Herald Square."

Donald, an Australian who later acted as a personal adviser to Sun Yat-sen, a couple of warlords and Chiang Kai-shek, had been close to the anti-Manchu movement in Hong Kong and around Guangzhou and southern China. He had followed the various uprisings in Guangzhou for both the Sydney *Daily Telegraph* and the London *Times*, and was close to both Sun and his millionaire backer Charlie Soong. Donald was effectively the only foreigner then in Shanghai who knew anything in detail about the movement; he had contacts in Hankou and was even acting as official adviser to the rebels and simultaneously adviser to the American and British consulates in Shanghai on developments up the Yangtze. When Sun Yat-sen eventually came back to China on Christmas eve 1911, Donald was immediately by his side advising him too on everything from democratic process to leaving prostitutes alone.

Events in Hankou eventually reached such a peak that Millard decided to dispatch Crow on the four-day steamer up the Yangtze to the city for another eye-witness account. Crow passed several sleepless nights with dreams of finally becoming a real live war correspondent. However, he also suffered from a nasty bout of Ningbo varnish poisoning, a particularly painful affliction then common along the China coast which Crow likened to "being stung by a thousand especially vicious mosquitoes who come back and sting you again as soon as the fire from the last lot of stings begins to die out."[4] Ningbo varnish poisoning was a major hazard of life on the China coast at the time and was first observed in sailors who came into contact with new Chinese-made lacquer ware that caused a painful vesicular dermatitis not dissimilar to poison oak or ivy. Crow was stuck in Shanghai, frustrated and itchy but ultimately closer to the center of the story as the fighting and rebellion started to spread rapidly down the Yangtze towards the International Settlement.

For Crow, the uprising in Hankou was difficult to understand. The rebels had no direct links to Dr. Sun's *Tongmenghui*, or United League (Sun himself being in America at the time of the uprising). The mutiny at the garrison was somewhat chaotic but the mutineers had done what no one had managed before by successfully rising up and mostly keeping their heads. The mutineers of the 21st Mixed Brigade in Hankou established a provisional republican government under their local commander Li Yuan-hong (1864–1928), later to be the only man to be President of the Chinese Republic twice. Li was chosen as he was the most senior officer present, though he was neither a revolutionary nor particularly sympathetic to the cause. Indeed, Li was dragooned into the role having decided to hide, then been discovered under his bed and threatened with death unless he joined the revolutionary forces as their leader. Given the choice, he agreed. A snowball effect started across China with more provinces joining the Wuchang rebels and declaring independence from Manchu rule. Crucially, unlike during the last major threat to the Qing during the Boxer Rebellion, the Great Powers, led by Britain, decided not to intervene and remained sitting firmly on the fence observing.

Crow tried to get to the heart of what was happening but Manchu court politics remained an obscure subject to foreigners. He consulted Dr. Wu Ting-fang, LLD, a former Chinese Minister to Washington, "health faddist", vegetarian, Shanghai restaurateur and director of the *China Press*. Dr. Wu tried to translate the machinations for him as well as suggesting that edicts from Beijing were always too late to quell rebellions as the lack of an alphabet in the Chinese language meant that the use of morse code in a telegram was impossible. To circumvent this problem, the Chinese assigned each individual character a number which involved one clerk in Beijing transcribing the written telegram into numerals and sending it, and then another clerk somewhere along the Yangtze translating it back into characters from numerals – a lengthy, frustrating and time-consuming process which became further lengthened when the telegram was passed along to the offices of the *China Press* for final translation into English. This did not make for rapid news reporting and also meant that translating took hours and stories were filed without all the lengthy and flowery telegrams being fully translated.

Consequently, Crow came to rely increasingly on Dr. Wu to interpret events. Though Wu had an intimate knowledge of the Manchu court, he was a complicated character with a varied career behind him. He had been a Chinese Minister to Spain, Peru, Mexico and Cuba before becoming Chinese Minister in Washington. While in Washington he had annoyed the Americans by referring to those Chinese who converted to Christianity through the efforts of American missionaries as "Rice Christians," only converting for a free meal. He also stood in the ambiguous position of having taken British citizenship while being a practicing lawyer in Hong Kong and, therefore, becoming a Foreign Ambassador of the Chinese government while not technically subject to Chinese law, as the extraterritoriality laws meant that British subjects in Shanghai could only be tried by a British court.

While this had never been much of an issue to Beijing, it did mean that elements in the republican movement distrusted Wu's motives and suggested he might be secretly working for British interests. Dr. Wu solved this problem by conferring openly and highly publicly with Crow, an American, as well as cutting off his pigtail, the sign of the anti-Manchu forces. This open consorting with an American national apparently absolved Wu in the eyes of the republicans from charges of complicity with the British. Wu was also well known for his book *America Through the Spectacles of an Oriental Diplomat*, in which he had praised the independence of American women but also criticized some other aspects of American life. Later, he became well known as a scholar in America where he provided the introduction to M. M. Dawson's book *The Ethics of Confucius* that was a best-seller during the First World War.[5]

This chance contact turned out to be more useful for Crow when Dr. Wu was officially appointed as head of the delegation of the *Tongmenghui* that was set to meet with the government to negotiate a peace treaty, see the Qing dynasty pass into history and the first Chinese Republic formed – an announcement that shocked everyone including Crow who, despite his daily in-depth briefings from Dr. Wu, had never been told by the man himself that he was even a member of the *Tongmenghui*, let alone a senior official. In fact, Crow had once asked Dr. Wu if he thought Sun Yat-sen would be the first President of a Chinese Republic if one were successfully established, but Wu denied any knowledge of who this Sun person was. Wu later became the Republic's first Minister of Foreign Affairs and then Premier of China under President Li while Sun became the first President of the Chinese Republic on December 29, 1911.

Sun had been in Denver, Colorado, on a fund-raising trip when the Hankou uprising broke out and had to read about it in a telegram. He hurried to New York to catch a ship to London where he tried to enlist British support for his republican movement, but Whitehall considered him a "windbag" and ignored him. Sun moved on to Paris but he received little more encouragement in the French capital than he had in the British one. He eventually got back to Shanghai on Christmas day and was hailed as a returning hero. In his absence, United League loyalists such as the wealthy Bible printer Charlie Soong, had made sure that Sun's legacy had remained alive and that he was seen by many as the true inspiration behind the rebellion. With Charlie Soong and Soong's daughter Ai-ling, Sun headed up to the new republican base of Nanjing where he was hailed as a returning conqueror and installed as the unanimously elected Provisional President of the Republic of China.

A year later Crow was to interview Sun in Nanjing after he had become President. This was good timing by Crow as Sun's tenure as President was short. Crow's contacts in Nanjing led him to be introduced directly to Tang Shao-yi – another original investor in the *China Press* and a head of the Manchu delegation – who agreed that Crow could report daily to him for an on-the-spot review of the negotiations. Mr. Tang, strangely both Cantonese and a Manchu official, was traditionally not well disposed to the press, Chinese or foreign, but he was willing to confide in Crow. Crow's ignorance of Chinese meant that he was allowed into the conference itself, which was a strange decision as Crow understood none of the proceedings. Crow believed that his presence was useful for two reasons: firstly, to show that the foreign press was able to cover the conference in a spirit of openness (it was hardly the delegates' fault he didn't speak Chinese); and, secondly, to impress him with their frequent wisecracks in English. Crow's initial contact with Tang – who, despite his role in the talks, was close to Sun – came through chance but was to last for over 20 years until Tang's assassination in 1938 for suspected collaboration with the Japanese in Shanghai. Much later, when Crow was a respected and long-term member of the Shanghai foreign community as well as President of the city's American Club, he successfully proposed Tang as the first Chinese to be accepted as a member of the club.

Eventually Wu and Tang reached a decision to dissolve the Manchu court and establish a republic in China. Crow believed that Tang was at heart sympathetic to the republicans. He was a southerner, a Cantonese with no blood links to the Manchus, and also, as a court insider, had seen more than most of the rot inside the Forbidden City and the internal warring between selfish factions. Tang was also a consummate survivor and saw which way the wind was blowing in China. The Qing dynasty effectively passed into history though it was several months before they left Beijing. Crow had been witness to what was then perhaps the most monumental change in 5,000 years of Chinese history: the ending of the 267-year-old Qing dynasty; the inauguration of China's first (and only) republic; and, most importantly for Crow as a practicing newspaperman in China, the elevation of China from being worthy of only a few lines of copy to a headline-grabbing nation. Within six months of arriving in Shanghai and fearing himself relegated to a backwater of international affairs, Crow found himself witnessing the death blow dealt to the old China, the formation of the world's youngest republic and himself in close contact with its new leaders about whom the world was curious to know more. Millard and Crow's dream for the *China Press* to report real news now seemed eminently more viable.

Life in the Republic – Between the Shoulders of a Snake and the Hips of an Eel

Crow would have agreed with the response to the events of 1911 of another increasingly prominent foreigner living in China, the head of the Yale-in-China program, Edward Hume. Surveying the events shortly after Sun had become President of the fledgling Republic, Hume commented: "This is the day of opportunity. The Rebellion of 1911 throws wide open the doors of reform and progress in China. It means that educated men, in the modern sense, are to lead the nation hereafter."[6] Certainly, Crow and the *China Press* immediately supported the Republic's existence.

However, at first it seemed that Crow would remain reporting the more quirky stories of China, such as queue- (or pigtail-) cutting. Of course, however quirky and "inscrutably Oriental" the severing of the traditional pigtail may have appeared to editors in New York or London, it was a dramatic sign that the revolution in China was real and that people were committing to it. Crow realized that the pigtail had become a sign of nationality to the Chinese, whatever its oppressive origins may have been – the Manchus had originally forced the plaited hair upon Han Chinese men as a symbol of their servitude. To cut it off was a significant sign of liberation and political change. For many Chinese men, including those as sophisticated internationally as Dr. Wu, the pigtail may have attracted attention abroad and been somewhat embarrassing but to cut it off remained a major act of personal change, a political declaration and a serious commitment. Western Christian missionaries grew their own pigtails, or stuck on false ones, in order to be more readily accepted in inland China.

The cutting of the pigtail was also a way of solidifying the rebellion. Unlike a badge or a uniform the pigtail, once cut off, could not be grown back quickly. Those that severed the hair from their head also severed their traditional loyalty to the Qing. For those queueless rebels that found themselves captured by imperial troops, the penalty was death, their offence immediately proven. Hence, to fight for the rebels was to fight for your life. It was perhaps this unique symbol of commitment to the new order, as much as the politics it espoused, that ensured that defection rates from the rebels were so insignificant. Crow himself fully appreciated the fate of those who did or did not cut off their queues – on his first visit to Nanjing he had seen decapitated heads hanging from telegraph poles by their queues.

By October 1911 Crow was witnessing the cutting of queues in Shanghai itself as millions of pigtails were shorn off across the country. The Chinese editorial and printing staff at the *China Press* held a ritual queue-cutting day after all had been convinced of the soundness of the action. Crow himself entered the debate on whether or not to cut with Chefoo, his houseboy, who desperately wanted to lose his pigtail against his more traditional and concerned mother's wishes. She, like many older Chinese, still remembered family tales from the days of the Taiping Rebellion. Chefoo, though described by Crow as his "houseboy," was in fact over 40 with children of his own, but he still feared his mother's wrath in his home town of Ningbo. When Chefoo did finally submit to the chop, he confided in Crow that it was the first time he had ever defied his mother's wishes.

Meanwhile, China was gradually switching allegiances and coming out publicly in favor of the Republic until only the Forbidden City itself remained as a fortress of Manchu power. The court promised reform, apologized for previous injustices and begged forgiveness to save itself. Eventually the six-year-old boy Emperor Pu Yi issued a statement (naturally drafted by the princes) accepting responsibility and swearing allegiance to the Republic. It was too late. Crow observed that when the floods had devastated the Yangtze, the rulers had done nothing to help, offered little compassion and only made a few "stingy contributions."[7] Crow noted that by the time of the Hankou rebellion, the Manchu's political stock with the people was exhausted. Shortly before her death, the old Empress Dowager had promised more charitable donations but few ever appeared. Now time had run out and the regime was finished.

In the fall of the Manchus and the success of the Republicans, Crow saw no great political organization but rather stored-up distrust and hatred for the Manchus in the Forbidden City among the people. He believed that the rebels were given more credit than they deserved for spreading the rebellion which, for most people, was more an unleashing of pent-up anger than a conscious political movement. Crow noted that the leaders of the anti-Qing forces, such as Dr. Sun, had always worked, largely overseas, for a rebellion among the upper echelons of society, more a coup than a popular uprising. To Crow, the rebellion was partly accidental, sparked by the premature events in Hankou, and ultimately haphazard in nature. Just why the rebellion in Hankou had been successful against the odds was not entirely clear to him. He pondered why the Imperial Navy had only briefly shelled Hankou and then remained adamantly silent – was it support for the rebels among naval officers or lack of ammunition after years of paltry armaments spending? Certainly many of the shells in the navy's armoury were wooden and many bullets turned out to be made from papier-mâché – fake ammunition largely manufactured in Japan.

Ultimately, Crow concluded that Chinese dislike of the Manchus was stimulated by years of Manchu garrisons stationed in Chinese towns as occupying forces, the obligatory forced payment of "tribute rice" to the garrison and the refusal of the troops to partake of daily life. The Manchus became parasites on the Han Chinese while simultaneously looking down on them as inferior beings. As Crow commented, the revolution for most ordinary Chinese was about the injustices they suffered on a daily basis rather than lofty Jeffersonian ideas of democracy:

> All he [*the average Chinese peasant*] had to do was look at the fat Manchu who slept in the sun all afternoon while he ploughed the fields, sowed the seeds and grew the food the Manchu pensioner ate.[8]

Crow also saw that the hatred of the Manchu court did not extend to a hatred of everyone with Manchu lineage. Despite their roles throughout Chinese society as everything from rickshaw-drivers to shop-keepers, there was no general massacre or revenge exacted upon the ordinary Manchu people, many of whom had long ago assimilated into wider Han Chinese society. While sporadic killings did occur in northeastern China, in other areas funds were established to ease the impoverishment of needy Manchus. In the treaty negotiations between the Republicans and the Qing, Sun had guaranteed the royal family protection and the right to continue to reside in the Forbidden City, as well as giving them a fixed income of four million Mexican silver dollars annually and permission to use their former imperial titles.

Crow noted that the traditional Chinese dislike of soldiering as an occupation was weakened by the mass unemployment and poverty that resulted from the Yangtze flooding and so swelled the ranks of the anti-Manchu militias – though he also noted that, even in Shanghai, where food was not scarce, many sons of prosperous Chinese families joined the cause and signed up for the rebel army. The republicans had become heroes and the nature of nationalism and patriotism was changing in China. Where once nationalism had been defined as an appreciation of China's past cultural heritage or allegiance to the current rulers, it was now increasingly defined by contemporary politics. Crow saw an interweaving of Nationalist traditions – the new republican heroes were likened to the mythical heroes of the Chinese classics and embodied in the new volunteer units, such as the Shanghai group who called themselves the "Death and Glory Boys" and another, comprising women only, who marched under the banner "Dare to Die" and a third that topped that with "Determined to Die." Sadly, many got their wish either on the battlefield or the imperial execution grounds. These volunteer groups were a motley bunch. One group was commanded by a young Chiang Kai-shek for a time while others comprised members of the city's major criminal cartel, the Green Gang.

Crow reported extensively for the *China Press* on the new mood of republican patriotism in China. He was based as the *Press*'s special correspondent in the new capital of Nanjing for a time and wrote a summary of Sun's first proclamation in which he outlined his ambitious plans for the new government. Crow wrote in the *Press* of the early days of the Nanjing government:

> The Republic of China is less than a week old now, but in that time it has begun to set its house in order. It has equipped itself with electric lights, and in the business-like atmosphere of the place an old style Chinese official would look as out of place as a sedan chair in New York.[9]

Crow also met Chen Qimei, the Shanghai revolutionary and blood brother of Sun who had been appointed Governor of the Chinese portions of Shanghai after 1911.[10] Chen had acceded to the demand by some war widows to be allowed to fight for the cause; 120 women volunteered, some with bound feet, and were issued with rifles and wore scarlet trousers as a uniform in the style of the French *Sans Culottes* of 1789. The *China Press* not only reported the revolution but was also intimately involved in its progress. Charles Webb, the *Press*'s managing editor and a correspondent in China for the Hearst press, worked with Wu Ting-fang on drafting the new government's appeal for worldwide recognition which concluded with the not entirely correct statement that

> "The most glorious page in Chinese history has been written with a bloodless pen."[11]

Certainly, when imperial troops had briefly retaken Hankou, they had slaughtered anyone found without a queue, as did the Manchu General Chang

Hsun in Nanjing. Crow rushed to Nanjing to cover what was expected to be a decisive battle in the revolution as rebel troops from Guangzhou steamed up from the south to confront the Imperial Army. However, the Manchu forces retreated under cover of darkness before the Cantonese soldiers arrived. Crow, who had been told by a local correspondent that the streets of Nanjing were "a foot deep in blood" had dashed to the city in the hope of finally covering a battle only to discover "… no bloody streets, only a correspondent who had mixed gin with Chinese brandy … There wasn't even a donkey left in Nanking."[12] Once again Crow missed his chance to be a war correspondent.

Crow did stay to see the Cantonese troops enter the city of a million people and was not impressed by their thin uniforms which were more suitable for temperate southern climes and antiquated muzzle-loading rifles which Crow referred to as similar to "the squirrel rifles of our pioneer ancestors."[13] He was also bemused to see that the troops had brought braziers with which to manufacture bullets as they needed them and also that many of the soldiers carried umbrellas rather than rifles. Though the Cantonese troops bolstered the revolutionary forces in Nanjing, there was little interaction; they only spoke Cantonese dialect and the garrison became what Crow described as a "Chinese Tower of Babel,"[14] with all communication and war councils having to be conducted through time-consuming written notes.

Crow settled down to cover the new Republican government, known as the *Xinhai*, and attended the First Republican Convention held in Shanghai which he described – and given his youth and religious family he would have known – as having an atmosphere similar to that of "an old fashioned Methodist revival meeting."[15] The mood, according to Crow, was certainly fairly euphoric with delegates feeling that they could achieve anything now they had overthrown the Qing and the worst problems were behind the movement.

Speeches invoked Jefferson, Washington and Lincoln and one inspired young republican actually concluded his speech by cutting of the tip of his little finger and daubing the Chinese character for "republic" on the wall (the character had had to be invented by Sun Yat-sen as the Chinese language had never had need of it before). Crow witnessed the somewhat confused proceedings noting that, despite the applause every time the word "republic" was uttered, it seemed most of the delegates had only a sketchy notion of what representative government entailed. To be fair, nobody could blame the generally young and idealistic delegates given China's 5,000 years of autocratic domination by one dynasty or another. Crow believed that if real democratic republicans existed in China, they were to be found largely in southern China around Guangzhou where secret political societies had existed for a century or more and where the old adage "the mountains are high and the emperor is far away" was coined to show a certain streak of independence. Unlike other pockets of republicanism, such as Shanghai, southern China was largely free of foreign dominance and a certain Chinese-style of republicanism had been able to mildly flourish. Southerners read foreign books and formed the bulk of those Chinese who emigrated to America and elsewhere and returned to their native villages with new ideas or wrote letters home to their families detailing new experiences and ways of thinking. It was also where Christian missionary work had traditionally been concentrated and conversion rates had been highest (including Sun and Charlie Soong). In short, the south was markedly less conservative and also markedly more open to new ideas than the rest of the country.

The new government was rocky from the start and Crow was one among many foreign observers who didn't think that it could last and would ultimately metamorphose into a new dynasty taking on all the trappings of previous regimes. Sun remained President of the new Republic, and head of the newly formed *Kuomintang* (KMT) that replaced the Unity League in August 1912, only briefly, soon transferring power to the experienced military commander who had largely supervised the training of the Imperial New Army[16] before 1911, Yuan Shih-kai. Yuan succeeded Sun as President and lasted until 1916. Crow felt sure that this marked the end of the Republic and the start of a new dynasty, or monarchical movement, headed by Yuan, who swiftly emerged as a virtual military dictator and did eventually attempt to declare himself Emperor. Yuan, whom Crow had identified as China's "sole strong man," was an enigmatic character in Chinese history, known as China's Machiavelli, and famed for his 16 sons and 14 daughters courtesy of his wife and a dozen concubines. He was not trusted completely by Sun who thought him overly ambitious and lacking in scruples. Sun was right.

Born in Henan province in 1859 to a family of mandarins, Yuan had been classically educated. However, he failed the civil service examinations that were the major guarantor of advancement in China and decided on a military career where he had been taken under the wing of an influential general. Still only in his twenties, he had been posted to Korea between 1885 and 1894 to command a brigade to maintain, ultimately unsuccessfully, Chinese suzerainty over the peninsula. Yuan returned to China in 1895 after Japan's annexation of Korea and settled in Beijing with the job of overseeing the modernization of China's army. He supported Ci Xi against the reform movement of the young Emperor Kuang Hsu in 1898. For this service, the Empress Dowager had rewarded him with the Vice Regency of Zhili (now Hebei) Province where he successfully contained the Boxers, which made him popular with the local foreign population that in return largely turned a blind eye to the sizeable military force he subsequently built up.

Yuan may have opposed the reform-minded Kuang Hsu but he also knew that China's army was still mainly composed of outdated bowmen, cavalry and foot soldiers and was bound to suffer defeat against a modern army. He slowly, and with little additional funding, crafted the New Army, sometimes known as the *Beiyang* (Northern) Army, with improved weaponry, field medical services, supporting battlefield logistics and a stronger command structure.

Despite these achievements, attempting to elevate himself to the Emperor's throne was a step too far. Though Yuan had won some adherents with his attempts to sort out China's chaotic finances and build up a national treasury through domestic tax collection and foreign loans, he had a tendency to centralize power around himself and showed little tolerance to those whose opinions differed from his. Yuan's intimidation of pro-Sun National Assembly members in Beijing led Sun to eventually call for the overthrow of Yuan. In July 1913 China's so-called "Second Revolution" broke out when some provincial warlords and military commanders challenged Yuan. The Chinese Machiavelli suppressed the rebellion and put in Duan Qirui, a noted hardliner, as Premier. Duan had been a commander in the New Army and had come to prominence during the suppression of the Boxers in 1900. Yuan had chosen him to go to Wuchang in 1911 to try to suppress the garrison mutiny there. Later he was a delegate on the imperial side at the peace talks, though he supported the abdication of Pu Yi. This allowed him to be trusted enough to be appointed as Minister for the Army in Yuan's government and subsequently to become Governor of Hubei province.

Duan was a complicated character: a military hardliner and a political conservative while also a devout Buddhist. Though he became Premier, he delegated much of the work, preferring to concentrate on military training matters, and retained his post as Minister for the Army. It was thought that the moustachioed and stern-looking Duan leaned towards cabinet government and open discussion, but he largely kept quiet and maintained a Confucian pupil-teacher relationship with Yuan. More cynically, it may have been that Duan saw that Yuan was increasingly in poor health and that his teacher wouldn't be around much longer anyway.[17]

Feeling confident in his position, Yuan then amended the 1912 Provisional Constitution consolidating power further and even banned the KMT altogether in 1913, ordered Sun's arrest and execution and looked to forge an alliance with Japan to ensure funding for his government. This later encouraged the Japanese in the Twenty-One Demands they made on China in 1915. All of this led to economic decline and a rise in warlordism and, eventually, Yuan's plan to become Emperor. He developed a taste for lavish ceremonies in true imperial style and swapped his military clothing, which had always been heavy on the braid and medals compared to most of his contemporaries, for even more imperial robes and ceremonies at Beijing's Temple of Heaven.

The situation was resolved when an outcry was heard from many quarters at Yuan's rise and the increase in what David Bonavia in his history of China's warlords called "military centrifugalism."[18] General Cai, the *dujun* of Yunnan, openly rebelled and declared his province independent, followed swiftly by Jiangxi and Guangdong. The impetus was flowing away from Yuan, but he died anyway (of natural causes) on 6 June 1916. By the time of his death, the short, squat Yuan was relying increasingly on military dictate to govern China and had become unpopular with the Chinese people, especially in the south of the country. Despite this, his funeral in Beijing was still a major state event attended by thousands in silence.

Sun returned to power on the back of popular discontent with Yuan, support in his southern strongholds and the rise of the National Protection [*Huguo*] movement. However, Sun was not the ideal man to run China anymore. The most unwarlike Dr. found Yuan's legacy, the military centrifugalism, unmanageable. Again, later, when the unreformed Qing General Chang Hsun, who had rampaged through Nanjing in 1911, tried to usurp power with the help of his private army, Sun had to deal with would-be leaders with grand visions. Chang got as far as reinstating Pu Yi briefly in Beijing after bombing the imperial palace from an aeroplane, but public protests and the rumor that the whole coup was a plot by the German Kaiser to take over China forced Chang to flee the city and Pu Yi to step down again.

Crow monitored the Republic's power shifts as the situation dissolved into warlordism, Yuan came and went and Sun, as well the Soong clan, went on the run in Japan. He felt that maintaining a detailed record of the shifts was probably valueless in the long run. He shared the majority opinion among foreigners on the China coast that, as long as the fighting stayed away from Shanghai, it would be better; though when it did inconvenience Shanghailanders, they usually managed to resolve the crisis. Crow lost one weekend of golf after a warlord dug some trenches and built machine-gun nests on the British course near Shanghai at Hongqiao. Apparently the golf club president remonstrated with the warlord who made good the damage and apologized after moving his troops to less contentious ground. Crow described these early warlord clashes as "semicomic."[19] At one battle, close to the International Settlement, in the suburb of Xujiahui, the fighting was briefly stopped while American missionaries entered the area to save some tethered and apparently terrified goats. Once the goats were escorted to safety, the potshots started again.

Crow's feelings about the warlords were mixed. He shared the popular view among the foreign community that most of them were outright exploiters bent on taxing people in areas under their control in order to accrue fortunes which were then stashed in American bank accounts. However, he believed that some of them were true patriots and genuinely believed in restoring the Qing dynasty and a monarchical system as the best thing for China and its future stability. They may have talked sometimes abstractly about parliaments and constitutions but, as Crow recalled a friend of his commenting at the time, the difference between the average warlord's conception of a constitutionally convened government and an absolute monarchy was "like the difference between the shoulders of a snake and the hips of an eel."[20] Later, as the warlord period gathered pace, he was to find himself up close and personal with several warlords.

These experience of the 1911 period and Yuan's rise and fall led Crow to believe firmly that attempts to establish dictatorships in China would all be doomed to failure. Looking back on the events of the early years of the Republic in his book *China Takes Her Place* in the 1940s, Crow commented: "An attempt to introduce anything resembling the Nazi salute or the "Heil Hitler" greeting would have been met with the raucous laughter of 400 million people who never overlook an opportunity to laugh at the absurd and the incongruous. Things like that are not done in China."[21] Reminiscing later, Crow felt that he had dismissed the stumbling attempts at forming parliaments and writing constitutions too quickly at the time. They were at least starting points from which reform movements could grow, base points from which people could have potentially advanced reformist agendas and demands.

A Silent Press Baron and an Unpretentious President

Crow's support for the new Republic in both his journalism and in acts such as helping Chinese papers thwart the intrusions of warlords had been strengthened by his personal contacts with Sun Yat-sen. In January 1912 Crow had traveled up to Nanjing to meet Dr. Sun personally when he had then been President of the new Chinese Republic for only a fortnight. Nanjing was also technically a treaty port and had been since May 1899. A rail link to Shanghai had been completed in 1908, along with the regular steamer service, which also increased the traditional heavy flow of missionaries into the city. Though now officially the capital of the Chinese Republic, few countries moved their embassies to the city. They preferred to remain in Beijing, presumably not wanting to go through the bother of a formal move in case the whole republican experiment failed and things returned to normal as many ambassadors suspected would occur.

Sun was quartered in the former *Yamen*[22] that had been the traditional home of the Viceroy who oversaw the imperial court's rule throughout the lower Yangtze delta and Jiangsu. Crow's interview with Sun was arranged for 6 a.m., which shocked the normally late-rising Crow, but was typical of the tradition of China's former imperial rulers to start work early and was in fact a compliment and courtesy to the American writer. However, the *Yamen* Sun was living in was eight miles from Crow's hotel which entailed a 3 a.m. wake-up call and a bumpy journey in a pony and cart along a severely rutted road.

Nanjing was the old capital of the Ming dynasty and Sun's decision to relocate the government there from Beijing indicated at once a break with the immediate Manchu past but also a continuation of a royal city for the country's capital. Sun added a few personal touches. As an urbane Christian Chinese, as well as a qualified doctor who had pioneered the blending of Western and Chinese medical practices while living abroad, Sun had learned to enjoy some more modern comforts than the Manchu rulers he overthrew. Crow arrived at the *Yamen* to see a shiny new car parked outside (though it was unable to traverse many of the poor quality roads around Nanjing) and the new five-bar flag of the Republican government flying over the building.

Dr. Sun greeted Crow on time dressed in an unpretentious uniform devoid of braid and frills. Crow focused on Sun's plans for Nanjing's rebuilding into a capital city fit for a republican China. Crow already knew from Sun's private secretary Ma Soo, who was an acquaintance of his, that Sun was drawing up big plans for Nanjing's transformation. The new President was planning a series of wide boulevards, parks, swimming pools and sports facilities. Most of the plans shown to Crow by Sun and Ma Soo that day were eventually carried out, transforming Nanjing completely though retaining many of the more traditional Chinese architectural sites of the city intact. This meeting with Sun was in fact one of the first major scoops of the *China Press*, and Crow's first scoop as a journalist in China. On January 4, 1912 the *China Press* trumped the rest of the English language newspapers in Shanghai by publishing a summary of Dr. Sun's first proclamation that took up the entire front page and in which the Provisional President explained his plans for the government and expressed his thanks to the friendly sympathy which had been aroused abroad for the Chinese republican movement. Crow and the *China Press* repeated their scoop two days later on January 6 when they published the next proclamation to be issued by the Republican government, in this case signed by both Sun and Wu Ting-fang. This proved that Crow's and the paper's relationship with Dr. Wu, now the Republican Minister for Foreign Affairs, was still proving useful.

For the Chinese New Year holiday in 1912, Crow also visited the city of Hangzhou, 125 miles from Shanghai and the capital of Zhejiang Province, which had a population of about 400,000. He described Hangzhou as "this beautiful lake city,"[23] later praising it highly in his *Handbook for China*, and observed that a major reconstruction of the town was occurring after it had fallen relatively quickly and peacefully to the young Chiang Kai-shek's advance. The Manchu garrison had been pulled down and the square mile or so of new vacant space was being rebuilt with broad streets designed for car traffic. Crow observed at the time that Sun had ordered the demolition of many old buildings in order to build boulevards capable of taking cars, though the first were not really to appear in the city for another 20 years.

After arriving in China in 1911, Crow had seen the country swiftly transform from the ancient dynasty of the Manchus to the new Republic. He liked the change, supported it and became rapidly pro-China when the vogue among foreigners was to remain indifferent and concentrate on business and the maintenance of Great Power privilege. Though Millard influenced Crow, he also drew his own lessons that led him to his not always popular conclusions.

Crow's reading of Chinese history led him to draw parallels between the so-called "unequal treaties" China had been forced to sign under the threat of British gunboats and Britain's treatment of colonial America where gunboat diplomacy had been used to limit the ambitions of those favoring independence. Crow also felt that the 1911 revolution was a chance for the Chinese to finally govern themselves free of Manchu control. He believed that China had been subjected to corruption, foreign influence and foreign "bad manners" for too long. As a proud American, he was also keen to see a nation like China move from under the yolk of autocracy and foreign influence, believing that in these new circumstances China would flourish as America was doing but retain strong links with foreign countries, just as the United States maintained a good relationship with Britain. Likewise Crow saw occasional problems such as the continuing bouts of anti-foreign sentiment that still periodically spilled over into violence as natural growing pains of an emerging country, much as an often xenophobic isolationist tendency lingered in America. Indeed, Crow was always quick to draw comparisons between China and America to show that some of the things that outraged or mystified foreigners, such as peasants throwing rocks at the first trains that arrived in China, had all happened before.

Despite Crow's enthusiasm for the new Republic and Sun's plans for China, he eventually came to the conclusion that Sun had largely been a failure as a President of China. Despite his strong patriotism and obvious abilities, he was simply not practical enough when it came to the business of day-to-day politics and economics and had got himself into various potentially compromising situations, such as considering offering the Japanese concessions in return for support when Sun was in exile in Tokyo in 1912. Crow was proved right when

Yuan Shih-kai eased Sun out of power with relative ease only a few months later.

Crow continued to cover the developments as best he could in Shanghai. When the warlords largely stopped speaking to the Chinese press, tried to censor them or force them to close and only talked to foreign-owned newspapers, Crow stepped in to help two publications. He became the nominal owner and chairman of the board of two Chinese-managed daily papers, one in Tianjin and another in Jinan. As an American citizen, this made both papers technically foreign publications. Crow never wrote an editorial or even actually visited the offices of either paper and declared that he "… had no more to do with the management of the paper than with that of the London *Times*."[24] He did not even draw a salary: his only contribution was to eat the sumptuous banquets that the editors of both papers provided for him as thanks for his help. This was not an unusual measure against censorship. For instance, the *Sin Wan Pao* [*Xinwenbao*], which Crow estimated to have a circulation of 10,000 copies daily rising to 35,000 at times, had been technically founded and owned by an American, Dr. John C. Ferguson, who also played an intimate role in the paper's management and editorial policy. Ferguson's *Sin Wan Pao* was registered at the American consulate in Shanghai, while other papers were under Italian or Portuguese protection, as well as a few under Japanese control. Crow noted that the two papers he helped were just two of half a dozen that approached him for assistance.

Crow's actions in Tianjin and Jinan were partly inspired by Ferguson whom Crow had met through their joint work in the Famine and Flood Relief Movement in Shanghai. Dr. John Calvin Ferguson was actually a Canadian who became a naturalized American and was a recognized China Hand who had acted as a journalist, had been an advisor to the Nationalist Government of China and, for a time, the President of Nanjing University and Nan Yung College. He had also served as Secretary to the Chinese Minister of Commerce as well as with the Chinese Imperial Railway Administration. He was a delegate for the Chinese Government at the Ninth International Red Cross Convention in Washington in 1912 and later represented China at the 1922 Washington Conference on the Limitation of Armaments and Far Eastern Questions. Ferguson went on to write a book on China – *Outlines of Chinese Art and Chinese Mythology* – and remained in China until the Japanese occupation when he was repatriated to Canada and spent the rest of the war campaigning in support of the Chinese in their resistance to Japan. He also had the honor of having a street named after him in Frenchtown – Route Ferguson.

Of nine Chinese newspapers in Shanghai surveyed by British Intelligence in 1918, seven were registered with the Japanese consulate and others with the

French authorities though their shareholders were mostly Chinese.[25] However, though Crow, Ferguson and others helped the Chinese press to register so as to avoid the censors, their actions did little to endear them to many of the traditionalists in the International Settlement. Many influential voices, including the right-wing *Far Eastern Review*, saw their actions as potentially eroding the privileges of extraterritoriality and handing over foreign papers to Chinese control.

That the *Far Eastern Review* attacked Crow was no surprise nor was it for the first or last time. An American journalist, George Bronson Rea, well known for having covered the Spanish-American War of 1898 had founded the monthly magazine in 1904 in Manila. He relocated to Shanghai in 1912. It was anti-American and pro-Japanese (being part subsidized by Tokyo) and so was bound to collide with the likes of Crow. Likewise, Bronson Rea constantly annoyed Crow with his pro-Japanese propaganda, particularly his 1935 book *The Case for Manchoukuo*[26] that argued that Japan had a territorial right to annex Manchuria. The *Review* eventually changed hands and was managed by Charlie Laval, an Old China Hand, but with equally right-wing opinions.

However, simply being foreign-owned was not a guarantee of untrammelled access. Crow was still an employee of the *China Press*, a paper that remained majority-owned and controlled by American nationals, but it still managed to incur the wrath of one small-time local warlord by writing an unfavorable profile of him. The warlord ordered the Shanghai Post Office to cease distribution of the *China Press*. Though this was illegal, the Post Office was concerned enough with the possibility of retribution to comply; and for a time the paper was shipped to nearby Suzhou by express train and mailed out to subscribers from there with the active support of another local warlord who intensely hated the first one.

Crow estimated that at any one time the combined forces of the warlords controlled no more than one percent of China's landmass and were able to tax no more than one-tenth of the population. First as a journalist and later as an advertising executive, Crow continued to travel the country and go about his business largely undisturbed by the warlords' activities. However, he was forced to write a number of letters home to friends, family and business acquaintances in America who were concerned for his safety after reading reports of warlord-induced chaos throughout China.

Crow's induction into Shanghai had been a busy and a testing one – starting a new life in a new country; launching a newspaper and establishing a bureau for UP; deciphering the collapse of the Qing dynasty and the rise of the Nationalists; and then watching a new government form and fracture as warlords proliferated. But it clearly hadn't all been work. On December 27, 1912, he found time to marry Miss Mildred S. Powers in Shanghai. Mildred had been a member of staff with the *China Press* before becoming manager of the Underwood typewriter department at Dodwell and Company where she was in charge of the firm's business in China and Japan. Crow must have met Mildred almost immediately upon his arrival in Shanghai – the two were the same age and were also photographed together in a souvenir program from the 1911 *China Press* Christmas Eve staff party.

Married, employed and chasing one of the biggest stories in the world, Crow had certainly arrived in the Far East – he was on his way to becoming a confirmed China Hand. However, with his initial contract at the *China Press* expired, he opted for a change of scene.

5

Intrigue in Tokyo and World War

Marriage, Manila and Around the World

The newly-married Crows left Shanghai at Christmas 1912 for their honeymoon, sailing to Manila en route to New York. He had finished his first book *The Travelers' Handbook for China*, a guidebook to China that was to be reprinted many times over the years. It was to become the major travel guide to China between the wars, going through a series of reprints and gaining a place as the "standard reference book for the foreign visitor to that country."[1] Four editions appeared between 1913 and 1933, the first being published by the Hwa-Mei Book Concern in Shanghai while the celebrated Shanghai book publisher Kelly & Walsh published later editions. Each update slightly expanded the previous one to reflect the growth of facilities throughout China and the arrival of modern hotels, the railways and airplane services. Crow called upon friends and colleagues to help put the *Handbook* together. K. C. Chow and Y. Obie, both later to be staff at Crow's Shanghai advertising agency contributed, as did his fellow Missouri University alumnus Hin Wong who worked in Guangzhou. His proofs were checked by Shanghailanders Reginald Sweetland (the Shanghai correspondent for the *Chicago Daily News*) and T. O. Thackery, who was later to work with Crow on a film script of his 1937 book *Four Hundred Million Customers* and worked for the *New York Post*; and the editor of the *China Journal of Science and Arts*, botanist and adventurer Arthur de Carle Sowerby,[2] wrote the section on the flora and fauna of China. In later additions the *New York Times* correspondent Hallet Abend contributed too.

After a brief stop in Hong Kong, Carl and Mildred arrived in the Philippines in early January 1913 and stayed in Manila for several months to gather material for a book Carl was planning on the country, which was eventually published in 1914 as *America and the Philippines*. In Manila, Crow took time to see the city and examine the American occupation of the archipelago. He seems to have found it a rather pestilential place (he arrived during one of Manila's periodic cholera outbreaks) and was not overly impressed with the American approach to governing the country or the grip of religion on the nation. As regards the latter, he declared that "the priest had usually seized on any epidemic to point out that it was the direct result of the sins of the people, visited on them through San Roque, the saint who controls cholera, smallpox and the plague. When these diseases appeared, great religious processions were held in which sacred images were carried through the infected districts."[3]

The Crows' brief stay in the Philippines got of to a disastrous start after one of their trunks was accidentally dropped into the sea while being discharged from their cruise ship, the *St. Albans*. The trunk contained some antiques from China that Crow had to admit were ruined by the ocean-dipping.[4]

After finishing his research (it is not known whether or not Mildred appreciated his researching a political text while they were supposedly on their honeymoon), the Crows sailed from Manila to San Francisco. They traveled cross-country to New York, spending several weeks in Manhattan. Then they headed off to Europe to begin a leisurely round-the-world trip visiting several European countries, followed by a voyage through the Red Sea that Crow particularly enjoyed, and then on to Egypt and Karachi.[5] They finished their round-the-world honeymoon and returned briefly to America in November 1913.

Crow had a reason to return to Missouri in late 1913. A family crisis had occurred when his younger brother Ray, who ran the local newspaper in Fredricktown, had left for work one morning never to return. The family was frantic. His mother, Elvira, was at her wits' end, while Ray's wife Mabel was distraught and left alone with her three-year-old son George. Carl used his many connections in Missouri to involve the police, FBI and others in the search for Ray but all to no avail. Ray was never to be seen again. Despite the local rumor-mill throwing up a number of possibilities, it was noticed six months later that Ray's former secretary, a noted Fredricktown beauty, left to look for a new job in St. Louis and then also disappeared without trace. Small town propriety forbade too much open gossip but two and two added up to a rather large four in the case.[6]

He had also become something of a local Missouri celebrity and talked about his experiences in China and the Philippines to the local press. He told the *St. Louis Times*: "The one deplorable thing about the American occupation of the Philippines is the fact that Americans know so little about it."[7] Eventually Carl could do no more in the fruitless search for Ray and had to leave. The Crows left St. Louis with Carl carrying on talking about Filipino politics, though the local Missouri press seemed more interested in his adventurous life. The papers made much of the fact that Carl left Missouri for San Francisco to sail for Japan to take up a new job in Tokyo while Mildred travelled overland to New York, sailed for Europe and took the Trans-Siberian Railway to get to Japan – a not inconsiderable trip for a single woman at the time. They both arrived in time to spend Christmas 1913 in Tokyo at their new address – 17 Mikawacho, Akasaka – in the center of the city, only a stone's throw from the imperial palace in Chiyoda and the Hie Shrine.[8]

Intrigue in Japan

Crow had only been in Tokyo a few months when he witnessed the full pageantry of Japan. On April 19, 1914 the Empress Dowager Haruko died. Her Imperial Highness Empress Dowager *Shōken* of Japan was the *kogo* (empress-consort) of the Meiji Emperor. She had been born in 1849 and was the third daughter of Lord Tadaka. Her original name had been Masako but she adopted the name Haruko after her marriage to the Emperor in 1867, after which she also started regularly wearing Western clothing while the vast majority of upper-class Japanese women continued to wear *kimono*. She was a highly revered figure in Japan, being the first imperial consort to receive the title of *kogo* in several hundred years. Although she was the first Japanese Empress to play a public role, she bore no children (though the Emperor had 15 children by five official ladies-in-waiting). She had assumed the role of helping the poor and promoting national welfare and women's education; and she also established the Japanese Red Cross Society during the first Sino-Japanese War (1894–95), an act that earned her the title "Mother of the Nation." Her funeral was a major state occasion and also the first time Crow had witnessed the famed discipline and micro-management of Japanese society. He joined the crowds thronging the streets for her funeral cortege and found his attention drawn from the procession to the people around him:

> I was a spectator at the funeral and found the tedious ceremony relieved by the actions of the police who took care of the crowd with maternal care. "Now is the time to stop talking," they would observe to the crowd. "Now you must remove your hats." "Now you must not move or talk," etc. The great outward show of respect, the draped flags, the funeral decorations on the humblest house, the band of crêpe univerally worn – all the things which so impressed foreign visitors may be attributed to the efficiency of the Tokyo police.[9]

By the summer of 1914, with the First World War underway in Europe, Crow was settling into his new job in Tokyo as the business manager of the *Japan Advertiser*,[10] at that time a well-known American-owned daily English language newspaper. He was employed on a salary of ¥500 a month and was responsible for 75, mostly Japanese, staff. B. W. Fleisher, a Missouri School of Journalism graduate who had founded the paper, was running the *Japan Advertiser*. In Tokyo, Crow was once again among Missouri News Colony members who, along with Fleisher, included Frank Hedges (Tokyo-correspondent for the *Christian Science Monitor*), Vaughn Bryant and Duke Parry, both Tokyo-based correspondents for various newspapers; and in 1915–16 Frank L. Martin, an Associate Professor at the Missouri School of Journalism, was the acting editor. Hedges was the best known of the group and was considered highly knowledgeable about Japan. He contributed regular sketches of Japanese life to the *Monitor* as well as the London *Times* and the *Washington Post* where descriptions of shrines, mountains, traditional drums, misty rains and the shrill wailing of Shinto music were all prominent features of his brief, lyrical pieces.

As well as taking care of much of the business side of the paper, Crow was also still an active journalist, moonlighting as a correspondent for UP as he had in Shanghai. However, in 1914, Crow's correspondent duties were light. He was an American in Japan and the isolationist US was not involved directly in the European conflict. Though technically an ally of Britain, Japan's role in the war was minimal and largely involved the seizure of the German treaty port of Qingdao in Shandong province in September 1914. China had declared neutrality in August but, at the urging of America and Britain, was to come out on the side of the Allies and declare war on Germany in the summer of 1917. For several months after the Japanese annexed Qingdao, nothing happened in Japan or China that could edge the growing slaughter in the European battlefields off the front pages of the American press. Crow didn't plan to stay long in Japan, only from Christmas 1913 to spring 1915, and so did not seek to involve himself in covering the machinations of Japan in great depth – but those machinations found him anyway.

While newspaper editors in the US were concentrating on Europe and ignoring the Far East, Crow became dramatically embroiled in local events. He recounted the story of how he had been a bit player in the events surrounding Japan's ultimatum to China in 1915, the so-called "Twenty-One Demands," in his 1937 book *I Speak for the Chinese*. This book, which was written during his last months in Shanghai, was an attempt to alert the American reading public to the dangers of Japanese militarism and the threat to China.

Crow was an early believer that Japanese intentions towards China would be a problem. Having made a study of Japanese history, Crow believed that Toyotomi Hideyoshi (1536–98), whom Crow later called "a Hitler of that period,"[11] had ignited Japanese expansionist ideas towards China as far back as the sixteenth century. To Crow, Hideyoshi had risen to power in Japan and saw Japanese influence naturally extending over China, Korea and the eastern part of India. His plans were never realized and his armies never crossed the frontiers of China, despite years of brutal warfare on the Korean peninsula. After his death and the end of the Sengoku period in 1598, Japan's territorial ambitions retreated somewhat, but in Crow's opinion Hideyoshi's reign had cemented the belief in Japan's imperial destiny firmly in the Japanese military mind with everybody being taught about his plans. Prior to his death, he had managed to unify the feudatories of Japan and had begun active planning for his conquest of China. In 1592 and 1597, he invaded Korea and seized much territory in order to prepare a jumping-off point for the conquest of China from the peninsula.

Following the end of Japanese seclusion and the treaty with Commodore Perry of the US Navy in 1854, which opened the then poor and unattractive ports of Shimoda and Hakodate to American trade, Japan embarked on a rapid modernization program to try to achieve some sort of parity with the Western Powers. This was demonstrated in the defeat (albeit finally more diplomatic than military) of Russia in the early twentieth century that led to the eventual formal annexation of Korea away from Chinese influence in 1910 and paved the way for the future annexation of Manchuria.

The Japanese watched events in China carefully, maintaining negotiations with the failing Manchus and becoming intricately involved in the intrigues and duplicity of the imperial court and the warlords and, at times, with the Nationalists. Though not necessarily part of a grander scheme, the Japanese did contribute to the fall of the Qing by having provided sanctuary to revolutionaries such as Sun Yat-sen and training for future generals such as Chiang Kai-shek.

However, as Crow pointed out later in his book *China Takes Her Place*, "The Japanese secret service was just as efficient then as it is now and must have known what Revolutionist Sun's plans were."[12] Crow believed the Japanese had been in a position to benefit from any potential scenario in China. If the Qing continued to rule, then they could influence them; while if the revolutionists succeeded, a period of unrest and division in China would offer them alternative opportunities; and Tokyo rightly believed a major war in Europe was imminent and that they could pursue their expansionist plans in China while the Great Powers were concentrating their attentions elsewhere. Crow ultimately believed that Japan's opportunistic strategy would finally lead to conflict with the Great Powers and the US. In his 1916 book *Japan and America*, he wrote:

> … a number of events of the present generation have in a striking and unmistakeable way placed Japan and the United States as the champions of opposing and conflicting aims and interests. The conflict of interests of the two countries is not a possible development of the future; it is an immediate and at-present-existing fact, which no amount of peace-advocate logic can reason away.[13]

This view had been brought home to Crow dramatically and with not a little intrigue during his Japanese sojourn.

Tokyo Scoop

In early 1915 Crow received a telephone call at his Tokyo office informing him that the Imperial Russian Ambassador to Japan would like to see him personally regarding the Embassy's *Japan Advertiser* subscription. Crow was instructed to appear at the Russian Embassy at 3 p.m. that day. Naturally, Crow wondered just why such a high personage as the Tsar's man in Tokyo would have such an urgent need to see the business manager of an American-run newspaper. At the time, Russia was still run by the Romanovs and the Embassy in Tokyo reflected all the glory of the rulers of Russia, which was fighting on the side of the allies.

Crow arrived at the appointed time and was greeted by a Secretary to the Ambassador who requested he wait in a small study off the main hall. The room was large but relatively bare with chairs around the walls and a lone table and single chair placed in the middle of the room. On the table was a single sheet of paper positioned face up. Crow himself in *I Speak for the Chinese* continues the story:

It was a large white sheet, covered with a typewritten message, and I could no more avoid reading the first lines than I could help seeing the paper. In capital letters the message began: THE FOLLOWING 21 DEMANDS WERE PRESENTED YESTERDAY BY THE GOVERNMENT OF JAPAN TO THE GOVERNMENT OF CHINA.[14]

Crow instantly realized that the letter's presence was not an oversight and that Russian ambassadors were not noted for leaving important documents of state lying around for visiting American newspapermen to browse. Crow took the hint, folded the letter in half and slipped it into his pocket. Moments later the Ambassador entered the room, and spoke quickly and perfunctorily about changing the address of his subscription while never once mentioning the piece of paper, and finally escorted Crow back to the foyer. The meeting was over. Before Crow left the embassy the ambassador's secretary pointedly told him that he had been the only caller the Ambassador had received that day.

Naturally Crow rushed back to his office, read the letter through and instantly realized that this was a major news story. The Japanese demands were in effect an ultimatum to the weak Nationalist government in China that, if agreed to, would mean China effectively becoming a protectorate of Japan. While the eyes of the allied Great Powers were averted to the mounting carnage in Europe, Japan intended to annex China.

To Crow, Japan's Twenty-One Demands would redraw the map of Asia in a way more profound than the ultimatum presented to Serbia by Germany in 1914 that at the time was seen as the cause of the First World War. Crow had a scoop, the ultimate newspaperman's dream – and he believed it was an exclusive one at that.

Crow never revealed the source of the document until 1937 by which time the Tsar's government was gone and Stalin was in firm control of the Soviet Union. He never did find out why he had been the man chosen to receive the scoop from the Russian secret service. Revealing the source of the story was a later problem. The immediate one was how to cable the news from Japan to the US with Japanese intelligence rigorously censoring all outgoing cables. Crow mailed a copy of the document to a friend in Shanghai with instructions to cable it from China to New York and, simultaneously, he mailed five separate copies to friends at UP's offices in America. Crow hoped it would get into the Shanghai newspapers, especially the *China Press*. He was less hopeful of the *North-China Daily News* as the paper was a rival of the *Press* and he preferred the American-run paper to get the scoop. Also, the *News* was usually considered to be "soft" on Japan as the paper generally admired the success of Tokyo's modernization efforts since the Meiji Restoration. It also wished to keep the peace in the

International Settlement (there was a large Japanese community, represented on the largely British-controlled Council of the International Settlement and the Rate Payers' Association) and, being British-owned, recognized that Japan and Great Britain had a formal alliance before and during the First World War.[15] Anyway, the letter never arrived in Shanghai and only one of the other five copies mailed was ever received. But one was enough and UP was the first news organization to publish the full version of the document.

However, Crow was partially trumped by Beijing which had leaked an incomplete form of the document to the press, despite the fact that the Japanese had told the Chinese they would be punished severely if the ultimatum became public knowledge. Still the world concentrated on Europe. In May 1915 Washington officially banned American citizens from traveling to Europe, the Austro-German armies were advancing through Galicia and the Russian army was in retreat in Hungary. Although America remained neutral and isolationist, alarm was rising as news of the German use of mustard gas against the British Expeditionary Forces in Belgium and France became public knowledge. On the day the Twenty-One Demands were officially submitted to the Chinese, America's newspapers were full of one of the major stories of the First World War – the sinking of the *RMS Lusitania*, torpedoed and sunk by the Germans off the Irish coast with over 1,000 lives lost. The list of the dead included 114 Americans, which ensured that the sinking dominated US front pages.

The Twenty-One Demands – "Sordid and Ruthless"

Crow broke down the essence of the Twenty-One Demands in *I Speak for the Chinese*. While most commentators at the time concentrated on Japan's territorial ambitions, Crow saw that the demands went a lot further than just territory and described them as "… revelations of the sordidness and ruthlessness of Japanese diplomacy and the value that can be placed on Japanese pledges, even when given by her highest and most renowned officials."[16]

The Twenty-One Demands were divided into five groups, with the first two series of demands being territorial and demanding that China recognize Japan's "rights" in Shandong, Southern Manchuria and Inner Mongolia. The Shandong demand was an extension of Japan's annexation of Qingdao, though this was extended much further than the territory the Germans had previously controlled and now claimed all of Shandong province. The Chinese, as Crow pointed out, found this particularly galling as the claimed area included the birthplaces of China's most influential philosophers – Confucius and Mencius – and were seen by many as the country's philosophical "Holy Land." The Japanese claim in

Southern Manchuria related to the lease arrangement at the end of the Russo-Japanese War in 1905 that had originally been forced on China by the Russians. It was due to expire but the Japanese demanded that it be extended and enhanced for a further 99 years. This encroached on the negotiated treaty rights of Russia, a Great Power ally at the time, and was bound to have annoyed loyal Russians such as their ambassador in Tokyo. The Japanese claims regarding Inner Mongolia were even less logically tangible as they were based largely on the dubious, yet opportunistic, notion of Japanese links with Inner Mongolian princes who were trying to reject Chinese sovereignty over their traditional lands and saw an alliance with Japan as a way to achieve this.

Another set of demands related specifically to the Han-Yeh Ping Company and argued that, due to the close relations existing between Japanese capitalists and Han-Yeh Ping, it should be restructured as a Sino-Japanese company with severely reduced Chinese control and that no competitors to Han-Yeh Ping be established. Han-Yeh Ping was an iron mining and smelting business originally established by Li Hung-chang (1823–1901), a prominent Chinese statesman and general, with Chinese and Japanese capital. Li had long been a thorn in Japan's side as he had been the chief negotiator of the Treaty of Shimonoseki (1895), which ended the First Sino-Japanese War and had granted Russia the right to build the Trans-Siberian Railway across Northern Manchuria. He had also shown himself powerful when he had protected foreigners in southern China when Viceroy of Guangzhou during the Boxer Rebellion and afterwards had managed to somewhat reduce the reparations demands of the foreign powers. As someone who had defied Japan in the past, had minimized their interest in Han-Yeh Ping, and was partially responsible for the modernization of China's army and railroads, Tokyo had long been annoyed with Li.

Japan had a direct commercial interest in Han-Yeh Ping, which was China's principal supplier of iron and steel as well as being a major supplier to Japan from the Tayeh iron mines on the Yangtze River. Additionally, the company's Ping Shang coalmines were major suppliers to resource-poor Japan. The Japanese claimed that, since Han-Yeh Ping had been established in 1898 partly with a loan from the Yokohama Specie Bank, which had various interests in Manchuria, the Japanese should have more say. In 1880 the Meiji government had granted a monopoly for foreign exchange and trade financing to Yokohama Specie while Tokyo supplied one-third of its capital and awarded it a special relationship with the central bank.[17] Yokohama Specie had made various loans totalling US$40 million, although the Japanese bank had no voice in the management of the business beyond some role in overseeing expenditures. The company was important for the Chinese as its products were being used to build railways and other infrastructure across the country as China slowly modernized, and the company also controlled China's largest arsenal. Japan's attempt to take complete control of Han-Yeh Ping clearly threatened China's military autonomy and economic growth.

Also related to military autonomy was Japan's fourth set of demands that referred to the lease of harbors along the coast of Fujian province. Japan wanted exclusive leases and demanded that China not lease the harbors to any other country. Fujian was strategically important to the Japanese as it lay directly opposite Taiwan which Japan had taken control of during the Sino-Japanese War. The creation of a string of Japanese naval bases along the Fujian coastline, along with a garrison in Taiwan, would effectively give Japan naval domination of the whole of southeastern China, the mouth of the Yangtze and the International Settlement of Shanghai, as well as control of the straits that allowed shipping to move from northern China down to Hong Kong.

Clearly acceptance of any of the four groups of demands would be tantamount to a Chinese surrender of a significant part of the country's sovereignty and would be difficult to reverse without going to war with Japan. However, other demands were an attempt at the effective colonization of China. They required China to cede control of all military and naval training to Japanese officers and to use Japanese officials to reorganize China's financial system. This would reduce China to the level of a Japanese dependency along the lines of Korea. As Crow pointed out, acceptance of the fifth group of demands would make China "Japan's slave."[18]

However, the demands didn't stop there. They also included the requirement that Japan be allowed to open schools, that would presumably be funded by the Chinese, to teach Japanese on the presumption that eventually Japanese would be the main language of education and that the whole Chinese educational curriculum would be modeled on that of Japan. Lastly, and perhaps most strangely, Japan demanded the right to send missionaries to China. This was odd, as Japan had received its Buddhist religion from China. In reality, Crow believed that the Japanese entertained the notion of switching the allegiance of the Chinese people from the Manchu "Son of Heaven" in Beijing to the Japanese "Son of Heaven" in Tokyo. The result would be the subjugation of the Chinese in territorial, military, economic, educational and spiritual terms.

The weakness of the Chinese government at the time was such that the demands were verbally accepted by a clique within the government that was partly panicked, partly scared and partly cowed by the Japanese while some took bribes to support the demands. Eventually the foreign powers stepped in and only seven of the original Twenty-One Demands were acceded to by China. The particularly dangerous fifth set that would have effectively colonized China were thrown out completely; and without leasing Fujian's ports to Japan, China agreed not to lease them to any third country. Most of the other demands were watered down or rejected though, as Crow pointed out, rarely in the real interests of China but rather to safeguard the position of the Great Powers and their treaty rights.

The immediate crisis eventually passed, but the Japanese never formally withdrew any of the Twenty-One Demands and they became the basic Japanese policy towards China until the Second World War. As Crow commented, "They were conveniently pigeonholed where they would not attract public attention – that was all; they could be drawn out at a moment's notice when the time was opportune."[19] Japan continued to promote the general destabilization of China with more "advisers" sent to the courts of various warlords, soft loans advanced to warlords to purchase Japanese arms and ammunition, the encouragement of Mongolian tribes to establish independent governments, and even funds and advice to rogue bandit groups to generally accelerate the chaos in the countryside. In China, public outrage at the Twenty-One Demands led to widespread boycotts of Japanese goods that were rigidly enforced and expressed the people's anger.

Among the Citizens of the Mikado

Crow considered Japan more modern in many ways than China and yet also more traditional; he found Kyoto to be a "beautiful" city,[20] but declared that "Life for the foreign resident of Tokyo is unusually dull."[21] He also expressed concern at the level of anti-Americanism in Japan, noting that Uncle Sam always seemed to be the character chosen as a villain in Japanese newspaper cartoons. However, he appears to have liked the ordinary "citizens of the Mikado" as well as the beauty of the countryside – though the mixed sex squat urinals then still common were something he claimed never to have got used to and maintained that, despite repeated use, he was still always self-conscious "at having to use a public urinal with a Japanese woman squatting on each side of me."[22] Crow found living in Japan generally tougher than living on the China coast. As he wrote in the late 1930s: "At the present day the foreigner who moves into a house in Japan finds the task of getting himself comfortably settled tedious and difficult, for the Japanese do not use any of the furniture and utensils which are necessities in the foreign household."[23]

While he was in Tokyo, Crow furthered his interest in Japan's history and culture by making several excursions to small villages around Japan that often still had open sewers running through the streets and thatched roof houses. As was his way, he started researching subjects of interest to him in his spare time and collecting voluminous notes with the idea that eventually he would produce several books on Japan. However, his work schedule on the *Japan Advertiser* as well as the distraction of the war meant that he never got any of his projects finished. It was to be after he left China in 1937 that he had time to return to these notes and finally write them up. As well as several books he had planned on China, Crow also published his book *He Opened the Door of Japan – Townsend Harris and the Story of His Amazing Adventures in Establishing American Relations With the Far East* in 1939. Crow felt that Harris, the first American Ambassador to Japan, had been largely forgotten in America to the point that visitors to the American Embassy in Tokyo were routinely shown a portrait of Harris that was in fact not of him at all but of his boss the American Secretary of State Lewis Cass. Similarly, Crow found out that the portrait of Harris on file at the New York Public Library was also not Harris but another American, William E. Curtis, who, like Harris, had served for a time as the President of the New York Board of Education. While in Japan, Crow had found references and remembrances of Harris everywhere he went. At the time, both of Harris's homes in Japan – the American residence in the once small fishing village of Shimoda and the American legation in Tokyo – were marked and preserved as shrines to his memory.

Crow wrote his biography of Townsend with help from several friends he made in Tokyo, including Roland S. Morris who had been the US Ambassador to Japan between 1917 and 1920 and Nelson Trusler Johnson who was to become American Consul-General in Shanghai and US Ambassador Extraordinary and Plenipotentiary to China, and was later to move on to Australia where in 1942 he presented the West Point Medal of Honor to General MacArthur. He also got back in contact with two former journalist colleagues who had been in Tokyo during his time there, Miles Vaughn, who like Crow spent a lot of his time studying Japanese propaganda techniques, and Glen Babb, a Missouri News Colony member who worked in Tokyo and Beijing for AP.

Leaving Tokyo, Crow travelled to Petrograd (*St Petersburg*) and Moscow in 1915 – both cities in the grip of political change – making the two-week train trip across Russia on the Trans-Siberian. He smoked Russian cigarettes all the way and traveled with the journalist Sam Blythe,[24] a friend and correspondent for the *Saturday Evening Post*. Crow had a vivid memory of arriving in Berlin and taking his first bath after crossing Russia from the Chinese city of Harbin. He suffered the trip but didn't have much to say about it except that he was disappointed in the sunrise beyond the Arctic Circle as he had expected much more than seeing "a sickly looking orb sink behind the horizon about midnight and crawl shamefacedly above it about an hour later."[25] He headed down to Sweden, Norway and eventually England where he boarded a boat heading to New York and arrived back in America in July 1915. Crow described the trip from Japan, across Siberia and via London to New York, with atypical understatement, as "uneventful,"[26] despite the maelstrom of world events swirling around him. However, the war did briefly interfere with his travel plans when after setting sail from Christiana, in Sweden, his boat was intercepted by a British cruiser and taken to the Scottish port of Stornoway in the Western Isles where a German passenger suspected of being a spy was taken ashore and interned. Eventually Crow and the ship made it to England.

There was a postscript to Crow's experiences in Tokyo. George Bernard Shaw once quipped that "all biographies are lies," and Oscar Wilde once remarked that "The one duty we owe to history is to rewrite it." Crow often exaggerated and was fond of inserting himself into history at a place somewhat closer to the action than might have been the case in reality. Sometimes it is hard to know whether Crow was exaggerating or inventing, or if it was simply the case that several versions of the truth were possible. Crow claimed the scoop on Japan's Twenty-One Demands for himself and UP. However, among others, both the *New York Times* Correspondent Frederick Moore and Bill Donald also claimed the scoop as theirs. Crow knew both men well. Moore was a veteran China Hand who had established AP's China operation in Beijing around the same time Crow was establishing UP's presence in Shanghai. Hallet Abend, who was appointed *New York Times* China correspondent in 1927 when Moore left to return to America, wrote that Moore had scooped the Twenty-One Demands but that AP in New York had ignored the story and binned it as the Japanese Ambassador in Washington denied it.[27] In another version of the story, Earl Selle[28] – Bill Donald's biographer and also a former Shanghai foreign correspondent – wrote that Donald was told early of the demands by the veteran China Hand Roy Anderson and Paul Reinsch, the then American Minister in China, both of whom were also close friends and colleagues of Crow's over the years. Donald, according to Selle, cabled the story of the Demands to the *Times* in London but the paper also ignored it. Selle also claims that, as the *Times* was ignoring Donald, he gave the story to Moore making him promise not to reveal that Donald was the source. In a further twist, Selle claimed that Donald, after sharing that AP had ignored the story too, then gave the story to William Giles, the China correspondent for the *Chicago Daily News* who did get it published and claimed the scoop for himself. So half a dozen characters who knew each other well over a long period of time all arrived at different versions.

Roy Anderson never told his version of the story in print; Moore's version was left to Abend to tell; Donald's version was told by his rather sycophantic biographer; and neither Reinsch himself nor his biographers ever mentioned any leaking of details to the press. Whoever really did the get the scoop, Carl Crow's story of Tsarist ambassadors, strange meetings and Tokyo censors was typically by far the most entertaining.

6

From Fruit Rancher to Spy

After Japan, Crow decided not to return to Shanghai but to buy a fruit farm in California's Santa Clara Valley. For a Missourian who had enjoyed living in Texas, visited Mexico, the Philippines, Shanghai and Tokyo, married a Canadian in China and cruised around the world, the decision to farm fruit in California may not have been an obvious one. However, it was a decision he clearly felt comfortable with at the time. For the most part, the decision seems to have been based on the fact that Mildred was pregnant – his daughter Mildred Elizabeth "Betty" Crow was born on December 4, 1916.[1] He had arrived back from Europe in July 1915 to a New York he found "full of feverish and irritating energy"[2] and appears to have needed a break away from bustling and crowded cities.

Before heading to California, he visited old friends in Fort Worth and also stayed in Manhattan for a while quickly getting "into the swing of things"[3] and working on a series of articles which dealt mostly with his experiences in China and the Far East. He had become something of a celebrity in correspondent circles and briefly became part of a roundtable of globe-trotting journalists and writers that met at the Judson, a hotel on Manhattan's Washington Square.[4] Crow was actually temporarily living at the Judson as were many other authors, journalists and artists. In a profile of the roundtable published by the *New York World* newspaper, Crow was described in rather exaggerated terms as one of the major figures:

That smallish man with glasses and a ready laugh is Carl Crow. His Chinese name is Kai Low. Years spent in China on newspaper work and in Mexico and India have supplied him with many tales of peculiar experiences, particularly in China, where things are a bit different. His rooms upstairs are choked with swords and carved camphor wood boxes, while the latter are in turn filled with silks and hangings of various kinds. One of his cherished possessions is a magnificent ermine robe and muff worn by an Empress of the Celestial Empire who lived centuries before the Christian era began.[5]

Clearly one thing Crow had learned since he left for China was the art of self-promotion. By many standards he was still a China coast "Griffin" and had spent only a short time in Mexico and visited India only as a tourist as part of his round-the-world honeymoon. As for the "magnificent ermine robe and muff worn by an Empress of the Celestial Empire", clearly Crow was learning the first art of the China Hand – proclaim yourself to be one first and pretty soon no one will question your status. However, the Judson roundtable was real enough and also included A. Travers Ewell who had spent most of his life in Latin America and been awarded a gold medal by the Bolivian government for saving many lives when a dam burst; T. H. Marsoner, who had traveled throughout Cuba; and Vilhjalmur Steffanson, an anthropologist and Arctic explorer who had been on expeditions with Sir Ernest Shackleton.[6] It included also the magazine writer, explorer and anthropologist Gregory Mason[7] who actually once found pirate treasure in the Caribbean; Robert C. McElravey who had caught a gang of bank robbers in Missouri when he was 14; and University of Missouri graduate Homer Croy who had worked on the *Havana Post*.[8] It was a mixed but fascinating bunch that Crow easily fell in with.

He was also starting to achieve some notoriety as an author. His *Handbook for China* had been published to acclaim in 1913 and updated and reprinted in 1915; and his study of the American occupation of the Philippines, *America and the Philippines*, had come out a year later to mixed reviews and stirred up some controversy both in Washington and Manila. The Philippines book was sub-titled an *Official Guide and Handbook*. He hadn't been overly impressed with the country or America's role in its history and development. He described the archipelago as a bureaucratic form of government, thinly disguised as a democracy – "Indeed, if every elective office … were abolished tomorrow, the machinery of government would not be seriously hampered, and one can believe that it would go on ever more smoothly than at present."[9] Crow also, controversially for the time, asserted that the American administration had failed lamentably in the Philippines, causing a rice shortage because the seeds had been kept too long in storage and could not germinate; and the introduction of carabaos imported from China to replace those that had died from the viral disease rinderpest was a costly waste of time and tax payers' money as most of the animals died anyway and the government was out of pocket.

Even more controversially for many Americans and Filipinos was Crow's assertion that the Philippines national hero José Rizal had been a creation of US interests and that America's greatest success,

> ... was the artificial manufacture of a hero for the Filipino people. Among things the Filipino people lacked to make them a nation was a hero – a safe hero, the only safe ones, of course, being dead. Aguinaldo was considered "dangerous" as the leader of the recent insurrection. It was necessary to establish a hero whose fame would overshadow that of Aguinaldo, and thereby lessen that leader's ability to make future trouble.[10]

Crow finally concluded with the argument that Americans were not really that well-suited to British-Empire-style colonialism. He noted that early "mistakes and failures" in colonial rule had proved vastly amusing to the British, especially those connected with the British Colonial Service, who had offered advice with a typically patronizing air and pointed out how much more professionally things were being done in Hong Kong, Singapore, the Federated Malay States and other nearby places under London's control.

Eventually, Crow headed westwards to San Francisco and in 1916 while moving across country his third book, *Japan and America*, was published. The book had been written while in Japan, sent to America, and edited and printed while Crow had been slowly making his way to California from Tokyo.

Picking Fruit with Spies

By the start of the twentieth century nearly 14,000 acres of orchards and vineyards were under irrigation in the Santa Clara Valley. Crow's fruit ranch was 30 miles or so from San Francisco. He commuted into the big city for a drink with friends at the San Francisco Press Club in a small Ford he had bought. He lived on the farm with his wife and baby daughter Betty in the ranch house. Crow was essentially taking one of his retreats into a "simple life" that occasionally gripped him. The everyday chores of fruit-picking as well as doing small jobs around the ranch seemed to satisfy him after the last few hectic years. Of course, just as a trip to Shanghai had ended up with Crow witnessing the fall of a dynasty and meeting Sun Yat-sen and a job in Tokyo had ended with a major scoop, so intrigue and excitement inevitably followed Crow to the Santa Clara Valley.

The peaceful life of a fruit farmer was rudely interrupted in 1917 with the announcement that America was eventually joining the war. Crow had been waiting for this moment and had long argued that America should join the British, French and other Allied nations against the Germans. He got into his Ford and drove to the recruiting station in San Francisco to offer his services. At 34 years old, he was not necessarily prime fighting material but the captain in charge was intrigued by Crow's experiences in China and Japan and thought him probably useful as a propagandist in military intelligence given his newspaper background. Crow remembered that he "... drove home in great elation, speculating on how my young daughter would like me in shoulder straps and wondering whether or not an intelligence officer would have to learn the manual of arms." Again Crow's sense of the poetic got the better of him for at the time Betty was still a babe in arms and probably not well versed in army ranks and insignia.

However, when Crow returned to see the recruiting captain he was told bluntly that he had been rejected as unfit for service. It turned out that Crow had previously entertained "one of the most notorious and cleverest German spies on the China Coast" at his ranch. This had led to Crow being branded as a German sympathizer. He was flabbergasted. It turned out that a young Canadian girl traveling on a British passport that he had hosted at the ranch was the spy. Crow never found out the true story till after the war when he became acquainted with the head of British intelligence in Shanghai who revealed all to him – and had indeed himself received a medal for unmasking the girl spy.[11]

Crow had known the girl four or five years prior to the war in Shanghai where she had borrowed some phonographic records from him. At the beginning of the war she had been employed as a typist in the American consulate in Vladivostok and collected information of use to the Germans as well as stealing stationery that was used to forge official documents. She returned to Shanghai in some luxury on the German payroll, claiming she had won the lottery. There she spent her time seducing young naval officers and diplomats and then securing forged British and American passports for use by German spies. She was also implicated in a plot to blow up a British shipyard in Shanghai and to ferment unrest among British-Indian troops in the International Settlement, part of a wider plot that eventually developed into the Singapore Mutiny in 1915.

She had managed to slip away from Shanghai to Manila and then on to San Francisco. Immediately upon arrival in America she had taken a taxi to Crow's ranch where she volunteered to work for a while in exchange for a chance to enjoy the countryside. She told Crow she had contracted a fever in Manila and been ordered by her doctor to recuperate in California.

Only later as Crow heard the story over drinks at the Shanghai Club with his contact in British intelligence did he piece together her strange behavior in California. Crow had wondered why the girl took a lot of solitary morning walks and he had once seen her talking to a strange man, and she always seemed to have plenty of cash. She had also struck up a flirtation with another guest of Crow's who stayed at the farm – a friend who had just passed through Petrograd and Stockholm and had been in Latin America investigating Mexican nitrate supplies. All this, Crow's British intelligence friend informed him, would have been valuable information once America joined the war effort. The girl managed to seduce Crow's guest away for a lovers' tryst in San Francisco after which she disappeared, heading to New York by way of the Panama Canal. Crow had unwittingly helped her escape by chaperoning her to a meeting with the British Consul-General in San Francisco to get her passport validated for the canal trip.

Even more to Crow's alarm was the fact that he had probably been on the German payroll too as one of the lady-spy's best tricks was to tell her German controllers that she had recruited other people and then collect their salaries, pocketing them herself of course. Apparently she later ceased her covert activities and moved to New York where she was being watched by American intelligence, had married a businessman, had a baby and was last reported to Crow as "… a typical middle class housewife living in the Bronx who spent her days cooking, washing and scrubbing and was devoted to her husband and children."

Crow's colleagues at the San Francisco Press Club tried to get the mess sorted out but army red tape meant Crow remained firmly rejected. With no reason given, Crow had to forget all his dreams of fighting against the Germans and returned to the cultivation of prunes and apricots.

However, as one door closed another opened. Crow was offered the job of Far Eastern (exclusive of Siberia) Representative and Chair of the Committee on Public Information (known as Compub), America's war-time propaganda organization, on a salary of $600 Mexican a month. He was posted back to Shanghai to set up an office for Compub. He sold the farm, packed up his family and his bags and booked his passage once again to the China coast.

Useful at Last as a Jekyll and Hyde

Crow found that things had changed in Shanghai. The city was modernizing fast. The odorous Yangjing Creek on the border of the International Settlement and Frenchtown had been filled in and renamed Edward VII Avenue (and on the French side of the road Avenue Edouard VII) in the spirit of cleaning up one of the city's most malodorous creeks and *L'Entente Cordial*.[12] Tom Millard had sold the *China Press* to Chinese interests in 1915 while Crow had been in Tokyo and had gone on to found *Millard's Review of the Far East* in the meantime with J. B. Powell on the editorial board. Crow's new employer, Compub, had been established initially as an organization devoted to popularizing the war at home in America and then spread its remit to include any country where America had interests. Crow noted that he was lucky to get the job as someone "... who had helped to establish the first American newspaper in China and while living in California had written a number of magazine articles about China which gave me a rather exaggerated reputation as an authority on the country... ."[13] – one of his rare admissions of "Griffinhood."

The American Legation in Peking around 1917/18.

Crow split his time between the American consulate in Shanghai and the American legation in Beijing. He was a propagandist and worked on a daily basis with legation and consular officials and earned their trust and access to many state secrets. His job, popularizing the war in China, was by his own admission "rather a large contract."[14] Crow's belief that the Japanese were not retreating from their strategy of Twenty-One Demands but just waiting for an opportune moment to re-present them was shared by many American officials; and Crow noted that a great deal of the work of the American diplomatic community in China was concerned with checking Japanese activities and seeking to prevent them from exploiting opportunities to once again advance the demands. The final victory over the Kaiser's armies in Europe was seen as the supreme task but in the Far East the job was to prevent China, with its potentially rich market for American goods, falling into Japanese hands and ensure that Allied gains in Europe were not offset by losses in Asia. This was a tricky position as Japan was officially an ally of America in the war against Germany but in China it was actively hampering the work of the Americans in every conceivable way.

Crow received daily news from London and Washington in Shanghai through his American Navy wireless. This news digest of events in Europe was translated and supplied to the Chinese newspapers as copy. The Japanese were also intercepting these messages through their listening post at Jinan and sending out an alternative version of events that minimized, distorted or ignored completely America's role in the fighting in order to create an atmosphere where American and Allied fighting power was seen as ineffectual compared to Japanese military strength. Many in China saw America as a firm ally at this period and it was crucial for the Japanese to break that faith in the Americans and portray the US as too weak and ineffectual to counter Japan in the Pacific. This campaign by the Japanese went so far as to report in the Tokyo newspapers American defeats in Europe that never actually occurred. Crow claimed that it was common knowledge that, though technically an ally, Japan wanted a German victory in Europe. For Tokyo, negotiating on the future of Asia with one power – Germany – was preferable to negotiating with a batch of victorious Great Powers with imperial and commercial interests in China. The military clique that held a high degree of political power in Japan at the time had not wanted to support the Allies at all but Japan had been forced to honor its obligations under the Anglo-Japanese Alliance with Britain signed in 1902. Despite the Alliance, there had been instances of the Union Jack being ripped down in Tokyo and trampled on by mobs supporting Germany, while the newspapers continued to extol Axis victories over the Allies.

The Japanese pro-German sentiment was not just political opportunism; many in Tokyo believed that Germany would support a special place for Japan in Asia. The support reflected the close ties between the two countries that had been developing for some time. The Japanese military was largely based on the Prussian model, down to the levels of uniforms and rank definitions, and Bismark had inspired the Japanese constitution. Crow himself noted that no German prisoners were as coddled as the Germans captured in Qingdao who were well housed and fed both there and in Japan and, according to Crow, were even provided with local prostitutes for their comfort.[15]

Crow set about trying to set up an effective propaganda machine, enlisting help from enthusiastic British amateurs who were already trying to disseminate news of the Allies' war victories and aims in China. With the help of the American Consul-General in Shanghai, Nelson Trusler Johnson,[16] Crow established a local committee of Americans, many of whom were old friends from his *China Press* days. The French provided access to their wireless services, which complemented Crow's US Navy radio. Dispatches from British, American and French radio were translated into Chinese and circulated to the local press. Crow had to establish a dummy company and sell the dispatches to the local papers that would not accept them free, regarding free news as propaganda. Crow kept the charges low and did not chase up payment. As both commissioner of Compub and also the manager of the dummy Chinese-American (Chun Mei) News Agency, Crow started to live what he described as a "Dr Jekyll and Mr Hyde existence."[17]

By the time of the Armistice in November 1918, China had reason to believe that it had a just claim for the wrongs it had suffered to be righted – the Japanese seizure of Qingdao as well as the "unequal treaties" with the Great Powers that still rankled Chinese sensibilities. China had joined the Allied cause partly at American insistence and persuasion and Crow felt partly guilty for the sense of gloom and disappointment in China when it became clear that the Treaty of Versailles would right few wrongs. He had continued to co-ordinate the publishing of propaganda from America including, upon instructions from the State Department in Washington, having all President Woodrow Wilson's speeches translated into Chinese and circulated to the Chinese press which duly published them to an enthusiastic response.

Wilson's rhetoric of self-determination and the rights of weaker nations against the Great Powers had struck a chord with the public. Crow, when asked by the Chinese if Wilson was genuine and if China would see some redress for past wrongs, told Chinese acquaintances that their hopes were justified, as he believed this to be the position of the American legation and Wilson. However, it was not to be and both Crow and China were to be bitterly disappointed by the outcome of Versailles. Indeed the China question was not even discussed by the Great Powers, though Japan took control of the former German possessions in China and the Pacific, which Tokyo eventually fortified as part of its military campaign across the region. China had been betrayed long before the start of the conference as the British, French and Italians had previously made a deal with Japan, offering her Germany's Far East possessions in return for support in the European war.

Crow was not the only one disappointed by the cold-shouldering of China at Versailles. The May Fourth 1919 demonstrations that broke out across China mobilized millions of Chinese in outrage. Students, teachers, intellectuals and merchants all took part in demonstrations against the wartime victor's marginalization of China. May Fourth became a symbolic day in the Chinese Nationalist calendar, a key date that marked the emergence of a new modern patriotism in China which stemmed from Great Power bullying, Western obstinacy, Japanese aggression and territorial slights.

As part of his Compub duties, Crow regularly had to travel to Beijing and mix with the city's diplomatic crowd – indeed he ultimately reported to the American Ambassador. Though he never lived there, Crow liked Beijing. He always got a thrill when he arrived in the ancient city by train at the Qianmen Station (where camels still gathered nearby at the end of the Silk Road), and then entered the Tartar City through the Water Gate that led into the Legation Quarter. However, he found diplomatic Beijing disagreeable. The obsession with rank and status rankled Crow's American libertarian soul and he found himself having to fulfil all manner of social obligations – "... whether I liked it or not I had to attend innumerable dinner parties and listen to stupid Peking gossip as detailed by fat old dowagers."[18] Crow managed to escape as often as possible to the Peking Club where the city's foreign press corps gathered, but again the Beijing obsession with rank became a problem. The head of a British news agency and the longest-serving foreign journalist in the city, and therefore the doyen of the press corps, became angry that Crow had visited other journalists in town before him simply because they were old friends. Crow claimed the obsession went so far that the British journalist "... hated me up to the day of his death."[19]

Crow's work with Compub also brought him into contact with the Missouri News Colony again. Despite the world knowing about Japan's Twenty-One Demands, Tokyo's diplomats in China still kept pressing them on Beijing. Eventually China's Foreign Minister Dr. Lou Tseng-hsiang decided to urge the newspapers to report the incessant Japanese pressure on China. To do this, he had called up the editor of the *Peking Daily News*, Colony member Holly Tong, who immediately called J. B. Powell who arranged a meeting between himself, Tong and Dr. Paul Samuel Reinsch, the American Minister in Beijing and an experienced China Hand, to organize a public defence of China. Powell interviewed Reinsch who strongly urged Japan to cease its intimidating activities and then sent the story to Crow at Compub. Crow cabled the story to Washington and thereafter all the foreign journalists in China were ordered by their papers to investigate it. Eventually the Japanese backed down somewhat, at least in terms of overtly applying pressure. However, their behind the scenes maneuvering continued.

Inevitably Reinsch himself, and Compub, became increasingly compromised by Washington's foreign policy. Crow and Reinsch had hit it off immediately despite the background gossip that Reinsch, whose family was of German extraction, was too pro-Berlin. As well as the general let-down at Versailles, Reinsch's position had been problematic since November 1917 when the US Secretary of State Robert Lansing signed an agreement with Baron Ishii, Japan's so-called "Ambassador of Good Will," agreeing to Tokyo's "special position" in Shandong and Manchuria. Washington never formally informed Reinsch that such a deal – the so-called Lansing-Ishii Pact – was about to happen. This had caused a storm even though most of the European powers had already signed similar deals with Tokyo – secretly.[20] The Lansing-Ishii Pact and the shunning of China at Versailles combined to force Reinsch, a supporter of parliamentary democracy for China, to resign in disgust in 1919 and take a post as an advisor to the Chinese government in Washington.

Before Compub was wound up, Crow was instructed to publish a collection of Wilson's speeches in Chinese. The book was duly assembled by Crow, translated into Chinese and published by the Commercial Press, the foremost Chinese book publisher of the day. It was an instant best-seller, as many Chinese blamed the Great Powers, rather than Wilson, for their Versailles betrayal, and ran into many reprints. Crow provided a foreword for the book and asked for any comments from Chinese readers to be sent directly to him in Shanghai. This was a decision he came to regret when thousands of communications came flooding into his office from all across China. At first all the letters were translated for him to reply to but soon the trickle became a flood and the best Crow's staff could do was open each envelope to see if it contained money for additional copies. The warlord general Feng Yu-hsiang,[21] the so-called "Christian General," ordered 500 copies alone, one for each officer in his army. Eventually Crow received over 10,000 letters. He couldn't possibly translate them all and eventually his office staff sold them for scrap paper.

The book did so well that Crow paid a 15 percent author's royalty to his dummy news agency. By now the agency was making such a profit that he had to spend it all on more advertisements for the book and took full-page advertisements in most of the major Chinese language newspapers. Crow also came up with another use for the profits. In order to make sure that the real provincial leaders of China read the book, he first had to admit that nobody knew who they all were as there were no directories of local people of importance. In what may have been China's first direct marketing campaign, Crow mailed postcards to every American missionary throughout China explaining to them that he wanted to send a copy of the book to all local notables. The missionaries, who were better acquainted with the interior regions and the local dignitaries, then posted the cards back with the names and addresses of all the people in their localities who should receive a copy. The missionaries were so taken with the project they established ad hoc committees to ensure they missed no one and also roped in their British colleagues to help add to their lists.

The postcard scheme was a roaring success and Crow ended up with a fantastic mailing list as well as identifying one or two Americans who were German sympathizers and replied admitting as much and refusing to take part. These he forwarded to Reinsch and they were summarily expelled from China. Crow then extended the scheme to the many local in-country representatives of America's largest oil and tobacco companies with similarly good results. Altogether, Crow got 25,000 names and addresses of local dignitaries across China and sent them each a copy of the Wilson book along with a letter asking them to recommend any friends who should also receive a copy. His list grew and grew.

As a supporter of the 1911 revolution and an admirer of Dr. Sun, and feeling frustrated at the betrayal of China at Versailles, by 1918 Crow felt himself becoming increasingly estranged from the mainstream position of the older China Hands in Shanghai. Majority opinion in the International Settlement was that if the Nationalist government gained strength then that very success would speed up the unity of China and eventually spell the end of Shanghai's special privileges. The bulk of the foreign press in Shanghai supported this view and painted grim pictures of foreigners being subject to Chinese law and ending up in Chinese prisons, or worse. The advances of the Nationalist government in starting to restructure and rebuild the country were mostly overlooked. Crow found himself rebelling against this downplaying of Nationalist progress while the Japanese were, to Crow's observation, increasingly interfering in Chinese affairs with apparently tacit foreign connivance. Slowly foreigners felt themselves more embattled. As Crow had observed of the days before the revolution of 1911, "We had been accustomed to barging around the country wherever we pleased, counting on the color of our skins in the place of a passport."[22] Now, as Crow had found upon his return to China in 1917, a passport and a travel permit were required – restrictions many foreigners found irksome.

Whatever the changing circumstances, Crow was happy to be back in Shanghai and started to renew old contacts and explore new opportunities as the city recovered economically and became a booming commercial center. His wife Mildred was also getting in on the act by starting a company that sold Chinese handicrafts to American stores. By 1921 she was trading as Mildred Crow Inc. and opened a wholesale showroom for her Chinese decorative products named "The Jade Tree" that was followed by a retail store of the same name, making her an extremely entrepreneurial foreign wife by Shanghai standards.[23] Carl was casting around for business opportunities too but first he had another appointment with Dr. Sun.

7

Sun Yat-sen and the Biography That Never Was

Afternoons with Dr. Sun

After the war, Sun Yat-sen was to re-enter Carl's life. Crow had kept in touch with Sun after his "retirement" and replacement by Yuan Shih-kai. He had eventually moved to a house provided for him by overseas Chinese supporters at 24 Rue Moliére[1] in Shanghai's Frenchtown where he worked on plans to develop China's governmental institutions, railways and industrial base. Both Crow and Tom Millard believed that Sun had been unfairly treated by Yuan and, despite his shortcomings, such as managing to alienate many potential allies after stepping down as President and his womanizing,[2] remained the brightest hope for the long-term success of the fledging Chinese Republic.

Millard decided that he would provide continued blanket coverage of Sun and his ideas despite his political sidelining. This plan entailed Crow meeting with Sun at least once a week for many months. Crow's interviews with Sun were popularly received by the readership of *Millard's Review of the Far East* and were translated and reprinted by the Chinese press for the local audience where another receptive readership was discovered. Crow found Sun to be a lonely and disappointed man in Shanghai. He remained somewhat isolated at the shady Rue Moliére house, set back slightly from the street, with some gardens and adjacent to the relatively new French Park.[3] Sun felt largely deserted by his former followers and was lacking in humor, but he was remarkably open in their interviews and prone to change his mind frequently on political and philosophical issues.

Sun lived in the house with his wife, Ching-ling, the second oldest of the famous Soong sisters. Sun had been close to, and harbored designs on, the eldest Soong sister, Ai-ling, but was rebuffed in no uncertain terms by the family's patriarch Charlie Soong who pointed out the small problem that Sun was already married. Ai-ling married the banker and descendant of Confucius, H. H. Kung, while Sun turned his affections to her sister who had replaced Ai-ling as his secretary in Japan where he and the Suns were living. Ching-ling was a dedicated *Sunist* and a graduate of the Methodist Wesleyan College in Macon, Georgia. The two soon fell into a clandestine romance despite an almost 30-year age gap (Sun being nearly 50 and Ching-ling just 20 at the time). The romance hit problems when Charlie Soong took the family back to Shanghai to move into a new house on Avenue Joffre.[4] The Soongs believed they would be secure in Frenchtown under the protection of Huang Jinrong, also known as "Pockmarked Huang," who, as well as being a criminal and boss of the city's Red Gang, was also handily the Chief of Detectives for the French *Sûretè*. Charlie Soong was an old acquaintance of Huang's, having handled all his gang's printing needs for many years. Ching-ling was due to be married to a suitor of her father's choice but resisted with the characteristic stubbornness of the Soong sisters. Sun wanted Ching-ling back in Japan, and she wanted to be with him but Charlie would not countenance any further liaison between the two. She eventually climbed out a window of the Avenue Joffre house and eloped to be with Sun in Kobe. Sun, who claimed to have sorted out a divorce from his first wife by this time, married Ching-ling the day after her arrival in Japan in 1914.

Back in Frenchtown, Charlie Soong took the elopement badly. Not the least of his concerns was that Sun's divorce was questionable. Certainly Sun told everyone that he considered himself divorced but no official papers were forthcoming which meant that not only was Sun possibly a bigamist but that Ching-ling was an adulteress, a mistress and a concubine. All of this was very disturbing to the deeply-Christian Charlie who rushed to Kobe to retrieve his daughter but was too late to prevent the marriage. Sun and Soong fell out, and Charlie threatened to have the marriage annulled as Ching-ling lacked parental consent. However, Sun remained adamant that the marriage would continue. Charlie disowned his daughter and returned to Shanghai. As well as her father, Ching-ling's brother Tzu-wen (usually known as T.V.) and younger sister Mei-ling were also stunned by the news of the marriage, as were Sun's family. Despite all this opposition, Sun's political supporters rallied to the marriage and largely overrode Charlie's objections. In 1918 Charlie Soong's death largely lifted the scandal that had surrounded Sun and Ching-ling's marriage and they were able to settle into living in the Rue Moliére house.

After the upheavals of the revolutionary period, many believed that Sun was still in some personal danger. When Crow and others visited him, they would often be met at the door by the cigar chomping Morris "Two-Gun" Cohen, Sun's personal bodyguard who had managed to rise from poverty in London's East End via New York, Chicago and Canada to Shanghai where he stayed to escape gambling debts. Cohen reportedly saved Sun from several assassination attempts.[5]

Crow felt that Sun had been treated badly politically despite his weaknesses, which included having flirted with the Bolsheviks in Russia. Also, as Crow said, "the leader's ideas of economics may have been faulty and he had the unfortunate habit of surrounding himself with fools and flatterers, but no one can cast any doubt on the intense fervour of his patriotism, his honesty and sincerity."[6]

At one point, Crow and Sun's former private secretary Ma Soo, were retained by S. S. McClure of *McClure's Magazine* to ghost-write a biography of Sun for what Crow described as a "fabulous sum."[7] Crow liked the idea of writing for McClure, a Scotch-Irish immigrant to America who had risen from a poverty-stricken boyhood on a farm in Indiana, written for several cycling magazines and eventually founded *McClure's* in 1892. *McClure's* specialized in publishing famous writers at a low price for a wide audience. The original staff had included such American journalistic luminaries as Ida Tarbell and Lincoln Steffens and became a home for many of the muck-raking writers of the time.

Crow and Ma Soo did write four sample chapters, all of which were jointly initialled by Sun and Crow. Sun then suddenly withdrew his support from the project, much to Crow's bemusement, claiming he had not understood the original agreement. Crow would meet with Sun in his study on Rue Moliére and the two would drink tea and talk. The small study was adjacent to Sun's bedroom on the first floor and lined with dark wood bookshelves. At one end of the room was Sun's desk complete with his collection of calligraphy brushes and ink. In front of the desk was a long sofa on which Sun would sit and then a small table and several dark wood chairs for guests. Occasionally the two would sit downstairs on Sun's shady back porch on rattan furniture, drinking tea and looking out onto Sun's small lawn garden and shrubbery. Crow later recalled that Sun preferred to speak in English and was fluent and fast in his replies to Crow's questions but eventually he seemed to distance himself from the discussion of past decisions and events before finally cancelling the whole interview process.[8] These were predictably long drawn out afternoons; while in internal exile in Guangzhou Sun had picked up the nickname "the Great Cannon" from Chen Chiung-ming, the so called Hakka General,[9] for his endless monologues. Even more unkindly, Guangzhou merchants had referred to him as "Sun the Windbag."

Crow's earlier contacts with Sun had tailed off after the Bolshevik Revolution in Russia survived the wars of intervention, consolidated power and looked to become a permanent state of affairs. Like most foreigners in Shanghai, Crow was extremely concerned at the dramatic turn of events in Russia and what the implications would be for China. While Sun had gradually moved towards a tacit acceptance of Marxism and had given the Russian Revolution his support, in the 1920s Crow had become involved in the British-led Constitutional Defence League (CDL) in Shanghai, an international committee on which Crow served as chairman of its sub-committee on propaganda at the same time as working for Compub. Much of Crow's free time was spent overseeing the production of anti-communist pamphlets and statements for dissemination and mailing throughout the International Settlement. He admitted to being very worried about the spread of communism from Russia to China, but he was less convinced that his propaganda efforts did anything to dampen the growth of the communist movement in China. Anyway, the CDL didn't last long and quickly ran out of funds a few months after forming as initial concerns over the spread of bolshevism receded and the organization attracted some poor publicity for including a few Fascists and admirers of Mussolini in its ranks.[10]

Though the initial fears of a repeat of the Bolshevik Revolution in China calmed down in Shanghai and the CDL ran out of steam, Crow remained extremely skeptical of radical socialism and distrustful of "The brain trusters at Moscow who were enjoying the delusion that they could convert China to communism."[11] In this sense, he was a product of his roots. He was a fiercely independent American who rarely missed a chance to reflect on the War of Independence from Britain and the success the USA had had in building a strong nation and independent manufacturing base that, just prior to the First World War, was growing in power and self-consciousness and preparing for a formal entry onto the world stage. Crow was no lover of the British Empire and was highly skeptical of the role of Europe in world affairs, but he was an unabashed capitalist, and though friendly with many more leftist colleagues was far from being what, at the time, was called a "parlour pink."

Crow's anti-communism, though more visceral at this time than later, was largely formed by the work of a now long-forgotten and rather heavy-going political writer Dr. Maurice William, a Ukrainian-born dentist based in New York whose book *The Social Interpretation of History* was a favorite of Crow's. William's book caused a minor stir in both socialist-inclined and anti-socialist circles at the time of its publication in 1920. The doctor had been an American Socialist Party activist, but around the time of the First World War he had become increasingly disillusioned and started to question the basic doctrines of Marxism that lay behind the slogans he had been championing in Manhattan and Brooklyn. Crow had been impressed by *The Social Interpretation of History* as it contained many ideas he rapidly accepted and also because William had not been formally educated and wrote his book after studying the Marxist canon from scratch. As Crow moved from being a journalist to being a businessman, he began to become increasingly interested in consumer behavior, the development of consumer culture and its impact on the wider society. William's book argued that Marx had wrongly seen the proletariat simply as wage-earners and ignored their increasingly important role as consumers – a perspective which fitted Crow's own philosophical evolution perfectly. This notion that the producer is also a consumer, and that as such workers enjoyed gains in their standard of living and benefited from capitalism while also working for capitalists had a strong appeal to Crow.

William had been born in Kharkov and emigrated with his family to America at the age of eight. He had been educated to a basic level but left school to sell newspapers and then work in a dairy for 12 hours a day. While involved with the socialist movement, he decided he needed a new career and was advised by one of his socialist friends: "Become a dentist, comrade. Under the most perfect system of society, there will still be rotten teeth." He did so and later established one of New York's first free dental clinics. Crow had become what he described as an "intimate" friend of William's[12] whose theories weren't popular with the American socialist movement and he had eventually parted ways with them permanently. Though *The Social Interpretation of History* remained largely unread in the US outside Socialist Party circles, a few copies did find their way to China.

Later, during the spring of 1924, Sun's pro-socialist speeches were to become increasingly radical. Sun was delivering a series of lectures on his political philosophy, called the Three Principles of the People. Once a week, like clockwork, for 12 weeks Sun expounded on his philosophy. But when it was time for the 13th lecture, Sun stopped, and did not resume for more than a month. After the summer he resumed his lecture program with a greatly toned-down version of the theories he had espoused earlier in the year.

Crow claimed that Sun read, appreciated and agreed with William's book, which Crow had given him a copy of, and that this caused him to rethink certain critical issues and tempered his former flirtation with socialism. When Sun resumed his lectures, he spoke not in terms that were overtly Marxist or Communist, but rather in terms of "livelihood," a phrase of William's. Though largely ignored in America, William later received plaudits and honors from the Nationalist government in China for his work and influence on Sun. He also became an organizer and fund-raiser for the American Bureau of Medical Aid to China in 1937 and Chairman of the Fundraising Committee of the United Council for Civilian Relief in China, along with Albert Einstein, Herbert Hoover and Henry Luce, the founder of *Time* magazine.[13]

Through his conversations with Sun, Crow came to believe that the Russian Revolution had been perceived by the Chinese Nationalists as something of an upstaging of their own revolution. The Bolsheviks had moved swiftly to crush their own civil war, while in China there was ongoing feuding and warlordism. They had also expelled all the foreign powers that intervened and had established a functioning national government that appeared to be efficient and also united the vast country. Communist propaganda portrayed the USSR as a utopia and many Chinese, including some senior leaders in the Nationalist government, believed this. Chiang Kai-shek himself was sent to Russia by Sun to investigate the successes of Bolshevism and came back much impressed with the efficiency of the government in Moscow and the Red Army, if not the politics of Marxism-Leninism.

With the war over and the job of building a post-war world underway, times were changing for Crow. His life as a dedicated newspaperman was over as was his time as a government propagandist. The fact was that the Shanghai newspaper business did not pay well, significantly below American rates, while stringing for American papers provided little additional income. Government pay was even worse. Now, in a changing Shanghai which was enjoying an economic boom fueled by Europe's thirst to rebuild, he felt the pull of the opportunities commerce and entrepreneurialism were offering to bright men. His years working on newspapers had shown him that the driving force of the business was advertising, while his time as a propagandist has shown him the power the press had to influence people. So it was this industry that he now looked to as a business opportunity in the new rapacious boom-time environment of post-war Shanghai. It was in advertising that Carl Crow was to make both his name and his fortune.

8

Four Hundred Million Customers and Bringing Billboards to China

A Brutal Metropolis on the Make

In 1918 Carl opened the doors of Carl Crow Inc., a firm of "Advertising and Merchandising Agents." In the years after the war Crow described Shanghai as "prosperous" – an apt though not always obvious statement. Perhaps a better description was provided by Jonathan Fenby, a biographer of Chiang Kai-shek's, who described Shanghai at the time as a "brutal metropolis on the make."[1] With the war in Europe over and the continent getting down to the business of rebuilding, order books in Shanghai were full and the wartime depression in exports starting to ease – Shanghai even had its own version of Monopoly, sub-titled "The Game of Shanghai Millionaire." An influx of new foreigners into the city found modern Western-style housing difficult to come by and had to resort to staying for long periods in hotel suites or suffer poorly but rapidly constructed new accommodation.

Industry boomed as Western merchants returned to the Far East and local and overseas Chinese money also emerged once again. Europe needed just about everything China could produce – rubber, coal, soybean oil, cotton and silk as well as other goods such as cigarettes, and there were fat margins to be made on deals to supply most commodities as prices rose daily. The banking industry blossomed to cater for all the new enterprises needing financing and trade deals needing underwriting, while the newly rich looked to spend their money and display their wealth after a period of relative austerity. The rejuvenated foreign community and the *nouveau riche* of Shanghai were both back in the market for consumer goods, the products that became the bread and butter of Carl Crow Inc.'s business. The wealth spread up the Yangtze to cities like Hangzhou and Suzhou and down south to Guangzhou. Foreign brands were attracted by low import tariffs as much as the dream of a seemingly limitless consumer market. With foreign business and Chinese capitalists prospering, Shanghai was their primary meeting point. However, the Shanghailanders never stopped worrying that the boom would end; as the American journalist Vincent Sheean said at the time, "Shanghai is the city par excellence of two things, money and the fear of losing it."[2] The fledgling Communist Party of China held its first Congress in Frenchtown in 1921, thus introducing a new element to the city's varied mix of ideologies.

As well as a trade boom the city was going through a property boom with more new, and grander, buildings planned along the Bund and the streets running off it. This was the period that saw the construction of the great edifices that still define the Bund – the Hong Kong and Shanghai Bank, the Chartered Bank, Victor Sassoon's Cathay Hotel and others. Soon the Bund rivalled the best the British Empire had to offer in architectural terms. It was a time of mass consumerism with department stores, such as Whiteaway, Laidlaw and Co. appearing, as well as the Chinese-run trio of great department stores – Wing On, Sincere, and Sun Sun[3] – all packed full of new and imported goods. Also, Nanking Road, "the Oxford Street of the Orient," became a sea of lights and was congested with all the new motorcars on the city's streets, which competed with the rickshaws whose safety became more perilous now they vied with cars and trolley buses for space. Nanking Road had formerly been known as Park Lane and was best known to the Chinese population as Great Horse Road [*Dah Ma Lo*]. By 1920, it had become the most modern commercial street in Asia.

Of course, there was a downside to all this phenomenal growth. The rise of industry led to factories, some of which could compare with the worst the Industrial Revolution had had to offer with child labor, long hours, low wages and dangerous machinery – a phenomenon that allowed for the rapid growth of a labor, socialist and communist movement. The number of dead the Settlement authorities had to collect in the streets every morning started rising; and the number of beggars grew. There were also the fatalities caused by the escalating warlord clashes that reached Shanghai's suburbs which not only saw members of their private armies killed but also led to the destruction of much-needed agricultural land and crops. The result was terror, famine, shortages, hoarding and the inevitable price rises for many lower down the economic scale.

Shanghai's new-found wealth was not evident on all the city's streets either. The port may have been one of the world's largest but it seemed as if most cargo was still moved along the Huang Pu by junk. The population had risen to 1.5 million but the city still had few paved streets; and the electricity and telephone systems were primitive and in summer most office workers relied on *punkah* fans to keep cool. Stomachers, or woollen cummerbunds, were almost universally worn in the belief that they warded of chills and stomach ailments. Little could be done about the plagues of mosquitoes beyond using kerosene and nets and it was some time before the SMC decided to clean up the city's canals and ponds. Shanghai was not a healthy place in 1918; typhoid, cholera and dysentery were all common. City services still seemed ad hoc: the fire brigade consisted solely of volunteers who relied on pumps and fire engines imported from England several decades earlier. Only a couple of buildings in Shanghai exceeded five storeys and had elevators. For foreigners Shanghai remained small; virtually the whole foreign community turned out for concerts in the Bund Garden and most lived nearby as the Western Roads' residential district was at this time still fields. Sewage disposal and rubbish collection were virtually non-existent, modern plumbing rare, flush toilets unknown and chamber pots the norm. This was the city that was to be transformed over the next two decades, not least by the arrival of modern advertising techniques.

Carl Crow Inc. – China's Major Advertising Agency

Carl Crow Inc. was technically a successor company to the Chun Mei News Agency, a specialist agency providing "translations of editorial comments, special articles etc from the Chinese press." Crow had helped found Chun Mei and it had started by translating articles by Millard, Crow and others that then appeared in the local Chinese language press. As the agency had grown, Crow and his partners found it profitable to handle advertising from American companies that needed their advertising translated and placed in local newspapers. The success of this placements service led Crow to redirect the focus of the business in order to capitalize on the growth in advertising, and so his new agency was spun off from Chun Mei. Carl Crow Inc. was a private limited company technically incorporated in Delaware. After several smaller homes, he established the office that was to be the agency's main premises for many years on the third floor of a building at 81 Jinkee Road. His office, in a large neo-classical building, was just east of the Bund and west of Szechuan Road, at the very center of the International Settlement, or what the Chinese called *shili yangchang* (literally, "ten-mile-long foreign zone"). The firm traded as *Ka-loo-kwang-ko-kung-sze* in Chinese.[4]

Jinkee Road was an oddity in Shanghai and remains a narrower street than most of the grander thoroughfares that run west from the Bund. The first streets laid out running off from the Bund were originally named in alphabetical order to make them easy to remember, among them Canton, Foochow, Hankow, Kiukiang, Nanking, Peking and Soochow Roads running from east to west. However, at a later date, Jinkee, between Nanking and Peking Roads, was created by turning a formerly private lane that led to the offices of the British traders Gibb, Livingston & Company Ltd. into a public street.[5] Gibb, Livingston's hong, or trading, name was "Jin Kee." It seems that the alphabetical order first used to lay out Shanghai's road system had been forgotten and so the name was never changed. Since then the road had become home to several major office buildings including the headquarters of the Metropolitan Land Company, one of Shanghai's largest real estate firms.

Carl Crow Inc. got off to a good start thanks to the post-war boom and the massive investment pouring into the city from both new companies seeking to tap into the potential of the China market and continued investment from longer-established firms such as Jardine Matheson, British-American Tobacco (BAT) and Standard Oil. With Shanghai's population expanding rapidly and soon to approach three million it was becoming a sizeable consumer market in its own right, attracting many brands and manufacturers who needed to place advertisements or run marketing and promotional campaigns. Manufacturing industry was flourishing, particularly in Pudong and Zhabei, and industries from the new shipyards to the textiles plants all wanted what would now be called "a corporate presence" in China. Department stores were flourishing too, stocking all the new goods being launched into the market and they also needed their own advertising to attract custom. Shanghai remained the national center of foreign business, investment and fashion and Crow was able to make a lucrative living quickly out of placing advertising for foreign companies in the press and on billboards throughout the country.

The city's role as a nightlife capital was also starting to take off as Shanghai became rich. The "outpost of empire" mentality was giving way to a new prosperity and changed attitudes after the war. The global trend of flapperdom, albeit with Chinese characteristics, and a devil-may-care attitude mixed with a seemingly transient lifestyle for many foreigners and lots of money – helped by a less than rigorous tax system and extremely favorable international exchange rates – were combining to make Shanghai a fun place. Visiting celebrities and writers started to trickle in and then took back to America and Europe stories of Shanghai as the equal of a Paris or a New York. Those that visited Shanghai were as varied as the hard-living Wallis Simpson to the teetotal travel entrepreneur Thomas Cook. All went home with tales of wild nights in Shanghai, though to the rather stern Cook this was not a positive thing. "Good, very good" was the future Duchess of Windsor's verdict, while the writer Emily Hahn described "… enormous feasts that lasted several days …" (which did little to help Crow's expanding waistline that he constantly bemoaned after the war). This was the period of the trademark mock Tudor villas of Shanghai, tennis, pony races, the many clubs of Shanghai, the jazz and the dancing. "It girls", "Fast Set", "Bright Young Things" – Shanghai had them all in the immediate aftermath of the First World War and this all went to building the city's reputation as a center of consumption, fashion and modernity.

Crow was also in a strong position to take advantage of the new wealthy Chinese industrialists and traders. Shanghai was gradually emerging as a city in which they could also make money and they too needed the services of advertisers and marketers. From the start Crow accepted clients of any nationality. This reflected a slight thaw in the old colonial racism of Shanghai. By and large foreign and Chinese society had kept to themselves but the social dividing lines were becoming a little more blurred both in business and society as the so-called "Shanghai Tycoons" emerged as well as another new class of overseas Chinese businessmen. The formerly whites-only Shanghai Race Club had started to admit Chinese members after the war. However, rather than embracing multicultural liberality, this was more a reflection of whose pockets the gambling revenues that sustained the club came from.

Crow remained President of the company, according to the *Shanghai Dollar Directory*. However, at various times he employed a K. C. Chow as his Chinese manager and had a Y. Obie as his art director, who also helped him on the design of his *Handbook for China*. Occasionally, Crow would also use old friends such as the Russian cartoonist and artist Sapajou. His chief accountant was C. C. Wolfe who was assisted for several years by B. L. Wang. The company included an outdoor advertising department, also run by C. C. Wolfe, that specialized in placing poster and billboard advertising across Eastern China, largely in Zhejiang province.

Over the years Crow invariably maintained a staff of about a dozen who were engaged in various activities, including buying space in local newspapers and magazines across China, and organizing direct mailing campaigns. They also dealt with "electrotypes," "advertising stereos" (plates cast in molten metal on which a replica of the type and any illustrations was impressed), and "matrices" which were moulds in which type was cast in line-casting machines. The adverts arrived from various destinations, including London, Berlin, Paris, and New York. If the client needed it, Crow could supply the artwork and the copy text too. As he was placing advertising in newspapers and magazines across the country, he started to produce a regular directory of every newspaper in China; and, as his clients often needed manuals translated, he ended up back in the translation business too. At the same time, foreign clients wanted detailed information on their prospects or sales in China and so Crow also found himself in the market research business providing information on competitors, consumer habits and spending patterns – a business Carl enjoyed immensely as it allowed his amateur anthropologist tendencies to run riot in his lengthy reports to clients.

He also developed another sideline by employing half a dozen crews of men to act as billposters for adverts. These crews worked their way from Shanghai up the Yangtze as far as Jinsha in Hubei province covering 60 cities, some of which were over 1,000 miles upriver. The posters, usually about 30 x 40 inches in size, were "sniped" on blank walls in what would now be called "fly posting," as well as pasted onto permanent boards in leased locations. The men constantly experienced problems with local officials who demanded all manner of bribes and unofficial "taxes" for permission to post the bills. Crow had to have identification cards printed with photos and the seal of the US Consulate-General in Shanghai (unbeknown to the consulate but very impressive nonetheless) to show that they were working for a foreign company, which usually ended the dispute without any payment having to be made. Eventually sniping became too difficult and Crow had to make more use of officially-leased boards across the Yangtze valley – at one point he had 15,000 of these locations each costing $6 a year in rent while he sold poster space to clients for a month at a time at good profit margins. Despite having been expensive to start, Crow's extensive network was a lucrative business and popular with advertisers as it was the only guaranteed billposting service in terms of number of bills posted. Other agencies had to either rent space from Crow – if he had any to sell, and then obviously at a high premium – or engage in the haphazard practice of sniping.

Crow preferred his network of leased multiple poster locations to the larger billboard sites as these were rare and more expensive (costing more than in America for standard 24-sheet billboards at the time) after fluctuating and often quite arbitrary local rates and taxes were factored in. In some cities, taxes were excessive and Crow refused to do outdoor advertising in these locations, which included major markets such as Tianjin. However, the major problem with billboards in the cities, as Crow saw it, was the lack of movement of the Chinese:

His [*the Chinese*] teahouse and the shops which he patronizes are all in the immediate neighborhood and his activities rarely take him outside of a radius of a few hundred yards. This means that outdoor advertising must be placed as to reach all the individual communities. Instead of a few large signs it is necessary to use a large number of small ones.[6]

For the same reason, Crow was not keen on either electrical neon light signs on streets (when they were introduced in the late 1920s) or advertising on trolleybuses, believing that outside the major centers of Shanghai and a handful of other places in China everyone went to sleep early and nightlife was virtually non-existent. Impressive as a neon sign may have been, in Crow's experience, it was not necessarily effective.

Crow, His Artists, and Shanghai's Sexy Modern Girls

We always redraw the picture in China

It was perhaps Crow's art department that was to be his strongest asset, as almost from the start Crow's attention to detail with illustrations was notable. Over the years Crow worked with a number of well-known cartoonists, artists and illustrators of the time, hiring them both to provide artwork for Carl Crow Inc. adverts and for his own books. Under his long-term chief of the art department, Y. Obie, Crow built one of the largest commercial art departments in Shanghai after the major in-house operations established by the Commercial Press ("The Largest Publishing House in the Orient") and BAT, whose art department was so large it operated out of a Pudong warehouse. During the life of the company

Crow employed many artists, including Chen Jianhong, D. Doo, Y. C. Hsu, K. T. Yang, Tewei, Hu Zhongbiao, Xie Mulian, Ye Qianyu and others, perhaps most importantly T. K. Zia. Most worked on a freelance basis and Crow had a wide range of commercial artists to choose from as their living was precarious given the plethora of short-lived magazines and publications they competed for work from. The way to a regular salary was to either find a permanent job with one of the large in-house production centers, such as BAT's, or to gain regular work with one of the major publishers or advertising agencies such as Carl Crow Inc.

It was these artists that were to realize Crow's basic philosophy that images were more essential to successful advertising in China than copy:

> When all is said and done, there is only one rule which may be laid down for the preparation of copy, no matter whether it be for newspapers or posters, and that is that a picture of the product must be shown and, if possible, its uses illustrated. So large a proportion of the population being wholly illiterate, the ideal advertisement would be one complete in its picture without one word of text.[7]

Carl Crow Inc. virtually always used illustrations in its in-house designed advertisements – except notably adverts for Carl Crow Inc. itself in a wonderful example of "do as I say not as I do" – and as such contributed to the phenomenon between the wars of the sexy modern Shanghai girl in advertising and the city's distinctively visual commercial art. The sexy modern girl image was primarily directed at a Chinese audience but was much admired by consumers across the spectrum. Many featured attractive modern-looking Chinese women in domestic or leisure scenes advertising everything from soap and skin cream to cigarettes and cars; one of Crow's first and most defining sexy modern girl images was for Pond's Vanishing Cream in 1920. Newspaper advertising with strong and modern visual images was, for Crow, a natural direction as he was in the business of organizing large promotional campaigns for foreign clients aimed at raising brand awareness. Crow concentrated on print adverts and posters and didn't become involved in the popular calendar girl business that was later to define Shanghai's unique advertising style to many, commenting that, "considering the high cost of calendars, it is doubtful that their distribution is ever justified by the advertising results obtained."[8] However, as he had some of the best calendar girl artists working for him on a freelance basis, and he was after all a businessman, he did advertise that Carl Crow Inc. could produce and print calendars at competitive rates for clients who insisted on producing these glamorous calendars. He had the artists and the printers, so why not?

Crow believed that his advert for Pond's Vanishing Cream that appeared in the Chinese newspaper Shenbao *on March 7, 1920 heralded the modern girl image in Shanghai advertising that was to become ubiquitous throughout the 1920s and 1930s.*
(This image appears through the courtesy of Tani E. Barlow and her work on the history of the sexy modern girl advertising image.)

Crow also required skilled artists, as he believed that the Chinese consumer was naturally distrusting – they expected advertising to exaggerate, make outlandish claims and downright lie. To be fair, the consumer had good reason to be suspicious given much of the advertising available. Therefore, for Crow, representations of packets of cigarettes or bars of soap should be accurate, show the contents honestly and use vivid colours. By the 1920s and 1930s the market was flooded with adverts, many of which came from the art studios of Carl Crow Inc. and could often be spotted by his trademark sailing ship logo in the left hand corner of the print. In his studios perhaps the most important artist was the aforementioned T. K. Zia, who was also known as Xie Zhiguang.

Carl Crow Inc.'s artwork was noted for its sophistication, which encompassed ideas from the Western art nouveau style, adapted for a Chinese audience. Crow and other advertising practitioners in Shanghai would meet regularly at the forums organized by the Advertising Club of Shanghai, that had both foreign and Chinese members, to discuss the latest advertising trends from America and Europe. Xie Zhiguang's art almost always adhered to Crow's basic philosophy by featuring the product prominently as well as blending Western and Chinese artistic styles.

Born in 1900, Xie had originally studied under several of the recognized masters of the calendar school of art in Shanghai and was a graduate of

Shanghai's Fine Arts College. He drew for Crow and other clients (notably the Nanyang Brothers Tobacco Company) in a dynamic style, either as drawings or full watercolors often featuring extremely pretty modern Shanghai girls in Westernized interior settings. His watercolors sold independently as works of art, while his commercial work in the 1930s pushed the boundaries as they featured increasingly buxom and curvaceous ladies in tight-fitting *qipaos*, smoking, relaxing and full of "come-hither" looks. He was one of the first artists to draw nudes in advertising while his portrait of the young movie starlet Chen Yunshang is perhaps the most copied Shanghai calendar girl poster in history.

Pictures of modern-looking girls had started to become popular around 1910 but they had usually been demure and restrained to suit traditional Chinese values. As dresses grew tighter and the figure-hugging *qipaos* replaced the previously fashionable blouses with three-quarter length sleeves and looser, longer skirts of the early-to-mid-1920s, Xie's sexual messages became more explicit and his models wore ruby red lipstick and translucent *qipaos* with high slits up the legs, and had the artist's trademark penetrating eyes that drew the consumer's attention.

Xie himself was a complicated character who was regarded as a handsome and charming man who indulged in a series of extra-marital affairs to his wife's very public fury. Xie pushed the boundaries of artistic and social tastes while also being an ardent Chinese patriot who spoke out vocally against Japan's occupation of Manchuria in 1931. This did little but endear him to Crow who hired him repeatedly; and Crow later hired Xie's talented artist nephew Xie Mulian too.[9]

Crow also worked with several fellow foreigners, including Esther Brock Bird, who provided the illustrations for his book *Foreign Devils in the Flowery Kingdom* (eventually published in 1940). Brock Bird was an American artist who had become relatively famous for her paintings of anthracite mines and other industrial buildings in America and had later worked on illustrations for Pearl S. Buck's children's book *The Dragon Fish*.[10]

However, the most regular foreigner that Crow used was Sapajou, a good friend who provided illustrations for his books *Four Hundred Million Customers* and later *The Chinese Are Like That*. Sapajou's distinctive line drawings both revealed Chinese daily life and idiosyncrasies as well as the decadent life of the foreign Shanghailanders in the 1920s and 1930s. Sapajou was the pseudonym for Georgii Avksentievich Sapojnikoff. He was a graduate of the Aleksandrovskoe Military School in Moscow, a lieutenant in the Russian Imperial Army, and an aide-de-camp to Dmitrii Leonidovich Horvat, the Tsarist general and relative of the Romanovs' (while he was overseeing the completion of the Trans-Siberian railway). Sapojnikoff was also a veteran of the First World

War where he was wounded on the battlefield. When invalided out of the army, he enrolled in evening classes at the Moscow Academy of Arts to study drawing. The tall, thin and bespectacled Sapajou always limped and walked with a cane as the result of his war injuries but he had maintained a pretty good social standing by marrying the daughter of a Tsarist general while in exile in Beijing.

With the victory of Lenin's Bolsheviks and the ensuing civil war, in the early 1920s White Russians had come to Shanghai – many via spells in Harbin or Beijing – to escape the revolution back home. By the 1930s more than 20,000 lived in the city which, as an open city, accepted just about anybody without passport or visa requirements. Sapajou fell instantly in love with life in Shanghai where he continued doodling and drawing local scenes while he worked out how to rebuild his life. Like many White Russians he had led a relatively privileged life until 1917 and business was a largely new and unknown concept to him.

His idle sketching launched a new career in which he worked as a cartoonist for many of the major Shanghai newspapers, as a commercial artist for a range of companies, and on special commissions such as Crow's books. Despite job offers from major newspapers around the world, in 1925 he joined the staff of the *North-China Daily News* and continued to produce cartoons for them until 1940 despite only being paid a relatively meager salary. In his memoir of Shanghai, the Englishman Ralph Shaw, who worked as a reporter for the *North-China Daily News*, described Sapajou as "the star of the office."[11] For 15 years Sapajou published a daily cartoon in the newspaper while Kelly & Walsh also produced several albums of Sapajou's sketches of Shanghai life.

Sapajou became a fixture in the International Settlement and, as was rare for a White Russian, also became a member of the exclusive British Shanghai Club where he could be found at the famous Long Bar, which also became a regular subject of his cartoons. He was also a member and regular at the Cercle Sportif Français, the French Club, on Rue Cardinal Mercier. In addition, he was a well-known figure in the heart of the White Russian community along Avenue Joffre (known locally as the "Nevsky Prospekt" due to its Russification) that between the wars was littered with Cyrillic signs and shops selling Russian furs and books as well as black bread, borscht and blinis for the taste of a home they could not return to. Though a stateless refugee, Sapajou was always considered distinguished in appearance and popular with the ladies as a "charming Russian gentleman."

As well as being a cartoonist, he was an accomplished water colorist and man-about-town. While he mixed with Shanghai's foreign elite, he remained involved in White Russian community affairs as a director and shareholder of the Shanghai-based Russian publishing house and popular newspaper *Slovo* [*The Word*]. When not at the Shanghai Club or the French Club, Sapajou mixed with other White Russians. These included the songwriter and cabaret artiste Alexander Vertinsky. Vertinsky became something of a cult figure in Russian art circles and owned a club in Shanghai in the 1930s and 1940s that occasionally featured the famous Oleg Lundstrem jazz band founded by the composer, pianist and violinist Lundstrem in 1934 in Harbin, where thousands of Russian refugees lived. Lundstrem's band employed nine young Russians from the Russian-Chinese Eastern Railroad staff. Lundstrem, who was inspired by Duke Ellington records, moved to Shanghai in 1936, where his band quickly gained a reputation as the city's best dance band, and he stayed there until 1947.

As a refugee who was broadly sympathetic to the Chinese, Sapajou was a natural supporter of the underdog and this made good ground for his friendship with Crow. His cartoons often made fun of Chinese manners and customs but they were never malicious. As well as providing drawings to Crow and the *North-China Daily News*, he also contributed some illustrations to a book that was essentially a satire on the changes affecting Shanghai during the war: *Shanghai's Morning After* by the notorious anti-communist, monarchist, journalist, soldier of fortune, pilot and spy Hilaire du Berrier. Sapajou also recalled his Beijing days in illustrations for a book of remembrances of the city called *Peking Silhouettes*.[12]

After the Japanese invaded Shanghai, Sapajou found work hard to come by as his major employer, the *North-China Daily News*, was closed down. He avoided the fate of many Allied Shanghailanders and, as a stateless person, wasn't interned. However, this situation left him mired in poverty and in 1942 Sapajou was forced to become the cartoonist of a Nazi-controlled German newspaper to make ends meet. When the war ended, Sapajou found that the *North-China Daily News* would not rehire him due to his wartime employment by the Nazis and he was reduced to once again living in extremely poor and deprived conditions in the docklands of the Hongkou ghetto and the streets of "Little Vienna," getting by largely on hand-outs from friends. The United Nations Relief and Works Agency (UNWRA) finally moved Sapajou, his family and many other White Russians to a temporarily-built displaced persons' camp in 1949 on the small island of Tubabao in the Philippines. Conditions on Tubabao were appalling. Various tropical diseases were prevalent, the island was located in the path of seasonal typhoons, and relocation was a slow process with, at one point, over 5,000 refugees on the island. Calls for the more rapid resettlement of the White Russian refugees started to reach Washington's ear, particularly those from the influential Archbishop John Maximovitch who had formerly been well known at the Russian Episcopate in Shanghai. Sapajou managed to secure a job with the Hearst newspaper group in America. However, in October 1949 he died of lung cancer in Manila.

Commerce Was the Beginning, the Middle and the End of Our Life in China

A Shanghailander in the nineteenth century summed up life in the city – "Commerce was the beginning, the middle and the end of our life in China. If there were no trade, not a single man, except missionaries, would have come there at all."[13] This situation only accelerated in the twentieth century. Crow too became absorbed in the frenetic business of business in Shanghai. As his turnover rose, he moved from the third floor of 81 Jinkee Road to the fourth. By the early 1930s Crow had approximately 25 key accounts with major foreign brands including some, such as Pond's, he had had since virtually the start of the business. Crow was still well known in advertising industry circles for his breakthrough Pond's advert of 1920. He wasn't slow to claim credit for this advert either and was fond of claiming that with his early Pond's campaigns he had personally revolutionized the female beauty market in China with his combination of sexy modern images and accompanying text. His by now proven abilities at self-promotion must have encouraged some to trust him to promote their brands as successfully as well.

Crow claimed that his Chinese staff insisted on the move to the plusher fourth floor at Jinkee Road as they believed it had better *feng shui* than the third. The new office was considered lucky by the staff and Crow went to the trouble of having the offices feng shuied by a local geomancer who officially blessed the premises before Crow moved in. It turned out that not only was the office lucky but that the whole building was lucky, according to the geomancer. Crow himself claimed not to believe in *feng shui* but felt that assuaging his staff by going through the motions would mean a happier and more productive workplace. Whether the building was truly lucky or not is a mute point as Crow admitted to having bribed geomancers several times over the years to get the right result that kept everybody happy and productive.

The new offices were purposely decorated in the style of a New York advertising agency with blackwood furniture, linoleum on the floors and classical eighteenth century English prints on the walls, mostly Hogarth reproductions. According to Crow, the Chinese staff always hated the furniture and he eventually capitulated and changed some of it to appease them. The office had modern equipment for the time with typewriters and electros, a telex and a switchboard. Daily business took place in the offices which were up four flights of stairs with various couriers coming and going while deliveries arrived in the so called "luggage lift." A secretary greeted clients in the reception area, in reality a counter at the top of the stairs. Statements and invoices were issued at the start of every month, a busy time for everyone, even for Crow who hated the activity of balancing the books.

The boss headed up to work by way of the building's elevator, which was staffed by an attendant who spent all his spare time knitting socks for extra income. Crow estimated that the nimble-fingered man made more from his handicrafts than from his lift-operating duties. At one point Crow's building was partially empty with few tenants due to the landlord's refusal to redecorate, and so the knitwear productivity of the elevator attendant skyrocketed. When it was eventually refurbished and smarter tenants filled up the empty offices, the management decided the attendant had to wear a specially-commissioned uniform and stand to attention in the elevator. Crow congratulated him on what seemed to be a sort of promotion. However, the man was inconsolable as his new routine allowed no time for knitting, he had to pay for the uniform in advance from his wages and the influx of new tenants meant he was constantly going up and down with no time for anything else.

The staff all took a two-hour lunch at noon in the *tiffin* tradition that was common in Shanghai and all of them ate their lunches in the office. Some of the workers brought food from home while others formed occasional lunch clubs and ordered up baskets of cheap food from local restaurants. The food would come steaming with baskets of rice and an assortment of meat, fish and vegetables that served about six people. After lunch coolies from the local restaurants would come back to retrieve the baskets and any left-over food, which was customarily given to local beggars who would congregate around the office buildings at the end of the *tiffin* period to feast on the remains of the workers' lunches. Sometimes the staff would venture outside to the traveling kitchens and lunch carts that appeared in the business district and were instantly recognizable from the offices above by the proprietors banging their mobile kitchens' wooden frames with a bamboo stick. These food carts traveled the city all day and all night long and Crow recalled hearing their traditional banging as they made their way along his street calling out to anyone who fancied a late-night snack.

Despite the traditionally long *tiffin* breaks, Crow thought his staff worked hard and exemplified his belief that China "was a land of unremitting industry ... with all working patiently and industriously."[14] Crow noted that his office staff did work unremittingly though not often strenuously in the American way – "If it is true that the devil can only find work for idle hands, then China must be a place of very limited Satanic opportunities."[15]

He admitted that his staff worked long hours but that they would stop en masse if something interesting "such as a dog fight or the visit of foreigners" occurred. The staff, like their boss, all took some time to rest and have a cigarette or a pipe. Though working hours were somewhat eased under the Nationalist government, Crow still considered the Shanghai workday a "health-breaking routine of early risings and midnight conferences." He commented that in his opinion it would not be an exaggeration to "say that nine tenths of China is out of bed and at work by sunrise."[16] The bad news for Crow, who appreciated his sleep and enjoyed a long breakfast, was that most staff expected the boss to keep even longer hours than they did. Crow knew many managers who rose before 6 a.m. to go to work and did not finish till 11 p.m. Crow tried to instil a discipline of reasonable hours, but he found that his many Chinese clients insisted on long conferences that stretched into the wee small hours; and he constantly had to try to come up with new strategies to avoid having meetings with clients on Sundays which he preferred to spend quietly at home. He could only content himself with being grateful he did not run an American factory.

After visiting several car factories in Detroit on a visit to the US in the 1930s, he returned to Shanghai and visited a client at a local cotton mill. He had gone to the US to see one of his largest clients, Buick. Wages in Buick's Detroit plants at that time were among the highest in the world for factory workers while wages in Shanghai were among the lowest. However, Crow contrasted the contentment he believed he saw in the Shanghai workforce with the general grumpiness of the American workers he had observed. He admitted that this was not precise sociology and also that he wasn't sure exactly what it meant except that it convinced him that as factories were a relatively new phenomenon in China they were seen by many workers as veritable bastions of enlightenment compared with many other workplaces and occupations available – particularly subsistence farming. This analysis, of course, tended to forget how quickly workers in these new factories embraced the nascent labor movement and political action.

Crow's office may or may not have been in a lucky building but it was certainly well situated. Facing the front door of the office building was the new Bank of China created by T. V. Soong, while to the south was an American bank and in the opposite direction the Metropolitan Land Company building, near the imposing British consulate building at 33 The Bund, one of the best-known venues in Shanghai at the time. From his office Crow could see the Huang Pu River, across to Pudong and the so-called "Dollar Boats" (the boats that sailed from the docks of the "Grand Old Man of the Pacific" Robert Dollar and his Dollar Steamship Company). Crow constantly referred to the Dollar Company; he was friendly with Robert Dollar and the Dollar Line was a client of Carl Crow Inc. In the mid-1930s he helped his nephew George to escape the stifling female-dominated Crow clan in Missouri and get a job with the company. He arrived in Shanghai as the head of the passenger division with an office close to Carl's on the Bund. Carl's regular lunchtime walk would take him along the developing Shanghai Bund from the Cenotaph at the junction of the French and International Concessions which commemorated those fallen in the First World War[17] along to the Garden Bridge and across Suzhou Creek. The Creek was a sight in itself; it was invariably packed with junks, lines of barges, sampans, ferries and perhaps also the sculls of the Shanghai Rowing Club.

Crow thought his staff very skilled in being able to concentrate and think without making mistakes in what he considered a very noisy atmosphere. He claimed to need silence to think but quietness was not the way of a Chinese-dominated office in Shanghai. Crow was constantly annoyed by noise, but he realized that it was just the Chinese way – he even devoted an entire chapter to the subject of the Chinese and noise in his book *The Chinese Are Like That* entitled "The Home of the Firecracker." He moaned about two Chinese brothers that lived next door to him for a time for talking loudly at 3 a.m. and keeping him awake; and he complained about the noisy funeral processions that made their way through Shanghai playing such strange Western standards as *Ta-ra-ra, Boom-de-aye* and *There'll Be A Hot Time in The Old Town Tonight*. He was also known to complain to the police about noise and once managed to get a neighbor to turn off a blaring radio at midnight after requesting the police do something about it. The setting off of firecrackers by children was a constant source of stress on his noise-sensitive nerves.

For Crow, punctuality was also important. He admitted that he was always infuriated by his Chinese clients' inability to turn up on time for meetings and that he could never shake off the Western obsession with timekeeping. He always felt the need to be on time and openly admired the Chinese for being far more casual about things like train schedules or boat timetables or meeting appointments while he worried himself sick about being five minutes late or missing a bus. During his time in China, Crow noted that the Chinese were becoming noticeably more punctual than when he had first arrived and ascribed this to the growth in the importance of transport timetables as well as, perhaps less explicably, a growth in interest in sports such as athletics where split seconds suddenly started counting for a lot. He also noted that when he had arrived in 1911, building sites in Shanghai were fairly leisurely places, but the boom in skyscraper and apartment building in the intervening period had been phenomenal with buildings going up in record time. The city's boom had ended the leisurely pace of life Crow had enjoyed before the First World War when he considered the city to be a calmer, quieter and generally more placid place.

However, Crow could do nothing but admire the aspirations of his staff. One occasional staff member, a carpenter, who helped fix things and make promotional signs, once consulted Crow about an idea he had for a small business renting out bicycles to visiting sailors, on the grounds that the British and Americans appeared to have a strange passion for pointlessly riding bicycles or horses all day in their leisure time. Crow considered the business plan but advised the carpenter that it might be hazardous – returns would be low as you couldn't charge very much and having foreign sailors as your target market was risky given their propensity for leaving port without a care, particularly for any unpaid bills left behind. The man agreed with Crow but stated that he wanted ultimately to get into the trucking business but didn't have the capital for a truck; and so he figured he'd start with bicycles and reinvest with some other members of his family in motorcycles and eventually trucks. Crow agreed that on that basis the proposition might be sound eventually. Seven years later Crow was delighted when the man came to visit him at home, driving a new truck into his garden and presenting him with a pet monkey to thank him for his early encouragement.

This sort of diligence in wealth accumulation and attention to detail always impressed Crow and he never objected to the added expense of the 13th month's wage that was traditionally paid at Chinese New Year. He was once faced with a printing job for a client that involved 100,000 Chinese language booklets that he had contracted with a local printer to produce. When the final copy was delivered, it was noticed that two strokes from one character had been missed out, thus completely changing its meaning. Nobody wanted to reprint the entire book and lose all the profits or had the time to do it as the client was demanding shipment and would have certainly demanded an entire reprint if he noticed the oversight. Crow noted that the solution was found by the printer who instructed his staff to open every single booklet, after Crow had suggested perhaps making the correction in every hundredth book, and individually ink in the two strokes so no one would ever spot the typographical error. As often appears to have been the case his diligent staff dismissed his short-cut solution as typical crazy foreign thinking and insisted that all 100,000 must be changed.

A Furnace for the Making of Men

Chiang Kai-shek once described Shanghai as a furnace for the making of men. As Crow's advertising business prospered, he became a relatively well-known and commercially successful citizen who had made it; the insurance tycoon C. V. Starr later described Carl Crow Inc. as an "extremely lucrative" business.[18] He had a good business model and soon started to reap substantial profits which made him a comparatively wealthy man.

Carl Crow Inc. grew quickly. He soon expanded to Ningbo and had a full-time business manager to cover the Zhejiang area, though he often personally took the overnight steamer that left Shanghai at 5 p.m., taking 12 hours to go down the coast to see clients. He claimed that the clamor of foreign

*Crow's message to his clients of accentuating the image in their advertising in China
clearly didn't extend to his own corporate ads.*

manufacturers to make a killing in the China market was such that even when Shanghai was hit by a cholera outbreak in 1923, causing many foreigners to send their families home and evacuate the city for a time, the advertising business continued to boom. Real estate prices collapsed along Nanking Road and vacant shops littered the city as businesses went bankrupt, clubs found that members couldn't afford to renew their subscriptions and the stock market went into a tailspin – but still everyone advertised and still Carl Crow Inc. prospered.

Crow had started Shanghai's first major advertising agency catering to foreign clients. Through his occasional trips abroad he also became a local source for major agencies and large concerns such as the J. Walter Thompson agency which hired Crow to handle its clients' China needs. Most of these clients were American but Crow also spent time on trips to Europe in which he visited agencies in London, Paris, and Berlin. Others soon realized it was a good business and followed suit. In 1927 F. C. Millington, an Englishman, started an agency that concentrated on British clients in a similar way to Crow's focus on Americans. (Crow did not concentrate exclusively on Americans, however, and was inordinately proud to have one client from the Duchy of Luxembourg and also included Chinese clients on his list as well as, perhaps oddly given his overt political views, several Japanese clients.) By the 1930s, Crow and Millington's agencies as well as two Chinese-run agencies – the Chinese Commercial Advertising Company and the United Advertising Company – were dubbed the "Big Four."

Crow's business gained recognition through his poster sites, billboards and modern artwork in newspaper adverts. However, the main source of his not insubstantial revenues came from the relatively simple business of placing advertisements on behalf of his foreign clients in the Chinese and English language press. Of course, few if any in Shanghai had better connections with the press than Crow. He had been directly involved at a senior level with the *China Press*, was later to be closely involved with the formation of the *Shanghai Evening Post*, and was a close friend of many other major publishers in the English language sector. It is hardly surprising that Crow's advertisements appeared regularly in his friend Arthur De Carle Sowerby's *Journal of China Arts and Sciences* or J. B. Powell's *China Weekly Review*; indeed Powell was a small investor in Carl Crow Inc. Crow also had connections with the major Chinese language newspapers and periodicals through the work of his Chun Mei Agency, contacts within the Missouri News Colony, friendships with his Chinese journalist colleagues over the years, and his role as a silent director of several newspapers to help them avoid the attentions of the censors. Buying space, placing adverts, and earning commissions (Crow preferred the more professional sounding term "service fees") both from the client and from the publication involved little more difficulty for Crow than a simple telephone call or a conversation over lunch at one of the city's clubs. Adverts for his foreign clients could be large, often full-page, and run repeatedly as rates were very low in Chinese papers. In 1926 Crow estimated that column inch rates in China were less than one-fourth of the average American rate. As most Chinese language newspapers were subsidized by a political party or an individual politician (or in some cases a warlord), deriving profits from advertising was not that important for their proprietors.

As well as getting preferential rates from old friends and colleagues, Crow could also negotiate favorable rates from the rest of the press by buying in bulk. His agency's major selling point was that Carl Crow Inc. placed twice as many adverts in newspapers as any other agency. He was able to get the best possible rates and the highest agency discounts – even with his service fee included – as placing adverts via Carl Crow Inc. was cheaper than trying to do it yourself. The discounts Crow got could bring down the cost of an advertising budget significantly as the published rates were generally considered as no more than a starting point in negotiations over the actual price finally paid. All newspapers in a given city published the same rates regardless of circulation numbers. It is not surprising that when Crow traveled round the country he was invariably treated to sumptuous banquets by the proprietors of regional newspapers who appreciated the volume of business he brought to them and were more than open to talking volume discounts.

The outdoor advertising business was good too. Crow saw the hoardings and billboards he erected along China's emerging highways as an extension of his newspaper adverts to reach the masses. Again, due to problems of illiteracy, the strength of the image became even more crucial with outdoor hoardings and posters than with newspaper adverts. Crow's billboard and poster business grew rapidly with his team of snipers working flat out across the Yangtze valley.

Crow knew the newspaper and the advertising business and profited from his contacts and network, but his forays into other businesses were not always so successful. For instance, he once got involved in a short-lived watch-selling venture with a young American in Shanghai. Crow had been representing an American watch manufacturer and was looking after its stock in China. He was approached by the youthful American who assured Crow that he could sell the watches without interfering with the client's market. Crow was intrigued but the man would tell him no more. Crow sold him two watches at wholesale prices. After half an hour the young man was back and bought another three, then returned once again for a further five and so on until fifty watches had been bought and then sold. Crow was impressed and wanted to continue to expand but the man explained that he was leaving the watch business and moving on to Hong Kong. Crow wanted to know why, as things were looking promising. The young man then had to explain that he had pawned one watch at each pawnshop in Shanghai for a good price and so now his new market and customer base had expired and reached saturation point. The short-lived business venture was over.

Another poor business venture for Crow was when he agreed to virtually assume ownership of a Chinese friend's coal distribution business. The friend was worried about problems with local warlords and their rapacious demands for taxes and so thought he would be safer if a foreigner ran the business. Crow's involvement did end the harassment from the warlords but caused Crow a major headache when Chinese customers started calling up Crow to complain about the poor quality coal being delivered. He decided the coal delivery business was not for him and withdrew from the venture. He also regularly speculated on currencies though rarely with much success – he admitted that his gambles on falling roubles and rising sterling had not often paid off. Eventually he wisely decided to stick to advertising, a little freelance journalism and books.

Introducing Four Hundred Million Customers

They learned poker according to Texas rules

All of Crow's adventures in the advertising business were eventually condensed into the book that was to make his name as a successful and best-selling author around the world. Advertising, marketing and the fortunes of foreign businesses in China were the subject of Crow's widely read and often re-published book, and the one that most people were to remember him for – *Four Hundred Million Customers: The Experiences – Some Happy, Some Sad of an American in China, and What They Taught Him.* The original publishers, Harper & Brothers of New York, described the book as a "fascinating and hilarious book which is giving tens of thousands of readers a candid, discerning picture of our oriental neighbors." Though published eventually in the disastrous year of 1937 the book had been written in happier times and recounts a series of tales of advertising and marketing in China, most of which were the direct experiences of running Carl Crow Inc.

The book, with specially commissioned illustrations by Sapajou, caught on and was reprinted in a variety of languages and editions including later a pocket book edition printed by the American army for soldiers stationed in Shanghai. Upon publication, the book received universal praise from the British and American press, was a Book of the Month Club choice and a *Harper's* magazine "Find." The Pulitzer Prize winner, Carl Van Doren,[19] writing in the *Boston Herald*, described the book as "A feast of human nature for almost any reader;" the writer and O' Henry Prize winner Dorothy Canfield in the *Book of the Month Club News* said it was "One of the most convincing and lifelike descriptions of Chinese life we have ever had;" and the London *Times* stated that "No one who wants to do business in China can safely neglect it." Also, *Newsweek* described the book as "… a rollicking human interest story of Chinese eccentricity and immovability."

Crow's tone in *Four Hundred Million Customers* was to be amusing but informative. His fascination with the advertising business had been that it allowed him time to study the ordinary Chinese man and woman, as a consumer, a shopper and a person in a new society tempted by an ever-growing range of products and services to choose from (or reject) while looking at the misconceptions foreign companies held about China. The book achieved a level of fame that meant that Crow was still receiving fan mail up until his death and one radio announcer in America reviewed it as an essential read for the visitor to China – and that anyone going to Shanghai should look up Carl Crow. He came to dread the arrival of every passenger liner from America for a while as it brought eager readers and tourists to his office door demanding a tour of the city as promised on the radio back home.

The book's popularity derived as much from Crow's style and wit as from his contention that selling to the elusive Chinese market was much more difficult than most supposed – including himself back in 1918 when he admitted to stupidly agreeing with one of his first clients that the Chinese would buy anything if it was cheap enough. The next 20 years in the advertising business had disabused him of that notion and he set out to find out why the seemingly boundless market of China had proved to be more a money-pit than a goldmine for so many foreign businesses. His conclusion shattered many illusions about China – "No matter what you may be selling, your business in China should be enormous, if the Chinese who should buy your goods would only do so."[20]

Crow also spent some time with an old colleague T. O. Thackery of the *New York Post* putting together a movie script of *Four Hundred Million Customers*, which his agent Nancy Parker submitted to several studios – unsuccessfully. Crow was obviously hoping that Hollywood might pick up the idea. After all, the last best-selling book in America on China, Alice Tisdale Hobart's *Oil for the Lamps of China*[21] – another business-oriented book, though a novel, dealing with Standard Oil's ambitions – had been made into a film of the same name in 1935 that attracted some success.

Of course, almost inevitably, Crow did not always believe what he told others. Over the course of 20 years Carl Crow Inc. ran some of China's most original and novel promotional campaigns and published some of Shanghai's most modern and ground-breaking advertising artwork. Crow never considered that any of it made much difference and that the Chinese remained largely distrustful of advertising.

The advertising business suited Crow immensely as it allowed him to pursue his twin interests: China and people watching. Crow was a genuine China Hand by now but still a frustrated amateur anthropologist and sociologist. However, while he continued to prosper along with Shanghai, across the vast hinterlands of China political machinations and warlordism continued to rage. Crow was unable to remain isolated from the shifting fortunes of China, safely cloistered in the International Settlement, and found himself sucked into the conflicts of the time.

9
Getting Friendly with Warlords

Bandit or advertising men?

Thick Streaks of Ruthlessness

Crow met his fair share of warlords during his time in China and found some
he liked and others he thought outright bandits. He couldn't very well avoid
them and, since arriving in Shanghai, had come into contact with them both as
a journalist and an advertising agent. Crow's time in China coincided roughly
with the warlord period (1916–39) sparked by Yuan Shih-kai's death that left a
power vacuum the warlords greedily filled.

Crow was later to drive out to Shanghai's suburbs to watch two warlords'
armies fighting during the Jiangsu-Zhejiang conflicts of 1924. In January 1925,
he watched the arrival at Shanghai's North Railway Station of a group of
mercenary White Russians and Frank Sutton – the old Etonian, one-armed ex-
British army officer turned arms-smuggler. They were all part of the sartorially
stylish, heavily moustachioed and well-equipped Fengtian Clique Army of the

Manchurian warlord Chang Tso-lin which controlled a territory the size of Western Europe.[1] Chang designed uniforms with more braid and sashes than even most European generals would have considered seemly; and Sutton, an armaments expert, eventually rose to the position of Chang's personal adviser. Crow met "One-Armed Sutton" several times on visits to Shenyang where he was based alongside his boss Chang who was known alternatively as the "Red Bearded Bandit" (a traditional term for northern warriors – the diminutive Chang lacked a beard) by the Chinese, the "Manchurian Tiger" by foreigners, and later as the "Old Marshall."

Most foreigners, including Crow, tended to see warlords as a traditional part of the Chinese scene and judged them as either friendly or hostile on a case-by-case basis. However, he noted that in his advertising business he had never met a warlord he couldn't haggle sensibly with over prices and taxes he had to pay to put up billboards in their territories; usually business got done somehow. Crow reckoned that the taxes levied against his adverts were pretty fair and that through negotiation he never paid more than one-tenth of the amount originally demanded anyway.[2]

He had also had some dealings with the various warlords that controlled Chinese Shanghai including Lu Yung-hsiang, a former general in Yuan Shih-kai's army, who ran the Chinese city for some years and established a highly lucrative opium wholesale business. He had also met the eastern warlord Sun Chuang-fang, who controlled much of the lower Yangtze and, for a time, the Chinese portions of Shanghai, as well as the "Christian General" Feng Yu-hsiang.[3] The latter had purchased 500 copies of Crow's Compub book of Woodrow Wilson's speeches despite having previously studied revolutionary technique in a class taught by the leading bolshevik Karl Radek.[4]

The warlords of the inter-war period were a contradictory phenomenon in many senses. Most were vehemently anti-communist; virtually all considered themselves patriots; and some later fought hard against the Japanese, often integrating their forces into the Nationalist army. Most of the major warlords[5] had military training and backgrounds in the imperial army and a number had studied in European or Japanese military academies, while others were more localized bandits who simply knew the lay of the land better than anyone else. In other instances, warlords emerged who had academic backgrounds and were Confucian scholars, such as Wu Pei-fu who was known as the "Philosopher General" as he had passed the Chinese Civil Service Examination. The warlord period saw sizeable armies form and dissolve: fortunes shifted with strong leaders and troops who switched sides. There were also others who acted as part-time mercenaries when the agricultural season allowed, and were generally young men who saw the warlord armies as quick routes to loot and a full stomach.

In the 1920s and 1930s bandits proliferated across the country. Ten years later the British journalist Peter Fleming traveled through Manchuria and northern China where he identified four distinct groups of bandits:

> 1) pseudo-political patriotic forces organised to promote a cause; 2) bands of religious fanatics such as the "Red Spears"; 3) old style bandits who survived through taxing the areas they controlled supplemented with a little pillage and; 4) bandits of despair, mostly peasants forced into lawlessness by poverty.[6]

Much of the actual fighting was fairly shambolic, such as the clashes Crow witnessed near Shanghai, but massacres and extreme brutality, torture, rape and pillage were all commonplace. Beheading was their preferred method of execution with the severed heads, a sight Crow saw many times on his travels throughout China, publicly displayed. If the warlords had an identifying characteristic, it was probably "a thick streak of ruthlessness,"[7] as David Bonavia suggests in his study of the period.

Becoming a Warlord's Elder Brother

Of all the warlords Crow met, the one he actually struck up a friendship with was the 25-year-old "Commander in Chief" Swen Miao.[8] In Crow's own words, Swen was "a real throat slitting bandit of the sort that splash blood on the pages of fiction and sometimes get into Hollywood."[9] Crow and Swen's friendship reached the point where Crow sent cartons of cigarettes to him while the warlord sent Crow bottles of brandy, though Crow noted that while he paid for the cigarettes the brandy was undoubtedly part of the bandit's swag from some looting expedition. Eventually Swen referred to Crow as *dage*, or elder brother – a rare privilege indeed.

The story of how Crow got to be such good friends with a bandit warlord was a major news story in Shanghai at the time. Swen was one of China's best-known and most notorious bandits in the 1930s and made the front pages of newspapers as far afield as London and New York. Crow's description of him as "throat-slitting" doesn't sit with the fact that Swen spoke English, was considered patient by his hostages and was generally thought to be a good and kind leader of his men – J. B. Powell called him a "young chap ... from a formerly respected family."[10] He had also received military training in the army of Chang Ching-yao, the pro-Japanese warlord who had taken control of Beijing briefly in 1920.

However, in the intervening decades Swen has largely been overshadowed in history by Chang Tso-lin, who was assassinated by the Japanese when his train was blown up in 1928 after forming an alliance with the Nationalists. Crow was forced to admit that Swen slipped pretty quickly from history: "He was not, however, a very successful bandit, for he was young and more ambitious than practical; but he might have traveled far after he had gained more experience if he had not been beheaded before he reached the prime of life."[11]

In fact, Swen's story was fairly typical of many bandits in China. He had come from a successful family which had managed somehow to annoy a local magistrate with its progressive political ideas. His father had ended up losing his head after a show trial on trumped-up charges. The magistrate then made every police station in the family's home province of Shandong exhibit photos of the execution and Swen was smart enough to realize that someone so obsessed with destroying his family would come after him next. So he wisely took to the hills with a few other endangered relatives and sought revenge on the magistrate. As Crow noted, "The Chinese learned many centuries ago that crooked officials can never be reformed and that the only practical thing to do is to kill them."[12] At least that was the biography of Swen that Crow believed. An alternative, somewhat less romantic, version has it that the Swen clan fell on hard times after idle, gambling sons squandered the family's wealth and so became salt-smugglers and bandits.

Whichever was the true story, Swen soon had over 700 followers as his ranks swelled with men after the Yellow River flooding in 1920 and 1921 which ruined many peasant farmers. Swen initially had a good stock of arms purchased with the proceeds of raids and robberies. However, the local population didn't care very much as Swen mostly raided police stations or ambushed armed police detachments patrolling the countryside. As their loot grew, many disaffected soldiers fed up with low pay and meager rations joined Swen. Poor peasants worked their farms and then when the harvest was finished would disappear for a little banditry until farm work called them back to their land. Swen moved on to raiding rich landowners and became a Robin Hood figure for many peasants; and he perpetuated the myth of his being an active agent of redistribution by naming his gang the Shantung People's Liberation Society.[13] All the time he kept on trying to assassinate the original corrupt magistrate who had killed his father, but the man kept a loyal force of bodyguards that made the job difficult. As time passed, the Shantung People's Liberation Society grew still further in a loose way with more bandits joining the "cause."

Eventually the Liberation Society set up a semi-permanent camp on the slopes of Paotzeku Mountain, which was virtually unassailable from below. Swen continued raiding and kidnapping to the point where his reputation grew to such proportions that he rarely needed to leave camp, and local merchants and wealthy landowners started paying him tribute and tolls (*lijin*) as protection money to leave them alone. The magistrate and his forces rarely entered Swen's territory. It was a stand-off between the secure Swen and the well-guarded magistrate.

This situation could presumably have carried on indefinitely to both men's benefit had Swen not decided on May 6, 1923, to attack the nearby Tianjin-Pukow Railway and derail the new deluxe fast train that plied the route between Shanghai and Beijing, the *Blue Express* – the first all-steel train in Asia. Swen and 1,000 of his followers kidnapped all the passengers in the early hours of the morning and looted the train near the town of Lincheng close to the Jiangsu-Shandong border (though technically in Hebei province), leading to the whole crisis becoming known as the Lincheng Outrage. His hostages included 300 Chinese and, crucially, 25 foreigners (foreigners generally fetched larger ransoms). The train was ransacked, all valuables were taken and even the mattresses and light bulbs were stripped by the bandits as loot.

Carl Crow onboard the Red Cross Relief Train during the Lincheng Outrage.

One short-term hostage was First World War veteran and *China Press* journalist Lloyd Lehrbas[14] who managed to escape and started filing stories about the incident almost immediately. The news that foreigners had been kidnapped from the *Blue* by a warlord and that a ransom was being demanded greatly excited the greatly excitable Shanghai foreign community, many of whom saw visions of the return of Boxer-like retribution and killing. To the insulated residents of the International Settlement, Chinese warlords terrorizing and kidnapping Chinese citizens was one thing but terrorizing and kidnapping Westerners was quite another. The kidnapped were probably relatively safe as dead hostages were worthless, but it was not unknown for prisoners to be slaughtered wholesale by warlords. The bandit soldiers were a mixed bunch. They included poor farmers and unemployed youth from the "university of the forest;"[15] a hard core of battle-trained soldiers who had seen action in Russia, Korea and China but had been discharged from the Chinese army and were aggrieved at their loss of status; and men who had formed part of the 140,000 strong "Chinese Labour Corps" recruited by the British and French during the First World War to do tasks such as clearing the dead from the European battlefields and keeping the trenches supplied. Needless to say, these men had seen some of the worst atrocities imaginable. They had become extremely battle-hardened and then sent home with some coppers once their usefulness ended.

In terms of news value, kidnapping of either Chinese or foreigners was not necessarily a shocking event at the time. Crow described kidnapping as a "well-organized business in China carried out with a large degree of success ...,"[16] although it was still something to be feared. Crow knew that traveling in the hinterland of China between the wars, as he often did, was to put yourself at a certain risk of kidnap whatever precautions were taken. It was a small comfort that it was relatively rare for foreign hostages to be abused severely and Crow worried more about lack of food and inclement weather than violent mistreatment.

He had had some experience of those who feared kidnapping and knew their concerns. Many of his Chinese friends lived in unostentatious houses and bought only second-hand cars to avoid becoming targets for the kidnappers. Crow had made friends with the successful Chinese manager of a Shanghai bank with whom he had some financial dealings. Kidnappers had attempted to capture the man several times but so far their attempts had all failed. The man's problem was that he had broken with the traditional Chinese way of keeping quiet about his wealth. At the time fear of kidnapping meant that most rich Shanghainese went unlisted in the phone book, traveled in bullet-proof cars and often hired heavily-armed White Russians to guard them. This form of protection was so successful that the kidnappers had to resort to moving down a notch on the social scale and taking hostages from those generally considered wealthy but not perhaps rich enough to employ small armies of hired guns. Crow's bank manager friend fell into this category and subsequently had to reinvent himself as a poor man.

The man, known as "Fatty" to his friends, put out the story that he had suffered a disaster on the stock market and owed money from losses at mahjong. He resigned from the bank and started wearing threadbare clothes to improve his impoverished image, thus making himself a poor subject for the kidnappers.

Crow found Fatty a job on a newspaper he was involved with, a publication known to not be making a great deal of money, on the grounds that this would enhance the illusion of his being just another "miserable underpaid wage slave." Fatty was hired at a low salary and put to work selling advertising. The whole thing worked well; Fatty enjoyed the work, and enthusiastically and successfully sold lots of advertising space to his former clients. Crow started to feel that the man deserved a wage rise but, despite selling more advertising space, Fatty refused a pay increase point blank. All the time Fatty gave discreet but elaborate dinner parties for the staff and even presented Crow's wife with a piece of jade Carl estimated to be equivalent to quite a few months of the man's official salary. Ultimately the kidnappers fell for Fatty's ruse and left him alone, and he died peacefully of a natural death in his own bed at home.

Kidnapping also wasn't a problem that went away soon. Later on Crow was to become involved in the locally high profile case of Feng Yixiang, also known as Y. C. Vong, a caterer who counted the American Club among his major clients. In May 1929 he was kidnapped in an alley behind the Club where he lived unostentatiously. The police failed to follow up the case and both the *Shanghai Evening Post*, J. B. Powell's *China Weekly Review* and Crow, as Vice President of the American Club, raised hell. The policeman involved was taken to task while Feng was eventually rescued from a boat hidden in a small creek just outside the International Settlement.[17]

Negotiating with Bandits

At first glance it may have seemed an odd choice by the American Red Cross to decide to send Carl Crow, a Shanghai businessman, to mediate with a warlord. However, Crow had helped the Red Cross to raise funds since the war. He had previously managed to secure large donations from wealthy Shanghai Taipans, including the phenomenally wealthy Baghdad-born Jewish property developer Silas Hardoon, as well as raising funds to open a relief kitchen for White Russian refugees in Shanghai after the Bolshevik Revolution. Also, the fact that foreigners were involved added a dimension to the situation; and Westerners had often historically acted as intermediaries in kidnappings and warlord disputes. For example, a former British Consul General in Chengdu, Sir Meyrick Hewlett, had in the past managed to mediate between warring armies from Yunnan and Guizhou who were rampaging in Sichuan. China Hands like Hewlett and Crow were seen as good potential emissaries and mediators.

Crow would have been aware of the reputation of Shandong as a major breeding ground for warlords. Shandong people had long had a reputation for being independently-minded and physically strong and had been much sought after by the army and police force as potential recruits. That China's most famous classic bandit story – *Outlaws of the Marsh* – is set in Shandong shows how long the image of Shandong folk as tough has endured. In fact, Swen's men were sometimes cruel to the hostages, particularly the Chinese, killing several while others died of hunger and exposure, as well as beating several of the Western hostages and forcing J. B. Powell to defend himself with his fists on one occasion. Nerves were strained after Joseph Rothman, a Romanian on a British passport, had been shot dead after refusing to surrender his valuables and throwing a teapot at a bandit's head during the storming of the *Blue*.

In his mountain hideaway atop the "sugar loaf"-shaped Paotzeku,[18] Swen eventually decided to let all the women and children leave after relieving them of their valuables, which defused some of the high-profile nature of the incident. However, it became headline-making when it was discovered that one of the female hostages who was traveling with her companion Miss McFadden and her French maid Mademoiselle Schonberg was none other than Lucy Aldrich, who was a sister-in-law of John D. Rockefeller Jr. and daughter of Nelson Aldrich, former Governor of Rhode Island. Among the remaining hostages was an assortment of Americans, British, French, Italian, and Mexican nationals.

Many of the hostages were well known in Shanghai and one, J. B. Powell, was a long-standing acquaintance of Crow and an old friend. Under Powell's editorship, the *China Weekly Review* was rapidly becoming a popular read with many nationalist-leaning Chinese and anti-colonial foreigners, not least due to its pro-Chinese stance and vocal criticisms of some of Shanghai's leading foreign dignitaries.

As well as Powell, who had been on his way to meet the US Minister to China Dr. Jacob Gould Schurman when captured, there was Guiseppe D. Musso, a bulky, wealthy and influential Italian lawyer who spent the crisis clad in his Roman nightshirt and was accompanied by his Secretary Signorina Pirelli; Lee Solomon, a bearded mahjong manufacturer rarely seen without a cigarette between his lips; British businessman Reginal Rowlatt; and US Army Major Roland Pinger who had been traveling with his wife and seemingly went through the entire hostage crisis without removing his waistcoat. The hostages also included Powell's cabin-mate for the journey, the smart and dashing Marcel Berube, a Frenchman who had previously worked for the Chinese salt monopoly and the Chinese Customs Administration and was a hero of the Western Front, and the only hostage to consider all the marching around on Paotzeku as just so much exercise. They also included M. C. Jacobsen of British American Tobacco; Frenchman Emile Gensburger; Fred and Eddie Elias, two British cousins of Gensburger's; their friend Theo Saphiere; Major Robert Allen of the US Army

Medical Corps in Manila who was on leave with his family at the time; the massive Leon Friedman, one of Shanghai's best-known car dealers who was forced to wear clothes several sizes too small for him throughout; the bearded William Smith, a stiff-upper-lipped Britisher known as the "Manchester Sexagenarian" who was clad throughout in the blue pyjamas he had been sleeping in on the train and proved invaluable in raising morale during the ordeal; and the hopelessly exotic and sharp-dressing Mexican industrialist and publisher Señor Manuel Ancera Verea of Guadalajara (who had already been kidnapped twice before in Mexico) and his new wife who were on a year long round-the-world honeymoon and refused to be parted by the bandits.

In addition, there were several prominent Chinese among the hostages, including Dr. Siji C. Hung; a Cambridge-educated Professor Cheng Chi; Charles Cheng his son; K. P. Koo, who was a member of staff at the Nanjing Teacher Training College; and Kang Tung-yi, the Sunday editor of the *Shun Pao* newspaper, who had also been travelling with Powell; and a train guard, Da Hu.

The bandits' mountain hideaway at Paotzeku was remote and involved a ten-day forced march for the captives. Powell noted: "The march from the train would have been worth a million to an American movie director. Most of the male passengers took the thing humorously, expecting to be taken but a short distance away while the work of rifling the train was completed. As we know, this expectation was not realized."[19] Conical, volcano-like Paotzeku – hostage Major Roland Pinger likened it to Tamalpais on San Francisco Bay – was not a particularly hospitable place. It had little food or supplies, and no medicines or clothes; their temporary accommodation in an old run-down monastery was flea-ridden; and soon dysentery and malaria were major problems. However, both Powell and his fellow hostage Rowlatt took time to report the scenery as stunning. The hostages were soon hungry as they had been fed little but some tinned sardines Powell had managed to beg from a bandit, some dog meat and a plate of scorpions with their stings removed. The first immediate task that was required before any negotiations could start was to get food and supplies to the hostages – which was the job given to Crow by the American Red Cross and the Shanghai Chamber of Commerce.[20]

Crow's brief was to travel to Shandong to start mediating for the foreigners' release if possible and to get supplies such as medicines, food and a change of clothing up the mountain. In Shanghai the hostages were rumored to be in bad shape after the long forced march to Paotzeku. Crow departed from Shanghai after being also made responsible for looking after and trying to release all the Chinese captives too. This meant a long process and it took him, and a host of other negotiators, six weeks to finally reach a deal with Swen.

Crow had visited Shandong several times before. In 1921 he passed through en route to Beijing with a client from New York. At that time a major clean-up operation to try to purge the area of bandits had been in full swing. He remembered having breakfast on the train in Shandong when it slowed to a crawl and passed 21 decapitated bandit heads on poles in plain sight which was intended to dissuade anyone from taking up banditry as a profession. Crow was shocked, though not as shocked as his suddenly unhungry New York client.

Crow headed up to Zaozhuang[21] on the Grand Canal in southern Shandong, which was the nearest town on the Beijing-Shanghai railway to the mountain hideout about 20 miles away. As he traveled north, Crow admitted to having "… allowed a sophomoric spirit of adventure to get the better of me; for I didn't have the faintest idea of how I was going to establish contact with a group of people who had been kidnapped and held for ransom by what was quite obviously a powerful and well-organized bandit gang."[22] He arrived with the first suitcases of supplies stuffed with food, letters and packages from the hostages' families. Zaozhuang itself was not that hospitable; it was a small town best known for its cherries, pomegranate farming, date trees and mutton soup made from young male goats, one or two years old, butchered in a special way and mixed with several seasonings and then boiled. Crow was to eat a lot of it over the coming weeks. The town had expanded with the establishment of the heavily-fortified Sino-German Chung Hsing Colliery which had high-powered searchlights that stayed on all night and machine-gun posts to prevent surprise attacks on the coalmines. Crow tried to make himself as comfortable as possible from his base in a couple of disused railway sleeping cars parked inside the walled coal mine about eight miles from Paotzeku.

Carl Crow marshalling supplies in Shandong for the hostages.

It turned out to be pretty easy to ship supplies up the mountain once Crow realized he could bypass the official channels that the Chinese government were trying to establish. Virtually as soon as he set foot in Zaozhuang, some local people offered to get supplies up Paotzeku to the hostages. Crow took a chance and handed over the supplies as he was worried that Powell and the others might be suffering unduly up on the mountainside. The average diet of a middle- or low-level northern warlord army recruit was little more than some bread and vegetables, with meat or fish only occasionally being available. Fortunately, the mild spring meant that the hostages weren't too cold. Crow addressed all the initial supplies, canned goods mostly, to Powell and asked his old colleague to send back a letter of receipt. When the first shipment of supplies arrived, Powell described the night's feast on Paotzeku as "a never-to-be-forgotten banquet."[23]

Although the porters Crow hired looked a little "raffish," the next morning he was awoken at 3 a.m. to be given a note from Powell saying that everything had arrived safely and in perfect condition. The first shipment started a daily courier service up the hillside and Powell sent back daily receipts for the goods that included bread, crackers, canned milk, sardines, bully beef, water, raisins, cheese, candles, bandages, cigars and cigarettes, as well as newspapers, magazines and rolls of toilet paper. Crow could not be accused of being stingy in the supplies he sent up. Señora Verea, who refused to be separated from her husband and did not return with the other freed women, was particularly grateful for magazines with the latest fashions to keep her informed of what she was missing. To dissuade the bandits from raiding the supplies, Crow also started sending shipments of rice to Swen for his men. Recalling the ordeal later, one of the hostages declared that when Crow's supply trains arrived it was like manna from heaven and raised everyone's spirits.

Ultimately the shipments became so regular that a special mail service, the Bandit Express, was introduced between Paotzeku and Zaozhuang during May and June 1923 to serve the captives. Crow had a local printer produce special stamps from wooden dies, which became known as "Bandit Mail Stamps," for the service in an attempt to regularize it and make Swen feel more recognized and also to be able to account for the cost of postage to the Red Cross accountants in Shanghai.[24] About 500 of these special stamps were printed and a supply was sent to the hostages for use on their correspondence back to Crow. The rest were kept at Crow's headquarters for use on letters being forwarded to the hostages. For a time the stamps became recognized by the official Chinese post office. On the hostages' letters that were going further afield to their families and friends, Chinese stamps were used alongside Crow's personally designed ones, with the private letters then forwarded by diplomatic bag. This is the only time in the history of China's postal service that privately designed and issued stamps were ever officially recognized. Each letter cost 2.5 gold dollars to send to cover the cost of the 40-mile round-trip up and down the mountain. Crow's postman, whom he nicknamed "Fazzle Face" due to a prominent scar, would leave Zaozhuang at 9 p.m. each evening and arrive at the bandit camp around noon the following day, after which he would return with the new mail. Ultimately, however, the whole enterprise was only continuing thanks to the whims of their warlord captor. Crow figured that it would be best to make some overtures and try to meet the bandit.

Bandit Brandy, Senator for a Day and Betrayal

Crow got to Swen by writing personally to him and getting a covering letter from the American Consul General in Shanghai, Norwood F Allman, on US Consulate headed paper. This alarmed the Consul General back in Shanghai who was not keen to be seen to be officially recognizing and negotiating with a bandit.[25]

As it turned out, Swen was not the least bit interested in hearing from the US Consul General but did want to meet Crow whom he had decided was a genuine humanitarian and a gentleman. Crow's initial letter was returned with a kind note and two bottles of "very good" brandy. Swen assumed that Crow had been paying for the supplies out of his own pocket, expressing regret to Crow that other rich people could not be motivated to be so generous and quoting Confucius on the subject of corrupt officials. Swen also told Crow to keep the shipments of supplies coming and translate the invoices into Chinese, and he'd have one of his trusted Lieutenants check off the list as well to ensure the porters were honest.

Crow estimated that eventually supplies worth thousands of dollars had gone up the hillside, including medicines, iodine, tins of Sterno canned fuel and blankets that could have been of great use to Swen's men. Only one towel and one lantern ever went missing (and Crow admitted he may have miscounted the number of towels), though he did think this might be due to the fact that Swen, having guaranteed the safe delivery personally, was liable to behead anyone found pilfering. The missing lantern enraged Swen who apologized profusely to Crow and sent him half a dozen watches as a gesture of apology – watches he had stolen from passengers on the *Blue*. Crow chose to accept the looted gift as a sign of good faith. He found some of the watches had been over-wound and broken, and arranged for them all to be repaired. Then he sent them back up the mountain with a bill for $50 for the repairs. Fifty dollars in a sealed envelope came back down the hillside from Swen with a two-dollar tip for the messenger if he was honest and delivered the full amount.

Swen now started to refer to Crow as his elder brother – *dage* – in their daily correspondence. However, some foreign diplomats began complaining that Crow should have tried to return the watches to their original owners and one foreign consul general even called Crow an "accomplice." Crow reasoned he was there to earn Swen's trust and passing the watches along to their owners would just be viewed by the isolated Swen as Crow having pocketed the watches for himself – hardly a confidence-building measure. While the consuls debated asking the US representative to censure Crow, he urged the watch repairer to hurry and got the watches back up the hill before the diplomats could reach a consensus.

Crow also hosted two of Swen's sons on a visit to Zaozhuang for negotiations and treated them to dinner where they kept their pistols at the ready and bragged about their bandit exploits. One tried to steal Crow's camera but became instantly terrified when Crow threatened to tell his father of the 14-year-old boy's criminal intentions. Crow also enjoyed a good relationship with the local constabulary after he had presented the police chief with a bottle of "tomato catsup," which the man upended into an empty dish and ate immediately, apparently relishing it.

By this time, the foreigners had been held captive for several weeks. Crow figured his old friend Powell would be getting bored and asked Swen if he and Powell could meet to discuss the supply shipments. The next day the tramp-like looking Powell was sent down the hillside on a Shandong mule with a razor-edged backbone and Crow immediately treated him to a bath, a haircut and some dinner. The whole scene became surreal with Powell, American China Hand Roy Anderson (who had been hired by the Chinese government as a negotiator) and Crow enjoying dinner in a ransacked dining car of the *Blue* and being joined by another surprise guest, Roy Bennett, a Missouri University School of Journalism graduate who happened to be passing through Shanghai on his way to the Philippines to start work for the *Manila Bulletin*. Bennett, hearing of Powell's kidnapping, had temporarily taken over the editorship of the *China Weekly Review* during Powell's enforced absence. The next day Crow sent Powell back.

He also arranged for Dr. Paul Mertons, a Shanghai physician, to go and treat the rather ill Italian hostage, the portly "Commodore" Guiseppe Musso. He was a wealthy Italian lawyer of independent means (nobody was sure how exactly his wealth had been amassed though he did represent the Shanghai Opium Commission for many years and was close to Mussolini) with a somewhat affected military bearing, whom the bandits considered the most valuable of the foreign hostages. The Commodore had tripped on the forced march up Paotzeku and injured his spine, but medical supplies and trained personnel were almost non-existent in the warlord camps. Crow also arranged for several people to start direct talks about the captives' eventual release with Swen: Roy Anderson, the official go-between for the Chinese government, the American Consul at Nanjing John K. Davis, and the US Minister to China Jacob Schurman, who had originally sanctioned Crow's Red Cross relief effort.

Schurman, a former philosophy professor and founder of the *Philosophical Review*, had retired as President of Cornell University in 1920 after 28 years' service. He had also previously served as President of the First Philippines Commission in 1899 after being appointed by President McKinley, and had served as the US Minister to Greece and then China, arriving in 1921. Though Schurman was described as having a genuine concern for China's national interests and a desire to improve the life of her people, Crow described him as always speaking "… in the didactic manner of the schoolroom … and at too great length," and always feared his speeches "… afraid they were going to be boring and this fear was usually confirmed in the first five minutes." Crow would join in the Beijing Legation staff's "Schurman Oratorical Stakes" where everyone bet a dollar on how long the honorable Minister's speech would last. Crow got highly proficient at estimating Schurman's speeches and once missed the jackpot by just one minute. Despite this, Crow believed that Schurman's frustrations with the European powers for not adequately recognizing Chinese nationalism and sovereignty were heartfelt and genuine. Schurman virtually based himself in Shandong for the entire negotiations and urged the Chinese government repeatedly to ensure the safety of the hostages.

The supposedly unflappable China Hand Roy Anderson, also an American, was an old acquaintance of Crow's. They had met originally in 1911 when Anderson was working for Standard Oil, and he was described by Crow as "The most interesting character I ever knew."[26] He had been a Shanghai-based journalist for some time working for the *North-China Daily News* and writing under the pseudonym Bruce Baxter, as well as being an old friend of Powell's. That Anderson had taken on the job of hostage negotiation was a relief to Crow as the more experienced man would, Crow believed, make a better job of it than he ever could. S. T. Wen, the Chinese Commissioner of Foreign Affairs at Nanjing, assisted Anderson.

Anderson was a mysterious though well-known figure at the time and was arguably one of the most knowledgeable and passionate of all the foreign China Hands. He had been born in China, the son of the founder of Suzhou University; and while he had been educated in the US and married an American woman, he had spent all his life in China since his return in 1902. According to the journalist George Sokolsky's obituary of him in the *North-China Daily News*, he spoke eight Chinese dialects while Crow described him as "... always at heart a Chinese and thought like one."[27] Crow claimed he had spoken Chinese before he spoke English. He was a tall, portly man with a clipped bristly moustache who invariably wore khaki, a topi-style tan-colored pith helmet and riding boots. He had been an early convert to the Chinese Nationalist cause and had served with the Chinese Nationalist army. He also acted occasionally as an adviser and trusted middleman to foreign businesses, including Standard Oil and several mining companies that were looking to secure contracts in Yunnan province.

Crow had also known Anderson at the end of the war when he had worked for Compub under Paul Reinsch. As an assistant to Reinsch, Anderson had become known as his "right hand man." Several years before, Crow and Anderson had had to endure a couple of weeks in the company of a visiting delegation of American Congressmen who had arrived in China ostensibly on a fact-finding mission. However, it soon became apparent that they were on a mission to enjoy the very thing that was forbidden under America's prohibition laws – booze – following the passage of the Volstead Act in 1919. Crow and Anderson suffered the increasingly hung-over delegation across China, and had even traveled with them on the *Blue* to Beijing. The Chinese government had wished to impress the visiting American politicians and temporarily extended the extraterritoriality law to the train for the dignitaries' time aboard – which meant that American law applied to Americans on the train. While a nice gesture, this met with uproar from the Congressmen who realized that American law meant prohibition on the train; and the guards, fearing the loss of their jobs, did not want to serve liquor to any of them and closed the onboard bar.

Crow and Anderson felt that this was a good way to even the score after having put up with the delegation for days on end. After the delegates were safely asleep in their private cabins, Crow, Anderson and an English passenger broke open several bottles of champagne. Around midnight, the train stopped at a small town where all the local worthies had come out to see the visiting Americans. Anderson, keen not to disappoint the local Mandarins, and having consumed a couple of bottles, immediately appointed Crow as a Congressman and himself as his secretary and translator. Consequently a speech was given – "The three hundred pounds of his [*Anderson's*] great bulk towered over the platform of the car and his great voice rolled out over the plains."[28] Anderson spoke the local dialect and announced that he and Crow were the only two delegates to have survived the trip so far after a surfeit of wine in Nanjing. He then gave a long talk on the problems affecting China. Crow surmised that, given Anderson's highly informed views on China, the locals may have been surprised to be so knowledgeably addressed by a member of the US Congress. With that, they rejoined the train and settled back into the Club Car and the remaining champagne.

The downside to the story though was that their English drinking companion who worked for the railway had cabled ahead to their next stop explaining the mix-up over the lack of alcohol on the train. Consequently, when Anderson, Crow and the Congressmen walked in for breakfast with some more local dignitaries at 7 a.m., the breakfast table was stacked from end to end with bottles of Scotch, bourbon and gin which dutifully had to be consumed before a planned climb up the scary Tianshan mountain with yet more bottles of booze waiting at the summit. It was a tough and hung-over day for Crow and Anderson.[29]

It turned out that, despite some initially sky-high demands, Swen was really seeking $100,000 from the Chinese government for the captives' release. Everyone involved in the negotiations, which on the government side included Huang Jinrong, the gangster and corrupt boss of the Frenchtown police in Shanghai, agreed that this was fair as Swen had become reasonable after some bargaining and it had to be admitted that with a private army in excess of 700 men the warlord clearly had overheads. Finances were the major problem for all the warlords who had to keep their men fed, armed and paid or watch them desert overnight. Mutinies by unpaid soldiers were not unknown. However, Swen also demanded the dismissal of the original corrupt magistrate who had killed his father and many of the bandits wanted reinstatement in the Chinese army. Anderson negotiated with Swen in his local dialect and, as the official envoy of the Chinese government, was also pleased with the deal. Despite this, getting the official sacked was decidedly trickier until Crow and Anderson managed to persuade the Governor of Shandong to agree. Crow then arranged for $100,000 to be portered up Paotzeku after Anderson had personally signed the treaty document.

At this point, Swen made a major tactical error in releasing the captives before the money arrived on June 13. The Governor's troops seized the money and returned it to the Shandong coffers; the Chinese post office cancelled Crow's specially designed stamps ending the Bandit Post service; and the Governor never did fire the magistrate who had started all the trouble in the first place. Six months later, Swen's group was surrounded and outgunned as they had little more than pre-First World War vintage weaponry. The bandit leader himself was shot and wounded in the chaos, eventually captured and then beheaded while 600 of his men were machine-gunned on the orders of Shandong's Governor Tien Chung-yu.

However, the hostages were released safely though Commodore Musso came down Paotzeku on home-made crutches. The others looked ruffled but in generally good health, including Powell who looked positively vigorous after his ordeal and was photographed for the *Illustrated London News* arriving from Paotzeku at the Nanjing Ferry to return to Shanghai with a fresh suit on. When Powell, Musso and the others came back to Shanghai, there were large crowds to greet them at the North Railway Station, along with the Russian Cadet Band and an impromptu singing of "See the Conquering Hero Comes." According to a rather overblown report in the *North China Herald*, "Hats were thrown into the air and men cheered themselves hoarse, while tears streamed down the cheeks of those near and dear."[30]

Crow and the other negotiators felt the whole business was a pretty bad show: "Foreigners shared the general Chinese indignation at the shabby duplicity of the Chinese government and Swen Miao went down to a fame as one of the thousands of Chinese Robin Hoods who are revered as heroes and patriots."[31] In the overall scheme of warlord China, Swen was not a *tuchun,* or one of the big warlords. He didn't have the large bank accounts in Shanghai or overseas and had not made the heavy investments in treaty port real estate that some warlords had. Warlordism could be a route to wealth; indeed the British journalist and China Hand J. O. P Bland estimated that the accumulated wealth of the 22 biggest *tuchun* amounted to four-fifths of China's national debt.[32] Swen was not among this elite group: he lived in a district too remote to be able to extort vast amounts of money and did not indulge in the trappings of Western luxury such as cars, planes, women and jazz. His rise to warlordism appears to have been based on genuine grievances which Crow thought meant that he was someone you could deal with.

The Chinese authorities were not the only ones that came out of the whole affair badly. Crow and some others also felt that some nations had not done all they could. While the Americans seem to have been generally keen to secure the release of their nationals along with the rest of the hostages, the British appeared keener to exploit the crisis to gain control of the Tianjin-Pukow Railway and to secure the right of British investors in the project. With the train's derailment and the subsequent crisis, passengers were no longer so keen to take the *Blue.* Sir Ronald Macleay, British Ambassador to China, may have called the crisis the most serious event to affect foreign nationals since the Boxer Rebellion, but he spent most of his time during the events concerned about British business interests. When the bandits threatened to shoot two foreign hostages, one American and one British, a debate about the crisis in the Houses of Parliament saw politicians complain about the railway line defaulting on its loans to British investors and had nothing to say about the possible murder of a British national in Shandong.

The whole business at Paotzeku convinced Crow that the Chinese would always cling to their right to revolt. He thought that Swen's band of brigands grew to such numbers because many ordinary Chinese shared Swen's general outrage at corrupt officials even if they didn't care too much what had happened personally to their leader's clan. Many of them had all-too-similar stories. The 1923 Lincheng Outrage had made the headlines throughout its duration and inspired a rash of further kidnappings of foreigners throughout 1924 and 1925, as well as partly inspiring Josef Von Sternberg's 1932 film *Shanghai Express*, starring Marlene Dietrich and Anna May Wong. The story remained news for some time afterwards, not least after Lucy Aldrich published her memoirs of the event in the *Atlantic Monthly* and revealed that she had buried her diamonds under a rock during the forced march. Later a clerk from Standard Oil's Tianjin office had been sent out to Shandong with a map drawn by Lucy to recover the jewels. He successfully located them under the rock.

Throughout this particular period of warlordism, Crow covered events both for the occasional article and for his own interest in all things related to China. In 1924 he visited a warlord battle at Liuhe near Shanghai in Jiangsu, seeing men shot, hearing "the cannon like bang of burning bamboo as the expanding air burst the joints of houses, saw wounded soldiers fall and die."[33] Crow recounted the battle as he saw it, but many more traditional and imperialist-minded foreigners from Shanghai saw things differently.[34] Most of the fighting, such as the skirmish at Liuhe, was free of modern artillery with airpower only used on rare occasions, and even then bombs were short and often just large stones or logs were thrown out of the planes onto the enemy troops below. David Bonavia quotes the American military historian William F. Whitson who wrote "a Chinese military commander of 1924 could expect to fight with weapons and at a speed approximating to American Civil War conditions."[35] For his part, Crow claimed that he had journeyed around covering these skirmishes for many years and that he and other China Hands were "... veteran military observers and had learned how to watch a war with little less personal danger than one would face at a golf tournament."[36]

Warlordism continued to plague China, its people and the government. Shandong, Swen Miao's old stomping ground, was to get significantly worse in the years to come with the ascendancy of the Shandong warlord General Chang Tsung-chang, one of the most feared and reviled warlords in China who ruled the province between 1925 and 1928. Chang had been a poor street kid who joined a bandit gang in 1911 and rose through the ranks rapidly. As military governor of Shandong in 1925, he became notorious for splitting the heads of executed people in two and hanging them on telegraph poles. He taxed the local people to a vicious extent and accepted no excuses. The semi-literate warlord, once described as having "the brain of a pig," was known as the "Dogmeat General" and the "Lanky General" (though he personally preferred to be called the "Great General of Justice and Might") and, at well over six-feet tall, had a fearsomely tough appearance. He bolstered his Chinese troops with former Russian Tsarist soldiers turned mercenaries who also manned his formidable armored trains. Negotiating with the "Dogmeat General" would undoubtedly have been a tougher proposition than with Swen Miao.

By the late 1930s Crow reported that kidnapping was becoming less common as police forces improved. Things got so good that one of Crow's Shanghainese acquaintances, who had for many years feared kidnapping and lived like a pauper despite considerable wealth, felt confident enough to start actually spending and had all the hardware in his house gold-plated at a cost of $50,000; and another spent even more for an Italian marble staircase and wainscoting.

Warlords were to continue to cross Crow's path and soon he didn't need to travel to far-flung Shandong to meet them; instead they came to an increasingly troubled Shanghai.

10

Rumblings in Shanghai

A Man's Town

Crow's bachelor status had presumably been a point in his favor when he was first hired by the *China Press* to work in Shanghai. Most of the larger foreign companies in China in the late nineteenth and early twentieth centuries only employed single young men who invariably did not marry until completing several years' service. Crow noted that this tradition had had a lasting effect on the China coast's foreign society – "Even after a great many women came to China, the predominant influence of the bachelor remained and foreign society in China still retains a robust and boisterous masculine flavour … Everything was run by the men and for the men."[1] Indeed until a greater number of European women started moving to Shanghai there were few socially acceptable options but to find a bride during a home leave, as marrying Chinese girls was still next to impossible and frowned upon by just about everyone on all sides and could lead to dismissal and social ostracism.

However, having married early on in his Shanghai life, Crow had not been able to enjoy the tradition of living in one of the bachelor messes that were run by the older and larger hongs. The *China Press* was not big enough to justify one. However, Crow regularly dined as a guest at several, including the most popular ones that were maintained by the crews of the volunteer municipal fire companies where Crow was often left the only diner after all the other residents had had to dash out to extinguish some flames somewhere. Crow liked this masculine life and, along with most other single men, had joined the Shanghai Volunteer Corps (SVC), being assigned to the Special Police for three years. Apart from being part of an ethos of civic service in the International Settlement, this also provided a social network of other bachelors.

In 1925 Crow separated from Mildred and they divorced. The split seems to have been amicable and Mildred took their daughter Betty with her. Mildred continued to run her Chinese handicrafts business and soon remarried Norris G. Wood, the Manager of Standard Oil's Hangzhou office.

Shortly after his divorce from Mildred, Carl also married for a second time – to Helen Marie Hanniger in Shanghai. Helen, an American, gets few mentions in his books or papers, though several of his later books were dedicated to her, including *Four Hundred Million Customers*. She features largely as a sensible block on Crow's sometimes more wild schemes, though remaining somewhat of a mystery. He saw Helen as more kind-hearted than him when it came to dealing with their servants at home and she always took responsibility for ensuring that the house was full of freshly-cut flowers. Most of the servants were Helen's choices. As was the way on the China coast, Crow's personal houseboy had left his service soon after Crow remarried. Most personal servants preferred to work for bachelors where life was considered easier or, if they had worked for married men, felt it easier not to continue with them when a new mistress entered the scene. Crow felt no lack of loyalty from the man as he had hired him after his former boss had got married and the man needed a new post.

Crow also appreciated Helen's ability to bring a certain order to his often-chaotic living arrangements, noting that "The usual helplessness of the unmarried man is increased by life on the China Coast where he has well-trained servants to anticipate his every want."[2] Certainly, when he had been a bachelor, Crow had not really bothered too much with his daily living arrangements, commenting that "… a cook employed in a foreign household for years can be as mysterious and unknown as the chef who makes canned soup imported from a distance of thousands of miles."[3] Crow recalled that he once got into a taxicab in Shanghai and the driver took him straight home without asking for directions. Crow asked him how he knew where to go whereupon the cabbie informed him that he had once been his cook for four years.

Helen certainly seems to have been as adventurous as Mildred had been and enjoyed life in China. She accompanied Carl on trips around the country, including a Christmas and New Year break to Chongqing as well as regular house-boating trips along the Jiangsu canals.

It appears that Helen, like Mildred, was a strong woman who had adapted to life in Shanghai and China. Crow claimed that many foreign women got hysterical at the slightest thing in China from mistaking firecrackers for gunshots (which, to be fair, Crow himself had done on his first week in the city), to being distrustful of rickshaw pullers and being unnecessarily worried about hygiene – "I have known personally of a half dozen American women who arrived in Shanghai to join their husbands and took the next boat back in a state of collapse."[4] The Crows were popular party hosts and Helen was apparently known for shaking a mean cocktail.

Rumbles in Shanghai

1925 was a tense year for Shanghai. In January the six-foot-seven-inch tall witch's son, former wharf coolie and Shandong warlord Chang Tsung-chang – the "Dogmeat General" – had swept into Shanghai with an army of 60,000 men. As mentioned previously, Chang was one of China's most feared warlords. He also maintained a multi-cultural harem that, according to the *New York Times* correspondent Hallett Abend, consisted of "… nearly forty women and girls – Chinese, Korean, Japanese, two French girls, and one bedraggled female who said she was an American;"[5] while the historian Stella Dong notes that "… each of the foreign members of the seraglio was provided with a washbowl with the flag of her country painted on its side."[6] Chang had rolled over the army of Jiangsu's Governor Chi Shi-yuan who had fled to Japan, though not before his soldiers tore up the town a little. In Shanghai, Chang's army faced off with that of the Jiangsu warlord Sun Chuang-fang, a situation that made for tensions and unease in the International Settlement and not a little looting and vandalism in the Chinese areas of the city. It seemed that the Shanghai underworld favored Chang who was a Green Gang member and an old friend of Pockmarked Huang. In October fighting broke out between Sun and Chang's forces and the northern warlord skulked back up north to the comfort of his harem. Sun, a bit of a social climber, was more favored by the foreign community and managed to actually unite the disparate Chinese parts of the city into one municipality. Sun, Huang and Du Yuesheng soon reached an accommodation and the opium business continued to be as profitable as before all the interruptions and disturbances.

Sun Yat-sen died on March 12, 1925. He had been terminally ill for some time and had long suffered digestive problems. He had been diagnosed with a malignant tumour on his liver in December 1924 and had repeatedly gone to the Rockefeller Institute in Beijing for treatment. Since the announcement of Sun's terminal condition, the question of succession had remained tense. As well as the military leader Chiang Kai-shek, other contenders included: Wang Ching-wei,[7] who was best known for having tried to assassinate the Imperial Prince Regent in 1910; Hu Han-min, who stood on the right of the Nationalist movement; and Liao Chung-kai,[8] who represented the left wing. Unknown to most people, another candidate was also lurking in the wings – Du Yuesheng, the boss of Shanghai's Green Gang. It was a time of tumultuous change in many countries, with a power struggle going on in Russia between Trotsky and Stalin after Lenin's death that looked like becoming bloody. Many thought China's succession struggle might also turn ugly. Sun seemed to leave no instructions as to his successor himself though Chiang, who was at the Whampoa Academy near Guangzhou at the time, claimed Sun's last words were "Chiang Kai-shek."

Sun's death was a major event in China and half a million people filed past his body in Beijing as it lay in state before being conveyed to the Western Hills just outside the city to be placed in the Azure Cloud Temple. Though born a southerner, Sun's wish had been to be buried in Nanjing and plans were already afoot to build a mausoleum to house his body though it would take another five years to complete. J. B. Powell later recalled that a major row broke out at the time between Sun's family and his Soviet advisers who wanted him embalmed and put on permanent display in similar fashion to Lenin in Moscow. The family considered this macabre.

In the meantime, the power struggle continued. Most alarming to many of those in the know were the behind-the-scenes intrigues of the gangster Du who appeared to want to run the KMT through a proxy, given his well-known criminal activities and hopeless opium addiction. Du thought that either the fiery-tempered Chiang or Chang Ching-chang, usually known as Curio Chang in the English language press,[9] would be the best proxy. Curio Chang was a crippled Zhejiang millionaire businessman with Green Gang connections who had been a long time devotee of Sun. He was a major "kingmaker" in the background of the KMT, and had amassed a fortune selling antiques and souvenirs to foreigners in China after working at the Chinese Legation in Paris, a job he got largely because his father had bought him an imperial title. He had set up a company dealing in gold, tea and silk and had also invested in bean curd factories, as well as having been one of Sun's major financial backers and also becoming a supporter of Chiang.

Wang Ching-wei, though lacking a regional power base, was the choice of Borodin, the Comintern's man in China. Wang and the principal rightist candidate Hu Han-min entered into a left-right struggle of their own that ultimately put both men out of the running. Hu was seen as tough and had studied in Japan but was too overtly sectarian. This left the leftist Liao Chung-kai, who was liked by Hu despite their political differences and his being Madame Sun's favorite. After Wang dropped out, Borodin, who was wielding significant influence since his arrival in China on Moscow's orders in 1923, championed Liao's cause. Eventually warlord-induced confusion around Guangzhou led the KMT Central Committee to compromise and form a triumvirate National government leadership composed of Hu, Wang and Liao. It seemed the left wing of the KMT, and Borodin, had triumphed.

There was also the continuing and seemingly close threat from the ongoing warlord feuds across China to contend with. The leaders of Shanghai's foreign community on the SMC had resolutely and consistently opposed any warlord troops entering the International Settlement. In 1925, and again in 1927, the International Settlement police along with soldiers of the concessionary powers had to intern and disarm large numbers of warlord troops found in the city who had either deserted or were on food-foraging excursions. Though most of those interned were actually half-starved, ill-equipped and poorly-trained young men, their presence in the sanctuary of the Settlement alarmed many foreign residents. This alarm was heightened when the Council mobilized the British-dominated SVC, the international military division formed in 1854, headed by a British army regular and made up of about 1,000 volunteers complete with cavalry and artillery components. The SVC, of which Crow had briefly been a member when he first came to Shanghai, drew its membership from the various foreign communities, as well as White Russian and Jewish detachments, and mostly formed a sort of part-time army that drilled and paraded at various events. The warlords were also a distraction from the normal routine of life. Crow would skip his usual weekend golf game and head out to watch some of the clashes between the competing warlord armies on weekends around Shanghai once spending "… an hour crouched behind what was fortunately a high and long grave mound while bullets whistled over us. What a tame thing a golf foursome was by comparison!"[10]

In 1925 trouble had flared after a series of anti-foreign demonstrations and strikes led by the Communist Party and the left of the KMT. In May tensions between the Chinese and Japanese communities had spilled over when a Chinese worker was killed in a clash with the manager of the Japanese Naiaga Wata textile mill. A resultant demonstration by Chinese workers got out of hand and the police opened fire, killing 11 Chinese and wounding dozens more. The reaction was a massive demonstration on 30 May that eventually became known as the May Thirtieth Incident, when International Settlement police shot and fired into the crowds killing 12 people and wounding 50 others. This was the biggest clash in Shanghai between the Chinese and the Settlement powers since the May

Fourth 1919 protests. A new wave of demonstrations rumbled across China in reaction to the bloodshed in Shanghai, with further protests in the Settlement. In Guangzhou the international community based on Shamian Island was threatened, and there was a general strike in the British colony of Hong Kong that lasted into 1926. Meanwhile the power struggle in the KMT continued and, as chaos increased, Chiang Kai-shek and his backers resolved to get rid of the party's left wing and restore order.

Shanghai became a center of strike action led by the Communist-controlled General Federation of Labor. This militant group and the negative economic fall-out from the strikes annoyed Du and his Green Gang as well as Pockmarked Huang in Frenchtown as the Communists appeared to be cementing an alternative power base to the gangsters in Shanghai. In August Liao was assassinated in Guangzhou. A witch-hunt for the assassin followed and hidden forces appeared to be stoking up seemingly baseless accusations against Hu Han-min, despite the known friendship between Hu and Liao, that neutralized Hu's position. With Hu and Liao both out of the picture, Chiang, now 38, was free to make his bid for power. He did, eradicating or exiling many of his opponents in Guangzhou, including Wang Ching-wei (who fled to France). He installed Chiang loyalists in key positions in the troublesome southern city and formed the 30,000 strong National Revolutionary Army (NRA) out of his own loyal troops and men once loyal to his deposed enemies. Chiang had shown a decisiveness and ruthlessness in decision-making rare in Nationalist politics and was now in a position to finally realize Sun's dream of launching a Northern Expedition. After a costly (in terms of men's lives) but successful initial battle against the "Hakka General" at Shantou, Chiang's position was further bolstered. In early 1926 the NRA took Hainan Island from a local warlord and Chiang felt ready to march northwards.[11]

However, Chinese politics between the wars was nothing if not Machiavellian. Du's friend and Chiang's patron Curio Chang was appointed Chairman of the KMT's Standing Committee in May 1926, due largely to back-room maneuverings by Chiang which secured to an extent the power of the right wing of the KMT and further sidelined the left. Chang took over for just long enough to arrange for Chiang to be elected as his replacement that July. With the highly secret help of his Soong family financial backers as well as the Shanghai Green Gang, Chiang had become China's leader. As modern Chinese history entered another crucial phase with the rise to power of Chiang Kai-shek, Crow was settling in to his new marriage and financial security as his advertising agency prospered, a life he found extremely congenial in Shanghai.

11

The Life of a China Coast Man

At Home with the Crows

Shanghai was moving on from the convulsions and revolution of 1911 and the First World War into a new phase in the life of the fledgling Republic. Sun was dead and the interim power struggle in the KMT was seemingly resolved with Chiang now in power. However, despite Chiang's pledge to restore order, China continued to fray at the seams with internal power and unity far from secure, warlordism still rampant, a rising communist threat and Japan remaining menacingly in the wings.

Crow continued to be involved in the day-to-day business of Carl Crow Inc. as well as various journalistic interests and also found time for other activities such as rescuing hostages. Chiang's new China was to be a new China for Crow too, though in the late 1920s and early 1930s as events unfurled Crow was also enjoying life in the city and, as ever, observing the minutiae of society around him. He openly admitted that the life he enjoyed in Shanghai was not possible anywhere else – servants, gardeners, houseboys and chauffeurs were all privileges Shanghai offered to those without necessarily great wealth. Certainly there had been no servants back in Missouri.

Crow settled into a new home at 883 Connaught Road,[1] in the International Settlement. Connaught Road was a relatively busy street with houses, lanes and various businesses lining its length. As well as a plethora of shops there were less established businesses that also attracted Crow's attention, including a fortune-teller and a professional letter-writer. Both predated Crow and, as far as he could work out, neither paid any rent or taxes for their pitches on the street. Crow passed some work the fortune-teller's way with many visiting guests insisting on having their fortunes told in return for a few silver coins, which was good business as the mystic's regular local Chinese clients paid only a few coppers. The fortune-teller had few accoutrements other than a portable table and saw no problem with a crowd building up to hear his customer's future being broadcast, as this was all good promotion for his services. The letter writer similarly had few props or belongings and soon anyone who cared to stop and listen would know the contents of the letter. Occasionally, the street would also be home to an itinerant sweet meats vender who would spin a wheel for the local children in return for a copper to see if they would get a small bag of peanuts or a piece of candy.

Connaught Road was a wide street. Those Shanghai streets that had been laid out around 1845 had had a required width of between 20 and 25 feet. It was not until 1863 that all subsequent roads were specified to be 40 feet wide, including Connaught Road. The street wound its way down to Suzhou Creek. Fortunately, Crow lived at the opposite end from the Creek, which J. B. Powell described as having "the consistency of spinach soup and being a breeding ground for clouds of mosquitoes."[2] During Crow's time, Connaught Road was a fairly major thoroughfare and was briefly in the headlines in 1929 following a notorious murder involving kidnapping, criminals and Shanghai's underworld that captured the city's insatiable lust for nefarious doings for a time.

Though Crow moved several times, his main home in Shanghai was Connaught Road. The road ran parallel to several other major thoroughfares including Peking Road, which was then a haven for antique, "curio", shops and small stores selling everything and anything imaginable. Connaught Roads had appeared all over the British Empire's far-flung territories in a naming spree which reflected the contemporary notoriety of the General HRH The Duke of Connaught KG KT KP. The Duke, born in 1850, was the third son of Queen Victoria and a brother of King Edward VII. He had a glittering military career, including commanding a Brigade of Guards during the 1882 Egyptian Campaign. His imperial credentials were extended after he served in India between 1883–85 and again between 1886–90 as the General Officer in Charge (GOC) Bombay Command. He was promoted to Field Marshal in 1902 and acted as the Governor General and Commander-in-Chief of Canada from 1911–16. Though he lived to the age of 91, dying in 1942, his royal birth and staunch defence of the empire ensured he got his name on streets around Britain's dominions, including Shanghai. However, he did have a Shanghai link, having visited the city in 1890 to unveil the statue on the Bund to Sir Harry Parkes, the celebrated British Consul to China in 1882–85.[3]

Crow's house had a long veranda for relaxing during the sultry and humid Shanghai summer nights. Visitors entered the premises through the front gate and attracted Crow's attention by banging his large brass doorknocker. Brass was popular in the Crow house and Thursdays were designated brass-polishing day. The house had a separate kitchen with its own yard which, like most household kitchens in Shanghai, suffered from an infestation of cockroaches. The cockroaches bothered Crow but he admitted that he took relief from the old Chinese kitchen god's saying that a house lacking cockroaches was clearly in desperate straits and not even able to feed a cockroach let alone an entire family.

In his living room, Crow was fortunate to have two real fires to stave off the cold Shanghai winters and there was always a supply of kindling wood. He remained annoyed at the unevenness of the floors and the fact that his tables were invariably wobbly. In the summer, electric fans kept the rooms cool. He enjoyed a smoke in the evening and was apparently proud of his collection of ashtrays. The same servants stayed with him for most of the time he lived there. Crow was always aware that his lifestyle was based on low wages. Later, after he had left China, when he was comparing the relatively low wages of South America with China and the level of services available, Crow was chastised by expatriates living in Peru for tipping on the grounds that this would upset the delicate economic balance of Lima and eventually lead to everyone having to pay higher wages and tips. Crow noted that "Foreigners on the China Coast used to be the same way and many of them still are. Servants were satisfied with such low wages that the poorest white man could enjoy the comforts reserved for the rich in other lands. Everyone seemed to think that this was just too good to be true. And there was a general conspiracy to keep the servants in their place."[4] Crow went on to describe the trouble a foreigner could get into when suggesting that this situation was not perhaps ideal for the Chinese: "One of the most heinous offenses one white man could commit against his fellow white man was to rouse the lowly ambitions of cooks or coolies or houseboys by liberal tips in hotels and restaurants or by paying his own servants anything above what was looked on as the standard wage."[5]

Crow often complained about how much foreigners talked about their servants in so much "back fence gossip." He himself claimed to pay his houseboy Chefoo $7 a month "… out of which he was, in theory at least, required to feed and clothe himself and provide for his old age …"[6] He noted that many visitors to Shanghai would look at him aghast as a great exploiter, but Crow believed that Chefoo actually thought him quite generous. In all the years Chefoo worked for Crow, 12 in total, he was constantly employed and had two pay raises which made him, according to Crow, "something of an aristocrat around Connaught Road ... envied by all his friends in the neighbourhood."[7] Crow admitted that Chefoo, who carried out his duties clad in a long white gown, worked hard: he rose on most days at around 5 a.m. and was busy until 9 p.m. or later. He knew Chefoo saved hard and could probably have provided a loan to Crow at very favorable interest rates had he needed one. Chefoo went on a two-week vacation every year to Ningbo to see his relatives, gossip and view progress on the family tomb he was building with his savings. Crow would always let Chefoo use his car and driver to go to the dock to take the Ningbo ferry to make sure his standing on the boat was high and ensure an annual triumphal homecoming. Helen, whom Crow saw as "more soft-hearted than I am," would also give Chefoo a couple of extra dollars. While Chefoo was away, a substitute would take over his duties – a post for which Chefoo insisted on finding and paying the replacement as he was naturally concerned that his position in the household would not be usurped while he was away. Chefoo would return after a fortnight with two chickens for the Crows and occasional ornaments as gifts from his relatives in Ningbo.

As well as Chefoo, for many years Crow employed another servant called Ching. Ching's main duties appear to have been to bring Crow his morning cup of tea and take care of Crow's clothes. Crow admitted that he submitted to a general bossing about by Ching. He knew of course that Chefoo, Ching and the other Crow family household staff had a variety of ways to augment their incomes, known in China coast pidgin English as "squeeze." The staff controlled the collection and sale of items that could be sold, such as waste paper, empty bottles and discarded clothing. Crow realized there were often slight discrepancies between the amounts of some items bought and the amounts used, for example for shoe or furniture polish. While he did not condone this, he did not see it as theft or pilfering but rather the normal Shanghai way of things and the amounts were never enough to be concerned about. Chefoo and the other staff would also occasionally get tips, *cumshaw* in the local slang, from visitors to the house and an extra month's pay at Chinese New Year. Crow reckoned Chefoo's actual earnings at around $10 a month, not counting the income he made from being a rather successful local moneylender. Chefoo and some other household staff lived in a small servants' house adjacent to the main house and therefore had their rent, water, electricity and heating covered. Crow also provided Chefoo with work clothes while Helen treated his minor ailments or sent him to the hospital for anything serious. While he worked for Crow, Chefoo remained unmarried though he supported his elderly mother.

There were other ways in which the staff profited from working for Crow. They could command commissions from the grocer (or "compradore shop" as it was more generally known in Shanghai), usually five percent of all purchases. The staff then divided the commission based on varying factors. For instance, whoever served Crow his drinks and cigarettes or passed him his shaving soap kept the squeeze on those items, while the coolie of the house got the squeeze associated with the brass and boot polish as he did the polishing while the cook got his percentage from all the food purchases. Crow also knew that small liberties were being taken with weights and measures, prices and somewhat adjusted invoices. Crow understood that the cook was invariably the boss of the servants.

Crow's chauffeur needed a higher salary as petrol companies didn't pay commissions (and traditionally chauffeurs lived away from their employers' houses and had rent to pay), so his opportunities for squeeze were necessarily limited though a new car purchase usually meant a good payday from the dealer. Chauffeurs had to rely on squeeze on the items a car needed such as dusters, polish and chamois leathers. Crow was mystified that a tin of metal polish seemed always to last exactly one month, regardless of how often the car was used or cleaned. He commented, "… in a period of ownership of cars extending over about 20 years I have always bought exactly 12 tins of metal polish a year and each tin has been exhausted on the last day of the month. The same has been true of feather dusters which start out bravely on the first of every month but are damaged beyond either usefulness or repair by the end."[8] During harder economic times, Crow had words with his chauffeur about the life of chamois leathers and managed to get the man to eke out their existence to two months on account of Crow's stretched financial circumstances. Crow even managed to persuade a new chauffeur to continue the practice of the last one with chamois leathers and saved himself a little money every month ever after.

It didn't stop there. Crow noticed that his gardeners got through an amazing number of brushes and bamboo baskets and that both always seem to expire on the last day of the month. Again Crow had to resort to subterfuge and, when he hired a gardener, who also happened to be a devout Catholic, he challenged him to prove the sincerity of his faith by making the galvanized watering cans last a little longer. The man's faith was so strong that he actually did, voluntarily cutting into his squeeze in the name of Jesus. Crow would annoy friends simply by showing them his year-old watering cans, an unheard of sight in Shanghai.

Crow's staff conversed with him in English, or at least the pidgin English then common along the China coast (a sort of bastardized China coast *potpourri* of mangled English, Chinese, Portuguese and Hindustani words), and in which Crow was fluent. He liked to prick the pomposities of many foreigners who delighted in giving orders to their staff in bizarre pidgin sentences. Crow wrote a series of six pidgin English short children's stories for *Liberty* magazine adapted from traditional Chinese stories and legends. Crow was also a proficient curser in Chinese and knew some rather rudimentary sign language and hand gestures. He learned the latter when, waiting for a delayed train, he fell into conversation with a railway porter who taught him at least 30 different obscene hand gestures "every one of which would have meant, in Texas, a case of more or less justifiable homicide."[9] Though Crow became reasonably proficient in Chinese he knew that he was still at a loss in comprehending many more subtle insults.

Additionally, Crow believed that the Chinese had attained a high level of English language proficiency rapidly. He commented after being somewhat surprised at the poor English proficiency he encountered during a tour of South America in 1941 that "Even in remote cities of China and Japan, the average hotel servant knows all the English he needs to know to carry out his duties."[10]

For most of the time he lived at Connaught Road, Crow enjoyed a good relationship with an English neighbor and a less amiable one with two Chinese brothers who occupied the other neighboring house and often kept Crow awake by talking and shouting late into the night. Crow's hatred of noise never slackened and extended to hating the insistent ring of the International Settlement's church bells on Sunday mornings.

He kept dogs and claimed to be fond of all things canine. He was inordinately proud of owning a Scottie dog that went on to win the prize for Champion Scottie at the China Kennel Club, of which Crow was a member. In 1936 *The China Journal* reported that the China Kennel Club's annual dog show was being held at the Race Club on May 17, when it was "expected to see an unusually fine turnout of Shanghai's canine aristocracy."[11] Membership of the Kennel Club had reached 246 by that year, an increase of 82 since 1935, with nearly 500 dogs being registered by the club. As well as raising champion dogs, Crow was also involved in animal welfare and was active in the Shanghai Society for the Prevention of Cruelty to Animals which collected stray dogs as well as taking in the washed-up and aged Mongolian ponies retired from the Shanghai Race Club.

Later, while touring South America, Crow traveled from São Paulo to Santos to visit Pat Mulcahy, a well-known foreigner who lived there. He was an Irish-born naturalized American who had moved to Brazil and been extremely successful in the coffee business, an industry Crow was keen to see at first hand. One night Crow went for dinner at Mulcahy's Santos penthouse, the only penthouse in the town. During dinner, Mulcahy's middle-aged Scottie dog called Sandy came into the room and Mulcahy ordered it to "pray for the poor Chinese."

Crow was both interested in the dog and the strange command, upon which the dog had "put his forepaws on the couch and his head between them in an attitude of supplication." It transpired that Sandy had been born in Shanghai and, after tracing his history, Crow realized that it was in fact a dog he had once owned and given away some time around 1932 to an American sea captain who plied the route between Shanghai and Seattle. When the Japanese started harassing ships along the China coast, the Captain had been given a new route down the west coast of South America, around the Horn and back to Seattle via the Panama Canal. The Captain's wife had moved to Santos as this both reduced her living expenses considerably and also meant that she could join her husband onboard in Buenos Aires and travel north to Santos with him. She had brought Sandy the Scottie with her to Santos. At the time Crow visited, the Captain and his wife were aboard ship and had left the dog with Mulcahy though the Captain and his wife had no idea Crow was visiting Santos or Mulcahy.[12]

Crow enjoyed his garden, and once admitted that he wished he had had the time to study botany, though he wasn't green-fingered himself. Both Connaught Road and the other couple of houses he inhabited for periods in Shanghai, including one he leased for a while in the edge-of-Settlement Western Roads area, had large gardens and at all of them he had to employ watchmen to keep out visitors curious about their layout – "When they saw the flowering shrubs in bloom in the spring, they took it for granted that they were welcome to come in and view them at close range." Crow felt that forbidding entry probably annoyed many of his neighbors and commented: "I have always had a sort of guilty feeling that they were right."[13] Gardens were certainly important to Crow. Of the three houses he lived in during his Shanghai years, he described one as having a garden big enough for two tennis courts, another with room for a croquet lawn and the third having "a couple of dozen square yards."

Crow later recalled that he got through about a dozen gardeners during the time he resided at Connaught Road. He found that when it came to maintaining his garden he was required to give very precise instructions if he needed a branch cut or a hedge trimmed. He assumed that a country with a history such as China's where wood had long been hoarded, most gardeners considered simply lopping of branches to tidy the garden a sinfully great waste. Crow observed that others had this problem too and that Shanghai's private gardens were "full of privets and other shrubs which have grown into trees of monstrous size and of hideous aspect, but no Chinese gardener will touch them."[14] However, this desire to preserve fuel had another side to it and during the winter Crow and his gardeners had to be constantly on the look-out for "a class of thief none of us heard of as existing in any other part of the world" who would come along at the dead of night with a long bamboo pole with a steel hook on the end of it and start surreptitiously cutting and purloining the limbs of trees for sale as fuel. This unique Shanghai crime rose to manic proportions when the temperature fell below freezing and branches broke easily, and then disappeared almost entirely in the summer months when the more flexible branches were tricky to snap.

Crow's love of gardening and his desire to imagine himself as some sort of a son of the soil – combining his love of the Chinese countryside and his rural Missouri roots – culminated in a rather ill-fated scheme between Crow and some friends to become occasional farmers. Crow became a partner in what he described as a "very jolly, clubby enterprise – more jolly and clubby than business-like" to lease a farm along with 20 other Shanghailanders. Each of the partners was assigned to be responsible for certain farm duties on the weekends. However, there was a problem. Most of the partners undertook their weekend farming duties when they fancied it but more often preferred to stay either in bed or on the golf course out near Hongqiao, which a *Fortune* magazine profile of the city in 1935 described as being of "the Westchester County variety except for the attendants in white nightgowns."[15] Crow recalled that, while it lasted, the farm was fun but a financial disaster. Presumably as he was the ancestor of pioneers, he was assigned the task of taking care of improvements to the farm such as building fences and digging wells. Crow admitted that he simply employed some local farmers to undertake most of the tasks, somewhat undermining the whole "back to the earth" ethos of the project.

One job Crow could not delegate was the hiring and supervision of a *feng shui* geomancer to determine the location of the farm's well. To start digging a well without the endorsement of a geomancer was unthinkable and likely to raise the ire of the local villagers. A noisy and colorful ceremony was required to assuage their concerns but it had to be at the point on the farm determined by the project's members to be the most likely to actually yield a supply of water to irrigate the vegetables. Crow let the geomancer's agent know that he had a wager with his colleagues that the geomancer would pick a spot on a certain piece of the farmland. If Crow were to win, he would split the winnings with the geomancer's agent. The trick worked – "… on the eventful day the geomancers wandered all over the farm with their divining rods and other mysterious paraphernalia, but in the end I won my imaginary bet and gave the feast." The agent received his cut, with presumably some passed along to the geomancer, and the farm was irrigated.

The other problem the farm presented for Crow was the presence of a number of temporary Chinese graves comprising a coffin above the ground surrounded by a wall of bricks and covered with a tile roof. This was a typical sight in the countryside and a temporary resting place until the bereaved family could find, or afford, a more permanent one for their esteemed ancestor. Though the lease on the farm stipulated that the coffins had to be removed, there was no timetable for the process. Crow's partners hassled him to resolve this problem as summer approached and the farm's first crop of cabbages was ready and they felt prospective customers wouldn't be keen on vegetables grown adjacent to dead bodies. Crow was told in no uncertain terms by the farm's Chinese agent that it was unlucky to move the bodies except during the mid-winter and appeared shocked that an Old China Hand like Crow didn't know this. Crow protested that this was superstitious nonsense but the agent simply asked him if he had ever tried to move a corpse in the summer. Crow considered this and retreated from the fight by draping the burial structures with vines to disguise them. As Crow noted, the problem was eventually solved in the mid-winter "without doing violence to any silly Chinese superstitions and without scattering any bones over the heads of lettuce."[16] After all that hassle, Crow and his partners gradually lost interest in the farm.

As well as trying his hand at farming, Crow became a keen photographer and liked to take pictures of wild flowers on his trips into the countryside around Shanghai. He included his daughter Betty on trips that included climbing to the top of the seven-storied Lunghwa Pagoda to look out over the surrounding farms. He occasionally fished, though apparently with little success, but he enjoyed the tranquility of a day's angling on Hangzhou Lake. Crow admitted that, for him, fishing was a leisure activity while for the Chinese it was a more serious business: "No one fishes for fun in China and since every man with a rod and line would be looked on as a trespasser and poacher, angling is not likely to become a popular sport."[17] He was "a disciple of Isaak Walton," that is to say a rod and reel man, when he fished but he always noted the local Chinese fisherman who preferred a trap and net laughing at his poor attempts to presumably feed himself. It was also the case that Crow avoided small boats, except steamers and houseboats, at most times as he never managed to learn to swim beyond a few pathetic strokes and some basic floating.

Sport played an important role in the overtly masculine world of foreigners on the China coast. However, Crow was not much more of an athlete than he was a swimmer. He would spectate but rarely took the field, except for rounds of golf. He watched games at the Shanghai Baseball Club and the annual steeplechase between teams from the big foreign firms. He tried his hand at cricket but decided that appreciation of the game was a peculiarly English affliction and quickly gave it up. The other major sporting pastime in which Crow indulged, along with nearly everyone else, was the Shanghai Race Club, which was as much about gambling as it was about ponies. The opportunities to gamble and watch racing became even more regular after greyhound racing became popular too though Crow, despite liking dogs, never took to racing them.

Hangzhou was a favored destination and he visited regularly, sometimes rising early on a winter's day and climbing the surrounding hills to watch the sunrise over the West Lake, a scene immortalized by the Chinese poet Su Tung-po in the Sung dynasty. Crow admitted that the first time he did this climb to the small pavilion where Su reputedly wrote the famous description of the view, it was more out of journalistic curiosity than a love of Chinese poetry, and he was feeling very depressed with wet feet, cold hands and no breakfast. However, all skepticism disappeared with the dawn and "the distant river became a silver ribbon, the hills changed from black to purple, before the sun brought out their daytime colors of brown and green. A few stray bits of fog which had been caught in the valleys shyly tiptoed from place to place before the sun drove them to cover, and they seemed to merge with some isolated low-lying clouds."[18]

Crow would often take clients who visited his advertising agency on the five-hour train ride out to Hangzhou for a weekend, though he found that most decided to opt out of seeing the sunrise and choose instead the sumptuous breakfast the hotel provided. Crow would extol the beauties of the Hangzhou sunrise to any who would listen and eventually came to the conclusion that he was considered a bore on the subject and thought of as not a little "queer" when it came to the beauties of Hangzhou. The Yellow Mountains in Anhui were another of his favorite scenic destinations for impressive sunrises.

Sodom and Gomorrah Shanghai-style

Crow's depictions of Shanghai were invariably of vibrancy, opportunity and fascination. However, it was of course a city of contrasts. A Christian evangelist in the early 1920s declared "If God lets Shanghai endure, He owes an apology to Sodom and Gomorrah." Crow never seemed to find the city quite Sodom or Gomorrah but he did observe both the poverty and the raucous nightlife.

Crow's favorite leisurely occupation was simply walking the streets where he would become absorbed in watching local life for hours – anything from the local temples, to the itinerant menders of fine porcelain who traveled throughout Shanghai and whose skill was such that they could earn a few dollars on the side by hastily repairing dentures, to workshops where mahjong tiles were meticulously made from small blocks of bamboo with a precision that amazed him. Indeed, Crow himself regularly played mahjong for over 10 years after finally learning the game and had a set of hand-made tiles that he claimed were still in perfect condition despite being dropped repeatedly and having to endure the climate of a steam-heated house. He was also a great walker and often headed out as far as Zhabei to visit the bird market before Japanese bombing destroyed it.

On his walks, beggars often attracted his attention. When escorting visitors around Shanghai's Chinese city he often felt that his guests might consider him heartless for his ability to ignore a beggar's dramatic entreaties. Crow felt that most begging in Shanghai was simply good showmanship and "... that wailing and having the appearance of being about to starve to death is a part of the stock in trade of every Chinese beggar."[19] It wasn't so much that Crow dismissed the poverty around him; it was just that he believed that he could tell genuine misfortune from professional begging – "To us tough old China Hands the beggar merely provides local color which we could quite cheerfully dispense with, but decline to get steamed up about." Crow was harsh on the subject of beggars believing that "a lot of exceptionally good Hollywood talent was going to waste in China."[20]

Whatever his opinions, he rarely came to any of them without exhaustive research. On the subject of beggars, he researched the market by getting to know one local female beggar whose pitch was along the Garden Bridge that crossed Suzhou Creek at the start of the Bund. This beggar happened to be Chinese though at that time there were also a great number of White Russian and other European beggars in the city. It was a good pitch as thousands of people walked across every day, and it was a center of traffic congestion. It had been named after the Public Gardens at one end of the bridge that once bore the twin stipulations banning dogs and excluding Chinese (excepting servants accompanying their employers) that have since passed into legend.

A child always accompanied the woman. After engaging her in conversation several times, Crow learnt that the beggar woman rented the child and had to pay a percentage of her earnings to the child's mother. Though the child slept a lot, Crow found that when he woke it the child cried with a lustiness not normally associated with starving children. Crow monitored the woman's progress over a number of years until the child became too large to be easily carried along the bridge. Over the 10-year period Crow knew the woman, she used five different children. She then sadly died of smoking too much opium! During her years on the Garden Bridge the local police religiously respected her turf rights. This all seemed to Crow more enterprising than trickery. Though he investigated many of the rumors about beggars that were a major source of bar-room chatter among the foreign Shanghailander population, he never found any examples of the famous detachable scabies or any beggar claiming to be missing a limb who actually wasn't. However, these stories kept on circulating and among others were tales of beggars rolling around in mud, smearing themselves with pig's blood or using fresh corpses as props. Stella Dong, in her history of Shanghai, provides an exhaustive list of these theatrical deformities as well as some local characters such as "Light in the Head" and "The Weeping Woman", but Crow stuck firm to the opinion that most were not tricksters though they did elaborate a bit.[21]

Crow became quite an expert on beggars and befriended a few in his local area as well as around his Jinkee Road office. When he returned from business trips outside Shanghai he found it necessary to make a financial contribution before restarting the friendships. He considered this a good investment in pursuing his research and, anyway, as he commented once "If you cannot live in a state of mutual tolerance with your fellow men who are beggars, what hope is there for humanity?"[22]

One of Crow's best beggar friends was a small girl he met one day who chased him after he had dropped a pair of gloves. He got to know her on the level of "chummy intimacy" and though she was extremely dirty (Crow assumed this was part of her "stage props") had a sweet smile and sparkling eyes. Crow briefly considered adopting the girl and was distressed when at a later date he passed by the row of beggar shacks where she seemed to live alone and saw that Japanese bombing had destroyed them. He never saw the girl again.

When Crow went to the office or to the American Club he had a car with a chauffeur, which eased the nightmare of Shanghai's heavy and congested traffic, but he was not averse to using rickshaws. By the early 1930s Shanghai had 16,300 private cars licensed, 9,900 in the International Settlement and 6,400 in Frenchtown.

Rickshaws provided a cheap and convenient alternative. However, Crow was a stickler for not being overcharged and would haggle with the "pullers," mercilessly examining the conveyance and in hot weather ensuring that the puller had turned the seat cushions over to keep them cool. He prided himself on being an expert on all things rickshaw. For instance, he claimed he could spot the "green country boy" who had recently arrived and would not know the shortest routes as well being unused to traffic and a menace to himself and his passenger. Crow was forever formulating strategies for getting the fare down to the same as local Chinese paid. Though many visitors to Shanghai rejected rickshaws as they believed them to be exploitative, Crow dismissed this argument believing that rickshaws provided much needed jobs.[23] The pullers may have been low-paid and hard-worked but they could feed themselves, labored honestly and did not fall upon charity, which would be extremely demeaning to any Chinese man. He also argued that while there were many rickshaw pullers who, given a car, would make excellent New York cab drivers, there were few New York cabbies of his acquaintance who would make good rickshaw pullers and so their superiority was misplaced.

The American Club was his refuge and "sanctuary" and he eventually became Vice-President and then President. It was also here that he and Helen invariably celebrated the American community's major get-togethers of Thanksgiving and Fourth of July. After many years in Shanghai, Crow felt he needed somewhere to escape from the city's heady round of socializing which another Shanghai resident Emily Hahn of the *New Yorker* had described as "... the tremendous variety of activities – parties, temples, curio shops, having dresses made to order overnight, trips to Peiping [*Beijing*], embassy receptions, races."[24]

Crow preferred the clubs of Shanghai for his socializing more than the rougher bar areas such as the notorious Blood Alley or the infamous Badlands district that lay in the "extra settlement" beyond the SMC's control and attracted many with their distinctly more illicit and hedonistic attractions.[25] Crow had visited Blood Alley with its bars, "salt water sisters" and "nailers" who offered sex to those on a sailor's budget and been disappointed not to witness one of the famous and apparently frequent knock-down-and-drag-out fist fights between British and American sailors that were legendary. In his early years in Shanghai, before the city's boom of the 1920s and 1930s, Crow often popped into the private bars that many companies, including the *China Press*, maintained for their staff and clients. Whether or not Crow wanted a drink, he had little choice. Shanghai was a hard-drinking town and even the drinking water in those early years tasted acidy and was full of alum and needed to be flavored with whisky or gin, according to Crow, who also claimed that local doctors advised this practice to fight against germs. When the travel business entrepreneur Thomas Cook came to Shanghai, Crow claimed that he was so shocked at the amount of booze consumed by the Shanghailanders that he spent his time handing out tracts against the evils of drink – a pointless activity, Crow decided.

These private bars included one at the Lane Crawford general store where every day at 10:30 a.m. Mr. Crawford would empty a bottle of gin into a pitcher, add some other secret ingredients and serve his friends and regular customers "Crawford Specials" all day. The Hong Kong and Shanghai Bank's private bar was the best to gain access to, which made it a distinction to be invited to imbibe with the bullion brokers. As Shanghai developed and the private bars died out, Crow preferred an atmosphere where he could discuss politics and current affairs and, according to him, the city's clubs were the place for this – "Every club and every tea table on the China Coast, then as now, provided a forum for the discussion of international politics."[26] In her memoir of her life in inter-war Shanghai, Enid Saunders Candlin described expatriate Shanghai as "... seldom intellectual, often highly intelligent and with a wide international curiosity."[27] Crow enjoyed a good gossip about international and local affairs at the Shanghai Club's popular "tiffin hour" where talk was invariably about the goings-on at the SMC or the courts. He commented that in general the gossip of Shanghai was pretty harmless – "... in more than twenty five years of almost continuous residence I do not recall any gossip that did not dissipate itself in a day or two because it had nothing substantial to feed on."[28] Crow was himself a major gossip in a city built substantially on gossip.

The American Club at 29 Foochow Road[29] was adjacent to the Central Police Station as well as the administration building of the SMC, housing the headquarters of the SVC and most of the chief departments of the city government. It had been built in 1924 in American Georgian colonial style with bricks imported from America by the firm of the American architect, R. A. Curry; and it had been designed by Curry's new assistant, the Czech-born architect Ladislaus Hudec, who became famous for a variety of buildings in Shanghai, including the Park Hotel, the Moore Memorial Church, China United Apartments and the Green House that was shaped like a ship's prow after the wishes of its shipping magnate owner.[30] Foochow Road was famous for brothels, opium dens and gambling houses as well as publishers and the American Club. The Club was also home to the American Chamber of Commerce and the LeSalle Extension University, as well as having 50 "bachelor bedrooms" and two dining rooms for its members, a billiards room, a card room, a mahjong room, a writing room, a library and a bowling alley in the basement.

According to a *Fortune* magazine profile of Shanghai in 1935, the club contrasted with the "gloomy Shanghai Club whose furniture is heavy and sedate" while "The red-brick American Club is bright with American maple and Colonial furniture, its lobby faintly reminiscent of a well-decorated hospital. It is full of eager, smiling men who take you by the hand whether they have met you or not. And its bar is packed."[31] Crow himself admitted that the American Club was noisier than other clubs around Shanghai and put this down to the natural boisterousness of the American character. The Club allowed the popular practice of dice-shaking for drinks to decide who paid, a custom strictly frowned upon and banned at the more stuffy Shanghai Club though that bar – supposedly the longest in the world at 47 yards – could get so busy that those lucky enough to get their elbows on it spent a great deal of time passing drinks back to those stuck behind.

Until the First World War, the Americans in Shanghai had neither been numerous nor organized enough to have a club of their own. Crow claimed this simply hadn't been a problem as Americans just used British clubs and institutions. However, with the coming of the war, the American community in Shanghai became isolated and some Americans were refused membership of the Shanghai Club as many Brits distrusted the motives and isolationism of the USA during most of the war. Americans were neutrals and found many of their old haunts shut to them. After the war, the Americans started to carve a more permanent presence in the International Settlement with two American clubs, an American school, a community church and, with the British, a YMCA.

Crow, presumably one of the "smiling men" *Fortune* noted, was President of the club for many years during which time he nominated and had accepted the first Chinese member of the Club, Tang Shao-yi, whom Crow had met in 1911 and was to become a Prime Minister of the Republic of China in 1912. Tang was born in the same village as Sun Yat-sen in Guangdong and he had been an envoy for the Qing court, as well as Emperor Guangxu's Ambassador Extraordinary and Plenipotentiary at the Sino-British negotiations on the Tibetan issue in India. By the late 1930s, while the Shanghai Club remained solidly white, the American Club began to accept Chinese members who were close to American business or had studied in the US, though Ralph Shaw noted, "I never saw a black man there and there were many black Americans in Shanghai."[32]

Crow mostly frequented the American Club, which probably suited his rather male tastes, as one of its unique features was that for many years women were not admitted except on the annual Ladies' Night and for the George Washington Birthday Ball (though later in the 1930s a Ladies' Lounge was thoughtfully added), but he did visit many of the other clubs that composed such an integral part of the social life of the International Settlement. The Shanghai Club built in 1910 by the British at 2 The Bund, was the most famous and close to Crow's office and its famous Long Bar was also frequented by his White Russian friend Sapajou.

The Shanghai Club was a British institution but other nationals could be admitted to membership though women were barred. There was also the Country Club, at 651 Bubbling Well Road,[33] that had extensive lawns, flowerbeds and fountains. Another watering-hole for Americans was the Moorish style Columbia Country Club, at 301 Great Western Road (later Avenue Foch). This club, which then was really in the country, was purely social with spacious verandas, a swimming pool and an indoor squash court. Its cocktail lounge, pool and veranda made it a popular drinking spot on hot summer nights. Crow was also an occasional visitor to the Cercle Sportif Français, the French Club, Shanghai's most cosmopolitan club (that is to say it allowed different nationalities and, daringly, also women, even if only 40 at a time and with hundreds wait-listed); and there was also the Astor House Hotel Bar as well as the hotel's courtyard where an orchestra played in the evenings or the American University Club which was open to former or current students of American universities. For a quieter drink, he would walk from his office over into the French Concession to a small French-run hotel where he would talk with a mysterious Korean prince that he became friendly with who had no apparent earned income and spent all afternoon in the bar of the hotel sipping Italian vermouth. Crow would pitch ideas at him to see if he really did have any money. He suggested a subsidized newspaper dedicated to restoring the Korean monarchy but the prince never committed to the idea.

Crow would also occasionally visit one of the city's casinos or gambling houses though described himself as a "timid gambler." His wariness of the roulette table was heightened by the fact that he could sign a chit for any gambling expenses or drinks without even looking at the sum and that this could easily lead to recklessness. Crow preferred to change $100 into chips and go home when the last chip disappeared. He did enjoy the various lotteries and numbers games that attracted massive interest with syndicates being formed and people eagerly awaiting the results. He never recorded a winning ticket.

The rickshaw pullers who waited outside the American Club at night got to know Crow so well that when he left they would cry "Ko Lo, Ko Lo", Crow's Chinese name, as they patted the cushions on their seats to show how soft, comfortable and inviting they were after a hard night's debating and drinking. To the Chinese, the crow was a bird of ill repute and evil habits and so most of the drivers enjoyed the irony of his name. If the chauffeur was not available and Crow didn't fancy a rickshaw, there were other forms of public transport but Crow, by his own admission, was an irregular user. He would occasionally take a motorbus though these were usually horrendously crowded and, once aboard, more passengers crowded on at each stop until the potential for suffocation was reached and getting off at your stop became a major battle. He noted that neither the complaints of the conductor nor his fellow passengers would stop more people piling on at each stop.

Crow maintained a hectic schedule throughout his time in Shanghai and the Far East, traveling regularly throughout China. His health was not perfect and from the mid-1930s he became self-conscious about putting on weight: he started at five feet 10 inches and 196 pounds and then expanded from there. Over the years he suffered from a variety of ailments, including the painful affliction of Ningbo varnish poisoning, bouts of Hong Kong foot (a version of athlete's foot caused by the humid weather) and gastritis, and he also lost his teeth. His workaholic regime didn't help with a busy schedule as both a newspaperman and an advertising executive, as well as being active on any number of committees. He was a smoker and liked cigarettes (indeed some of Carl Crow Inc.'s biggest customers were tobacco brands) though he could not abide "unpalatable" French-made cigarettes nor Chinese-made matches ("as thin as toothpicks"). The matches annoyed him as it is "sheer folly to attempt to light a cigarette with a single match. The only sensible procedure is to hold four or five of them like a bunch of fagots and strike them altogether in the hope that one of the lot will ignite and that one or more will be inflammable enough to hold the flame."[34]

An Expanding Waistline

Crow noted that many foreigners managed to spend a lifetime in China without ever eating Chinese food, but he claimed to have tried everything put before him in China including shark's fin, fish lips, bird's nest soup and thousand-year eggs, as well as once eating a locust. He constantly complained about chicken in China as those deemed fit to kill and eat were invariably old, scrawny and past their egg-bearing days. However, pheasant, duck and venison were all available along with beef and, of course, pork. Crow found fresh vegetables to be tastier and generally better in China than America and decided that he actually liked cucumber after previously having thought it a rather boring vegetable. He also constantly marveled at the huge squashes and marrows he was served and experienced new vegetables such as lotus. Specialties abounded with oysters on Thursdays when the boat from Dalian arrived, giant crabs from Vladivostok, fresh fish and squid from Japan, Ningbo clams and Yantai prawns as well as Hangzhou peaches, Yantai pears and Qingdao grapes. However, he also noted that a soft-boiled egg seemed beyond the otherwise excellent capabilities of every Chinese cook. This infuriated Crow, but he was never sure whether it was really because of cooks' inability or whether the staff were having a little harmless fun at his expense.

He claimed that he preferred every variety of cooked fish in China to the tasteless English-style boiled fish that was served in Shanghai's clubs. Things did not improve at home as far as Western food was concerned as Crow's cook had previously been trained by a British employer and so naturally equated Western food with blandness. Joints of roast beef, Yorkshire pudding, cold toast and boiled fish were the best he could expect, which further encouraged him to eat Chinese-style.

The cook would shop daily carrying his own scales to the market as, according to Crow, no Chinese cooks would trust a merchant to whom they had to pay out money. Though he liked Chinese food, Crow admitted that he never adopted the traditional Chinese breakfast nor did he like a continental breakfast or cereal and preferred to start the day with a cooked meal. And quite sumptuous it was too – usually involving a combination of ham, bacon, eggs, waffles, hot cakes, finnan haddie (smoked haddock) and salted mackerel with boiled potatoes. Contemplating his breakfast in the mornings, Crow recalled the sounds that greeted his waking up. "When I was awake at daybreak in Shanghai there were several familiar sounds I always heard. One was the monotonous clang of a little gong with which a Buddhist nun marked her prostrations on her daily pilgrimage to Bubbling Well Temple, kneeling to the ground and reciting a prayer with every third step. Another was the concert of that glorious songster the *minah*, who, except in rainy weather, always greeted the dawn from my willow trees and then flew away on his business for the day. The third was an inarticulate cry coming from the foreman of the ordure collectors warning poor householders, or the servants of the wealthy, to place the night soil pales outside the door so that their contents could be collected. Before the sun was well up the collection would have been completed and before office desks in Shanghai were opened, farmers many miles distant were carrying well-filled buckets of fertilizer to the fields."[35]

The good cooking he got at home, as well as the meals he took outside, all eventually added to his weight problem, which annoyed him; and his sweet tooth led to his need for dentures. Food was just too plentiful and too good, leading Crow to declare that "... the married man in Shanghai learns as much about food as a traveling salesman with an expense account ..."[36] Crow lunched well and particularly favored the curried prawns served at the Cathay Hotel. Emily Hahn described the Shanghailanders' insistence on dinner parties, where full dress code was observed religiously, as an "insane fashion;"[37] and *Fortune* magazine described them as invariably "rigid and pompous, seated with painful precision"[38] that all added to Crow's consumption and waistline. It didn't help his sleep either as dinner in Shanghai was rarely served before 8 p.m. and in summer servants would walk around the diners spraying their ankles with a solution of kerosene to deter mosquitoes. Crow noted that his cook rarely measured out amounts of ingredients but judged them all by hand and eye which meant that there was usually more butter or cream in a dish than necessary, all adding to his calorie intake. "Butter", according to Crow, "is spooned out with lordly disdain for exact proportions," though he also noted that "The results, while arrived at by unscientific means, are usually entirely satisfactory."[39] However, he clearly liked his fine foods, noting his purchases of American tinned food, Australian butter, Scotch kippers, Italian cheese, New Zealand and English marmalade, and fresh fish from Japan.

Sometimes Crow was unable to avoid the gut-busting banquets that were laid on in his honor. Several times a year he had to attend various banquets thrown for him by clients. One client, a Chinese publishing house he worked closely with for many years, threw a banquet in Crow's honor and called the Columbia Country Club to ask the barman what Crow's favorite tipple was. The barman told them champagne and whisky and soda. This then entailed Crow sitting down to a banquet at noon one day with each course accompanied by glasses of champagne, whisky and soda all mixed together.

He was scrupulous in recording just how much food he bought – for instance he noted that his household's flour quota was a strict 25 pounds per month. Crow wasn't necessarily tight with money or lacking in it (though he called himself a "spendthrift"), but Silas Hardoon[40] had taught him that frugality in the small things in life allowed you to be reckless with the bigger things. Crow saw the evidence of this when he met Hardoon in his spartan office, which had no heating, and also in his opulent Bubbling Well Road mansion, the largest in Shanghai, as well as his equally opulent Chinese-style house on the shore of Hangzhou's West Lake. Apart from recording his household expenses (and noting to his delight that pheasant was cheaper than chicken in China), Crow claimed that he rarely followed Hardoon's voluminous advice except on the issue of accounting.

Crow's growing weight problem meant that for a time he was forced on his doctor's orders to cut his consumption of pastries and starchy food. He was just as bad with other household expenses, calculating that a match was used in his house every 15 minutes throughout the day all year round. However, he realized that the custom of "squeeze" meant that he could go away on business for six months and the same amount of matches, flour and sugar would somehow be consumed.

Like most of Shanghai's foreign community, Crow was not averse to a drink and favored gin and bitters or whisky and soda known as "stengahs" or, when drinking with the British China Hands in the Shanghai Club, a *chota peg*.[41] He developed a good appreciation of Scotch whiskey in the Shanghai Club and one former colleague at the UP news agency in China later described Crow as a "two fisted" drinker.[42] In the summer, he always looked forward to a cold beer after exerting himself. When Crow had first arrived in Shanghai, beer had been a big disappointment to him as the only available brews were rather flat, tended to be drunk warm English-style and had been shipped to Shanghai from Suez. Later the beer market improved and Crow often visited the private bar of Caldbeck, McGregor and Company, the largest wine and spirits merchants in the city, who built a replica of an English taproom in their offices.

Boating and Poker

The Crows found house-boating a particular pleasure and he and Helen would make elaborate plans to navigate the canals in a hired boat with a party of friends from Shanghai over a weekend. His regular house-boating trips in Jiangsu also featured mammoth games of bridge with seemingly endless rubbers late into the night. Crow and Helen took regular house-boating trips on the canals of

Jiangsu and Zhejiang with stops at towns such as Changshu and Wuxi where he would hire a *loadah* (house-boat skipper) for a weekend. Boating allowed him to gather a group of friends and see new places. Over the years he explored all the tributaries around Shanghai including the Yangtze and around the port of Zhakou.

Crow, of course, saw the whole trip as a further opportunity to try to understand the Chinese way of doing things and delighted in understanding the rules of the boatmen – such as smaller craft giving way to more heavily-loaded boats, with boatmen blatantly lying about the amount of cargo they were carrying to try to get the other boats to give way. Occasionally, the house-boat would come to a stop, stuck in a boat-jam on the often-crowded waterways. When there was a complete jam, all the boatmen would start shouting at the top of their lungs until by some method, never detected by Crow, one boat would move aside and everyone would manage to wiggle through and continue their journeys. He would also occasionally take pleasure in playing to the Chinese opinion of foreigners as rude and ignorant by simulating a loss of temper to gain right of way, much to his hired captain's delight. However, as Crow noted, this was a strategy that the Chinese understood as being as devious as their claims to be carrying non-existent cargos: "Some foreigners assume this courtesy to be a tacit acknowledgement of their own superiority, thus giving the Chinese something else to laugh about."[43]

Crow earned a reputation for being a somewhat competitive house-boater, always seeking out new creeks, views and canals that had not been traversed before. House-boating became a Christmas and New Year ritual for the Crows and their Scottie dogs as well as assorted friends. The travel was broken up by hikes and sightseeing with the aim of driving the Shanghai soot from their lungs. Again, Crow overindulged on food on these trips. As house-boating had been a craze started by the British, house-boat menus tended to follow British traditions with roast ham, beefsteak and kidney pudding, sides of bacon and kippered herrings for breakfast, and any game bagged along the trip such as goose, duck, pheasant, pigeon or partridge, as well as the occasional mouse deer, all of which were often prepared as a traditional China coast "game pot" soup.

When in Shanghai, apart from visiting the American and other clubs, Crow occasionally visited the cinema. By 1933 Shanghai had over 37 cinemas and a thriving local movie industry. Like many other Shanghailanders, he relied increasingly on the cinema newsreels for details of deteriorating world events as well as footage of local events. He also attended the numerous amateur dramatics performances staged by the various foreign communities. Many were staged at the Lyceum Theatre before it became a cinema in 1931.[44]

His other more sedate activity was playing poker, a game he had learnt while working the night shift on the *Fort Worth Star-Telegram*. Poker was a distracting relaxation for Crow, though not necessarily a successful endeavor, as he declared that he was "… one who has figuratively lost his shirt in many a poker game…"[45] However while a deck of cards and the mahjong tiles attracted him, he never developed an ear for Chinese music or opera. He admitted that after 25 years in China he did slowly come to appreciate it, but he never found any tunes he could claim to truly like.

He appears to have been an amiable and well-liked man – one who moved easily in Chinese and foreign society. In the 1935 edition of the *Shanghai Municipal Gazette* Crow is listed as a "person qualified to be elected as councillor for the foreign settlement of Shanghai."[46] In the highly stratified European society of Shanghai, Crow retained his all-American Yankee spirit and slightly funny Missouri accent but he made friends across all the nations including the English and eventually even the Belgians. Crow had taken an instant dislike to a Belgian he met once before in Tokyo and transferred this opinion to all Belgians. However, he later admitted that he eventually decided that he liked everyone, including the Belgians. When the Second World War broke out in Europe, Crow was quick to state his abhorrence of Hitler but he still fondly remembered many German friends from his China days, including Julius Eigner, a German journalist, a Herr Breuer of Mechers and Company in Shanghai, and even the one-time boss of the Nazi Party in Kunming who once threw a cocktail party for Crow at the city's French Club, as well as an old German consul who provided "a marvellous luncheon" for Crow in French Indo-China.

To look at pictures of Crow, at least those that have survived, he seems a sterner man than is revealed in his journalism and books: formally dressed, invariably in a black suit with white shirt and black tie, round glasses and a double chin that revealed his battle with his weight. While in Shanghai, he had most of his suits tailor-made. At various times he tried a British, an American, and a Spanish tailor but he invariably used an old Chinese tailor, Mr Lao Hai-shing who, he noted, soon realized that good tailoring, a perfect fit and Crow's large frame were all incompatible and stopped attempting a perfect fit or even to claim one was possible. Crow soon learnt that when Mr. Lao commented that a new suit he had made for Crow "can pass", he was "bestowing a sartorial accolade, the highest praise his sincerity will allow him to bestow."[47] Crow had a reputation for always being slightly out of fashion and friends would joke with him about his threadbare suits with worn elbows.

Life may have been good and comfortable in Shanghai but work beckoned and Crow was also interested in the rise of a character he had watched closely for some time – Chiang Kai-shek.

12

Fear in Shanghai, the Generalissimo and Three Stripes on the Arm

Chiang Kai-shek, Heading North and Confusion in Shanghai

Through chance and his work for the *China Press*, Crow had grown to know Sun Yat-sen on a personal level, and he also followed the eventful rise of Chiang Kai-shek, though from more of a distance. Even after Chiang secured control of the KMT, Crow still saw him as essentially an outsider in Chinese political circles, "a southern rice eater,"[1] as opposed to the apparently stronger northern noodle eaters who dominated Nationalist China's politics and warlord circles. Sun had also been a southerner but a more overt revolutionary than the Generalissimo (the title he was officially granted in 1932), which endeared him more to the northern political elite.

Chiang rose to prominence in China through his involvement in Nationalist politics as a result of his time as a student and his study of the 1905 Russo-Japanese War. The defeat of Russia, a great European imperialist power whose empire stretched from the Baltic to Vladivostok, had had a profound effect on many Chinese intellectuals who saw the possibilities for Asian countries emerging from seclusion to stand up to the seemingly invincible Europeans. However, the progress Japan had made from isolated nation to strong military power under the Meiji reign also highlighted the continuing backwardness and weakness of China in comparison. It also didn't escape the notice of men like Chiang that the Russo-Japanese War had actually been fought largely on Chinese soil. At the time the strength of Japan seemed revolutionary, but many did not know the role of America in the war and President Theodore Roosevelt's efforts (for which he received the Nobel Peace Prize) in convening the Portsmouth Peace Conference in 1905 to prevent the defeat of Japan in an attempt to limit Russian expansionism.

What the Russo-Japanese War did do in China was lead a generation of intellectuals, including Chiang, to decide on military careers rather than the more traditional path of intellectual pursuits. Chiang had rejected his family's ancestral occupations of farming or small business, cut off his queue and tried to enrol in a Japanese military school. He wasn't accepted, being told that he needed some training in China first before the Japanese would take him. Consequently he ended up moving north and enrolling in China's National Military Academy in Baoding, south of Beijing. In a twist of fate, it was the Qing government which provided him with the opportunity to go to Japan to study the military tactics he would eventually use to help overthrow it and consolidate a Republic. Chiang made it to the Tokyo Military Staff College in 1907 and spent time stationed in the freezing port town of Takada where he met Sun. Crow likened Chiang's later defence of the Qing against Japanese invasion to George Washington's support for the British Red Coats against the French. Patriotism made strange bedfellows and led to temporary truces in the name of saving China.[2]

In many ways Sun and Chiang were strange bedfellows too. The "… quiet, persistent and persuasive revolutionist," as Crow called Sun,[3] was 20 years older than Chiang at the time of their first meeting but had an immediate and profound effect on the younger man, appealing to his fierce sense of patriotism. Sun convinced Chiang that China could best resist foreign encroachment and engender national recovery by removing the Qing rather than supporting them. Chiang soon became a close supporter of Sun and acted as his secretary for a period.

The Hankow revolt in 1911, which Crow had argued so vociferously to call a "revolution" in the *China Press*, led to Chiang's technical desertion from the Japanese army and return to China. Chiang commanded a voluntary militia unit in Shanghai and led it in a victory against a Manchu garrison in Hangzhou as well as sporadic fighting around Shanghai. Chiang also entered the world of publishing and journalism for a time after 1911, publishing a magazine on military science. He looked quite dapper in photographs of the time in a Western three-piece suit, tie and cane. He was just 25 years old and continued to drift about in a somewhat restless way, considered attending a German military academy, and then became a stockbroker in Shanghai for a time. Though still fiercely patriotic, Chiang also needed to be financially independent. Thus began his long-term links with many of Shanghai's wealthier Chinese business community and their tips led him to quickly amass a decent sum of money to fund his other activities. As chaos worried many wealthy Shanghainese families, they increasingly invested in overseas Chinese ventures such as Malayan and East Indies rubber plantations as well as in the London and New York stock markets. Chiang profited greatly from these inside tips and amassed enough savings to rejoin Sun and the struggle full-time.

He carried on expanding his horizons. Sun sent him to Moscow to take a look at the Red Army to see if there was anything the KMT could learn from Lenin's organizational model. He didn't find the USSR a true panacea for all China's ills but appreciated enough of what he saw to return and organize the new Whampoa Military Academy, which had been founded in 1924 to train military commanders. Chiang, out of his Shanghai-tailored suit and now back in military garb, was appointed the first Principal of the academy and made sure that all the Soviet instructors were thrown out after the break in relations with the Chinese Communist Party in the late 1920s.

The May Thirtieth Incident had seen student- and communist-led agitation spread rapidly across China which raised anti-British sentiments. Crow had, not surprisingly, been in the middle of a golf game, when he heard of the events in Shanghai and raced back to the city arriving at the scene of the killings only minutes after they had occurred. He saw the bodies hastily carried away and the blood-stained streets washed down to remove all trace of the incident. Despite the bloody scenes, unlike many foreigners in China, Crow did not believe that another Boxer Rebellion was in the offing. Political consciousness among many influential people was advanced enough in China to see that trying to murder all the foreigners in the country would not end foreign domination. It was the KMT that appeared to have the only workable political program for the country and consequently power gradually slipped away from the warlords and to Chiang.

Crow admired the new professionalism of Chiang's Nationalist army, initially led by Chiang on a white horse (he was later to absent himself from most of the major battlefields), as it marched on the ambitious Northern Expedition from Guangzhou in July 1926 to try to reunify the country and wipe out warlordism. At first it had not looked good – Chiang's army was poorly equipped, and many men had only just previously been warlord troops and were considered less than reliable, and the expedition threatened to break the bank. Chiang tried to win over warlords to his cause as he advanced and, if they proved truculent, fought them one-by-one as their forces combined would have outnumbered his. By August Chiang had advanced to Hunan and Hubei provinces, and on to Hankou and the Yangtze. Hankou fell and Chiang advanced into Jiangxi. Nanchang fell, as did the tea-production center of Jiujiang, leaving Nanjing and Shanghai in Chiang's sights. At the same time other divisions had moved up the coast through Fujian province and taken Fuzhou. Despite a run of victories, the cost had been high; 25,000 men dead, 15,000 of them killed in Jiangxi alone, while T. V. Soong was desperately trying to raise funds to pay the troops and prevent them mutinying.

However, Crow remained concerned at the left wing of the KMT's links to the Russian and Chinese Communists and the presence of the Comintern's Michael Borodin in close proximity to the left. With Chiang in Jiangxi, Borodin had stayed in the fallen city of Wuhan and was seemingly reorganizing the left of the KMT in a possible challenge to Chiang.

The tall, Stalin-moustachioed Borodin[4] was a shadowy figure at the time – a Byelorussian Jew who as a young man had worked floating logs down the Dvina River to Latvia, he moved onto smuggling and then joined Lenin in 1903. Hunted by the Tsarist police, he had moved through Britain and then on to America where he lived among Chicago's Lithuanian community. After the Bolshevik Revolution, he returned to Moscow. He undertook various covert operations for the Bolsheviks and was also Soviet Consul in Mexico City for a time. He returned to Britain to be an agitator for the Comintern during the coal miners' strikes in 1921 and spent a few months in a Glasgow prison. After he had made his way back to Russia, Lenin immediately dispatched him to Guangzhou. On the way he passed through Beijing and Shanghai before arriving with the job of helping Sun turn the KMT into a more disciplined mass movement. Borodin stayed for some time in Guangzhou and at one point had a keen young Chinese Communist as his personal secretary – Zhou En-lai. Borodin remained involved in Chinese politics, eventually also advising Chiang for a while though he was expelled from China in 1927 after Chiang had secured control and felt he had largely defeated the leftist elements of the KMT. Borodin eventually died in a Siberian labor camp in 1951. While in Shanghai, Borodin and his family lived a strange life – while he was out fomenting revolution all day, his two sons attended the American School while his portly, tough-faced wife Fanny, played a back-stage role supporting his work. He was technically the correspondent of the Soviet Rosta News Agency, but his real work in China was always widely known. He agreed to interviews with Western journalists, including an extensive one with Crow's old friend Randall Gould who described him as looking more like a big businessman than a revolutionary,[5] while Madame Chiang noted his unaccented English and personal magnetism.

Borodin and the other Soviet advisers decided that the issue that would unite China as a nation, and hopefully under a revolutionary flag, was the exploitative presence of the foreigners and the "unequal treaties" that had created the treaty ports and international concessions. As Crow wrote in the 1930s looking back on this time: "The ordinary man who drank tea and ate watermelon seeds in the teashop didn't know very much about the terms of these treaties but he did know that a group of Chinese students had been shot down and killed in Shanghai by orders of a British police officer."[6]

Crow was willing to give Chiang the benefit of the doubt when it came to the rising tide of anti-foreign propaganda that accompanied the progress of the KMT army from Guangzhou. Crow believed that Chiang did not fully approve of the tactic and, indeed, when some foreigners were killed in Nanjing, Chiang conducted a military investigation and executed over 50 Chinese found to be responsible. Further anti-foreign incidents occurred in Jiujiang and other towns along the Yangtze. The bloody incident in Nanjing saw several Americans killed and an American gunboat shell the city while the remaining foreign residents escaped. It was true that leftist elements had moved into the vacuum created as the Northern Expedition moved north from Guangzhou. Mao Zedong was now running a Committee on Peasant Affairs in Henan, and reports that churches had been forced to replace pictures of Jesus with images of Dr. Sun alarmed some in Shanghai.

On the whole, Crow saw the KMT army as well-disciplined, at least when compared to the warlords, though in reality the force was loosely composed of recent converts to the KMT cause such as the Kwangtung [*Guangdong*] Fourth (Iron) Army and the Seventh Army which hailed from Jiangxi province. Despite some incidents of looting, for the most part the army was disciplined and won the support of most of the Chinese people that encountered the troops. The whole expedition received the support of many of China's richest families and none other than the Harvard-trained economist T. V. Soong, Charlie Soong's eldest son, oversaw the army's finances after his sister Ai-ling stepped in and asked him to support Chiang.

T. V. was a major figure in Shanghai due to his family connections and his own wealth. His stocky frame and spectacles were a regular feature at society events, though he was a man of few unnecessary words, and a rigorous banker and accountant who had worked for the International Banking Corporation in New York after graduating from Harvard. He was noted for his sense of humor and belief in Western-style liberal politics. In 1917 T. V. had returned to China to become the secretary of the Han-Yeh Ping Company's Shanghai branch, the company singled out in Japan's Twenty-One Demands on China as so important in 1915. The Japanese now had a controlling influence in the company, something they had long coveted and finally managed to achieve. T.V. had apparently sorted out the books of Han-Yeh Ping in Shanghai and now his sister Ching-ling (Madame Sun) was urging him to sort out the KMT's finances. He largely did this by tackling issues such as import duties and how the government could best raise loans. He was a keen taxer and imposed additional taxes on most areas of life, including rickshaw fares, wedding celebrations, restaurants bills, and funerals. In 1924 he set up a Central Bank for China with help from a $10 million loan from Russia. Many ordinary Chinese saw T.V. as both economically and financially gifted as well as trustworthy and the Central Bank's deposits grew rapidly, while a nationwide tax collection system began to emerge backed by its own armed collection force under T.V.'s control which ensured maximum revenues and minimum squeeze.

Crow watched Chiang's progress from Shanghai. He did not agree with what he called the "club barroom strategists" and most of the diplomatic community who believed that the KMT would halt after securing the south and the Yangtze Delta to avoid challenging the bulk of the best organized warlords that remained in the north along with the Japanese. Crow believed that Chiang's army was well enough trained and well enough disciplined to continue. Chiang dealt with the Borodin-inspired leftist resurgence in Wuhan by executing Communist leaders, suppressing leftist organizations and wiping out Communist activity in many areas. Chiang was now secure again and ready to consider his position vis-à-vis Shanghai.

Defending a Thin Slice of Heaven and a Thick Slice of Hell

In 1927 the authorities of Frenchtown and the International Settlement were determined to defend their, as one commentator described it, "thin slice of heaven and thick slice of hell": their privileges and their treaty rights. Despite Crow's dismissing a Boxer-type scenario, the foreign portion of Shanghai was preparing itself for a siege, with Britain sending an additional 1,500 troops of the Durham Light Infantry and the French bringing in Vietnamese (Annamese) soldiers to guard Frenchtown. In all 20,000 armed men stood ready to defend the city. At the urging of his friends – Judges Thayer, Lobinger, Purdy and Helmick of the American court in Shanghai – Crow joined the Special Police which comprised mostly British and American citizens. He took lessons on how to use a revolver and actually donned a policeman's uniform; and he was given the rank of sergeant, something he found both amusing and slightly strange. Based in offices near the headquarters of the SMC on Kiangse Road[7] near the Anglican Holy Trinity Cathedral, Crow's job was to liaise with the floods of British-controlled troops arriving in Shanghai, which included Bengalis and Punjabis as well as the Coldstream Guards and other British regiments. The Americans sent Marines from the Philippines and over 20 battleships from a dozen nations were anchored on the Huang Pu while the Royal Air Force maintained a squadron of fighter planes ready to take off from the race course.

Crow was awarded the job (and his own service issue revolver), which he found "interesting", as a recognized Old China Hand and "man of good standing in the foreign community" attested to by his judge friends. According to Crow, the British troops couldn't tell the difference between the Chinese and their erstwhile Japanese allies, and so there was the threat of some premature fighting breaking out between supposed allies in defending the Settlement. Crow claimed that he once averted an outbreak of shooting after some British soldiers mistook a Japanese cavalry regiment for an attacking KMT force. Thankfully, the Old China Hand was available to advise the alarmed British sentry that these were indeed allies and not enemies.

To many, the situation looked perilous. The KMT had long been organizing in Shanghai and Zhou En-lai had moved from Guangzhou to the International Settlement to organize the Communist Party and the unions, while the Green Gang organized rival "Yellow Unions." Chiang moved on Shanghai in March 1927 through the city's southern defensive line and hordes of refugees poured into the International Settlement, now surrounded by sandbags, barbed wire and troops. Some fire-fights erupted between British soldiers and warlord troops who were trying to flee the fighting. The General Labour Union called a general strike, occupied Zhabei and helped the Chiang-supporting Guangxi Clique general Bai Chongxi to penetrate the city. Anti-foreign feelings grew in Zhabei where the union wished to establish a soviet. A mob tried to break through into Frenchtown. Chiang's forces were in position but he was unwilling to take on foreign troops despite having just taken Nanjing and declared it the Nationalist capital once again.

Chiang himself arrived on March 26 1927 by gunboat to a Shanghai seething with anti-imperialist students, restless unions, NRA soldiers and many more ex-warlord troops of dubious loyalty. Wang Ching-wei was returning from Europe to assume command of the KMT left wing. When Wang arrived, he pledged support to Chiang to prevent an uprising. The major unknown quantities were the Green Gang and the Communists. It was therefore little surprise that the first civilian visitor to see Chiang in Shanghai was Huang Jinrong. Chiang was determined to use the gangsters against the Reds. They agreed that the gangsters would back Chiang with men and arms in return for immunity and continued control of the city's lucrative drugs business.

The deal involved all the major players in Shanghai. Du Yuesheng organized his own militia – the China Mutual Progress Association – while the French Consul General called for a public struggle against the Communists, with French police guarding the headquarters of Du's Association and supplying them with guns. Du then used his contacts with Captain Fiori, the French Chief of Police, to meet with Sterling Fessenden, the Chairman of the SMC. Fessenden, a short, plump American, persuaded the SMC to allow Du's thugs passage through the International Settlement so they could slaughter the leftists.[8] Chiang would have liked to think of Du as either a patriot he worked with to do a good thing or someone he temporarily had to work with to achieve the right ends. However, the truth was that the Nationalists' links with the Green Gang went back to the founding of the Republic when Dr. Sun's confidant Chen Qimei had enlisted Green Gang support to seize Shanghai for the Nationalist cause.

The deal done, Chiang headed back to Nanjing leaving General Bai to clear up in Shanghai. On April 11 the Green Gang killed the city's top union leader and then the men of the China Mutual Progress Association moved into the city unmolested by either French or International Settlement authorities. They proceeded to attack union branches and leftist strongholds. Public executions followed with an estimated 400 leftists killed, though some claims run far higher – Edgar Snow claimed between 5,000 and 10,000 people were executed. General Bai and Du's men occupied the working-class areas of Shanghai.

Ultimately the situation calmed down as order was restored, often brutally. The Chinese army stood down and most of the foreign troops were sent back to where they had come from without seeing any action – as the historian John Keay has noted they departed "with only VD as a souvenir."[9] Chiang had exacted revenge against the left from Shanghai down to Guangzhou and everywhere between. Crow later reminisced that he might have been a little over-zealous in his concerns at the time and that Chiang was not reckless enough to take on all the world's major powers in the International Settlement at one go. This would have threatened the business interests of his financial backers such as T. V. Soong, who was that year also becoming a brother-in-law to Chiang after the General's marriage to Mei-ling Soong in a Shanghai ceremony where Chiang wore formal Western top and tails and Mei-ling a European flapper-style white wedding dress.

Life returned to some sort of normality in the International Settlement and Crow, who by now had discarded his sergeant's uniform, went back to work. However, what Crow and most other foreigners never knew was the deal done between Chiang, the French, Fessenden and the Green Gang. The Northern

Expedition had reached Shanghai successfully but achieved little more than cementing Green Gang power in the city and unleashing a vicious period of largely untrammeled gangsterism. Chiang had given the Green Gang the concession to sell narcotics in Shanghai, the profits from which, in part, funded the Northern Expedition's onward march from Shanghai to Beijing. Chiang's army pressed on while Crow took time to examine what exactly the new Republic meant and got back into the newspaper business.

13

Back in the Newspaper Business

The depression caused a drop in club bar receipts

A Hack Again Briefly

With Carl Crow Inc. a success, Carl felt secure enough to become involved in a new newspaper venture. He was one of several Americans who founded and edited the *Shanghai Evening Post* in 1929[1] with offices at 17–21 Avenue Edward VII. The paper was effectively a reinvention of the former *Shanghai Evening News* that had been supported by the tycoon C. V. Starr.

Crow founded the paper based on the principles he had learnt from Millard: essentially supportive of the Nationalist government and against Japanese militarism. The paper's major backer was Cornelius Vander Starr, or C. V. Starr, a leading life insurer in Asia. Originally from Fort Bragg on California's Mendocino coast, after a period in the army Starr got a job with the Pacific Mail Steam Ship Company in Japan and arrived in Shanghai in 1919 as stenographer with just ¥300 in his pocket. With Frank Jay Raven, another American who had come to Shanghai as an engineer in 1904, he founded American Asiatic Underwriters Federal,[2] which became extremely prosperous. Starr became wealthy and was described by *Fortune* magazine as "Shanghai's most bullish Taipan,"[3] investing heavily in the city through his Metropolitan Land Company (with offices close to Crow's own) and holding the major share in Raven's Asia

Realty Company. Starr lived with his maiden aunt on the eighth floor of the North-China Building (17 the Bund), where Asia Life and American Asiatic had offices. He was also something of a social reformer and gave equal working terms to his foreign and Chinese staff.

Crow felt free to compete in the fiercely competitive Shanghai newspaper world. After Millard's departure and then financial difficulties under Chinese ownership, the *China Press* had come under the control of N. E. B. "Edward" Ezra, a prominent British Sephardi Jewish merchant and landowner who had accrued a fortune running the local Opium Monopoly until 1917 and had a road named after him in Shanghai.[4] Ezra knew something about newspapers as he had edited the locally-published Jewish paper *Israel's Messenger* for many years.[5]

The *Shanghai Evening Post* continued to be a major evening paper in Shanghai through to the 1940s. The British soldier-turned-journalist Ralph Shaw who worked for the rival *North-China Daily News* described it as "a large-circulation evening newspaper ... whose editor-publisher Randall Chase Gould, was outspokenly anti-Japanese."[6]

From the start the paper was strongly pro-Chinese though it looked thoroughly American and included agony aunt Dorothy Dix, crossword puzzles, Ripley's "Believe It or Not" and columns from half a dozen news syndicates. After briefly editing the paper himself, Crow had personally chosen his old acquaintance Randall Gould as editor. He had got to know Gould when the bulky Minnesotan had arrived in Beijing as a UP correspondent. Gould was a friend of many of the Missouri News Colony. He had worked as a news editor on the *Japan Times* in Tokyo in 1923–24 before becoming UP's roving bureau manager in Beijing, Tianjin, Shanghai and Manila in the late 1920s, as well as the news editor of the *Peking Daily News*. Gould was hired in 1931 and stayed as editor of the paper for a decade as well as being a China correspondent for the *Christian Science Monitor*. He eventually went on to write two books in the 1940s – *Chungking Today* and *China in the Sun*. After Pearl Harbor, he returned to America as the US editor of the *Shanghai Evening Post* (a paper that blatantly espoused America's wartime viewpoint in China), became President of the Post-Mercury Company in 1946 and then, in 1949, moved on to the editorial team at the *Denver Post*.

Competition in the English language newspaper market in Shanghai remained strong, given that there were just an estimated 8,000 to 10,000 potential native English readers plus a few thousand more who read English competently as a second or third language. The readership was growing with a new generation of English-speaking younger Chinese who had a greater interest in the outside world between the wars, but it was still a limited market. Crow estimated that a not inconsiderable portion of the readership were Chinese students studying English.

In 1919, Crow had been commissioned to write a report for the American State Department on conditions in the newspaper business in China that was eventually published in 1921. In the report, Crow divided the country's press into three groups:

1) English-language publications by and for the English-speaking population of China; 2) bona fide Chinese newspapers published by and for the Chinese and; 3) a category growing in importance, consists of newspapers published in English, Chinese and other languages, but edited in the interests of a certain foreign power, while purporting to be either under British or Chinese ownership.[7]

The *China Press* had been a clear example of category 1 when it was founded. However, by 1929 the situation in the English-language press had become increasingly complicated. The *North-China Daily News* continued as ever before; the *China Press* repeatedly changed hands; the *Shanghai Times* and the *Shanghai Mercury* were nominally British but effectively under Japanese control; and the *Shanghai Gazette* emerged in 1918. The *Gazette* claimed to be aimed at readers requiring an "American complexion" to their news. However, it appears to have been largely under the control of Sun Yat-sen and San Francisco-born Liao Zhongkai who had met Sun in Japan, had developed the KMT's worker-peasant policy and was eventually assassinated in 1925. This was a fourth category that Crow omitted in his report to the State Department – Chinese language newspapers controlled by local political parties or prominent politicians. In 1926 Crow commented that "The number of newspapers published in any city will be found to depend almost entirely on the political activity of the place."[8]

The *Shanghai Gazette* fell into this fourth category. It was edited by two Trinidadian-born, ethnically Chinese British subjects, Eugene Chen[9] and Corinth Henry (C. H.) Lee, and also featured the questionable involvement of George Sokolsky. The *Gazette* puzzled Crow, as he admitted in his report to the State Department.

The thin, British-accented Chen was a shadowy figure who rose to prominence in Shanghai. Having been born in the British West Indies of a Chinese father and a black Trinidadian mother, he was to be Foreign Minister of China four times. After an English education, he briefly practiced as a barrister in London's Inner Temple, where he developed his reputation for being a "master of the stinging invective,"[10] before returning to Trinidad. After a brief stay in the West Indies, he soon emerged in China as a legal adviser to the Ministry of Communications in 1912. Unable to read, write or speak Chinese, Chen founded the English language *Peking Gazette* in 1914 and published raging editorials against the *North-China Daily News* as the bastion of British power in China. He also denounced Yuan Shih-kai in his editorials, for which he was thrown into jail in 1916 though, as a British subject, he used the extraterritoriality laws to secure his release soon after. After leaving jail he moved to Shanghai and became a personal adviser and private secretary to Sun (a position he held until Sun's death). The *Shanghai Gazette*, which he founded, continued to attack British interests for which he was thrown into prison again. In 1919 he was a delegate to the Versailles Conference where he tried to promote China's cause. Later on, he continued to agitate against the British in China with some success, including forcing a deal whereby London returned the treaty port of Hankou. At times when Chen was being held at His Majesty's pleasure, the *Gazette* was edited by C. H. Lee, another ethnic Chinese of Trinidadian birth. Adding to the mystery around the *Gazette* was the involvement of George Sokolsky.

Sokolsky was an enigmatic figure. The son of Russian-speaking Jewish immigrants, he had studied at Columbia University's journalism school. He had set out for revolutionary Russia in 1917 but came to China a year later and married a Chinese woman. He joined the editorial staff of the *Gazette*, which put him in close proximity to Sun and he became involved in the May Fourth 1919 demonstrations as a courier between Sun and the students. Sokolsky left the *Gazette* pretty quickly after a row with C. H. Lee, but he stayed close to Sun and wrote for a wide range of newspapers including the *North-China Daily News*, the *New York Post*, the *New York Times Magazine*, the *Philadelphia Ledger* and Fleisher's *Japan Advertiser*. He often appeared in the *North-China Daily News* as an editorial writer, under the pseudonym G. Gramada, reporting from Guangzhou and Shanghai regularly until he left China in 1931.

Roads to a Republic

In this heady and competitive atmosphere, the *Shanghai Evening Post* was to become one of the major sources of news on the fluctuations in the Chinese Republic. After a brief stint Crow parted ways with the paper and Starr replaced him as manager. Starr believed Crow was an excellent choice to establish the newspaper but wasn't best suited to the longer term management of the business.[11] Crow moved on; by now he was also interested in the myriad of different ways in which China was changing.

Chiang had marched onwards leaving foreign Shanghai to carry on much as before. His expedition had headed northwards, closing in on Japanese-controlled Qingdao (but as ever Chiang declined to fight a foreign army), while his second flank had penetrated Henan and his ally, the Christian General, had captured Zhengzhou. Changsha had fallen to republican forces and the so-called Northern Coalition of warlords had started to self-implode. Communist rebellions continued to break out but Chiang repeatedly suppressed them with extreme brutality following the launch of his ferociously harsh "Punishment Without Leniency" campaign in 1927.

In January 1928 Chiang had returned to Nanjing after defeating the remnants of the KMT's left. He was in largely undisputed control of the party, and he used this new power base to re-launch the Northern Expedition with 800,000 men in April to mount the final push to Beijing and oust the Old Marshall Chang Tso-lin who was still ruling the roost up north. T. V. Soong, with his seemingly limitless ability to raise funds, was once again called upon. The push began at Jinan and most of Shandong fell, unleashing a wave of Japanese brutality on the Chinese of the city.[12] By June Chinese citizens were fleeing Beijing, including the Old Marshal himself who retreated to his Shenyang stronghold. He never made it home; he was assassinated when the Japanese-controlled Kwantung Army blew up his train. The NRA fought its way into Beijing. Chiang arrived a few days later, his two-year 1,500 mile expedition completed and renamed Peking as Peiping.[13] In Nanjing, thoughts of military strategy and political maneuvering were now replaced with thoughts about building the new China.

After Chiang cemented power across most of the country, relations with the Western powers improved and the China Hands moved from monitoring warlords and the expedition's progress to seeing how the Nanjing government would shape up as an administration. Crow was giving even more praise to the now solidly-rightist Nationalist government, not least for its program of public works and road-building schemes initiated under the newly-formed National Economic Council and the National Reconstruction Commission. Ever the entrepreneur, he was quick to realize that with the road network around Shanghai expanding fast there was now the possibility of traveling more freely and independently around eastern China by car. He started a small monthly travel magazine, *China Highways*, which was technically the official journal of the Automobile Club of China. *China Highways* gave descriptions of the newly-constructed roads to cities like Suzhou, Hangzhou, Nanjing and Anhui's Yellow Mountains, as well as sites of historic or scenic interest that could be reached by car. The magazine was able to cover longer journeys as the road-building program progressed rapidly and, prior to the Japanese invasion in 1937, it became possible to drive from Shanghai as far south as Guangzhou and as far west as

Chongqing. Crow's magazine was supported by advertising by the major oil companies that were providing petrol stations for the new class of long-distance motorists and had begun issuing road maps of China.

As car ownership and China's road building program accelerated Crow saw opportunities for new publications.

The *Shanghai Evening Post* and *China Highways* both reflected Crow's interest in trying to understand and interpret what exactly was going on in this new China the Nationalists were building. Ultimately that entailed a meeting with Chiang Kai-shek.

14
The New Republic and the Soong Dynasty

Hot Porridge and Cold Toast in Nanjing

Crow's generally good opinion of Chiang had been boosted following a meeting with him after the tumultuous events of 1925 and 1927. He was part of a delegation of foreign newspapermen that traveled to Nanjing in 1928 at the Nationalist government's invitation in an attempt to try to challenge the perception of the new government as overly threatening to Great Power interests in China. Crow was not a full-time journalist at the time. However, he was preparing to launch the *Shanghai Evening Post* for Starr as well as *China Highways*, while also running his advertising agency, and so he decided to tag along anyway. Chiang, for his part, was now established in the new capital of Nanjing and was keen to soothe the concerns of Shanghai's business community whom he relied upon for support and finances. This meeting was one of a number Chiang orchestrated to try to rebuild links and keep the support flowing.

On the day of the reception, Nanjing was hit by a freak snowstorm and icy winds from the north but Crow still reported that he thoroughly enjoyed attending a tea party given by the General and Madame Chiang for about 30 journalists. Madame Chiang spoke English for her husband, but Crow was convinced that Chiang understood more than he let on but would routinely ask his wife to translate. After the obvious thrill of meeting Madame Chiang before the General's arrival, Crow assumed that his brief speech of welcome was typical of the somewhat publicity-shy leader and concentrated on the lavish spread of sandwiches and tea while huddled next to a warm stove pumping out much-needed heat. However, Chiang resumed speaking but this time in a tone Crow described as that of an "impassioned patriot pleading with us, as representatives of the foreign public, for understanding and for help."[1] He believed that the half-hour speech from Chiang on the positive future of the Republic was well received by the press, but when they got back to Shanghai their more closeted editors rejected it out of hand as a publicity trick played on them by the Chiangs. When Crow tried to persuade senior editors of Chiang's honesty, he was accused of being "pro-Chinese," an accusation he described as meant to be "not complimentary" and one he was to face many times over the years.[2] Overall, Crow saw Chiang as a modern general but deeply imbued with Chinese tradition, a lover of classical Chinese poetry with a "purely Chinese mind" but who had learnt from his observations of the Soviet Red Army and his Japanese military training.[3]

The trip to Nanjing had been an uncomfortable one due to the adverse weather conditions. Crow described the outing as "a three-coat day and at breakfast our teeth chattered on the hot porridge as well as the cold toast."[4] Crow also endured a miserable lunch where he was equally freezing and he told a Chinese official who raised the issue of special rights for foreigners in China that he would gladly relinquish them all right there and then for a warm room. Madame Chiang's sandwiches later that day were most welcome. In retrospect, Crow acknowledged that, despite the day's privations and the truculence of editors back in Shanghai, the party of journalists had seen something new in China in all the efficient and hard-working government offices. Before Chiang surprised the assembled crowd with his apparently heartfelt patriotic speech, their initial expectations had sunk as they had expected a rather grand, and warm, residence and were surprised to see that he was living in a somewhat unpretentious dwelling far smaller than the nearby *Yamen* where Crow had visited Dr. Sun back in 1912. In addition, Chiang had only the minimum number of security men in his entourage and was smartly turned out in his trademark American-style officer's uniform and peaked cap rather than looking as if he had just returned from muddy maneuvers on the Northern Expedition.

This was also the trip that started Crow's fascination with the character of Madame Chiang, Mei-ling Soong, the youngest daughter of Charlie Soong, who had worked the room when the journalists arrived and had what Crow described as a "charming presence" and a "personality that dominated the room."[5] She served Crow coffee and talked with his wife Helen, who had also tagged along for the ride, about the problems of runs in silk stockings and how to press men's trousers correctly, while complaining that the General usually looked as if he slept in his uniform.

Of course, being besotted with the formidable Madame Chiang was normal at the time and Crow was just one in a long line of foreign admirers of the woman. Ernest Hemingway dubbed her "the Empress of China," while the explorer Sven Hedin called her "refined" – a list of male tributes to Mei-ling would be long indeed. Madame Chiang was more than aware of her ability to seduce Westerners with her good looks, fashion sense, fluent English and long fingernails and used it mercilessly to get good coverage for her husband. Later, during the Second World War, her ability to charm the foreign press became legendary when she undertook barnstorming tours to raise support for China in its fight against Japan, addressed both houses of Congress and street meetings in New York, stayed at the White House and fed the gossip columns with tidbits by bringing her own silk sheets from China. Crow was instantly won over by her charms and after meeting her famously noted, "Madame's body was born in China but her mind was born in America," while constantly describing her as "a woman of striking beauty and charm."[6] However, she was far from universally popular in China and one Chinese language newspaper had declared "If Mei-ling were at the bottom of the Yangtze, then China would suffer less."[7]

Crow never had the good sense to do what President Roosevelt did during Madame Chiang's wartime visit to Washington and insist that a card table be placed between them, to avoid being "vamped." Roosevelt also had the good sense to warn Churchill of Madame's bewitching tactics when the two leaders met with Chiang in Cairo. According to Chiang's biographer Jonathan Fenby, "She [*Madame Chiang*] flew with her husband to meet Churchill and Roosevelt in Cairo. Instead of visiting the pyramids, as Churchill wanted her to do, she walked into the conference chamber, wearing a black satin dress with a yellow chrysanthemum pattern, her skirt slit high up the side. Since her husband spoke no English, she took over on the Chinese side, constantly correcting the interpreters and setting policy as she chain-smoked British cigarettes. At one point, according to the British chief of staff, she aroused a 'rustle' and a 'neighing' from men in the room when she shifted position and showed 'one of the most shapely of legs' through the slit in her skirt."[8] As Crow could testify in 1928, the Mei-ling that Churchill and Roosevelt met later had not changed her style much since that cold day in Nanjing.

The Republic of Soong

Mei-ling had not originally been a political animal. That had been more her sister Ching-ling's role as a fervent republican who had eloped with Sun Yat-sen. However, the Soongs were a political family and the three Soong girls soon emerged as a Chinese version of the Mitford sisters. As the youngest sister, Mei-ling had spent most of the chaotic time when the Soongs and Sun were in exile in Japan; and then when the Soongs returned to the relative safety of Pockmarked Huang's Frenchtown, she was at college in America. There she only vaguely followed Chinese politics in between her classes at Wellesley College near Boston. She, like her sisters, had previously attended Wesleyan College for Women in Georgia where she learnt to speak English with a slight southern accent. She then moved on to the prestigious Wellesley where she briefly adopted the name Olive, studied English literature and enjoyed Arthurian romances while taking up all the usual interests of college-aged girls of pursuing boys, sports (she made the college basketball team) and socializing.[9] She returned to Shanghai in 1917 where her contemporaries were now sipping cocktails, dressing in a Western style and living in a social whirl. She became an instant hit on the party scene and the toast of the regular soirées at the Soong's Avenue Joffre house. She dabbled as a socialite and a "committee woman" but soon tired of this life. Instead, she applied to the YWCA Employment Bureau in Shanghai for a job.

One of her first interviews was with Carl Crow Advertising Inc. The Bureau's director, Lucy Randolph Mason[10] felt he might have a need for a smart, American-educated Chinese girl. Crow considered her application and decided to pass, apparently not realizing who she was at the time. It was only much later at the tea party in Nanjing, when Mei-ling Soong was by then Madame Chiang, that Crow realized who he had turned down. Crow claimed that he had been prepared to take her on but that one of his major clients drastically reduced their budget at the time and he decided temporarily not to add any expenditure to his books. Instead, Mei-ling became whole-heartedly involved in the Child Labour Commission that had been established in Shanghai by the SMC, though the local press largely ignored her contributions. However, she was dedicated to the Commission and was able to force some change partly by using the power of the Soong name with factory owners. According to Crow's observation of her dedication at the time, it appeared as if she was destined to become "the childless mother of all the suffering children of China."[11] She also took to studying the

Chinese classics and improving her knowledge of Chinese culture, which had taken a back seat while she was studying in America.

The patriarch of the family, Charlie Soong – a broad-nosed, thick-lipped Hakka Chinese from Hainan Island who had converted to Christianity, been educated in America, and had then established a Bible-printing business which rapidly amassed a fortune – had died in 1918, aged just 52. Though diagnosed with stomach cancer, rumors of the *real* cause flashed around Shanghai at the time, hinting at dubious deeds including poisoning by his enemies, poisoning by his friends and, according to one biographer of the Soong family, probably a broken heart thanks to Ching-ling's elopement.[12] Mei-ling and her mother moved to a house on Seymour Road (now Shaanxi North Road) where the family influence continued to grow with Ching-ling married to Dr. Sun and another sister, Ai-ling (purportedly the first girl in Shanghai to own a bicycle) married to H. H. Kung, a successful banker as well as another Nationalist supporter. As the saying went, the Soong sisters all married: one for money (Ai-ling), one for power (Mei-ling) and one for China (Ching-ling).

Chiang and Mei-ling had married in 1927 in a manner similar, according to Crow, to "some American girls will marry into the army or the navy or the social register."[13] Chiang had been married before at age 14 in 1901 to a girl five years older than him, Mao Fu-mei, in an arranged ceremony in his home village of Xikou in Zhejiang province.[14] The marriage, which was set up by his mother, made little sense and by 1905 Chiang had started to read anti-Manchu tracts and cut off his queue, and was leaving China to study in Japan. Returning to Shanghai, he acceded to his mother's wishes and the couple had a son.

In 1921 Chiang arranged a divorce from Mao and married Chen "Jennie" Jieru in a Buddhist ceremony. He had started courting Jennie when she was just 13 years old, only four years older than Chiang's son. The new marriage didn't stop him also taking a concubine, a rather fat singsong girl called Yao, and also passing along a dose of gonorrhoea to Jennie. However, at a Christmas party organized by T. V. Soong at Sun Yat-sen's Frenchtown house, Chiang met Mei-ling. He had just divorced his first wife, remarried a second and also taken up a new concubine, but Chiang became obsessed with Mei-ling. He entreated Sun in Guangzhou to help him court her, telling him that he had divorced his village girl wife, and disposed of the concubine, but he omitted news of his marriage to Jennie. Sun promised to raise the issue of a possible matrimony between Chiang and Mei-ling with his wife. Ching-ling reportedly was furious at the very idea.[15]

For a man like Chiang, immensely successful yet still on the cusp of absolute power and isolated through his position, Mei-ling appeared the perfect match. She was beautiful, young and from a good family as well as having impeccable political credentials, wealth and an obvious social conscience. The match was good for both sides as it bolstered Chiang's image as the unifier of China and allowed Mei-ling to really effect social change. The major person to oppose the marriage was Charlie Soong's wife, Ni Kwei-tseng, the matriarch of the Soong clan. Though Charlie was dead, his widow remained a devout Methodist who read the Bible daily and enforced a Sunday visit to church on all her children. Chiang was a Buddhist and Mother Soong insisted he convert. T. V. and his sisters argued with their mother that this was not necessary and anyway what use was a convert if the conversion was merely to please her and not a true embracing of Jesus? A compromise was reached. Chiang, after denying Jennie was his wife and dispatching her to America out of harm's way, agreed to read the Bible daily and try to understand their faith. At first, Mother Soong felt she might have lost out in the deal. However, three years later, Chiang amazed his Buddhist friends by agreeing, apparently of his own free will, to be baptized a Methodist. The marriage used both Christian and Buddhist rites and the new couple set up home in Shanghai with Mei-ling now being known as Madame Chiang.

The connections between Chiang and the Soongs highlighted the interconnectedness of so many worlds and characters in inter-war Shanghai. Chiang was financially supported by Mei-ling's brother T. V. and her brother-in-law H. H. Kung. Chiang had been a protégé and senior lieutenant of her sister's husband Sun Yat-sen; and he was also known to Shanghai's Green Gang leader Du Yuesheng, "Big Eared Du," who was in close contact with the Soongs' original protector in Frenchtown Huang Jinrong. Born in Pudong as a wharf rat, Du had risen up the ranks as a fruit-peddler and then an opium-dealer. He had taken over control of the Green Gang in 1927 after leading the suppression of the Communists in Shanghai and controlled most of the city's prostitution, drugs and labor rackets as well as being an accomplished kidnapper and dabbling in "lifting rocks" (trafficking in boys) and "plucking mulberry leaves" (trafficking in girls). His reach extended into the heart of the International Settlement as well as the more lax environment of the French Concession. By the early 1930s, Du had an estimated 20,000 men at his beck and call, traveled around the city in an armored limousine and lived in the relative safety of Frenchtown surrounded by bodyguards. Though the premier gangster of Shanghai, this didn't stop Du being publicly lauded as a philanthropist and receiving a flattering entry in the local edition of *Who's Who*.

Killing Flies and Cleaning House

Crow observed that Chiang's modern vision of China influenced the streets of Shanghai too. Chinese restaurants added more Western-inspired dishes to their menus, men wore trousers and foreign-style suits more frequently, and the traditional black silk skull cap was increasingly rejected in favor of felt trilby-style hats usually made in Osaka. Crow interviewed his old friend Dr. Wu Ting-fang who had taken exception to these changes in style and had gone so far as to invent a new style of Chinese hat – a hexagonal cap. Only one was ever produced, and despite Dr. Wu's championing it by walking around Shanghai wearing one for a few weeks, it never caught on and he reverted to his silk skullcap. Dr. Wu also tried to design a complete range of silk clothing but it didn't catch on either despite some publicity from Carl.

As he traveled around Shanghai and eastern China, Crow saw signs of the new Chinese style everywhere from the use of knives and forks to Western clothing. He also applauded the changes in women's styles as a move away from many old conventions that had been repressive. Perms, bobs and bang hairstyles appeared, as did lipstick and silk stockings along with a nascent suffragette movement in Shanghai and Guangzhou. He attended the new mass wedding registrations at the KMT-built Shanghai Civic Center and observed the positive effects of the Chiang-inspired New Life Movement that sought to improve hygiene for ordinary Chinese and was taken up enthusiastically in many of the liberated parts of the country. He also noted that corruption was being tackled and reported on a meeting at the Shanghai Club where an English businessman who visited Nanjing to bid for a construction contract had not been asked for a bribe or "commission" – a tale that shocked a largely disbelieving audience who thought that there must be a catch in the contract somewhere.

The New Life Movement had its slightly comical side, which Madame Chiang acknowledged to Crow when she explained the policy to him. The rampant spread of signs urging people not to commit suicide or not to visit brothels were some manifestations of exuberance. Also, there were fly extermination contests in local schools where prizes were awarded to school children who brought the most dead flies to class for the teacher's inspection and counting by official tellers. Crow noted that exterminating China's fly population was probably an impossibility, but he did record with encouragement on a trip to Suzhou at the time that the vendors of ripe red slices of watermelon were now covering their wares with mosquito nets. The small changes, such as the local signs and wire nets over food stalls, were further indications to Crow that in China change always ultimately comes from below – be it school children collecting flies, the anti-gambling patrols that wandered the back streets of Chongqing listening for the tell-tale click of mahjong tiles late at night, or the train boys Crow noted on the Lung-hai railway who voted to forgo their tips for the sake of the Movement. This soon proved problematic as tips were an important part of their salary, so they revised their decision and decided to only forgo accepting tips from foreigners.[16]

Mei-ling's life had become hectic after her marriage to Chiang as she dashed around China following the General from one rebel uprising to another, always carrying a revolver and often ill. She took on a range of jobs: promoting women's rights; preparing to withstand a Japanese invasion; and even trying to reorganize China's Air Defence Force and rid it of the rampant corruption that had reduced it to little more than a financial burden rather than an effective military force. Crow described her approach to sorting out the corruption and nepotism in the Air Defence Force as similar to the way she tackled all the tasks she accepted during this period as "principally a housecleaning job and she took care of it like an efficient housewife."[17]

Crow maintained a relationship with the Soongs throughout his time in Shanghai. Perhaps this relationship clouded his opinions on the new Nanjing government. It was certainly true that many were struggling to build a new China after the success of the Northern Expedition but, alongside all the positive factors Crow noted, it was also the case that China remained largely backward and poverty-stricken. Outbreaks of anti-government rebellion flared in ever-troublesome Jiangxi and Guangdong. Famine remained a constant threatening shadow – an outbreak of bubonic plague appeared while a blizzard of locusts descended on crops and left farmers with nothing to eat but the insects themselves. Typhus and cholera spread across the country; and the destruction in the wake of the Northern Expedition remained, adversely affecting the rail network and slowing supplies of food moving around the country. Opium also remained a major problem as did corrupt officials, and all the time the Green Gang continued to extend its power in Shanghai. At the same time, Crow chose not to highlight the discrepancy in the New Life Movement that generally promoted positive virtues but also dictatorially told people to go to bed early or eat silently. These proscriptions against excess were hard to reconcile with the KMT elites' lavish banquets, not to mention their contacts with drug-dealers like Big Eared Du. Not everything in the garden was rosy but Crow chose to accentuate the positive.

In the late 1930s Crow had tea with the Chiangs again in Chongqing during a period when every day the Japanese were flying bombing raids across China, a major objective being the assassination of Chiang and his wife. Crow noted that over the time he had known them they had suffered terribly – they had built a nation only to see it being devastated by Japanese attacks. He commented a decade later on that sunny spring day in Chongqing in which he drank tea and chatted with the Chiangs while air-raid sirens blasted across the war torn city: "… there was no trace of tragedy in their faces, cheerful, smiling, determined."[18]

15

More Skirmishes and a City in Flux

Floods, Brinkmanship and the Shanghai War of 1932

In 1932 Crow was observing the growing Japanese threat to China with increasing alarm. Tokyo's occupation of Manchuria in September 1931 had led to a nation-wide boycott of Japanese goods and the establishment of Chinese-run societies to extend the boycott in retaliation for Japan's annexation and creation of the puppet Manchukuo state.[1] The boycott was entrenched in Shanghai not just by patriotic fervor but also by the fact that the Green Gang supported and enforced it. Big Eared Du had been elected to the French Concession Council in 1931 and was being referred to as the "Unofficial Mayor of Shanghai," much to the personal annoyance of the long-serving SMC Chairman Stirling Fessenden who had held the title previously. Du himself, despite his illegal lifestyle and opium addiction, was a fervent Nationalist (albeit one who sold large amounts of drugs, murdered people and controlled a vast prostitution ring, among other nefarious activities) who secretly funded Chiang and the KMT. He also helped to finance the growing anti-Japanese struggle and had used his thugs to brutally put down the communist and leftist movement in 1927, a process that had first brought Du and Fessenden into contact and collaboration.

    Times had been hard in China. Severe flooding along the Yangtze in the summer of 1931 killed 140,000 people, submerged 70,000 square miles of land and caused the inevitable flow of new refugees into Shanghai. The Year 1932 started badly too. Tensions began rising early in the year when a group of Japanese Buddhist monks was attacked by some Chinese in Shanghai. Then there was a serious clash in front of a locally-owned factory in the largely Chinese area of Zhabei that left two Japanese wounded, one fatally. Two days later a Japanese mob attacked the factory and set fire to it. Three Chinese policemen who were guarding the premises were injured and one eventually died. Three Japanese were also injured and one of them died too. It later transpired that the Chinese thugs had been hired to attack the monks and that the incident at the factory had been orchestrated by Japan's Military Attaché in Shanghai, Major Tanaka Ryukichi, as a way of diverting attention from Japan's consolidation and extension of power in Manchuria.

The Japanese Admiral Shiozawa immediately presented a series of demands to the real mayor of Greater Shanghai Wu The-chen[2] that required an apology from the mayor, the arrest and punishment of those deemed guilty by the Japanese and payment of damages and hospital bills. Other demands required the mayor to rein in the anti-Japanese societies and crush the boycott. The independently-minded and well-liked Mayor Wu, a distinguished Chinese soldier and political leader who had only been appointed to the post on January 1, 1932, was willing to consider the first set of demands but not the second. According to Crow, by this point the situation had moved along too far for this to be countenanced as politically possible anyway, and the mayor could not have had much influence on the activities of the patriotic movement without permanently undermining his own political career.

The Japanese authorities responded by issuing a notice that, should the mayor of greater Shanghai fail to give a satisfactory reply to the Japanese and not fulfil their demands without delay, the Admiral was determined to take the necessary steps in order to protect Japanese imperial rights and interests. Mayor Wu responded by perfunctorily calling on the anti-Japanese societies to refrain from inflammatory activities (without actually calling for an end to the boycott) and the police temporarily closed some of the societies' premises.

Crow considered that the mayor had done all within his power to comply with the Japanese demands and had served with distinction by allowing both himself and Admiral Shiozawa to save face. The situation appeared to have been calmed. As Crow commented, "Those of us who lived in Shanghai breathed sighs of relief, for it was believed that the crisis had been passed and that our city would be spared another unnecessary war."[3] However, Crow's relief was premature and that night Shiozawa issued another set of demands requiring all Chinese troops near Shanghai to be moved back and all defences in the city to be dismantled. Mayor Wu received the demand at 11.15 p.m. that night, and at a quarter to midnight the Japanese troops began their movements. It would clearly have been impossible for the Chinese authorities to comply with the demands in a mere 30 minutes.[4]

On the evening of January 28 Crow was awakened at exactly midnight by the sound of field guns, trench mortars and machine-guns. As he stumbled out of bed in Connaught Road, he saw Japanese reconnaissance planes flying over his house and disgorging flares to help identify the Chinese positions for the ground forces. The Japanese had moved up 20,000 extra troops by warship to Shanghai. It was clear, to Crow at least, that Admiral Shiozawa had never had any intention of letting the mayor defuse the situation peacefully.

The sporadic fighting continued for around a month, with Chinese troops resisting and the Japanese destroying much Chinese property and also killing many local Chinese residents. As usual, Zhabei bore the brunt of the attack. Crow felt sure that this policy of killing innocent local civilians was part of the Japanese army's strategy to "train and harden the new Japanese marines."[5] It has also been suggested that the Japanese troops in Shanghai were keen to show that they were just as aggressive as their comrades in Manchuria. Crow reported that almost all the caddies at the Kiangwan golf course – then part of the International Recreation Club just north of Shanghai, beyond Hongkew Park on Boone Road[6] – were killed as target practice for the Japanese marines. Crow was personally upset at this as many had been his caddies over the years and he only found out the truth after the parents of the dead caddies met with him to retell the story. The bloody events, the tone of the Japanese commanders and the deliberate battle-hardening of the Japanese troops all further indicated to Crow that Japan's intentions in China were more than simply extending its commercial influence.

The Japanese shelled Zhabei from their ships on the Huang Pu and used aerial bombing – the first time an air raid had been launched against a city that was not technically at war. The Cantonese Nineteenth Route Army engaged the Japanese marines fiercely around Shanghai's North Railway Station. Japanese troops used the safe harbor of the International Settlement to move into Zhabei from one direction while others moved up from Woosung. The SMC, as well as the League of Nations and London, lamentably raised few objections to Japan's use of the Settlement as a staging post for its attacks on Chinese Shanghai.

Eventually the fighting, in what became known as the Shanghai War of 1932,[7] receded in early March after considerable loss of life (11,000 Chinese military casualties, and an equal number of civilian casualties – Crow estimated over 4,000 soldiers killed, 6,080 civilians dead and a further 10,040 missing.[8]) The area north of the International Settlement, all the way to the old fort at Woosung, was the scene of the hardest fighting and Zhabei was all but destroyed.

A quarter of Shanghai's primary schools were also damaged and five colleges were heavily bombed, including Fudan University and the printing presses of the Commercial Press, China's largest publisher. Also lost to the fighting was the Commercial Press's priceless collection of Chinese rare books and ancient manuscripts, a unique collection of Chinese culture housed in the company's Oriental Library.

The government had reached a questionable compromise with the Japanese. The Chinese did withdraw some troops and closed the effectively defunct fort at Woosung. The Japanese objective of ending anti-Japanese sentiment had demonstrably failed and hatred of them by ordinary people had moved to a new intensity, and the city's economy was severely damaged which further frustrated the population. Chiang's government was reduced to bankruptcy as tax receipts declined and the costs of the war and then the reconstruction soared. T. V. Soong, who argued publicly that the government had compromised too much with the Japanese in Shanghai, resigned.[9] To counter criticism of Chiang's handling of the truce with the Japanese, the government chose to accentuate his growing cult of personality by formally conferring the title "Generalissimo" upon him – one he rapidly came to enjoy using.

Crow was amazed at the fact that so few Japanese in China were either killed or assassinated by angry Chinese in the aftermath of the events of 1932.[10] After all, as well as atrocities committed by Japanese troops in and around Shanghai, many had also been instigated by civilian groups imported from Japan who called themselves *Ronin* and urged Tokyo to be more aggressive in its dealings with China. He commented: "To foreign residents of Shanghai it was a constant source of surprise that there were so few of these fatal accidents. I feel sure that under similar conditions in America the life of no Japanese resident would have been safe."[11]

Thumbed Noses and Slapped Faces

Despite the partial end of actual armed clashes between Japanese marines and Chinese troops, the Japanese continued acting in a menacing way, according to Crow. The 1932 Shanghai War, it was alleged, had largely been instigated by the Japanese military to divert attention from their own land-grab in Manchuria. The eventual peace settlement in May was agreed to by Tokyo largely because the puppet Manchukuo state was by then formalized. The land-grab had worked – no foreign power or the League of Nations had taken any action. The Japanese rightly calculated that any attack on Shanghai that threatened the bastions of foreign privilege in the International Settlement and Frenchtown would concern the Great Powers far more than annexations in remote northern China. Eyes stayed fixed on Shanghai while Manchuria was swallowed up whole.

During this uneasy standoff, Crow saw American marines stationed in the Settlement teach the Chinese baseball and British soldiers playing football, while the Japanese continued to perform daily displays of military strength and never tried to interact with the local population. Crow recalled seeing long lines of Japanese armored cars and tanks paraded through the streets of Shanghai on a daily basis, all prominently flying the rising sun flag, while truckloads of Japanese marines would drive slowly along Nanking Road with rifles at the ready covering the side streets along the route. He was woken early on many mornings as the Japanese military insisted on moving armored cars and troops around the city in full war kit to assemble and then dismantle barbed wire entanglements and machine-gun nests. All this was of course inconvenient and provocative to Crow and the foreign community but it was truly terrifying to the Chinese population who were occasionally worried enough to flee the city temporarily. Crow also noted that the Japanese undertook most of these maneuvers in the Hongkou district of the Settlement, which was where most Japanese citizens lived and was also a middle-class Chinese district with pleasant residential streets and thriving commercial areas. As the Japanese stepped up their maneuvers, the area became understandably less popular and real estate prices dropped dramatically.

Interfering with business and property prices was bound to annoy the foreign powers with interests in the Settlement. Fessenden and the SMC asked the Japanese navy to provide notice of when they were going to start marching around disrupting life, especially at night. The Japanese promised to do so but, according to Crow, they rarely did which merely perpetuated the nervousness and uncertainty across the city.

As the situation continued, inevitably it became a normal part of Shanghai's routine. People coped and learned to live with the erratic maneuvers of the Japanese. In his 1937 book, *I Speak for the Chinese*, Crow remembered that as things got back to a sort of normality in the spring numerous amusing incidents occurred that to him demonstrated the total lack of a sense of humor in the Japanese character. He recalled one event where a group of Chinese were enjoying a lazy evening in a cabaret adjacent to the Japanese Naval Landing Party headquarters. Someone eating a pear tossed the core into the street where it accidentally hit a member of the Japanese Naval Patrol. The cabaret was raided but there were over 100 Chinese present and any one of them could have eaten and discarded the offending pear. The Japanese eventually applied the principle of collective guilt and for a month afterwards the Chinese proprietor of the cabaret was required to appear before the Commander of the Japanese Naval

Landing Party to promise repeatedly that he would not sell pears on his premises again and that he was deeply sorry for the incident. The Japanese periodically inspected his venue to ensure that the pear ban remained in effect. Ultimately the interference from the Japanese drove away all the cabaret's business and it was forced to close anyway.

Other incidents added to the bizarre atmosphere in Shanghai. Crow also recalled the case of a small Persian boy who thumbed his nose at the Japanese and was arrested and kept prisoner until his parents turned up to apologize to no less than the Japanese Admiral himself. Word got around that this gesture annoyed the Japanese and soon every boy in Shanghai was thumbing his nose at the troops before running away. Meanwhile, a luckless Chinese soap manufacturer fell foul of the Japanese when he launched a new bar of soap with the image of an open umbrella on the packaging. The Japanese objected, concluding that this was an insult to the Japanese Emperor Hirohito. As Crow reasoned it: "As the rising sun is the national emblem of Japan and as an open umbrella is designed to obscure the rays of the sun, the trade mark could only be construed as a wish that the rays of the sun be obscured. Hence the deadly insult." Of course no story in China was ever quite this simple – as Crow continued, "Piquancy was added to this incident by the fact that the Chinese manufacturer was feloniously copying the trademark of one of my British clients."[12]

However, despite the bizarre moments, many more events were less comic: bumping into a Japanese soldier earned many Chinese imprisonment and torture; schoolchildren and women were subject to random beatings, face-slappings and harassment with the aim always being to show that the Japanese were the real military force in the city. Crow thought ultimately that the campaign by the Japanese was successful "… for we foreigners gave them a wide berth."[13]

As well as the Japanese, Crow also watched the more overt emergence of the city's criminals as Shanghai, at least in the press, became a rival to Chicago with an image of being under the influence of organized crime. In Frenchtown Pockmarked Huang and Big Eared Du were still running the notorious Green Gang and were seemingly untouchable. These characters and other minor ones such as Cassia Ma – the Night Soil Queen, who made a fortune by controlling the collection of night soil (human waste) in Shanghai for shipping up the Yangtze to be sold as fertilizer at a huge profit – became popular public figures and were hardly discreet in much of their activity from extortion to prostitution, kidnapping to drug running. The Green Gang ran brothels, opium dens and gambling parlors in Frenchtown. It was a profitable business. By 1930 Shanghai had more prostitutes per capita than any other city in the world and the Green Gang got a healthy percentage of their earnings.

Crow was concerned that the links between the city's underworld leaders and the Nationalists were growing – like most others he was unaware just how long-standing and deep the links really were. It was common knowledge that Du and Chiang had reached an agreement for the Green Gang to help smash the Communists in Shanghai back in 1927. Now Du, though a criminal, sat on the Frenchtown Council. When the British poet W. H. Auden visited Shanghai in 1937 and met him, the gangster was introduced as the head of the Chinese Red Cross who had converted to Christianity and supported a number of charities. Du maintained his allegiance to the Nationalists and moved his operations to Chongqing during the war, eventually relocating to Hong Kong where he died peacefully a multi-millionaire in 1951.

All the while, Shanghai was changing fast. By 1934 the city was the world's fifth largest conurbation and home to more skyscrapers and cars than any other Asian city and more than the rest of China combined. The city was starting to look different too. The original vogue for British-Empire-styled neoclassical buildings that had lined the Bund when Crow arrived in 1911 was giving way to more American-inspired styles which gave Shanghai a fantastic legacy as an art-deco city almost without an equivalent internationally. Leo Ou-fan Lee argues that the changing skyline in the 1930s represented "a new 'mediation' between the neoclassicism of British imperial power, with its manifest stylistic ties to the (Roman) past, and the ebullient new spirit of American capitalism."[14]

Of the city's population of over three million, 70,000 were foreigners, and the downtown area was reputedly three times as crowded as London's East End. It was also arguably as ethnically mixed as New York. There was an influx of 20,000 Jews between 1931 and 1941 as the European situation once again deteriorated, creating a Jewish ghetto in Hongkou; 25,000 White Russians had turned Avenue Joffre into a Little Moscow; and there was a growing Japanese presence in Hongkou, creating a Little Tokyo. Since as early as 1915, the Japanese had been the largest non-Chinese group in the city. Along with them were the large British and French populations, assorted other Europeans and sizeable numbers of Mexicans, Canadians, Australians and Filipinos as well as, of course, Americans. At the same time Shanghai was witnessing a flowering of a new *avant-garde* Chinese culture of writing and expression, invariably left-leaning, and the city's movie industry was booming.

Crow played a major part in recording these changes to the city in both his writing and in a 1935 project when he produced an illustrated full-color map of the city with the White Russian artist and cartographer V.V. Kovalsky that had been commissioned by the SMC as a guide for tourists. The map was drawn by Kovalsky, while Crow added sidebar comments on the "history, customs and points of interest in this cosmopolitan city of Shanghai."

However, outside the relatively cosseted world of the International Settlement major events were occurring that in hindsight were to change China more permanently. In October 1934, the 41-year-old Mao Zedong set out on his Long March and in January 1935 he was formally installed as Chairman of the Chinese Communist Party. At the same time the Japanese threat to Shanghai, and ultimately all of China, continued to grow.

16

Swallowing Like Whales, Nibbling Like Silkworms

Chair coolies complain about my increasing weight

Up the Yangtze: Dolphins, Alligators and Men Overboard

Since 1911 Crow had traveled extensively and regularly throughout China but it was not until 1935 that he ventured west and travelled to Sichuan, the one part of the country he had not yet seen. He was combining business with pleasure, seeing clients as well as hoping to visit the famous Yangtze Gorges. Crow placed adverts for his clients in local and provincial newspapers across the country and this gave him the necessary excuses to go traveling and rub his "constant itch to explore every part of China."[1] These trips were really exchanges of information, with Crow eager to gain some local flavor while the provincial newspaper owners were eager for news from Shanghai.

As usual with Carl, what should have been a routine journey to Sichuan turned into a more informative trip than he could have hoped for. In the mid-1930s Sichuan was still considered hopelessly remote. The inland treaty port of Yichang[2] in Hubei, the "Gateway of the Gorges," was 1,000 miles from Shanghai while steam navigation went only as far as Chongqing, a further 410 miles up-river from the rapids at Yichang through the famous Three Gorges. Crow traveled by Yangtze River Steamer from Shanghai with Yangtze white dolphins dipping and diving in the boat's wake. The steamer departed in the late afternoon, passing Zhenjiang,[3] a city noted for the quality and the all-pervasive smell of its locally-produced vinegar, in Jiangsu, at the junction of the Grand Canal with the Chang River, and arrived in Nanjing a day later. Though the new rail service was only an overnight journey, Crow considered the standard of hotels in Nanjing so poor he preferred to stay on the steamer. From Nanjing it was a further four-day journey up-river through the commercial center of Wuhu, the tea-producing town of Kiukiang and Anking[4] with its famous wind moving pagoda before arriving at Hankow and the junction of the Yellow and the Yangtze Rivers. Along with the famous white dolphins, Crow also glimpsed the miniature Yangtze alligators; and he also experienced the famously volatile currents, known as *chow chow* waters by the ship captains, north of Anking.[5]

Between Shanghai and Hankow, the Yangtze was broad and deep and in the summer season, when the river was bulging with melting snow waters from Tibet, it was navigable by ocean-going vessels. However, above Hankow the Yangtze changed its nature considerably. The so-called middle Yangtze, between Hankow and Yichang, became narrow, crooked, shallow and far harder to navigate which meant that passengers had to transfer to smaller passenger boats for the remainder of the journey which could only be undertaken during daylight hours as by night the river was simply too treacherous.

Hankow to Yichang was a voyage of 400 miles and took longer than the 600 miles from Shanghai to Hankow. At Yichang the middle Yangtze became the upper Yangtze and a further transfer to an even smaller passenger boat was required to proceed and complete the 410 miles to Chongqing. The small vessels that traversed the Yangtze between Yichang and Chongqing were highly powered in proportion to their size to deal with the swift churning currents and rapids. It was still often the case that no amount of engine power was of use and the boat had to be steered through the Gorges and ominously named spots like the "Little Orphan Channel." This involved towlines being pulled by several hundred Sichuan peasants, or trackers, who dragged the boat by walking along narrow paths cut into the cliff face on either side of the torrent below. The upper Yangtze was at that time known as a "graveyard for ships" and, according to Crow, carried the highest maritime insurance rate in the world. As Crow's ship inched up through the Gorges, he could see the funnels of sunken ships dotting the water to remind passengers of just how unforgiving the Yangtze could be.

Eventually it was this very treacherousness that made Chongqing ideal as the capital of China during the Japanese attack. It was impossible to take an armada of ships further than Yichang without being destroyed by the power of the river or by even basic anti-naval defences; and, indeed, though the Japanese later occupied Yichang, they never managed to advance further up the Yangtze. All in all, this was no small trip even for the much-traveled Crow. He noted that in the time it took to get to Chongqing by steamer he could have sailed to Tokyo, done a week's business and returned to Shanghai or could have traveled to Singapore, Manila or Moscow and back in the same time.

The trip was a long one but not uneventful. As well as admiring the scenery, Crow witnessed two suicide attempts between Shanghai and Nanjing. The first, a middle-aged man, tried to kill himself by jumping overboard after losing heavily at mahjong. He leapt over the side of the ship and was hauled back by the crew before promptly jumping back over the side for a second time only to be rescued again and then tied up at the bottom of the boat for his own safety. The next day a teenage boy leapt overboard when overcome with homesickness. However, as soon as the boy hit the water he changed his mind and with the crew's help scrambled back aboard. His rescuers who had dived in after him gave the lad a good beating for wasting their time and risking their lives.

Sichuan and Preparations for War

When Crow visited in 1935, things in Sichuan had not changed much for decades. The memoirs of the former British Consul General in Chengdu, Sir Meyrick Hewlett, provided a description of the city in 1916 that still applied when Crow arrived 20 years later. Hewlett had noted that sedan chairs were the major form of conveyance and shops opened on to stone-paved streets that in summer were shaded by straw mats hung on bamboo poles to offer some protection against the intense heat.[6] The ancient frontier city was still divided into three parts: the Chinese city, the Manchu city and the Imperial city, with an eight-mile wall around the metropolis. In the city center there was a profusion of flowers, shrubs and trees which earned Chengdu the sobriquet of the "Hibiscus City."

The reality of Sichuan's isolation obviously meant that it was vastly different from Shanghai. Although Sichuan was starting to emerge somewhat – Chiang Kai-shek also visited the province for the first time in early 1935 – it was still seen as one of China's more isolated and backward regions. Crow highlighted the history of rampant warlordism in the region as well as the effects of the opium poppy cultivation that partly fueled the local economy from the major landowners down to the independent boat-owners. On this trip to Sichuan, Crow first noted the importance of opium, known commonly as either "that vile accursed drug" or *Ta Yen* (the "Big Smoke") to the region of Sichuan and neighboring Yunnan. He recalled that one American acquaintance of his, a member of the American Club in Shanghai and a prominent citizen ostensibly engaged in the fur and skins trade, unbeknown to his colleagues, was really engaged in the far more lucrative business of opium-trafficking. Crow had no idea of his friend's real life and, when the man died, he even agreed to be chairman of a committee that drew up a memorial expressing the regret of Shanghai's American community at the passing of a fellow citizen of such apparently flawless character. In 1935 opium still proliferated in Sichuan and had for a long time. G. E. Morrison, Morrison of Peking, had noted in 1894 that, "… from the time I left Hupeh till I reached the boundary of Burma, a distance of 1,700 miles, I never remember to have been out of sight of the poppy."[7]

However, Crow was also amazed at the changes that had been wrought in Sichuan since the new Nationalist government had come to power, at least compared to the newspaper reports of the region he had been reading for many years. Crow arrived in Sichuan to find Chongqing rapidly improving itself and remaking the city from generally being considered one of China's filthiest (rats the size of cats, one visitor noted) to one of broad avenues and modern buildings with a new highway being constructed between Chongqing and Chengdu. This new road would eventually become the final stage of the war-time Burma Road and was designed to eventually connect Chongqing with Rangoon via Kunming. Progress that had not occurred for centuries was now taking place in the space of a few years.

What Crow had walked into was Nationalist China's plan for a final battle with the Japanese, although Chiang did not finally relocate the government there until 1938. The city's natural defences – the swirling Yangtze and its remoteness – meant that Japanese planes taking off from Tokyo could not reach Chongqing without refueling which made it the perfect location for a Chinese army forced to retreat up the Yangtze valley. This fall-back plan had been Chiang Kai-shek's and started soon after he established the National government in Nanjing. Chiang had toured Sichuan slightly earlier than Crow to convince the normally somewhat complacent and remote Sichuanese of their importance in the struggle for a unified and free China. Chiang had won most of the warlords over to the cause, replaced a large portion of the opium crop with cotton and started the process of road-building and civic construction. Also, a new broadcasting station was being built with the power to send out messages across China; new airfields were being finished; and new mills were being established for the manufacture of military uniforms. Crow observed production lines being set up to make bone buttons, shoes, suitcases and a variety of other army supplies. He also saw a converted printing plant capable of manufacturing bank notes being built in anticipation of China's financial center having to be moved from Shanghai to Chongqing. To make sure this could occur smoothly, local banks in Chongqing were all enlarging their bank vaults to store silver and gold shipped from

Shanghai, and a new munitions industry was being created to supply the Chinese army, along with barracks for thousands of troops. Chongqing was turning itself into an alternative political, military and financial capital of China in case the worst scenario became reality.

Crow wrote back to Shanghai that the city was turning itself into a "fortress … a spot to which the government of China can move and feel secure from invasion."[8] Sichuan itself was not a small place – it had a population of 80 million (more than that of Japan at the time) and an area larger than that of France, with enough arable land to feed a population the size of the United States in 1935.

When Crow had completed his business and sightseeing in Sichuan, he returned to Shanghai with reports of the progress being made at the top of the Yangtze. The China Hands in the International Settlement largely dismissed him. Indeed, many of the Chinese intelligentsia and business community in Shanghai also rejected his opinions. The mood at the time was that, rather than preparing for the worst, Chiang was preparing to sell out Shanghai and hand over the whole of northern China and the Yangtze valley to the Japanese without a fight, leaving Chiang with a guaranteed "empire" of his own in western China. It was also rumored that the Japanese had agreed to this in a deal brokered by T. V. Soong and that Soong had received a major cash payment for making the agreement. The logic went that the Japanese would pay large amounts to Soong and Chiang for this deal as it would work out cheaper to pay them now to concede than to fight their way across the country. Crow himself believed that the rumor had been started by Japanese intelligence as part of its campaign to undermine Chiang and Soong and divide China internally. However, this was the story that in 1935 Crow found most China Hands in Shanghai believed.

With Manchuria now a Japanese-controlled area and Tokyo scheming to take over more of China, the Chinese coined the phrase "swallowing like whales, nibbling like silkworms" to describe the policy of establishing pro-Japanese puppet regimes across the country. The Japanese military was in the political ascendancy in Tokyo and was acting largely as an autonomous body in China with little overt political control from back home or even from Hirohito himself. Of course, nobody in Japan worried too much about this as the military forces were delivering victories at relatively low cost. After Manchuria, Japan easily annexed Jehol[9] in a 10-day campaign which gave the Japanese control of 100,000 square miles of Chinese territory. Jehol provided a direct route to Japanese control of Mongolia and Chinese Inner Mongolia as well as launch pads for military campaigns against both Beijing and Tianjin. Beijing was a city largely controlled by the foreign regiments of soldiers stationed there since the Boxer Rebellion in 1900 which comprised British, French, Italian and American soldiers, among others. By this time, Chiang had moved virtually the entire machinery of government from Beijing to Nanjing, though most foreign powers retained their legations and embassies there. Under the Boxer Protocols that had been forced on China by the Great Powers in the wake of the Boxer Rebellion, the Japanese also stationed troops in Beijing and used them on regular maneuvers in the countryside between the city and Japanese-occupied Manchuria. As well as trying to incite clashes with Chinese troops, further small-scale puppet regimes were encouraged such as the regional government of Yin Ju-kong in eastern Hebei, adjoining Jehol, which encompassed around four million people.

These changes in China affected Crow who was still engaged officially in the advertising business, placing advertisements across the country and producing an annual directory of all newspapers published in China. Several of Crow's major clients insisted that advertising be placed only in newspapers in KMT-controlled areas and in only those newspapers that supported the Generalissimo. This presented a major problem as he could not find a single newspaper in northern China that claimed to publicly support either Chiang or the KMT – the Japanese had suppressed all pro-government newspapers. According to Crow's research in 1935, "From Kalgan on the border of Hepei and Mongolia and a gateway of the Great Wall to Tientsin on the Gulf of Pechili there was not a single Chinese newspaper that dared say a friendly word about the government of the country. Nor could they so much as hint at the menace of Japanese aggression of which everyone was so conscious."[10]

The Whiff of Opium and Kidnapped Leaders

Crow himself could see the efforts of the Japanese to extend their control over China and disrupt the advances of the Nationalist government. One major form of sabotage was to introduce narcotics production and sale across China. The Nanjing government had been attempting to deal with the narcotics problem but the Japanese started mass-growing campaigns in Manchuria, forcing farmers to grow opium poppies at pain of losing their land and counteracting the ongoing poppy field reductions in western China. The Japanese army opened factories in Harbin, Dalian, Hankow and Tianjin where raw opium was converted into morphine and heroin. They then imported Korean workers to do the processing and protected the drug dealers who targeted the Chinese troops.[11] Opium-laced cigarettes were sold to impoverished Chinese soldiers at cheap prices while poppy acreage grew rapidly in Manchuria. When Crow himself was traveling back to Shanghai from Beijing in 1935 and was changing trains in Tianjin, he observed the Japanese-organized smuggling operations at first hand:

The station platform was packed but the usual Chinese guards or railway police were not to be seen. Japanese soldiers and police, accompanied by their officers, were everywhere. Alongside the platform were trucks piled high with boxes and bales of merchandise especially packed in small parcels for transportation in the compartments of a passenger train.[12]

Japanese police ejected most Chinese travelers from the train and replaced them with Japanese or Koreans with these small packets; some were frightened civilians press-ganged into drug-running while others were the more motivated *Ronin* gangs who had been causing so much trouble in Shanghai since 1932.[13] Crow, who was traveling with a British friend, was left unmolested by the Japanese police but during the trip one Japanese passenger tried to secrete some of his smuggled contraband in Crow's luggage. By the time their train departed from Tianjin it was entirely packed with new passengers and their small packages of heroin covering "every square inch of the compartment." Crow estimated that his train was now carrying "several hundred thousand dollars worth of Japanese merchandise."[14] Crow later made this Japanese support for the opium trade a subject for specific study, amassing notes and even starting a book that he never got round to publishing.[15] Opium remained a curse across China, fueled by the Japanese as well as gangsters like Du Yuesheng and his Shanghai network. In 1935 Chiang had been appointed head of the Central Opium Suppression Commission. This might have signaled an all-out war on opium production and selling in China if not for the fact that Du, China's major drug runner, was appointed Director of the Opium Suppression Bureau in Shanghai!

All in all, 1935 and 1936 had been good years for Carl Crow Inc. and the Crow family. The agency was prospering and Crow was a well-respected and noted figure in the Shanghai foreign community. By 1935, the foreign population in the International Settlement was about 40,000, of whom 2,000 were Americans, while another 3,400 Americans lived in Frenchtown. He had spent time in Chongqing as well as Sichuan and now he felt hardened to life in China. He commented that in China, "We [*foreigners*] see around us so much poverty and so much obvious physical suffering that we become hardened. If we did not life would be a perpetual burden."[16] Crow at least, unlike many other foreigners enjoying the relative safety and prosperity of life in the International Settlement, realized that he had become somewhat inured to the harsh conditions the majority of Chinese lived under – "It is only when I am taking visitors about and listen to their exclamations of horror and sympathy that I realize how hardened I have become through a quarter of a century of constant contact with distress. Hard-heartedness becomes a measure of self-protection. The wells of pity run dry."[17]

Crow was a little alarmed at the personal and emotional changes he witnessed in himself over his years in China. He commented in *The Chinese Are Like That*, "... I am myself callous to sights which sicken a visitor. I am sure I was not born that way. Indeed, I remember quite distinctly the physical shock I suffered at the sight of the first decapitated head which I saw hanging by its queue from a telegraph pole in Nanking."[18] Despite this, inevitably over time he had become inoculated to the shock and gradually hardly paused to notice what had originally been such cruel sights to his once Griffin eyes.

In a particularly cold December 1936 and January 1937, there occurred the strange incident of the Generalissimo's kidnapping at Xian by the 34-year-old "Young Marshall," really more of a warlord, Chang Hsueh-liang,[19] whose father had been Chang Tso-lin, the "Old Marshall." Though a former drug-addict and playboy, Chang had supported the Generalissimo against rebels in 1929 and 1930 and was rewarded with the title of Vice Commander-in-Chief of all Chinese forces and made a member of the KMT Central Political Council as well as being given a lot of braid and medals to wear. However, he had been ousted from Manchuria in 1931 by the Japanese and suffered a severe loss of prestige, disappearing to Europe for a time. In 1936 he kidnapped Chiang in Xian in a desperate attempt to compel co-operation between the KMT and the Communists to force a united front against Japan. A worrying fortnight for the Chinese people who supported Chiang followed (the kidnappers had shot Chiang's nephew dead during the raid) throughout what became known as the "Xian Incident" as little news of Chiang's whereabouts or condition were reported. The Nationalist government looked to be in dire straights. Zhou En-lai was sent by Mao to collect Chiang for trial by the Communists but this plan through when Stalin decided that the whole thing was a Japanese plot and that the Kremlin wanted the Generalissimo alive to run China in the event of war breaking out. Chiang's kidnapping even excited the normally unexcitable foreign community in Shanghai. Emily Hahn commented that though "We (*foreigners*) acted like ostriches most of the time in the treaty ports ... this development was of such magnitude that even we, the half-wits of the world, paused and looked at each other, and stopped chatting for a little."[20]

During the 1936 Christmas and New Year holiday period, Crow and his wife decided to spend 10 days on a houseboat anchored near the scenic Nine Arch Bridge [*Sanfangse*] in Jiangsu, one of Crow's favorite spots in China and where he once expressed a wish to be buried. One night they were awakened at around midnight by a burst of firecrackers in Suzhou, four miles away. Crow was surprised as in that part of the countryside everyone was normally long asleep by midnight. Eventually a passing peasant solved the mystery for Crow by telling his servants that news had come through that the Generalissimo was released and safe again on his way back to Nanjing. For the next few hours Crow witnessed fireworks exploding across the Yangtze valley. He noted, "Their importance and the quality of the joy to which they gave expression can only be appreciated by those who know the Chinese predilection for going to bed early and staying there until dawn."[21] The foreign community also breathed a sigh of relief at Chiang's release and then "… laughed shrilly, and poured out more cocktails."[22]

The kidnapping of Chiang was partly resolved by the involvement in the hostage negotiations of one of Crow's old acquaintances, Bill Donald. Crow had met Donald in 1911 when he had first arrived in China to cover the Hankow uprising and when Donald was the vastly more experienced *New York Herald* correspondent in China. At the time Crow had been impressed by the Australian's in-depth knowledge of Chinese affairs and listened to him closely. By 1936 Donald had passed through a number of guises in China, including being an adviser to Sun Yat-sen, to the Zhili Clique, to the Young Marshall[23] himself, and latterly to the Generalissimo – he was particularly committed to Madame Chiang. Donald's previous employment by the Young Marshall allowed him to gain access and help negotiate Chiang's safe release along with entreaties in Xian from Zhou En-lai, T. V. Soong and Madame Chiang herself. The final deal revolved around building a framework for a united front against Japanese aggression. It involved the Communists promising to stop propagandizing against the government outside the areas they controlled and accepting Chiang as head of the armed forces, while the Nanjing government promised a monthly stipend in silver dollars as well as supplies of rifles, ammunition and food to the Communists. In reality, neither side ever stuck to the deal.

The kidnapping clearly took a toll on Chiang who was photographed shortly after regaining his freedom. He looked decidedly worn out while Madame Chiang stood by his side looking as radiant and ready to be photographed as ever. Donald and Madame Chiang perhaps realized more than most that the kidnapping had finally made Chiang the symbol of Chinese unity he yearned to be. For his part, the Generalissimo awarded Donald the Order of the Brilliant Jade, Grand Cordon of Blue.

Crow was still happy in Shanghai and the continued prosperity of Carl Crow Inc. meant that he was still putting on weight because of all the good living. This had few disadvantages for Crow, though it did mean that rickshaw pullers could charge him more for the journey as he was heavier. As an inveterate haggler with the pullers over the fare, he was resigned to this – "I know that I am fat and must pay for it."[24] In the summer of 1936 Crow had visited Chongqing for a second time with his wife Helen and a party of friends. After embarking from their boat they hired chairs to get to the top of the city, which is on a steep mountainside. Each member of the party was charged 12 coppers for the journey except Crow whose extra weight meant he was charged 16. For the two weeks Crow was in Chongqing, the rickshaw pullers and sedan chair carriers never once failed to evaluate Crow as heavier than the rest of the party and consequently always charged him more. Crow did start to become a little self-aware of his additional girth – "I am conscious during all the preliminary negotiation that every ounce of my superfluous flesh is being tallied up and taken into consideration."[25]

By the start of 1937 life in Shanghai for many, including the Crows, looked good and prosperous and most were betting that it was likely to remain so. However, China was still China and 30 million people were threatened with famine in Sichuan, Shaanxi and Henan while plague and smallpox outbreaks were reported. The storm clouds were gathering over Shanghai too and were shortly to burst, changing forever life in the International Settlement, China and across the Middle Kingdom for both Chinese and foreigner alike.

17

Final Days in the City of the Dead

The old British merchant told me many stories

Black Saturday and Real War

The last days of old Shanghai found Crow dealing with his advertising agency and writing enthusiastic communiqués to his foreign clients on the continued growth of their businesses in China. In his book *China Takes Her Place*, Crow recalled sitting in his fourth floor Jinkee Road office on Saturday August 14, 1937. With a breeze blowing in from the nearby Bund signaling the end of a recent typhoon, he wrote to his client, the Colgate toothpaste manufacturing company in New Haven, reporting that sales were up despite there being more than 60 brands of locally-made competitor toothpaste on the market, all of which were cheaper than the American brand. While sales had been slower than expected, they were growing. Crow informed Colgate that prosperity was continuing to rise in Shanghai, the recent warlord-induced disruptions in neighboring Jiangsu appeared to have dwindled and the government was as stable as any Chinese government could be expected to be given recent circumstances. Crow wrote quickly as he had to catch the noon mail, but in his report he was bullish and optimistic about business in China, noting the growth in the sale of small cameras as a sign of increased purchasing power – 1936 had been a record year for retail sales.

With hindsight, perhaps Crow should have seen the storm brewing and the end coming. However, he tended to share the general Shanghailander opinion that there was always trouble somewhere in China and to put out of their minds that it would all eventually reach a disastrous climax. He also had personal reasons for feeling a renewed sense of bullishness despite his observations of the previous few years concerning the threat from Japan and the problems facing the government. Apart from the massive celebrations across Shanghai to celebrate the Coronation of King George VI in May 1937, all Crow's major clients were intending to increase their advertising expenditure in China over the remainder of the year, which would mean more commissions and profits for Carl Crow Inc. He was feeling prosperous enough to have started investigating property prices in Qingdao, with a view to possibly owning a summer home in the Shandong seaside resort. By 1937 Qingdao, known as the "Riviera of the Far East," was a relatively wealthy and prosperous town of 450,000 people, thanks to the popularity of its beaches as a holiday destination.

During 1937 Crow had also been working on a book to be called *The Chinese Are Like That*. It was to be another attempt by Crow to win over American public opinion to the cause of China, to highlight the dangers of Japanese militarism, and to try to engender additional respect for China in the US among mainstream readers. Though the book was not published until 1943, it does reflect how enthusiastic Crow was regarding China and Shanghai in 1937. Talking about Japanese militarism and expansionist aims was still, as late as the summer of 1937, unfashionable and considered unhelpful to Western business interests. In January, Crow had been rebuked in a letter from the US Commercial Attaché in Shanghai who asked him to soften his public criticisms of Japan.[1] He drew a distinction between the actions of the Western powers in China such as creating extraterritoriality and treaty ports and what he saw as "the studied system of terrorism"[2] that was practiced by the Japanese in China in the 1930s. Consequently, the Chinese came to hate the Japanese to a far greater extent than other foreign powers meddling in China. In the preface to *The Chinese Are Like That*, Crow declared: "... in the spring of 1937 the country was enjoying the greatest measure of peace and prosperity it had known for a quarter of a century."[3] Perhaps the atmosphere of Shanghai in its last glorious and hedonistic days was best described by the visiting British poets Christopher Isherwood and W. H. Auden in their memoir of their time in the city, *Journey to a War*:

> The tired or lustful businessman will find here everything to gratify his desires. You can buy an electric razor, or a French dinner, or a well-cut

suit. You can dance at the Tower Restaurant on the roof of the Cathay
Hotel, and gossip with Freddy Kaufmann, its charming manager, about the
European aristocracy, or pre-Hitler Berlin. You can attend race meetings,
baseball games, football matches. You can see the latest American films.
If you want girls or boys, you can have them, at all prices, in the bathhouses
and the brothels. If you want opium you can smoke it in the best company,
served on a tray, like afternoon tea. Good wine is difficult in this climate,
but there is whisky and gin to float a fleet of battleships. The jeweller and
the antique dealer await your orders, and their charges will make you
imagine yourself back on Fifth Avenue or in Bond Street. Finally, if you
ever repent, there are churches and chapels of all denominations.[4]

Internationally the situation was not as buoyant as it appeared to Carl in
the International Settlement. By the summer of 1937 the world situation had
started to deteriorate. In Stalin's Moscow, a batch of leading Communists had
undergone show trials accused of participating in a plot supposedly led by
Trotsky to overthrow Stalin's regime. In April the worsening situation in Spain
had erupted into open civil war with the German *Luftwaffe* bombing Guernica
with a massive loss of civilian life, and just a month later the Nazi Condor Legion
Fighter Group arrrived in Spain to assist Franco against the leftist republic.

Signs that the situation was deteriorating across China were growing too.
Conditions for poor Chinese in Shanghai were worsening whatever Crow's
bullish estimates – in 1937 the SMC collected over 20,000 corpses from the
streets of people who had either starved or frozen to death. In early July
Japanese and Chinese troops had clashed on the *Lukouchiao*, or Marco Polo
Bridge, in Beijing, in a Japanese-orchestrated "incident." In Shanghai too there
had been periodic problems – on July 7 Chinese and Japanese soldiers had
clashed once again and additional Japanese gunboats were reportedly sailing
from Japan to Shanghai; the Japanese were skirmishing with Chinese troops
between Beijing and Tianjin; and a couple of Japanese soldiers had been shot
by Chinese militia at the nearby Hongqiao Aerodrome. But none of this disturbed
the atmosphere in Shanghai's clubs and bars where Crow's optimistic mood
was generally echoed by the foreign community. In general the Yangtze valley
had remained calm and, as Crow noted, it was "all that the commercial city of
Shanghai was interested in."[5] It was effectively war in northern China but
many in Shanghai did not appear, or opted not, to notice. As Crow also
commented, he had learnt over the last few years since the Japanese occupation
of Manchuria that "There might be death and destruction all around you but
people still bought food and clothing and toothpaste."[6] All in all, 1937 looked
like being a record year for business and prospects were good for 1938. The

evening before what became known as "Black Saturday" and the Japanese assault on Shanghai, Crow recalled:

> The night before the thing really got serious, nobody in Shanghai thought much about it. I've covered or seen almost all the wars in China since Sun Yat-sen's revolution in 1911. I just thought the thing was a little squabble. I remember I spent an hour or so at my club and nobody even talked much about it.[7]

Crow never finished his report to Colgate. His office windows exploded and the sound of machine-gun fire ripped through the air, followed by the burst of shrapnel from an anti-aircraft gun somewhere nearby. Crow peered out of his shattered window to see mayhem on the streets below with abandoned rickshaws, wheelbarrows and terrified citizens running for cover. Explosions and gunfire continued and the Japanese gunboat *Idzumo*, anchored off the Bund opposite the Cathay Hotel, opened fire on the Chinese sections of the city. (Historically, the *Idzumo* had been Admiral Kamimura's flagship, and Kamimura had been largely responsible for the Japanese victory at the Battle of Tsushima in May 1905 when his fleet of armored cruisers operated semi-independently of Togo's battleships and performed well.) The *Idzumo* gunners got their ranges wrong and bombed Shanghai's crowded streets killing thousands, while the Chinese army returned fire on the *Idzumo*. Saturday August 14 suddenly became very black indeed.

Crow wrote that he became used to the nightly firing and shelling of the Chinese city including Japanese bombing raids on other parts of Shanghai as well as Nanjing launched from Taiwan. Ferocious blazes got out of control as fire-fighting services quickly became overstretched and the Chinese areas of the city rapidly became deserted as the population flocked into the International Settlement. Crow observed that before August 14 was finished "the usually gay city of Shanghai was a city of the dead with more corpses on the streets than coffins could be provided for."[8] The dead were piling up while the Japanese Blue Jackets (naval personnel) were growing bolder and even occupied part of the International Settlement.

According to Crow, the arrival of war in Shanghai dramatically changed the complacency that only a day before had been the norm in the club bar-rooms. It was dangerous for Crow personally as bombs were dropping nearby; "Some of them burst only a hundred yards from my office in Jinkee Road. We knew it was real war then."[9]

After what became known as "Black Saturday," Japan moved significant naval detachments to the city and their base in Hongkou. Crow, along with the rest of Shanghai's residents, wondered what Chiang's response would be. Most foreigners felt that he would not fight back or retaliate, still believing the rumor that he had done a deal with the Japanese in which he had surrendered Northern China and the Yangtze valley in return for a fiefdom in western China and Chongqing for himself. There was a precedent for this belief – when the Japanese navy had attacked Shanghai in 1932, Chiang had largely refrained from responding and remained aloof. It had seemed to many that Chiang was more intent on fighting Chinese warlords and the Communists than the Japanese, though Crow believed that he had rightly made a distinction between Chinese warlords and a major foreign power, the result of which could be to lose China completely. Crow was sympathetic to Chiang's policy of resisting Japanese aggression by playing for time, unifying the country and strengthening the army before fighting back. Looking back in the 1940s from the safety of America, Crow considered that Chiang's strategy had been broadly right in the circumstances.

With hindsight, the signs had been ominous. On August 10 all Japanese citizens had been ordered by Tokyo to leave Hankow, indicating that the Japanese were preparing to move into the Yangtze valley in force. Old China Hands largely derided this analysis as they believed the general wisdom that the Yangtze valley fell under the British sphere of influence and that this would protect it from Japanese incursions. Crow leaned somewhat towards this view, believing that the Japanese were becoming increasingly reckless and "cocky" but were not prepared to take on Great Britain just yet – hence his upbeat assessment to his toothpaste client only days later. Despite this, he rarely had much time for the older imperialist-leaning China Hands as he believed them to be mostly as worthless as missionaries of whom he declared: "I would not condemn them as a whole, for a few are honest and sincere and have accomplished a great deal of good work; but as a class would have been better for everybody including themselves and their children if they had stayed at home."[10] However, it was irrefutable that life was steadily changing for the foreign community in the International Settlement and, as the Japanese grew bolder, a few foreigners were thrown into jail for insulting the Japanese Emperor (by which was meant that they had been rude to a Japanese soldier or sentry at some point) as well as the face-slapping incidents.

On August 12, a 26-ship strong Japanese naval fleet had arrived in Shanghai, prompting Chinese troops to move in closer to the city, but there had still been no fighting. Again the Old China Hands interpreted the navy's arrival as a threat but not a declared intention to invade, repeatedly citing the British pledge to defend the city. Crow believed that the naval maneuvers were mostly designed to weaken Chiang's position in the eyes of the Chinese population and were part of a wider propaganda offensive by Tokyo. On August 13, sporadic firing began between Chinese and Japanese troops, leading to a growing sense of panic among those living north of Suzhou Creek. The start of hostilities on August 14 that blew out the windows of Crow's office was, accidentally, the Generalissimo's response.

His strategy had backfired. The bombs that shattered Crow's windows had been from a Chinese plane and were intended to hit the *Idzumo*. In a catastrophic error, a Nationalist Air Force pilot released his 550-pound bombs too early, missing the Japanese ship and hitting the crowded downtown area at the intersection of Nanking Road and the Bund, one small block from Carl Crow Inc. One landed in front of the Cathay Hotel and another crashed through the roof of the Palace Hotel across the road. The Cathay's clock stopped at 4.27 p.m. Two more bombs fell on bustling Avenue Edward VII.

In another disaster, a Chinese pilot tried to turn for home after suffering damage to his plane. To lighten his load so that he would make it back to Hongqiao aerodrome he tried to drop his bombs on the racecourse. He missed and the bombs landed near the New World Amusement Center on Tibet Road[11] that was then housing thousands of Chinese refugees. Again, many died or suffered appalling injuries. This event was the single largest act of aerial bombing carnage in a civilian area since planes had been invented – 1,740 people killed and 1,873 injured – eclipsing the aerial bombing of civilians that had shocked public opinion at Guernica in Spain earlier in the year. Photos of the carnage were transmitted around the world.

People argued for years about whether this disastrous bombing was the result of pilot error or was a cynical ploy by Chiang to drag the Western powers into the war in China by attacking the foreign-controlled areas of Shanghai.

Nothing But a Suitcase and an Overcoat

Politically events moved swiftly too. China was now at war as a nation, not just a portion of it. The pretence that normal life could continue along the shopping emporiums of the Nanking Road while Manchuria suffered under Japanese annexation was ended. Rapidly the Nationalists and Communists sealed a pact to co-operate against the Japanese for the national good, and warlords that had long held out against Chiang also pledged their allegiance to the anti-Japanese effort. Remote provinces, such as Yunnan, started to train troops while donations from overseas Chinese for the Nationalist effort arrived from San Francisco, New York, Singapore and Manila among the hundreds of other cities where Chinese immigrants lived, read the newspapers and worried about their families at home.

Many people subscribed to Chinese war bonds in one of the many signs of a new sense of unity and heightened patriotism across the country.

With his office a wreck, Crow stayed at home. There he watched Connaught Road swarm with refugees from the Chinese areas of the city marching up from Suzhou Creek past his house, while old friends started to bury their valuables in anticipation of a Japanese takeover of the city. As he lay in bed, he "heard the soft plodding of cotton-shod feet, the murmur of voices and the occasional wail of a baby"[12] as the stream of refugees from the flattened but densely-populated Chinese districts of Zhabei on the opposite side of Suzhou Creek from the Settlement, and Nantao, up-river to the south, continued through the nights. Many left the city altogether and headed for the relative safety of the countryside and their home villages, away from the Japanese army and the roaming *Ronin* looting gangs that were back in action. Another misguided Chinese bomb hit the Sincere department store on Nanking Road and also damaged the Wing On department store (Shanghai's largest) opposite causing many fatalities.

Though the Chinese army fought back – better than many expected – and slowed the Japanese advance noticeably, both Hangzhou and Suzhou eventually fell to the Japanese and Chiang pulled his troops out of Shanghai on November 8. Chiang's plan to retreat to Chongqing now made sense and the government moved en masse from Nanjing to the remote safety of the city at the head of the Yangtze in 1938. Shanghai continued to brace itself against the continual shelling. The Japanese bombing of Zhabei, much of it with planes launched from Taiwan and Korea, had made no distinction between military and civilian targets; indeed there were no garrisons in the area. Shanghai's North Station which had been rebuilt after being destroyed in 1932 was once again shelled. The Japanese plan was to erode resistance rather than hit specific targets, to thoroughly demoralize the Chinese people into believing that resistance was useless and Japanese military power supreme.

Atrocities began to be reported. A train of refugees moving between Shanghai and Hangzhou was machine-gunned. In Nanjing the Japanese army's brutality became openly apparent with looting, indiscriminate execution, rape and torture in what became known as the Nanjing Massacre and marked a new stage in brutality in international warfare. Nanjing has become the most famous site of a massacre on Chinese soil but it was far from the only one. However, it is Nanjing that is most vividly remembered in China for on the night of December 13, 1937 the Battle of Nanjing ended with the retreat of the Chinese forces and heralded a six-week reign of terror that left over 300,000 people killed and over 20,000 women brutally raped.[13]

Predictably, however, the foreigners of the International Settlement doggedly carried on much as before wherever possible. With the situation deteriorating rapidly in Europe and the depression still hanging over America, most did not feel inclined to leave until absolutely necessary. Emily Hahn described the period vividly as did J. G. Ballard in his memoir of his boyhood in Shanghai, *Empire of the Sun*,[14] with a continuing, though increasingly desperate, round of parties and socializing as the tension mounted.

However, a mass exodus was taking place in the wake of Black Saturday. An estimated 350,000 Chinese left the city on steamers up the Yangtze or on foot,[15] and others fled to the hinterlands to find some sanctuary from the Japanese invasion either in Chongqing or with the Communists at their secluded base at Yanan. Foreigners too increasingly began to decide that the game was up. Crow realized that not only was business largely over but that he might be in danger as an obvious and overt critic of Japanese aggression if he remained in the city. He wrote: "Over the tragic weekend, our business had been destroyed and there was nothing left for most of us to do."[16] It was time to go and, as he observed, "No one had to be warned to leave Shanghai!"[17] For Carl Crow, Black Saturday was the end of business, the end of Shanghai, and the end of a quarter of a century living in China:

I saw, after a few days, that it would do no good to stay on … shrapnel from the antiaircraft guns made living there dangerous – some of it hit the roof of my house a few nights before we left. So I came away – after 25 years – with the suit I'm wearing, a suitcase and an overcoat.[18]

18
Business Over:
The Escape from Shanghai

Persona Non Grata

Crow and Helen sadly packed up their belongings and joined some 5,000 other Americans and British as well as thousands more other Europeans and an equal number of Japanese civilians who boarded hastily-arranged evacuation ships in the aftermath of Black Saturday. With foreign business upping stakes and leaving China entirely or looking for a safe haven somewhere else, either further inland or in British-controlled Hong Kong, Shanghai started to grind to a halt. Crow also had good reason to fear what might happen if he remained. It takes a large dose of realistic fear to make someone pack up and leave 25 years of their life and a business they have built from the ground up. However, his anti-Japanese and pro-Chinese sentiments were well known and marked him as an obvious target for Japanese retribution. This was no idle fear. Crow's old colleague, fellow Missourian, friend and sometime business partner J. B. Powell chose to remain and found himself at the top of the Japanese occupying force's list of most wanted foreigners. Powell was regularly intimidated, even having a hand grenade thrown at him and his bodyguard – the bomb was faulty and didn't explode – as he left the American Club one day after lunch.[1] He was shot at twice and reduced to working on the *China Weekly Review* at night for his own safety, with the door guarded by tough Mauser-toting bodyguards from Shandong. Ralph Shaw, who stayed on too, described approaching Powell's office – "It was like entering a citadel."[2]

Eventually Powell was arrested, taken to the notorious Bridge House Jail and tortured. At Bridge House he developed beriberi: his feet swelled up and turned black from infection. He was eventually transferred to hospital by which time he had lost so much weight that the nurses called him "Gandhi." He finally left Shanghai in 1943 on one of only two repatriation ships allowed to leave the city during the war after the initial evacuations in 1937, and had to have both feet amputated during the voyage. He died just two years later.

Crow was widely known for his views too and had been involved in arguments in the American Club as late as July 1937 with fellow members who believed that it would be best if Japan came in and "cleaned up" China; and the Japanese singled out the *Shanghai Evening Post*, which Crow had founded, as particularly irksome to the Japanese military for its militantly pro-US and Nationalist Chinese views.[3] The Japanese intimidated Randall Gould, the *Post's* Editor, who had a bomb planted on the steps of his building, though it did not explode. Crow's original employer, the *China Press* itself, also came in for a lot of attention from the Japanese and the situation became even more hazardous as the pro-Japanese *Shanghai Times* had offices in the same building which were a target of Chiang's secret police chief Dai Li's Nationalist underground movement.

The situation in Shanghai worsened as the Japanese encroachment across China proceeded. Six gunmen raided the *China Press*'s printing works. When a security guard tried to stop them entering, the police became involved and a full-scale gun battle broke out on the street leaving two dead, including a local American bar owner, Tug Wilson, and several more people wounded. Shortly afterwards, in July 1940, Samuel "Sammy" H. Chang, editor of the *Shanghai Evening Post's* Chinese language edition, was shot in the back and killed by an unknown assassin while having lunch at a Nanking Road restaurant. A hired killer from the pro-Japanese puppet government was blamed but never caught. With hindsight, Crow's decision to evacuate himself and his wife may have prolonged his life. As the Sinologist and sociologist H. J. Lethbridge was to write in an introduction to a reprint of Crow's *Handbook for China*, "Strongly pro-Chinese, Crow was *persona non grata* with the Japanese authorities."[4]

Had Crow stayed, he might have shared J. B. Powell's fate, or perhaps arguably worse such as that of a Chinese assistant editor of the *Shun Pao* [*Shanghai News*] whose head was cut off and left on the street in 1940 as a warning to all journalists. Though C. V. Starr later remarked that Crow had been "panicky" in "abandoning" Shanghai, things were obviously becoming bad in the autumn of 1937.[5] A "stray" Japanese bullet killed one journalist, Pembroke Stephens of the London *Daily Telegraph*. There was no doubt the writing was on the wall. Japan's puppet ruler of Shanghai, the Chinese Pètain Wang Ching-wei issued a blacklist of 80 Chinese and seven foreign journalists in Shanghai that it wanted. That Crow's old friend Powell was the major target was not surprising as it was widely known that Chiang Kai-shek had been buying up large quantities of his *Review's* print run throughout the 1930s to have posted abroad at government expense, believing it to be the most effective form of pro-Chinese propaganda. Powell could also expect little support from the dignitaries of the Shanghai business community such as were left in the city as he had been an early advocate of the voluntary renouncing of the major symbol of Great Power privilege, extraterritoriality, and been expelled from the American Chamber of Commerce for his views which at the time, according to Crow, were considered "deranged" by many of the tycoons.

Other close and long-time associates of Crow were also on Wang's list, including Starr and Gould.[6] Also of interest to the Japanese was the South Dakotan broadcaster and journalist Carroll Alcott. Since leaving the *China Press*, he had become well known for his own shows as well as some joint radio commentaries he broadcast with Crow on the American-owned radio station XMHA that had studios at the Shanghai Race Course. Alcott's broadcasts became compulsive listening in 1939 and 1940 as the situation worsened. He purposely avoided repeating the Japanese official line and was forced to travel around town wearing a flak jacket for protection.[7] Others who were at risk included the "big, blond and bluff" Chinese-speaking, horse-loving and relentlessly self-promoting American diplomat turned lawyer Norwood F. Allman,[8] the entire staff of the *Shun Pao* and the vehemently anti-Japanese Woo Kya-tang who, as well as being the managing editor of the *China Press*, was yet another Missouri School of Journalism alumnus. Other journalists found themselves equally harshly treated. James M. Cox, a Reuters correspondent, was murdered at the Japanese police headquarters. *New York Times* correspondent Hallett Abend was seriously beaten in his Broadway Mansions apartment, though he eventually got out of Shanghai alive. By 1943, British and American nationals who had not been forced to leave, assassinated or arrested were interned by the Japanese for the duration.

The exodus of foreigners from Shanghai in the wake of Black Saturday was both chaotic and dangerous. There were simply not enough ships to cater for all those who wanted to leave. Eventually the Dollar Line Steamship company diverted several ships to Shanghai to start shuttling those Americans leaving for the relative safety of Manila, while British ships started transporting British refugees to Hong Kong. Waiting for the Dollar boats was a worrying time for Crow and Helen. People were dying daily in Shanghai and the city was rapidly grinding to a halt with limited supplies of food and a falling population as the Chinese residents continued to flee to the interior. Crow worried about the refugees' future and how they would eat, remembering a trip to a terraced farm in Hubei that was so small it contained room for only 14 stalks of corn yet somehow provided a living and sustenance to a family. Could this level of subsistence maintain even more people? Crow himself had to wait for a week after Black Saturday before eventually managing to secure passage on the third and final American refugee ship bound for the Philippines.

"The Day of the Old China Hand Is Gone"[9]

Packing up after a quarter of a century in Shanghai was a hurried and sad affair. Crow felt that he was deserting his faithful household staff and leaving them to a highly uncertain and certainly deprived future. As the foreign exodus gathered pace, there was little chance of them securing other jobs. He decided the best thing to do would be to give each member of staff a sum of money to try to ameliorate their financial worries for a while at least. His plan was thwarted when he arrived at his bank to withdraw the funds and found that severe restrictions on the amounts that could be taken out had been imposed to prevent capital flight. He could take out little more than a "driblet." It was just enough to cover a month's wages for each member of staff and didn't even stretch to the extra month's severance pay a discharged staff member could normally expect. Crow felt that, as most of the staff had been with them for between eight and 12 years, they deserved better but there was little else he could do. He had rarely needed to go to a bank as the Shanghai system of signing chits for most things and then settling by cheque at the end of the month was common for him; and he rarely needed to carry cash except a little "rickshaw money" as the pullers were the only people who demanded cash for their services. For years Crow had been able to eat lunch or drink at the American or the Shanghai Club, visit his tailor or gamble at mahjong without ever needing to hand over any money. He recalled that this system of chits seemed to work throughout China; in 1935 Crow, Helen and three friends traveled over 1,600 miles up the Yangtze from Shanghai and back covering all fares, food, tips and other incidentals without carrying any cash.

Crow's only alternative was to tell the staff they could take all the household belongings that the couple could not carry back to America – the refugee ships had strict limits on the amount of luggage each passenger could take: one suitcase each. He did not see much point in putting his household items in storage with little likelihood of retrieving them at a later date. His experiences with the Japanese army did not instil confidence that foreigners' property rights would be respected. With food short, goods were not that useful but Crow's long-loyal servant Ching gained possession of "one of the world's most complete collections of safety razors."[10] Crow felt bad about the whole situation but there was nothing to be done. He concluded that, "It was the first time I had felt what it meant to be ashamed of poverty."[11]

The violence continued around the Crows in Shanghai. He saw a Sikh policeman shot dead by a sniper and, from the roof of the American Club, a woman on a balcony opposite shot dead while hanging out washing. The city was alight with numerous fires every night and the sound of the overstretched municipal fire brigade dashing from one blaze to another. However, many other things continued as if all was normal. He attended the wedding of a New York newspaper correspondent; bridge games continued at the Columbia Country Club; and the Shanghai Club continued serving whisky for its much-depleted membership to drown their sorrows in. Crow watched Japanese and Chinese fighter planes dog-fighting in the sky over the city and the sudden bursts of anti-aircraft fire as Japanese bombers flew over Shanghai. It was dangerous to watch; deaths from shrapnel were alarmingly common and falling shrapnel in Connaught Road had seen Crow and his servants run out in their pyjamas with buckets of water to cool the roof. However, like many others, he still stood riveted, watching the deadly fights to the death in the skies over the Settlement with a self-confessed morbid fascination.

Crow claimed that his "heart was strained to breaking point at the sight of the poor Chinese refugees with their pitiful bundles, endlessly walking, escaping from old dangers and miseries, only to encounter new ones – a sad pilgrimage with no certain destination."[12] Crow, with two tickets to travel to Manila, had a destination but his journey was to be no less dangerous.

From Old China Hand to Refugee

The Crows had managed to secure a passage on the Dollar Line's *President Hoover*, which had docked upstream on the Huang Pu after bringing troop reinforcements from Manila and was now a repatriation vessel. The ship was relatively new having been launched in 1930 as a 635-foot luxury trans-Pacific liner sailing from America to the Philippines, down the China Coast and on to Hong Kong. Though the ship was carrying only refugees, this didn't necessarily guarantee its safety. Just before the *President Hoover* sailed, a series of bizarre incidents had raised alarm on the Huang Pu. Ten days before Crow sailed, the American destroyer the *USS Alden* had been moored on the river when sailors aboard noticed a small craft approaching upstream. Bill Wells, a crewman on the *Alden*, noted that something was different about the craft – "There was a boom running its length and a bamboo curtain was draped over it covering both sides from bow to stern. Suddenly, it came about, the sides flew up and without warning machine guns appeared and strafed both sides of the river as it raced back downstream."[13] The Captain of the *Alden* recalled all crew from shore leave and within a couple of hours the ship was underway, headed for the South China Sea and the relative safety of Filipino waters.

The *President Hoover* herself encountered an arguably even stranger incident. On August 20 the ship was moored off the mouth of the Huang Pu at Woosung, having just arrived from Manila. A Chinese plane bombed the ship forcing the captain to send out an SOS that Chinese planes were bombing him. Seven members of the crew and two passengers were injured, one of the crewmen later dying from his wounds. The Chinese government, which immediately assumed full responsibility for this untoward incident, stated that it was an accident, the bomber having mistakenly believed the *President Hoover* to be a Japanese transport carrying troops to Shanghai. The incident naturally alarmed those about to sail, as well as President Roosevelt in Washington who vetoed Admiral Yarnell's attempts to get a division of heavy cruisers into Shanghai to carry out the evacuation. Roosevelt was also worried by the fact that another Chinese pilot had accidentally bombed the British cruiser *HMS Cumberland* while it was approaching Woosung, apparently mistaking the British vessel for a Japanese warship; and yet another American cruiser, the *USS Augusta*, was first bombed by an inexperienced Chinese pilot and then accidentally fired on by a Chinese anti-aircraft installation, killing one crew member. Roosevelt's attitude towards Shanghai was to be further hardened in December 1937 after the sinking of the *USS Panay* by Japanese airplanes on the Yangtze where it had been evacuating Americans from Nanjing and was mistaken for a Chinese ship by the Japanese airforce. August 20 just happened to be Crow's designated evacuation date.

Admiral Harry E. Yarnell was keen to get into Shanghai to take out allied refugees. He knew the port and had served in the US navy's Asiatic Fleet during both the Philippine-American War (1899–1902) and the Boxer Rebellion. Though he had retired, he had been recalled to active duty during the period of emergency prior to the outbreak of the Second World War to serve in the office of the Secretary of the Navy as Special Advisor to the Chinese Military Mission. Now he had to divert all his ships to alternative ports on Roosevelt's direct orders. All this meant that the Crows were extremely lucky to have secured passage on the *President Hoover* as it was the last American refugee ship to leave Shanghai for several years. Probably the only luckier person in Shanghai was the inexperienced pilot who attacked the *President Hoover*. Chiang Kai-shek had a habit of executing officers whose operations didn't go as planned. He initially threatened to execute the guilty pilot but eventually relented.

The near-miss bomb attack on the *President Hoover* must have been on Crow's mind as he boarded the tender on the Bund that was taking the passengers downriver to Woosung. The tenders the Dollar Line had arranged were really converted tug boats which were overcrowded, open to the elements, rather vulnerable to attack and commanded by nervous Chinese pilots. An arrangement had been made with the Chinese army not to start any air attacks while the refugees were on their way downriver but delays occurred. At 9.30 p.m., when Crow should have been settling into his cabin onboard, he was still sitting uncomfortably in an exposed tender on the Huang Pu, watching a squadron of Chinese bombers flying overhead and shrapnel from Japanese anti-aircraft guns bursting all around him. Crow pretended to himself that it was a fireworks display to wish departing friends *bon voyage*. Though shrapnel fell among the passengers on the tender, nobody was injured.

Once onboard the *President Hoover*, Crow could see that his fellow passengers were a mixed bunch, including a group of American tourists caught up in the attack on Shanghai; "enough tap dancers, crooners, and minstrels to put on a complete old-fashioned vaudeville program,"[14] two complete Filipino orchestras, a mixed group of Filipinos from Shanghai ranging from wealthy *mestizos* to elderly *amahs*, millionaire heiresses and black jazz pianists as well as many babies who did a lot of crying. It was indeed a varied bunch of all and sundry caught up in Shanghai that August from the so-called "beachcombers" who were foreigners that bummed jobs where possible in the city, to Mrs Theodore Roosevelt, Jr. and her son Quentin.[15] Crow seemed to know everyone on board, including the Roosevelts, as Quentin was a close friend of a good friend of Crow's, the author Earle Looker who was at the time a speechwriter for FDR. However, their shared misfortunes appeared to create some sort of bond and as Crow described it – "Ours was the democracy and brotherhood of common disaster and Walt Whitman would have loved it."[16]

He was being optimistic: conditions onboard were far from perfect and morale far from high. He noted that children were a major problem, or rather their mothers were. For many of them, this was the first time they had been responsible for their own offspring with no *amahs*, nurses or governesses to rely on – "Even a diaper was a mystery to them"[17] – while there were too few crew members for the number of passengers and those that were working cared little for good service as the mostly penniless refugees were not in a position to tip

218   CARL CROW — A TOUGH OLD CHINA HAND

much worth making an effort for. Crow parodied the whole ghastly situation but it was clearly too much for some people. One wealthy, successful, family man whom Crow knew slightly committed suicide one night by simply jumping overboard.

Eventually the *President Hoover* made it to Manila and deposited its cargo of weary refugees in the Philippines. The ship then sailed on to repeat the exercise although its luck didn't hold and in December 1937 the liner ran aground off Taiwan where it stuck fast on rocks and was eventually salvaged by the Japanese. Carl and Helen managed to transfer to the steamship the *President McKinley* in Manila which was bound for Kobe and then Seattle. Helen shared a stateroom with eight other women while Carl had to bunk down below the waterline. A major problem occurred onboard when it was discovered that all the American passengers on the *McKinley* would be required to pass a cholera examination before the ship could land in Japan. The test involved the provision of a stool sample from each passenger for testing. Unfortunately the ravages of war, cramped conditions and a poor diet since leaving Shanghai meant most passengers were horrendously constipated. It seemed the *McKinley* would not be allowed to dock. According to the *Sandalwood Herald*:

> A demand was created – and Carl produced.
> Unknown to the Japanese authorities they analysed Carl Crow for cholera scores of times – and scores of passengers were grateful for the prowess and generosity of their gallant fellow passenger.
> All save one, who could not find it in her heart to accept this favor from a stranger. She was a nun. It wasn't so much the fact that she felt it would be unfair to Japan – but she knew that she would always have it on her conscience because she could never bring herself to confess the deception. So the boat waited three hours for her to come through.
> In times of war and strife one finds oneself faced with many unusual and difficult situations. Each situation has its hero. We asked Carl how he was able to do this, but he explained that he was an advertising man – and to advertising men such things are simple.
> Carl moves in mysterious ways his wonders to perform.[18]

Back Again in Familiar Very Strange Surroundings

The Crows eventually arrived in Seattle on the *President McKinley* in mid-September 1937 with other refugees from various war zones. When interviewed by the *Seattle Daily Times* after disembarking, Crow looked noticeably older and tired in a photograph taken at the time. He declared, "I don't know what is going to happen to my home and office and furniture. My wife and I are on our way to New York."[19] He told the paper that China was willing to fight for years and suffer heavy casualties and would eventually beat the Japanese. At the forefront of his mind was the terrible plight of the Chinese:

> The worst part of the war to me was not the bombing or the fighting. It was watching the thousands and thousands of coolies who are without food or shelter, trying to find some way of living.[20]

Crow's quarter century sojourn in Shanghai had come to an end and he had been forced to flee from the very forces he had predicted would cause havoc to the city if not checked. When he looked back on the period in his 1940 book *Foreign Devils in the Flowery Kingdom*, he admitted that with hindsight he could see that as he had sailed away from Shanghai an epoch had ended – "Japan, with a calculating eye, surveyed the West and adopted and adapted the things she thought would be useful to her. China changed in more leisurely and less calculating fashion."[21] In another interview given shortly after his arrival in America and travel across country to the eastern seaboard, Crow met the press at the Buzzard's Bay home of *Liberty* magazine publisher Charles Fulton Oursler. He bemoaned the fact that he had caught a cold in Japan on the evacuation voyage – "It makes me so mad, that I, a hater of their [*Japanese*] goods, should catch a cold manufactured in that country!"[22]

His Shanghai days were over and he was never to return to the city. The day of the Old China Hands had passed. While visiting America in 1917, Crow had exaggerated his experiences to appear an experienced China Hand; but by 1937 there was little doubting that he had served his apprenticeship and passed with flying colors. The China Hands who left Shanghai in 1937 had been a product of a particular period in China's history – the period of extraterritoriality, treaty ports and foreign influence – that was now over. Crow likened the Old China Hands after 1937 to aging gold miners in California who hung around in ghost towns long after the money had run out. He remarked that those who now did little but reminisce about the old days and bemoan the future were both mournful and sometimes bitter – "I know how they feel for I am an old China Hand myself."[23]

Once war was declared in China, Crow's posited scenario of a few years earlier that he had laid out in his book *I Speak for the Chinese* became a horrific reality. After leaving, Crow had published the book with the specific aim of providing a wake-up call that "the peace at any price Americans [*were*] virtuously sidestepping present problems for future generations to settle."[24] He had continued to publish articles in the US press arguing the case that America needed to be more aware of the growing Japanese menace. Typical of this was his article, *Have the Japanese Fooled Themselves?* in *Liberty* magazine.[25] He was convinced that ultimately the Japanese had bitten off more than they could chew in China.

Straitened financial circumstances meant that this was a prolific time for Crow who seems to have found the energy to prepare final manuscripts for many books he had been planning in Shanghai. With the success of *Four Hundred Million Customers* raising his profile substantially as an expert commentator on China, he delivered a number of finished books to his publishers, including: *The Chinese Are Like That*; *He Opened the Door of Japan: Townsend Harris and the Story of His Amazing Adventures in Establishing American Relations with the Far East*; *Master Kung: The Story of Confucius*; and *Foreign Devils in the Flowery Kingdom*. All these books were published between 1938 and 1940. The truth was that, after arriving home with one suitcase, the suit he stood up in and an old overcoat, he needed the money as he had little prospect of recovering the assets he had been forced to leave in Shanghai. However, *Four Hundred Million Customers* became a best-seller and the author was in demand for speaking at events across the country, including the 1937 Times Book Fair in New York.

Crow had outlined for the American public the extent of Japan's long-held desire to control China and all Asia, a desire that had been thwarted for a time by a combination of Great Power interests in China and the policies of the Nationalist government. Now, with the European powers occupied with the building conflict in Europe and America remaining stubbornly isolationist, Japan saw geo-political opportunities. Crow forecast that, once Japan had control of China, Asia would fall rapidly in a domino effect:

> Hong Kong could not be securely held without the possession of Singapore, the Dutch East Indies, and the Philippines – and so, if we follow the Japanese justification for conquest and expansion, we find ourselves in a series of vicious consequences to which there can be no logical end. After China, what?[26]

Crow's predicted scenario proved to be horribly correct.

After coming back to America, the Crows settled into a new home at 1 Wolf's Lane, Pelham Manor in New York. Before long Crow decided he liked the town so much he bought a house on Highland Avenue. In his later travelogue, *Meet the South Americans*, Crow claimed he loved the "austere beauty" of this part of the country, the architectural style of many houses and the English-style layout of many towns which often had their own village greens. Pelham Manor was, according to Crow, a town "… full of women who looked like Katherine Hepburn… ."[27] He became interested in the local history and would tell anyone who would listen how beautiful the town was. Indeed he went so far as to suggest to the town council that an "eyesore" should be erected at public expense to allow visitors a comparison that would further enhance the town's beauty.

After spending the best part of a quarter century in the Far East, Crow obviously noticed changes when he returned to America; not least changes in himself. He noted that he had less tolerance of beggars in New York after having become somewhat hardened to their presence in Shanghai. He also found himself somewhat inured against physical suffering, seeing it as largely the way of the world after China. He realized that much of this was a result of spending too long in China and having been around people who were used to deformity or had never known artificial heat such as a modern American house with steam heating. In 1943 as a preface to a book he had mostly completed in the seemingly balmy and prosperous days of early 1937 Shanghai, he wrote that "No one can live in intimate contact with the Chinese without coming to act and think like them, to take on a likeness which is more than superficial. Even the British and American missionaries have not been able to escape this. There is a great deal of the Chinese in every one of them who has lived long in the country."[28]

Crow noted all his renewed impressions of America and wrote "… the American who returns home after some years in the East always feels himself in very strange surroundings."[29] He observed that he had also inadvertently picked up what, in America, were "exotic tastes,"[30] such as curry and chutney, which he claimed to be unable to get cooked properly anywhere in America – "What a princely dish! And what a mockery it is when prepared by cooks in America."[31] Realistically, he may have been a little spoiled in his experiences of curry having been introduced to it by Silas Hardoon who had brought his own curry chef with him from India to Shanghai. In America Crow felt slightly depressed by the tendency to either roast or boil everything.

He also claimed to miss the gossip of the China Coast, the China Hand talk of political tittle-tattle and the American Club chatter about world affairs. He could find little to excite him in arguments about who was going to be state governor or local baseball scores, and one of his first tasks after settling in was to take out a subscription to Powell's *China Weekly Review*. Crow noted that "… when two old China Hands happen to meet at home they are much more likely to talk about the China Golf Championship or the duckpin bowling tournament at the Columbia Country Club."[32] It was a somewhat sad realization to Crow that, while he had been away, friends and family had died, got married, and moved away, and that he had more friends in China than in the whole USA.

However, he noted that this realization also forced him to admit that once this was the case you had become an official Old China Hand. Unable to let go of China he, like many other returned China coast men, joined the Shanghai Tiffin Club in New York which, according to Crow, "... meets at irregular intervals to hear some speaker but what really attracts them is the opportunity to meet together and talk about things that only the Old China Hand understands."[33] The speakers were invariably romanticizing about inter-war Shanghai and included the likes of Henry Luce and Anna Chennault[34] but also featured more radical speakers including Earl Browder, the President of the American Communist Party.

Perhaps most surprising to Crow, the fiercely "hundred percent and proud" American, was that he had absorbed many British ideas and manners during his Shanghai time and prolonged close contact with the English. He claimed that he had not expected or noticed this change in himself and like many other China coast Americans "... never realized it until they returned home and often found that they were mistaken for Englishmen."[35] Despite his affection for the British, Crow found this extremely disconcerting.

The Crows had been forced to leave most of their belongings, property and money in Shanghai when they fled. In the US they found themselves in relative penury, though later Crow was to estimate his earnings in the years between 1938 and 1942 at approximately $8,000 per year. Carl spent a great deal of energy chasing up interest payments and rental incomes to try to make ends meet and many of his personal belongings, including many items in his personal library, did not arrive from Shanghai until late in 1939 while the auction of the property of Carl Crow Inc. was still being finalized. However, these auctions didn't help much with two blackwood long tables and four matching chairs selling for $102.50 at an auction, and it was not until 1941 that Crow found a buyer for his business in Shanghai. Crow continued writing for a variety of publications, including the *Saturday Evening Post*,[36] preparing manuscripts and traveling to promote *Four Hundred Million Customers*. He also addressed the Society for Libraries and visited the Boston Book Fair in 1939, sending letters to the organizers concerning their late payment of his expenses for the trip. He also found time to make several broadcasts for the BBC to be aired in London dealing with the air raids over Chongqing.

Despite this, Crow's time in China was not quite over. He undertook one more trip to the country – an adventurous and potentially dangerous journey this time through the back door of Rangoon and the Burma Road to a Chongqing that was now a besieged wartime capital.

19

Through the Back Door into China

Wooed by both, won by neither

"The Most Interesting Assignment I Have Ever Been Given"

Throughout his quarter century in China, Crow had traveled the length and breadth of the country declaring "an insatiable curiosity"[1] about travel. In the summer of 1939 he returned to a China at war, this time through the back door. The return trip to highlight China's plight had first been mooted in late 1937 when Crow spent some time at the luxurious home of *Liberty* magazine's publisher and editor Charles Fulton Oursler[2] at Buzzard's Bay overlooking Cape Cod. Crow described it as "The most interesting assignment I have ever been given."[3] His brief was to travel along the Burma Road – by then China's major supply route – from Rangoon to the wartime capital of Chongqing. It would be a rough and potentially dangerous journey and Crow could expect trouble not just from Japanese bombers in China but from Shan State bandits, the weather and, not least, the treacherous Burma Road itself.

Oursler was very specific regarding what he should supply during the trip. In an office memo in March 1939 he outlined his desire for 1) a piece stating why Crow was making the journey; 2) a narrative dealing with the trip from Europe to Burma; 3) a narrative dealing with the Rangoon to Chongqing road trip; 4) a descriptive piece on Chongqing, including an interview with Chiang Kai-shek; 5) the story of the mass migration of Chinese to the relative safety of

Carl Crow, around 1940.

Chongqing; 6) a piece on the "Blue Shirt conspiracy" (by which Oursler meant the fascistic-leaning elements in the KMT); 7) some details of the guerrilla struggle in the countryside and; 8) a final summing up, discussing the question of how long China could resist the Japanese onslaught. Crow leapt at the chance to return to China and also hoped that his articles could help shift America's then still resolutely isolationist position on the brewing world war, which was an extremely hot issue already in China. The Madame Chiang-smitten Oursler reminded Crow "Don't forget to lay my heart at the feet of May Ling Soong."[4]

When he visited Chongqing before the war, Crow had considered the city "… generally isolated and remote and half forgotten by the more prosperous coastal provinces. American missionaries and representatives of American oil companies were stationed there, but few other Americans ever visited that part of China."[5] Those that did make the trip invariably traveled along the Yangtze River rather than the Burma Road, as Crow had before.

Crow had seen the first Chinese phase of the Burma Road being built in 1935 in Chongqing. Since then, the Chinese had been frantically extending the Burma Road across Sichuan to the Shan State and the border with Burma to provide a surreptitious entrance through which to supply and restock Chongqing and continue the resistance to the Japanese. As the Japanese armies were quickly overrunning China, the country's eastern seaports, including Shanghai, were occupied or blockaded and so Burma became a major and crucial supply route. The Chinese had calculated that the Japanese would not attack British colonies and so the route through Burma would remain open. They were wrong and Japan did attack British imperial possessions throughout the Far East with Hong Kong, Singapore and Malaya all falling rapidly to the Japanese onslaught. However, the Burma Road linking Kunming with the British-held port of Rangoon remained a vital route for the Chinese for some time.

Crow, and *Liberty* magazine, believed that American support for the war was essential. He had started corresponding with several Congress members who were isolationists to try to change their views and saw his trip to Chongqing – "a Gibraltar-like rock at the confluence of the Yangtse and Kialing rivers"[6] – as reinforcing the wartime-struggle imagery of the city.

As Shanghai was closed to him, Crow had to travel via Europe. When he arrived in London he drove to the English south coast carrying his regulation 44 pounds of luggage (his portable typewriter alone weighed 13 pounds) to meet his Imperial Airways flying boat from Southampton to Burma – a 7,000-mile journey that took six days. The flying boat was an expensive option: passengers travelled down from London to the flying boat's moorings in Southampton. The plane carried 26 passengers on two decks with a sitting room, clubroom and bar onboard, as well as cargo composed mostly of mail heading out to the edges of the British Empire. The plane cruised at 120 knots just 3,000 feet above ground stopping at Aix-en-Provence's Hotel Princess and then moving on to Rome, Alexandria, Basra, Karachi and then Calcutta for refueling and a night's sleep in each before finally arriving in Rangoon. The easy part of the journey was over.

"The Sky Is Covered with Carrion Crows and the Ground Is Carpeted with Priests"[7]

Crow launched his Burma Road journey from Rangoon in May 1939. He stayed a week, found taxis cheap and plentiful but too small for his growing girth, and thought the city would benefit from larger cabs to accommodate those with more bulk.[8] The British had administered Rangoon directly from India until April 1937, after which the country had achieved a degree of separation though a governor still effectively controlled the government. However, the strategic significance of Burma for the defence of the region was not lost on British senior commanders, and from 1937 onwards it was argued that the Commander-in-Chief in India should control forces in Burma. Crow found the Rangoon Brits a stiff bunch compared to those he had known in Shanghai. Rangoon's British community was more overtly colonialist and viewed India as the center of the Empire. Most of the Brits Crow had known in Shanghai were primarily interested in making money. He also saw evidence of Japanese propaganda activity in Rangoon aimed at stoking anti-colonialist sentiment against the British. Crow, like the Chinese and the Brits, feared that Burma would fall to the Japanese – London feared losing yet another territory (and weakening India's position once again), while Chongqing feared losing its essential supply lifeline.

Arriving on May 5, Crow contracted with a Hindu bearer called Doss to assist him on a salary of one rupee and eight annas a day.[9] As Burma followed the Indian system of not providing servants for visitors staying more than a few days, Crow was required to hire a local person to assist him in most things. He quickly became very attached to the short and slight Doss who had a small moustache and prominent sideburns, and dressed in the style of an English gentleman – at least to Crow's eye.

He had packed in a rush and only been allowed a limited amount of luggage on the flying boat from England. This was a problem on two counts – firstly, Rangoon still observed all the sartorial customs and traditions of the British Empire and, secondly, Rangoon was tropical. The Shan State, an area as large as England and Wales combined, would be mountainous and cool in the evenings, while Chongqing would be spring-like and moving quickly towards a high humidity as the furnace-like summer approached. Doss was shocked to see Crow had packed some heavy woolen shirts that were entirely unsuitable for Rangoon. He had some thinner cotton shirts in various colors but Doss, who had previously served many (and better-equipped) colonial Englishmen, advised Crow that colored shirts were just not the done thing. Crow was forced to wear one of several tennis shirts he had brought along which rapidly started to disintegrate through regular washings by his "Mohammedan dhobie or washerman." The flummoxed Doss was equally shocked to find that Crow had brought no dress clothes for the evenings but ensured that his one pair of semi-formal white trousers were kept spotlessly clean. All this led to some confusion. Doss had been expecting a proper gentleman; indeed, Crow was staying at the exclusive Pegu Club in Rangoon where even those dining alone were expected to dress formally for dinner. Due to his assignment, the war and the shortage of guests at the Pegu, the club kindly made an exception to its dress rule and he was able to enjoy several dinners of wieners and sauerkraut in his casual attire.

Doss quickly became indispensable. He took care of Crow's paltry assortment of clothing, and his bed linen, and made him tea and toast in the mornings. He also undertook his shopping requirements in Rangoon's Scott Market, getting discounts Crow could never have negotiated. For more menial jobs such as sweeping the floor or cleaning the bath, Crow had to hire a "sweeper" who was of a lower caste than Doss. Crow adapted to this new caste system though he claimed to be shocked when addressed as "Sahib" by policemen.

His sartorial inelegance became even more problematic when he was invited to luncheon at Government House, the home of the resident British Governor of Burma. This was a great honor which established the invitees' social status beyond any question of doubt, Crow likening Government House's importance in Rangoon to that of Buckingham Palace in London. Crow eventually arrived in a blue flannel coat, white trousers and extra-shiny shoes courtesy of Doss. Government House, the most imposing building in Rangoon at the time, was set in its own immaculately-tended grounds with guards that jumped to attention and saluted as visitors entered.

Carl always relished British pomposity and imperial customs and was delighted when the Governor's aide-de-camp whispered in his ear "You are to sit at his Excellency's right." Pre-dinner drinks of gimlets were served in a reception room lined with tall Sikh soldiers with broadswords at their sides. Several courses ensued, with some conversation that Crow found eminently forgettable, and then coffee and cigars. Crow rather liked the Governor, Sir Archibald Douglas Cochrane, whom he described as looking like a "Scottish bank manager," and who was generally regarded as a man who spent all his waking hours in a pose of stiff formality. Among Rangoon's British community, the Governor was known as "Popeye the Sailor." He had little experience of Asia; had been a British army officer; had enjoyed a brief but undistinguished parliamentary career; was rumored to enjoy a drink when traveling outside Rangoon; and had served for about three years in Burma by the time Crow arrived for lunch. Finally, Crow enjoyed another slice of British pomp when he was driven back to the Pegu in the Governor's car – the only one in Burma without a license plate, simply flying the Union Jack.

While not dining with governors or worrying about his attire, Crow took some time to note the city's architecture and the 2,500-year-old Shwedagon Pagoda. He found the pagoda deserted as the British residents of Rangoon were boycotting it. The Buddhist monks that ran it had decided that no shoes could be worn inside and the Brits had taken this as an insult directed at them. Crow didn't feel insulted, slipped off his shoes and enjoyed the stunning building. He found an excellent local guide who had read *Four Hundred Million Customers* and provided an informative tour in return for Crow autographing his copy.[10]

To Crow, the city was slow-paced and reminiscent of the Manila he had known before the First World War. He, like most foreigners at the time, considered the Burmans generally lacking in industriousness and most unlike the Chinese. However, this was changing slowly as the old trade route into China for tea, silk and jade became reinvigorated as a vital supply line.

Along the Burma Road – "Gosh I'd Give all the Beer and Whisky in Burma for a Drink of Good Water"[11]

The Burma Road in 1939 was a dangerous place. Though it had been an ancient trade route, it had traditionally been little more than a footpath. Without the benefit of earth-moving machinery, 100,000 Chinese laborers required two years, all of 1937 and 1938, to complete a basic 681-mile long road. Even then it was not much more than a rough, one-lane wide track that switched back and forth through the mountains alongside seemingly bottomless ravines where trucks often toppled over and disappeared forever. By 1939 this was China's principal lifeline.

He left Rangoon after securing the necessary passes and permits from a "mysterious" Chinese in Rangoon called Mr. Chi. He traveled by rail to the town of Lashio which was effectively the start of the Burma Road. The train was packed but Crow had his own cushioned seat. However, moving from the seat was problematic as the cars were sealed to prevent Burmese of different castes from mixing. It helped that Crow was the only first-class passenger on the train and so had a compartment designed for six people all to himself. Doss accompanied Crow on the trip as his personal "Pullman porter and redcap," but in seating reserved for lower castes. The train headed from Rangoon to Mandalay and then climbed the mountains to Lashio. In Mandalay the temperature was 110°C, but by the time they reached the heights of Lashio, in one of the Shan States, a chill had set in. Crow's varied collection of shirts was at last proving useful.

More problems with permits and passes detained Crow in Lashio for a few days. The town was cool and in a beautiful setting with dawn mists that were swept away by the sunshine in the early morning. On the morning of May 9, Crow finally got all the paperwork together and went to the Southwestern Transportation Company's station where cars and trucks were made ready for the trip to Kunming. The scene was chaotic as drivers milled around trying to get the all-important chops to travel into China, all carrying new thermos bottles which were presented as gifts from overseas Chinese charities in Singapore.

Lashio was the first, but not the last, bottleneck on the Burma Road which was crowded with trucks loaded with munitions and supplies for Chongqing and hired by the Nationalist government from Greek and Indian contractors. The Burmese insisted that convoys be assembled and then set off together. This caused a rush of demands on the Burmese and Malay mechanics in Lashio who were suddenly all required at once when word came through that another convoy was about to depart. The Malay mechanics were also making the trip, having been hired to work in Kunming's military repair shops.

At noon a convoy of 27 vehicles got underway with Crow, his driver and a mechanic in the last car's front seats and another six mechanics destined for Kunming in the back seat. These mechanics provided Crow with some good stories during the journey as one of them, an expert on batteries apparently, claimed to have been born in Timbuktoo, abducted by pirates, enslaved and sold to a Chinese couple in the Dutch East Indies – all before his tenth birthday!

When Crow traveled up the so-called "Road that broke the Japanese blockade of China" it was still in its early days – especially the first stretch through the Shan States that suffered from flooding and was virtually washed away in the rainy season. A further concern was the numerous reports of Japanese secret agents in the Shan States taking potshots at vehicles heading towards China or blowing up the numerous bridges through the mountainous areas.

Over the course of the war, 1,000 US army engineers and at least 20,000 Chinese laborers worked to finish the nearly 620 miles of road between China and Burma, often in extreme weather and under threat of attack. The American army's General Lewis Pick, who supervised the road's final construction, eventually announced its official opening in January 1945. He called it the toughest job ever given to US army engineers in wartime – although, of course, Crow and countless others had traveled the road previously.

In 1939 the Burma Road's final completion was still over five years away and Crow's car had to edge along paths cut into the side of the mountains, not an easy assignment for an overweight man of 56. There was barely room for two cars to pass, and Crow felt the fear of turning blind corners to be confronted by an oncoming truck and being on the wrong, or the outside, lane of the road, gazing down sheer 500-feet drops into the gorges and valleys below. Several times Crow's car nearly ended up in the bottom of a gorge and was once knocked half off the road by a truck, leaving their back wheels spinning in space and a nervous portly American writer in the back seat. Crow termed the Burma Road the "road of a thousand thrills and a thousand dangers."[12] Despite the excitement, he still kept notes for a diary that he intended to publish eventually.

When accidents did happen, they were invariably fatal. Crow personally saw one truck disappear over the edge of the road ahead of him near Lashio. The drop was so deep and steep that he couldn't see the wreckage below. He noted: "When this happens, you do nothing, for there is nothing you can do. Just drive on and try and forget about it."[13] The Chinese themselves described these always-fatal accidents as "four wheels to heaven." On another occasion Crow was high in the mountains outside the Shan State town of Manshih when his car broke down. Despite some tinkering from the driver, it stubbornly refused to start. As he dozed in the back seat, Crow was suddenly woken by the driver's shouting and forced to leap out as he realized the car was on fire. With no extinguisher or water nearby, there was no immediate way to fight the blaze. Remembering that his portfolio containing all his money, passport and papers, as well as his portable typewriter and spare ribbons, was still in the car, he rushed back to retrieve it all before the car was fully engulfed. The Chinese driver came up with the idea of throwing sand and dirt over the flames, which managed to put the fire out before the petrol tank exploded. Afterwards the engine appeared to be destroyed, but they started cleaning the dirt out in the hope that it might still work – enough to get to the next village at least. Somehow the driver got the vehicle started again and they were able to edge their way to the next rest stop.

Crow had faith in his driver who had been born in Beijing and, after seeing his father killed by the Japanese, had become a taxi driver negotiating the narrow streets and *hutongs* of the capital before being forced to drive army trucks for the Japanese. Eventually the Japanese came to trust him and when his guard was buying some cigarettes on a routine drive out to the country he roared off, stole the truck and delivered it, and its cargo of ammunition, to the Chinese guerrillas. Crow let the man do all the driving while he tried to sleep as much as possible in an attempt to ignore the perilous condition of the road. He knew they were on a safer stretch of highway when the driver started singing to himself, imitating the Chinese opera star Mei Lang-fang, after hours of rigid concentration on the more dangerous parts of the route. He knew the road was getting safer still when the driver switched from Beijing opera to one of the new patriotic songs then becoming popular such as *Build China's New Great Wall* or *Awake, Do Not Be a Slave*.

Eventually they made it from Lashio as far as the Salween River which watered the Shan States. This area was still then largely a blank on most maps, and was the second bottleneck on the Burma Road as traffic was reduced to a single direction and met trucks returning from China piled high with timber for shipment to America. The wait at the Salween was a mixed blessing. It was a good opportunity to get some food and ponder that the Salween flowed from the Tibetan Highlands down through Burma but, less romantically, it also allowed him to look at the bridge he would imminently have to cross – "an ancient suspension structure the cables being supported on stone piers."[14] It had been built for pack-mule trains, not convoys of trucks loaded down with men and munitions. Each vehicle had to cross the bridge alone and at a speed of exactly two miles an hour with an official walking ahead to check the structure wasn't about to collapse. Once across the bridge safely, Crow was traveling across plains that were somewhat less hazardous, though mud pools were an annoyance as the vehicles got bogged down and had to be dug out manually. There was also the additional problem that many wilder Burmese Shan tribes were around such as the colorfully-dressed Lolos, who carried swords, used poisoned arrows and raided the convoys at night.[15] They moved with caution through this area as the Lolos had a fierce reputation in Shanghai, the *China Press* once alarmingly commenting that "Any man who ventures into their territory may expect to depart there from in two sections."[16] To add to their problems, there were the traditional mule-trains that had followed the Burma Road for centuries and were still in operation. The convoys scared them and forced them of the road which angered the mule-train drivers.

At each Burmese town they reached, food supplies looked available until they saw queues of hundreds waiting in line. Crow's car continued onwards to save time but this left the *Liberty* correspondent with a rumbling stomach. As the road became less dangerous, the driver would sing louder which inspired in Crow a sort of confidence that he might actually make the entire journey in one piece despite other cars in the convoy having disastrous accidents with wandering water buffalos and other wildlife at night on the road. Sleep was problematic too. When the convoy did stop, Crow either slept in the car or on several occasions managed to find some shelter in the company of a herd of pigs. He admitted that "I was making myself the slave of silly old customs which decree that a civilized man must sleep under a roof." He gave up the pig-sties and crowded restaurant floors for the relative comfort of the car despite the inconvenience of the steering column.

Back into China and Old Friends

Eventually Crow and his party crossed into China after a brisk wash and a splash from a bottle of eau-de-cologne shared with a mechanic. The first town on the Chinese side of the border was a welcome sight, all the more so when one of the officials who came to greet the convoy turned out to be an old acquaintance from his Shanghai days. This lucky meeting led to a meal of tea, hot chocolate and cakes. However, Crow was still over 600 miles from Kunming and in the no-man's land of bandit country along the border between China and Burma. He felt himself in some danger still until they reached the Chinese-controlled town of Zhefang[17] where Crow bedded down for the night in an old Chinese temple full of ammunition en route to Kunming.

Zhefang was technically in a Shan State that straddled the border and Crow, as the only foreigner in the party, was given the king's bedroom for the night as the regent was away on business. The king had lined his wall with ancient Shan swords as well as old pistols and a rather new looking machine-gun. Crow enjoyed some time in Zhefang, visiting the hot springs, which were a relief after the dust and mud of the last few days. The food was starting to improve too and an old case of long-forgotten German beer was dug up from somewhere in the temple.

By now his car was looking a little worse for wear; it had no mudguards or fenders; a towel held one door closed; and the springs had literally fallen out, making for a bumpy and uncomfortable ride. He had also somehow managed to acquire the mysterious Mr. Chi from Rangoon as a traveling companion, as well as two Chinese doctors heading to Manshih. This seemed fine to Crow after the crowded journey from Lashio until three nurses joined them who, with the driver, made a party of eight.

The party reached Manshih on May 12 complete with two additional Chinese officials who joined their vehicle, so that ten people were crammed into one ancient Chevrolet. The body of the car had been altered with the addition of a bus body put on the chassis to increase the passenger load as well as an extra luggage rack tacked on the back. The once-comfortable seats had been removed and replaced with wooden benches to increase the number of passengers that could be squeezed in. Finally, Crow was one of 14 passengers in the car-bus, including a small boy who jumped aboard. Tiring of the wooden bench, Crow inflated his rubber air-pillow to provide some posterior relief until a particularly deep rut in the road on the way to the next stop at Baoshan[18] caused it to explode. While trying to repair it, his car-bus was hailed over by a Lashio-bound vehicle. Out of the car stepped another old acquaintance – His Excellency Chang Chia-ngau, the Chinese Minister of Communications, who was heading to Rangoon on government business and had heard Crow was also on the Burma Road.

Though it was nice to see an old friend, the Chinese Minister insisted that Crow return to Manshih where a better car would be found for him by a certain Mr. Wang of the Yunnan Highways Bureau. The Chinese Minister's chauffeur in the meantime repaired Crow's deflated air-pillow. Consequently, he spent a second night in the king of Manshih's[19] bed. He ate papayas from the king's garden and peanuts, and drank the regent's supply of tea, while wandering through his (deserted) harem and looking at his collection of radios and imported cars – none of which worked. Crow also got to use the king's magnificent bathtub though it had no plumbing and required water to be brought for a nearby well. As all the king's servants were employed on finishing the Burma Road, he was sadly unable to enjoy a royal bath. However, he duly marveled at the bathtub – "the only one in this part of the world."

As the streets of Manshih were unpaved and were traversed all day by pigs and cows, Crow decided against a walking tour of the town that was anyway renowned for its high rate of malaria and terrible stench. Malaria-ridden beggars lined the streets and, hardened as he was to disease victims in China, he was shocked at their state, commenting: "I am thoroughly frightened of being stung by a mosquito and will be happy to be on the road again and take my chances of being in a car when it topples over a precipice." To make matters worse, Crow had to wash his own clothes. He hung them out to dry only to find the next morning that the site he had chosen was below where a large number of carrion crows roosted at night and defecated repeatedly, forcing him to repeat the washing exercise once again. Things took a turn for the better when he visited a local temple and was presented with an oil painting depicting scenes from the life of the Lord Buddha.

Eventually Mr. Wang of the Yunnan Highways Bureau showed up along with the ever-mysterious Mr. Chi and all of them, along with a driver and Mr. Wang's assistant, started out again through the rice fields surrounding Manshih in a relatively new Ford car with an accompanying truck for their extra gas and baggage. Still, there were 11 people crowded into a vehicle designed for eight. Before he left, Crow managed to bump into yet another old acquaintance working as a radio station operator in Manshih. Crow had known the man when he ran a radio shop on the Bubbling Well Road in Shanghai and had once repaired a radio for him. Like many other Shanghainese, he was now a refugee.

The frequent stops and the delay in Manshih had meant that he had only traveled 500 miles in seven days. All the way along the mountainous and wild road from Manshih to Kunming, Crow started to see thousands of Chinese laborers, many of them refugees from agricultural areas now under Japanese control, working day and night to improve the road and ensure the safe consignment of supplies to Chongqing. They worked long hours carving the road out of the rock with iron hoes they had brought from their rice fields, carrying the broken-down rock and clay in baskets on their shoulders to smooth across the new road's surface, and then stamping it all flat with their bare feet. Crow likened their seemingly ceaseless laboring to ants, a "patient industry" that continued without stopping. Many of the engineers on the project were American-educated Chinese, and for many of the laborers this was the first time they had been commonly referred to as "workers" rather than simply as "coolies." The workers themselves referred to the Burma Road as the "Victory Road."

Crow finally arrived in Kunming where the food and accommodation improved dramatically. He checked into the Hotel du Lac, run by a Frenchman, Monsieur Arsene, who employed Greek porters and Tunkinese boys as staff. Crow delighted in a proper bed and private bathroom. Kunming was full of refugees from Shanghai who had all walked at least part of the way from the coast to Sichuan. He also met half a dozen Americans he knew from Shanghai who were working on various war-related projects for the Chinese government, including setting up radio transmitters and constructing a factory to make fighter planes. Kunming had become a major arms dump with both the munitions coming up the Burma Road from Rangoon and more matériel coming up from Haiphong and Hanoi in French-controlled Indo-China. The city was on full war alert and searchlights constantly roamed the sky at night looking for Japanese bombers.

Crow completed the last leg of his journey from Kunming to Chongqing by plane, hopping a ride with an American crew flying in supplies. The journey had been an arduous one for Crow – though he had traveled widely he was not used to having to take his baths in streams near the road in the company of five-foot-long monitor lizards, to take tea made with muddy water, to share rice with Malay mechanics and to sleep on just a rug by the side of the road. The weather had shifted almost hourly between blazing sun and bone-chilling cold. Despite its dangers, Chongqing was a welcome destination.

Crow's diary of his trip portrayed the Burma Road in 1939 as China's lifeline. It was to an extent, but more than anything else at this time it was symbolic of the isolation and desperate position of the Chongqing government. Crow was seeking to engender greater support for China's plight from the American public. Arguably, the Burma Road was never able to supply Chongqing with anything close to its true needs – at most 18,000 tons of war supplies were delivered via the road in any one month, and often far less. The lesser-known Indo-Chinese Railway delivered the same amount, if not more, every month. The Burma Road's usefulness was also hindered by China's lack of petroleum production facilities, which meant that half the tonnage going into China was made up of fuel for the return journey. Despite these drawbacks, the symbolic importance of the Burma Road as a lifeline and a sign of ongoing Chinese resistance to Japanese domination cannot be underestimated.

Chongqing – China's Wartime Capital

I welcomed the spring in romantic Chungking,
I walked in her beautiful bowers.
In the light of the moon, in the sunshine at noon,
I savored the fragrance of flowers.

(Not to speak of the slush, or the muck and the mush
That covers the streets and the alleys.
Or the reek of the swill, as it sweeps down the hill,
Or the odor of pigs in the valleys.)
General Joe Stilwell, the Chief of Allied Staff in Chongqing – 1943[20]

Crow found Chongqing much changed from the reconstructing city of the new China he had visited in 1935. Despite the city's remoteness, Japanese planes had been able to reach it, bomb it and set fires through dropping incendiaries. Chongqing was covered in a perpetual mist in the winter months that made aerial assaults on the city almost impossible, but Crow arrived in the late spring when the city was bathed in sunshine, and getting hot as Chongqing is one China's "Yangtze furnaces" where temperatures become sweltering, and therefore it was a somewhat easier target. 1939 was to be one of the hottest summers on record. Heavy bombing had started in early May on the north bank of the city and continued for several months while the skies remained clear.

The Japanese bombardment was most effective in the poor, more ramshackle areas of the city where the majority of the 600,000 population of workers and refugees were crammed in and where fire spread most rapidly and the wood buildings tended to collapse more easily. Bomb-damage clearance was taking place and piles of bricks from bombed-out buildings were neatly piled on street corners waiting for their eventual collection and reuse. The city's roads were pitted with large bomb craters. However, despite eight or nine Japanese raids per night in 1939, mass bombing was problematic and Chongqing's remoteness had saved much of the city while electricity and basic sanitation continued to work. Although people had been killed by the Japanese bombs, the city continued to function and Crow noted: "It was quite obvious that Japan was using up a lot of gas and explosives and accomplishing very little toward the winning of the war."[21]

Crow, of course, had experienced aerial bombing in Shanghai and, as was his usual manner, he had tried to rationalize his chances of survival. He believed that if he took reasonable precautions during an air raid he would probably be fine. He did fear low-level machine gun strafing from Japanese fighter planes but thought that, due to the large number of foreign diplomats in Chongqing, this was an unlikely strategy for the Japanese. In typically logical style Crow declared: "So from a statistical analysis of the situation I know that I will be just as safe from death by air raids in Chungking as I would be from death by taxicabs in New York."[22]

Chongqing was doing more than just surviving the Japanese attacks; it was actually becoming the manufacturing and munitions capital of China which fueled the Chinese counter-attack. The city's geographic location meant that large, deep bomb-shelters were relatively easy to construct and hard for the Japanese planes to hit. By the time Crow arrived, hundreds had already been built while thousands more were under construction backed up by an advanced air-raid warning system that gave an hour's notice of approaching bombers.

The industry that was rapidly being re-assembled had largely been broken down and shipped up the Yangtze out of the Japanese-controlled areas of China from as far downriver as Shanghai. By the end of 1938, 2,000 factories had been relocated to Chongqing. Machinery and raw materials – and the workers to operate it all – had been shipped en masse by junk up the river and reassembled. Crow visited one iron mill with 1,000 Shanghainese workers that he knew from the Yangshupu district of Shanghai. He also saw a cotton mill moved in its entirety from Shanghai's Hongkou district with its entire staff and 10,000 spindles all back in place and running again; and 40,000 more spindles were being assembled by the factory managers to increase the production of army uniforms and blankets for the coming winter. As well as existing plants that had been transported to Chongqing, he also visited ingenious new ones including a factory that was making gasoline out of wood oil. He found the Chinese working in Chongqing so proud of what they had achieved that they were more eager to talk about the industrial miracle of the city than the progress of the war.

As workers relocated to Chongqing from all over China, they brought their entire families. Crow visited refugee schools for communities from Shanghai, Tianjin, Guangzhou and Nanjing. School books, and whole science laboratories, as well as teachers, had all accompanied the factories hundreds of miles up the river or overland by foot to recreate their communities afresh. He was amazed at this ingenuity in the face of adversity, noting that in comparison "It was something like moving all the colleges and universities of New England to Albuquerque or Denver."[23]

Still Crow had a job to do in Chongqing – to report on the Nationalist government's fight to repel the Japanese and the KMT's uneasy alliance with the Communists, and to boost support for Chiang's cause in isolationist America. To do this he needed to go straight to the top, to get the story straight from the horse's, or in this case the Generalissimo's, mouth.

20
Tea with Madame Chiang and Whisky with Zhou En-lai

Waiting for a Mystery

Crow checked into the Waichupo Hostel after finding that his preferred Metropole Hotel was full. Mostly visiting diplomats were using the Waichupo and, as Crow arrived, a senior British official was leaving and he bagged the Ambassadorial Suite. He immediately met with his old Missouri News Colony friend Holly Tong who took him on a tour of the city's bomb damage. Tong was now the Vice-Minister of Information and was considered efficient (though a little too deferential to the Chiangs for many peoples' liking). He was a committed Methodist and a member of the United Board for Christian Higher Education in Asia along with Henry Luce, the founder of *Time*.[1] A secretary and typist, Miss May Fay, had been arranged for Crow and she accompanied him to interviews, often at the KMT's Military Council headquarters in the city, where he interviewed several of Chiang Kai-shek's senior generals.

Chiang himself was in town but access to the Generalissimo was hard to get and he had been awarded dictatorial style "emergency powers" by the KMT to secure his position. The whole government apparatus was up and running, including Dai Li's secret police and Chiang's two brothers-in-law. T.V. Soong was running the Foreign Ministry and H. H. Kung was overseeing the government's finances and deputizing for Chiang in the Executive *Yuan*.[2] To complete the relocation of all the old gang, Du Yuesheng was also living in Chongqing. Crow met up with his old friend Bill Donald who was still acting as Chiang's adviser, striding beside the Generalissimo wearing his trademark dark blazer and light flannel trousers. Crow had brought a book offer from Eugene F. Saxton, Crow's friend and the senior editor at his publishers Harper & Brothers in New York,[3] to Donald and another for Madame Chiang. Donald was being heavily courted by a number of publishers as rumors were circulating that he was working on his memoirs.[4] Crow told Donald that he would like to do a personality sketch of the Generalissimo for *Liberty* as he was seen as a man of mystery in America. Donald commented, "He's a good deal of a mystery to me and I've known him for 25 years."[5] Donald, whom Christopher Isherwood described as "a red-faced, serious man with … a large, sensible nose",[6] had by now worked for Chiang for several years, despite speaking no Chinese and claiming to dislike Chinese food.

While waiting to get access to Chiang, Crow carried on interviewing often with his old Shanghai colleague and former *China Press* writer Tillman Durdin who was in Chongqing as the *New York Times* correspondent, along with his popular wife Peggy, who had been born in China the daughter of missionaries. Crow also socialized with the former Shanghai playboy Norman Soong and with assorted other characters in Chongqing at the time, including the French air attaché, the former warlord turned Vice Chairman of the National Military Council Feng Yu-hsiang,[7] a Dr. Green who represented the Rockefeller Foundation and W. R. Peck who was then running the American Embassy in Chongqing.[8] Crow and Tong also stuck up a curious friendship with the self-styled Mr. Ma Ping-ho, an Irishman whose original name was, Crow believed, MacKenzie. He refused to read or speak anything but Chinese, claimed to have studied at Oxford, had taken Chinese citizenship, gave all his money to beggars and was working for Holly Tong.[9] At night Chongqing was relatively quiet except for the odd tea dance for foreign correspondents that he attended. His fellow tea-dancers included Julius Eigner, a 33-year-old German correspondent and the AP correspondent Karl Eskelund.[10] Crow considered that Eigner was generally pro-Nazi but against Hitler's persecution of the Jews; and that he was hoping to find a peaceful job in somewhere remote like the South Seas (Crow supposed he was a spy). All swapped stories, drank at the hastily-established Chungking Club and attended concerts put on by troops of Chinese Boy Scouts who sang medleys of popular tunes, including *The Song of the Guerrillas* and *The Air Raid That Failed.*

Crow spent two hot summer months in Chongqing in 1939, a time of constant air-raids over the city and blackouts. He was forced to flee to a bomb shelter on numerous occasions, where he passed the time listening to the wireless and the radio shows of Lowell Thomas, the pioneering American radio reporter who later followed US troops throughout the Second World War, or killing time with the French delegate from the League of Nations, René Cassin,[11] who was visiting the city. Crow spoke no French, and the Frenchman only a smattering of English; so they were reduced to passing the time until the Japanese bombers turned for home and the all-clear signal sounded by conversing in China coast pidgin English which both men knew. On one occasion, a bomb fell directly on the house next to his hotel killing eight people. He largely laughed off the Japanese attempts to bomb the city into submission in his despatches to *Liberty* though the death toll was high (6,000 to 8,000 dead in May 1939 alone, with a quarter of the city gutted by fire) and charred bodies were piled in the street for collection and burial while the city had no effective anti-aircraft defences in place. Chongqing became the most heavily-bombed city on earth that summer.

As well as visiting Chongqing to assess its wartime mood, Crow was involved in political discussions. The touchiest subject, according to Crow, was communism. He wanted to discuss relations between the Nationalists and the Communists but nobody in Chongqing wanted to talk about it. However, Crow found the three people who would, and could, talk about politics, communism and the war – the Generalissimo, Madame Chiang, and Zhou En-lai.

Tea with Madame Chiang – "Something Akin to Catherine the Great or Queen Victoria"

After hanging around Chongqing for some weeks, Crow finally got to meet the Generalissimo and Madame Chiang on June 13. Holly Tong arranged a tea and hinted to Crow that the meeting was with Madame Chiang but that there was an off chance that the Generalissimo might just drop in out of courtesy.[12] Another useful contact during his stay was his good friend Jimmy Shen,[13] a former *China Press* journalist and Missouri News Colony member who had left Shanghai to work for his old mentor, Tong, and was now the Chief of Liaison with Foreign Correspondents in Chongqing.

Tong was an active presence in Chongqing, helping foreign visitors and doing a variety of tasks which included arranging French lessons for Madame Chiang. He had been Chiang's teacher many years before and had since then tended to fawn over the Generalissimo somewhat and was later to produce a rather hagiographical biography of him. He was known to be devoted to the Chiangs; Emily Hahn described Madame Chiang at this time as the "busiest woman in China" and Tong as her "loyal slave."[14] However, his major role was as the head of the International Department of the Board of Information. It was engaged in various propaganda activities and, along with the National Military Council, also provided journalists, visitors and embassy officials with a regular weekly press conference. In addition to Jimmy Shen, Tong's team included Warren Lee, a former teacher in a Chinese School in Rangoon who was now in charge of the photographic section and Frederick J. Chen, or simply "Freddy," who headed up the business section. The Board of Information was publishing a number of bulletins, special handouts, state documents, speeches by Chiang and a monthly magazine in English, *China at War*.[15]

Tea with Madame Chiang had been arranged for 6 p.m. with just Crow and Tong in attendance. The couple had two residences in Chongqing, a squat villa on the heights of the city that served as the Generalissimo's operational headquarters and another, more remote and private residence, across the Yangtze. It was to this second home that Crow was summoned. At 5.45, news came through that a squadron of Japanese bombers was heading towards Chongqing from Hankow and Crow had visions of spending the night in an air raid shelter with China's two most powerful figures. Chiang was well guarded, though the steel-helmeted sentries remained outside the residence. He was in luck, and both Madame and the Generalissimo greeted him and Tong as they entered. Madame appeared first with the Generalissimo following several minutes later as was the couple's custom.[16]

Crow had been led to believe that in the intervening years since he had last met her – 12 years previously – she had morphed into something akin to Catherine the Great or Queen Victoria, but he recorded in his diary that he found her nothing but charming, gracious and without grandeur.[17] Certainly, since August 1937 she had emerged as the Nationalist's most effective spokesperson around the world. As before, Crow noted her beauty and dress sense as she wore a simple blue gown while the Generalissimo remained as ever in his plain military uniform. Even during the trials and tribulations of war, Madame Chiang retained what the writer Edgar Mowrer referred to quite bluntly as her "sex appeal." Despite this, Crow was fascinated with the Generalissimo who was trying to lead China in a war that, after a series of Japanese atrocities, was increasingly linked in his mind to the very survival of the Chinese race.

Madame was inevitably more than just the Generalissimo's wife in Chongqing. As well as her French lessons and continuing commitment to the New Life Movement and refugee problems, she had also taken on the task of running the Aeronautical Commission that was charged with reorganizing China's air force – W. H. Donald described her as "an elf with a dynamo." The Chinese air force was lacking planes and had few trained pilots. Italian advisers had largely trained those that could get airborne in the 1930s and a new crop of fliers was desperately needed. In 1937 Chiang had found that only one-fifth of the 500 planes in his air force were fully operational. Madame Chiang hired the former US fighter pilot Claire Lee Chennault, a Texan, to run the force after finding that no Chinese personnel had been trained in organizing bomber missions. Chennault described Madame Chiang in Chongqing as "… looking twenty years younger than I expected and speaking English in a rich Southern drawl."[18] Madame, like the Generalissimo who had hired a steady stream of foreign advisers, understood that if China's military was to match the Japanese it would need both foreign advice and support. She therefore made sure the Generalissimo saw as many influential foreigners in Chongqing as possible while she was about to embark on her famous fund-raising tours to America where her brother T. V. was to become Chiang's envoy in Washington.[19]

The Generalissimo appeared eager to talk with Crow, either actually remembering him from before the war, or having been well briefed by Tong that Crow was on an assignment. *Liberty* magazine had become one of a number of mouthpieces for the couple's views in America since Oursler had interviewed them in Nanjing in 1935 and been immensely impressed with the New Life Movement, and his adoration of them only grew once the war started. Chiang told Crow he appreciated his being a friend of China.

Crow asked Chiang a series of questions he believed were on the minds of his readers back in America. Would a post-war KMT-run China welcome back foreigners, asked Crow? Yes to foreign capital, no to technical help was Chiang's reply. China's industrial development would take a century, Chiang added. Would Shanghai be made a free port after the war, asked Crow? Chiang began to reply but Madame butted in asking why exactly China would take this step and hand back control of China's largest commercial city to foreigners? Chiang dodged the question and said he would consider it. Chiang then made his excuses and left – Crow had got his undivided attention for 15 minutes, better than most managed as few got longer and most assumed that Chiang had other business to deal with. Tong let Crow know that the unfortunate Generalissimo had been a martyr to the affliction of constipation since his youth.

Crow had carried with him from America personal letters to Madame Chiang from Eleanor Roosevelt, Oursler and other close acquaintances of hers,

including the book contract offer and some publicity in *Harper's* magazine. Mei-
ling served tea and marmalade that was reputedly made by her from fruits in
the residence's garden, and, in defiance of the New Life Movement's edicts,
smoked cigarettes. Crow interviewed her about her work with orphans, relief
work and the New Life Movement. He, rather elaborately, likened her patriotic
zeal to that of Joan of Arc – "I think she would seize a sword or more probably
a machine gun and go out and attack the Japanese invaders single handed if she
thought it would do any good. When peace comes I feel sorry for the first
Japanese diplomats who have to meet her!"[20] Crow saw Madame and the
Generalissimo as a perfect combination – he a traditional Chinese thinker but
with a penchant for Sherlock Holmes novels and morning *taiqi* exercises while
she was all too American in her rationalizations – "Neither is complete without
the other," he commented in his dairies after the meeting.

Whisky with Zhou – "The Most Interesting Man in Chungking"[21]

Zhou En-lai was living in Chongqing acting as a liaison between the Communists
and the Nationalists. In reality, of course, Zhou was a senior Communist figure,
one of the few Communist leaders to have been abroad and generally considered
an urbane man, being descended from a line of Tianjin mandarins. His offices
and residence were in Red Rock Village beside the Jialing River and they housed
the Communist's Chongqing operations and were stuffed full of rather
dilapidated furniture.

Zhou had already been the Communist's Political Officer in Whampoa
(where he had first met Chiang) and the leading Communist organizer in
Shanghai. During the 1936 Xian Incident, it had been Zhou who had initially
encouraged the Young Marshall to pursue a campaign for unity, though not to
go so far as to kidnap Chiang. However, Crow had to wonder just how cordial
relations between Chiang and Zhou could be, given that in 1927 Chiang had
tried to kill Zhou in Shanghai during his suppression of the Communists and
that in 1936 Zhou had traveled from the Communist headquarters in Yanan
across Shaanxi province by mule to bring Chiang back to Mao so he could be
put on trial for crimes against the Chinese people? The plan was only foiled
after Stalin decided he preferred Chiang alive and Mao, granting the Kremlin's
wish, ordered Zhou to help negotiate the Generalissimo's release – a task he
undertook after Madame Chiang and Bill Donald had met him in Xian and also
asked him to intercede.

In Crow's view, Zhou was the official ambassador of the Communists to
Chongqing. This was generally true as Zhou spent most of the Second World

War in Chongqing representing the Communist Party as its spokesman and working to resolve the endless spats and conflicts with the KMT. Zhou took the time to meet as many foreign journalists as possible to put forward the Communist viewpoint, invariably over glasses of Scotch or bourbon rather than tea. Zhou's legendary cosmopolitan qualities and ease among foreigners charmed many visitors, including Ernest Hemingway and T. H. White, the American novelist, who at the time was working as *Time* magazine's China correspondent.

Crow likewise found Zhou fascinating, describing him in his dairy as "… the most interesting man I have met in Chungking, not even excepting the Generalissimo,"[22] and living modestly in an obscure back street of the war-torn city without any personal security, flags or flunkies asking to inspect documents. Crow wasn't overly surprised at this as he was used to the low level of ostentation that surrounded Chinese leaders. At tea with the Generalissimo and Madame Chiang only days previously, there had only been a couple of guards and a servant who took his name and ushered him into their drawing room. While Crow had noted that the Chiang household was far from luxurious, by comparison Zhou's was positively austere.

When Crow arrived he found the Communist leader agitated after a Japanese bomb had caused some damage in one corner of the house. Zhou laughed off Crow's concerns commenting, "… the Japanese aviators were still too busy dropping bombs on women and children to bother about killing soldiers."[23] The Communist was lean and gaunt and was dressed in a basic uniform with no insignia of rank attached. Crow asked after Zhou's safety but the Communist leader again laughed and told him he never went to the bomb shelter. This was Crow's first interview with a noted communist and he had intended it to be a formal affair. He was wary of Communists and knew that he was there partly to confirm his dislike of Marxism. He had written out all his questions and wanted desperately to control the conversation and, if possible, trap Zhou in the contradictions of communist theory – "I considered my interview with General Chao [*as Crow referred to Zhou*] so important that I prepared for it as carefully as an undergraduate facing an examination at the end of a school term."[24] From the start Zhou wrong-footed Crow on the question of land redistribution. Crow realized quickly that he had made too many comparisons between the communism espoused by Lenin and Stalin in Russia and in China where the party was composed largely of peasants rather than industrial workers.

The full text of Crow's interview with Zhou was never published but a version of it that he prepared for publication –*The Puzzle of Chinese Communism* – remains in his archive.[25] Crow and Zhou talked for two hours in English – Crow noting that Zhou did not need an interpreter even though many Chinese officials who spoke English preferred to answer questions through an interpreter to avoid any misquotations. At the time, Zhou was one of the younger leaders of the Communist Party in China and was already identified, by Crow at least, as "… one of the half dozen men who might conceivably take the place of Generalissimo Chiang Kai-Shek if the Japanese should succeed in their threat to capture and behead the Chinese leader."[26]

Crow also believed Zhou's emphatic rebuttal of any Soviet influence in the affairs and policies of the Communist Party. As far as Crow could see, all aid to the Communists and the Nationalists was coming into China over the Burma Road and nothing was coming from the Soviet Union via the old Silk Road in Turkestan that was closer to the Communist-controlled areas. Crow believed the days of high-level Soviet influence in the 1920s and early 1930s with the likes of Borodin and Mahendranath Roy[27] were gone. He came away from his interview with Zhou far more impressed than he had expected to be. A lot of other American and Western reporters met with and interviewed Zhou in Chongqing. Jonathan Mirsky, in his essay *Getting the Story in China*, claims that Zhou "… charmed foreign reporters, even though they were occasionally shocked by his lies."[28] Crow never actually believed that Zhou lied to him but he did admit that he had not expected to be so charmed by a Communist leader despite, "… interrupting him and cross-questioning him as rudely as a prosecuting attorney who is trying to pin the guilt on a defendant."[29]

Crow moved from an in-depth discussion of land issues to the role of foreign capital in a Communist China. Zhou unsurprisingly advocated giving the land to the people who farmed it; and he thought the continuing role of foreign capital would be essential in a similar manner to the early years of the Soviet Union. The two also discussed the chances of democracy in a Communist China. Zhou believed they were good and that China was essentially a democratic country. Crow finished up the interview with what he believed would be the most problematic issue for his American readers:

> According to Chinese standards of courtesy and politeness, my question was so abrupt and pointed as to verge on rudeness. I knew this at the time, but I couldn't help asking it anymore than I could help sneezing once the sneeze had started … After I had asked him all of the questions I could think of and he had answered them all carefully and frankly, I impolitely blurted out: "And now will you tell me why you call yourself a Communist?"[30]

Crow interpreted Zhou's answer for himself in terms of believing that the Chinese Communists had adopted the term "Communist" as the one that seemed to best fit but it was not a direct imitation of what had been seen in Russia.

He thought that the uneasy anti-Japanese alliance between the Communists and the KMT that had held for a couple of years by the time he sat down for a whisky or two with Zhou was becoming a strained relationship in which distrust was becoming the main theme. Disputes between Nationalist generals and Communist commanders were growing, with a rising series of charges and counter-charges. The KMT side claimed that the Communists were actively recruiting among their ranks, and the Communist side argued that the KMT was disbanding Communist units and not supplying them to ultimately weaken them. Crow felt that all of this was unfortunate as it detracted from the overall united front to beat the Japanese.

Indeed, Crow's belief in the need and desirability of the KMT-Communist alliance to defeat Japan may have clouded his view of Zhou. At the time, with America becoming increasingly sucked into the conflict in Asia and Europe, a greater number of American reporters in China chose to be less critical of both the Communists and the KMT for the sake of the united front. Symbolic of this was Chiang's high profile in the American media, thanks not least to the efforts and looks of his wife and also the support of Henry Luce and *Time* that repeatedly featured the Generalissimo and Madame Chiang on the cover and named them "Man and Wife of the Year" in 1937. Veteran journalist Harrison Salisbury of *The New York Times* summed up the attitude of American reporters to China during the war years: "Just as the puritan image of the Communists stemming out of [*Edgar Snow's*] *Red Star Over China* influenced many, so the image of the Nationalists given by Luce, and his journals, *Time* and *Life*, influenced many Americans as well."[31]

When Crow questioned Zhou on the subject of KMT-Communist relations after the war, Zhou stressed that the two would not revert to civil war for control of the country but would work together for a quick reconstruction of China. Crow quoted Zhou as saying "In this work [*reconstruction*] we need the KMT and the KMT needs us. The development of a strong and independent China is of much more importance than any party differences."[32]

Crow was not inexperienced at propaganda himself. Though always wary of communism, he invariably underestimated the Chinese Communists' chances of success. After the rise of bolshevism, he had argued that it was not something that would catch on in China but that Soviet propaganda had to be countered; while later, when Sun Yat-sen and Chiang had both seemingly toyed with communism, he had dismissed their flirtations as expediency. Crow was convinced that Sun was drawn more to the utopian nature of communism rather than its practices, while Chiang admired the new Soviet state's ability to organize an independent army and government structure rather than its political ideals. Both Nationalist leaders saw parallels between the changes in Russia and what had occurred in China in 1911. Likewise in the late 1930s and on through the war, Crow still believed that communism posed no major threat in China and would never gain widespread popularity. Later, after an extended trip to South America in 1941, he likened the Chinese view of communism to that of the Chilean working class he had come into contact with: "Poverty has made him [*the Chinese or Chilean working man*] a philosopher and he is more inclined to laugh at his superiors than to revile them and join the Communist party."[33] The history of both countries turned out somewhat differently from what Crow had envisaged.

While he believed that the ordinary Chinese man or woman would ultimately reject communism he did admit, in the notes of his meeting with Zhou, that he was playing a crucial part in China's defence against the Japanese – "... it is equally certain that he [*Zhou*] will play an important part in the building of a new China which will emerge from the wreckage of the war."[34] Crow could not know how right he was in this respect.

At the same time, he was most eager to alert American public opinion to the threat from Japanese militarism which he felt was much more real and immediate than communism. In this sense, Crow was no archetypal "cold warrior." Though he continuously and relentlessly criticized Japanese policies and intentions towards the rest of Asia, at the same time he was not a racist in the way many critics of Japan at the time were. Indeed, as in his book written largely in 1937, *The Chinese Are Like That*, Crow was critical of the animosity and hostility being shown at the time to Japanese immigrants to America and also later criticized the establishment of internment camps for Japanese-Americans.

With hindsight, it can be seen that Crow misread the ambitions and abilities of the Chinese Communists. He was looking to build support for the Chinese resistance in America and he tended to gloss over the strains in the KMT-Communist alliance. He also glossed over the ideological Marxist-Leninist element of the Communist Party and, after meeting with Zhou, declared:

> There is nothing for the world to be afraid of in Chinese communism. Last year I asked about two hundred prominent Americans for advice as to what party I should join, and in an article in *Liberty* told about the replies I received. They were not very convincing; that is to say that at the end of the inquiry I was in just as much doubt as I was at the beginning as to which American party I should support. But if General Chao should organize a political party in America, I am inclined to think that I should join it.[35]

Clearly Crow was writing as a propagandist seeking to build American support for China. However, his seemingly contradictory positions of being historically anti-Communist and pro-Chiang and yet sympathetic towards Zhou after meeting him, are problematic. He probably naturally fell into what became the "China lobby", which saw the Generalissimo as a viable force to counter communism, and supported him despite becoming increasingly aware of his shortcomings. Indeed Crow did little to reveal them during the war – he cannot fail to have noticed that, despite the war, corruption among senior KMT officials remained rife. His friend Bill Donald eventually parted company with the Chiangs over the issue of their and the Soong family's corruption.

His work finished, Crow headed home. His old friend J. B. Powell got in contact and asked him to visit and investigate the situation in Shanghai for the American Information Committee but Crow had to get back to file his story for *Liberty*. He also had one last meeting with Madame Chiang when she personally escorted him around one of her pet projects; a school for training girls for war work. Madame arrived at the school in peasant clothes and sporting a broad-brimmed straw hat similar to that worn by women farm workers in Sichuan. Still her famed testiness and attention to detail was intact even if her usual sartorial elegance was not; on leaving she admonished the school's principal, commenting "There are more flies today than there were yesterday."[36]

Crow left Chongqing on Saturday June 17. He flew back to Kunming for a return visit to the Hotel du Lac and then down to Hanoi before returning to America via London. He traveled light, as it was the custom to leave as much clothing and other personal belongings as possible in Chongqing for division among the rather isolated foreign community remaining in the besieged city. In Kunming he managed to get a seat on the *Michelin* train to Hanoi.[37] The *Michelin* was really a large motorbus, "… about the size of a Greyhound bus at home, but not so comfortable," that ran on railway tracks. Once across the border and into French Indo-China, he was moved to a sleeping compartment that he shared with a Chinese merchant. He enjoyed the ride into Hanoi marveling at the lotus in bloom and the small flat-bottomed boats harvesting them, as well as the amazing engineering feat of the railway with 172 tunnels along the route.

In Hanoi Crow enjoyed the luxury of the French colonial Hotel Metropole, the "Grand Dame" of Hanoi's hotels; and he had his first haircut, and coffee and American cigarettes at the Café de la Paix and cocktails at the French Club.[38] He thought Hanoi prosperous. The department stores well stocked with Cambodian silverware for him to buy for his wife, and he decided that French women in Indo-China were much better looking than "… the leathery skin and the lusterless eyes" of British women in India. The staff at the Metropole took a great liking to Crow after discovering he was the author of the book *Les Amis les Chinois,*[39] a popular book at the time in Hanoi, and they brought copies to his room to be signed for local notables.

The planes out of Hanoi were fully booked but the French booking clerk at the Air France ticket office, who was apparently an avid reader of Crow's books, recognized him and got him on a flight to London and thence to New York. Crow mildly missed the chance to sail once again through the Red Sea but he needed to get back to America. As with the outbound flight, the return flight involved numerous stops: from Hanoi to Saigon; Saigon to Bangkok; Bangkok to Rangoon and a stop at the only luxury hotel in the city, the Strand by the Yangon River; Rangoon to Allahabad; then on to Calcutta, Jodphur, Karachi, Baghdad (for dinner by the Tigris), Alexandria, Benghasi, Tunis, Marseilles, Lyon, Paris, London; and then by boat to New York. By the time he arrived in America, the storm clouds of world war were gathering apace and it seemed inevitable that America, and Crow, would be dragged into the global conflict.

21

War Service and Being Proved Right

A Change of Scenery

In 1940 Crow, not long back from China, started to plan an extensive trip through Latin America. The latter half of 1939 had been spent writing and finishing new manuscripts in America as well as a round of fund-raising events for China, including public speaking and attending such events as a "Bowl of Rice Party" at the Worcester Club where Crow addressed the members on China's plight and raised money for medical supplies to be sent to Chongqing.[1] His long-time lecture agent Harris "Harry" Merton Lyons, in conjunction with the *Reader's Digest,* arranged the trip while the State Department helped out by providing a range of introductions for him. He spent the autumn months of 1940 traveling throughout the region on an extended lecture tour and typically his travels yielded him another book, *Meet the South Americans*, and a series of newspaper articles recounting the trip called *Carl Crowings.*

Crow traveled south on the Moore-McCormack liner the *SS Argentina*. He took the *Argentina* from New York, stopping at Rio de Janeiro, Santos, Montevideo and Buenos Aires. Onboard he was initiated into the Kingdom of

Neptune as is the custom when crossing the 180th meridian in the Pacific. On the voyage Crow reflected that "In the course of my journeyings I have both added and dropped days and a careful calculation shows that I have actually lost three whole days out of my life which I can never regain except by traveling three times round the world from east to west."[2] The *Argentina*'s Captain Simmons gave him a certificate to mark the occasion and also threw a cocktail party in his cabin for Crow's 58th birthday on September 26. At the party a fellow passenger, a particularly attractive brunette who Crow had been convinced was the archetypal Latin woman of his imagination, turned out to be 100 percent American, and a fan of *Four Hundred Million Customers* who lived near Crow's temporary home in Pelham Manor.

During the voyage he became friendly with Captain Simmons who had been born of Dutch ancestry on Saba Island in the West Indies and was a long time captain with Moore-McCormack. Crow was just one of the celebrities that sailed with Simmons; the Duke of Windsor, Clark Gable and Bing Crosby were all guests of Simmons and Moore-McCormack during his career.

Ostensibly, Crow's trip had largely been prompted by the success of *Four Hundred Million Customers*, which was bringing him considerable notoriety and recognition. However, a major reason for visiting Latin America was to look at the state of Nazi propaganda; hence the involvement of the State Department. Despite exhaustive research, Crow found little evidence of successful Axis agitation in the region. First he had to ascertain if the general belief that the Nazis were winning the propaganda war in Latin America was an accurate one. He had been told that Brazil was the center of German operations. With an assistant, he bought every newspaper in Rio de Janeiro he could find and marked every news item supplied by an American wire service with a blue pencil, everything from British agencies in red, everything from the German-influenced Trans-Ocean service in green and everything from the Japanese or Italian agencies in yellow. Crow then factored in the circulation figures of all the newspapers and multiplied the column inches each nation had got by their readership. What this revealed was a slightly different picture of the effectiveness of Nazi propaganda than he had been led to believe. According to Crow's figures, 82 percent of news coverage in Brazil emanated from America, 11 percent from Britain and only seven percent from Germany, Italy or Japan. Crow believed that, taken as a whole, the influence of the German media on Brazilian public opinion "… is probably less than of the *Daily Worker* on the public opinion of the United States."[3] What he did note was that the small amount of pro-Nazi coverage the Germans were getting in Brazil was being trumpeted out of all proportion back in Europe by Nazi propagandists such as Lord Haw Haw.[4]

When Crow did another comparison of the Brazilian press, this time counting the number of photographs supplied by each country, he found that Hitler, Tojo and Mussolini came in a poor second to Loretta Young, Norma Shearer, Bette Davis, Clark Gable and Shirley Temple in terms of public interest. He was also pleased to note that, "In Latin America the newspapers and illustrated weeklies published just about as many pictures of the author of *Four Hundred Million Customers* as of Hitler and Mussolini and without the aid of a press agent."[5] His conclusion was that the best way to fight any Axis propaganda in Latin America was simply to leave movies like *Gone With the Wind* running at cinemas to "... present a gripping and unforgettable picture of the way the heart of the North American beats ..."[6]

Meet the South Americans was written in Crow's usual jovial style with a range of anecdotes and stories as well as closer looks at various places including Rio, Buenos Aires, Montevideo, Santiago and Lima. He also looked at the possibilities for American exports and investment in the region and the success of American retailers. Again he used an illustrator, this time the well-known Oscar Ogg, to provide sketches for the book.

However, 1941 was a bad year for Crow as his wife Helen died suddenly in November at their Pelham Manor home. Crow continued working, propagandizing and pushing out books but ill-health and bereavement had set in by now. He sold Pelham Manor and moved to a smaller apartment in Manhattan's Washington Square where friends described him as "broken up" over Helen's death.

His growing fame combined with the debate over whether if, when and how far America should become involved in the Second World War also prompted some arguments. He was angry when the isolationist Harold Beckjordan misrepresented his views in a *New York Times* editorial and wrote to the editor demanding an apology.[7] He had also engaged in a vigorous correspondence with the radio broadcaster Lowell Thomas[8] and also with Carl Van Doren, who had enthusiastically reviewed *Four Hundred Million Customers*, over their off-hand and, according to Crow, inconsiderate use of the term "Chinaman." The argument had started at a lunch the three men had attended at the upscale Parker House Hotel in Boston in 1938 and through 1941 in an exchange of letters. This led to a correspondence between Crow and the compilers of the Oxford English Dictionary over the term. The editors of the OED in England accepted his argument that "Chinaman" had gone out of fashion and was now a derogatory term and therefore offensive. The OED replied that they would consider revising their entry – Crow was encouraged enough to fire of letters to the compilers of other English dictionaries encouraging them to alter their entries too.[9]

As his fame grew he received growing amounts of fan mail. He was proposed for membership of the rather prestigious Lotos Club in New York, a literary club for nationally known figures, though he rejected it claiming it was stupid. Also, his old friend the "Thinker and Drinker" Homer Croy recommended him for membership of the Players' Club in New York, which he did join (if only to be able to lunch with Croy) as well as the New York Advertising Club, which held meetings at the Stanford White Building on Park Avenue. He corresponded with Nelson Rockefeller about his Latin American trip and also got an entry in *Who's Who*, while perhaps less likely was an invitation from Bernarr Macfadden, the physical fitness guru, to stay at one of Macfadden's spa resorts as his guest.[10]

Quite what Macfadden and Crow had in common was not immediately apparent. Regarded by his acolytes as the Father of Physical Culture (what Macfadden called *Kinestherapism*), he was nicknamed "Mr Body Love" by *Time*. He was a flamboyant personality, millionaire publisher and life-long advocate of physical fitness, natural food, outdoor exercise and the natural treatment of disease. He became a highly successful magazine and newspaper publisher as he anticipated the trend towards sensationalist tabloids in America and even later tried unsuccessfully to establish his own religion – *Cosmotarianism*[11] – and to become American's first Secretary of Health. At the time many in the press branded him a charlatan; he was once arrested on obscenity charges and was regularly denounced by the American medical establishment. The only possible link was that Macfadden was from Mill Spring, Missouri, though he was Crow's senior by 15 years. Still, Macfadden abhorred tobacco and alcohol, two things Carl rather liked, and had strict rules about eating while Carl tended to indulge. Macfadden was also frankly a little odd: he commissioned statues of himself and regularly walked 25 miles barefoot from his Physical Fitness Institute in New Jersey to Manhattan. It seems likely that Macfadden would have liked to hire Crow in some capacity in his populist press empire. Over the years Macfadden courted such notable journalists as Walter Winchell and Ed Sullivan, but most found him too weird to be associated with.

Despite his personal losses and growing acclaim, Crow was still involved with old friends from China as well as elsewhere. He kept in touch with J. B. Powell until the latter's death, and his publisher and agent in Vienna, Viktor Polzer, asked Crow to help him and his wife get visas for America.[12] A former member of his staff also appealed to him for a loan as times got still tougher back in Shanghai under Japanese occupation. Also, his mother Elvira had been ill with a severe cold and age-related problems in early 1940; she was now well into her seventies, and required more of his time. Crow also contacted the FBI in the person of no less than J. Edgar Hoover himself with information on someone he thought should be registered as an enemy agent.[13]

Fighting the War from Behind a Desk

Three days before Christmas in December 1941, with Crow only recently having become a widower, he received his draft papers from the War Department. He had been expecting them since the start of the month and the attack on Pearl Harbor. The infamous attack on the American naval base was clearly a disaster for America's military prowess but it also confirmed what Crow had felt for a long time: that no matter what some in Washington believed, the US would not remain immune from war and would eventually have to confront Japanese militarism. America declared war on Japan.

In January 1942 he was appointed as a consultant on US$15 a day WAE (when actually employed) to the Foreign Information Services Publications Department. This was to become part of the Office of War Information (OWI). J. Edgar Hoover at the FBI ordered a routine investigation into Crow's background and judged him fit for service.[14] On his formal application Crow described himself as having been "… in business for myself or making a living at writing and lecturing for more than 20 years." His referees, who included C. V. Starr, Foulton Oursler, T. O. Thackery (the executive editor of the *New York Post*) and Roy Howard of the Scripps-Howard publishing company (and a former head of the UP news agency), all testified to his patriotism, loyalty, hard work and obvious ability. J. R. Record, the editorial director of the *Fort Worth Star-Telegram,* remembered Crow as "one of the outstanding young men of the city" during his time in Texas.

Crow's knowledge of China, and particularly Shanghai, was now considered important by the OWI. On December 8, 1941, the Japanese army had finally occupied Shanghai's International Settlement. The *China Press*, *The China Review* and the *North-China Daily News* were all shut down, while the *Shanghai Evening Post* was forcibly turned into a pro-Japanese paper. The occupiers took over all the grand hotels, luxurious houses and the American Club as barracks and offices. J. B. Powell and many other leading foreigners were in prison, while Powell's secret "underground" radio station that had kept transmitting out of China since 1937, the *Press Wireless*, was likewise silenced. One old China coast friend of Crow's, Francis MacGracken Fisher, better known simply as "Mac," and a long time correspondent in China for UP was in Chongqing running the OWI's office in the beleaguered capital. Another friend, Max Chaicheck, who had worked for the *China Press* in Shanghai had fled the city with the Japanese on his heels and returned to America where he had changed his name to Milton Chase and was working on the OWI's China desk in San Francisco. Most of the key cities in China were now under Japanese control and its entire coastline from Dalian to Hong Kong was in enemy hands. All American and British diplomatic staff in Shanghai had been deported or interned while a pro-Vichy administration was overseeing Frenchtown.

The OWI was created by Executive Order in June 1942 and Crow became one of its employees. On one level, it was purely a propaganda machine for American values and war aims promoting a vision of apple-pie America, but it also eventually produced a unique record of social change in the country during the war with its army of OWI photographers. Its mandate was twofold: at home to produce propaganda to support the war effort and overseas to engage in psychological warfare. Even domestically, the OWI had some tough issues to deal with, including discrimination against blacks in the army, the use of Japanese-Americans as soldiers and how to deal with social conflicts such as the Los Angeles Zoot Suit Riots and the public's dislike of rationing. Overseas, the OWI attempted to co-ordinate policy and propaganda in Europe, Asia and Africa. The Office generated countless propaganda directives in its efforts to undermine enemy morale and cultivate a pro-American post-war climate. Central directives were sent weekly to all OWI offices worldwide, containing the general propaganda themes that the OWI wished to see included in radio broadcasts, leaflets, newspaper articles and editorials. There were also regional directives targeted primarily at the enemy and tailored specifically for the target country, as well as special directives issued as responses to events that required immediate attention. A fourth category, long-range directives, laid the groundwork for the post-war American propaganda apparatus in such key nations as China, the Philippines and India.

Crow's boss was the highly-regarded China Hand Owen Lattimore who was based in San Francisco as the deputy director of Pacific Operations. Crow and Lattimore had come into contact previously. In 1939 Lattimore, as editor of the journal *Pacific Affairs* and Frederick V. Field,[15] the secretary of the American Council Institute of Pacific Relations, had contacted Crow. Field asked if Crow would consider reporting back to the Institute when he returned from Chongqing, while Lattimore was interested in the possibility of Crow's writing articles for his journal on his impressions of western and southwestern China.

Lattimore was an intriguing and influential character at the time and one that Crow was destined shortly to cross swords with, albeit briefly. From the start, the OWI's Asia section was rife with internecine war and office politics. A host of divisive issues led to schisms occurring between those who favored Lattimore and those who didn't, and those that Lattimore favored and those he didn't. One OWI insider wrote to Crow in July 1943 telling him that Lattimore had eliminated everyone who knows anything about China – Crow included. He already knew this. In the spring of 1942 he had been reassigned as Special Assistant to the Director of the Foreign Information Service and their Planning

Board for the Far East on a salary of US$6,500 per year, based in New York. In reality he shuttled between New York and San Francisco in what was a move from the OWI's Pacific Operations section to its South East Asia section.

Despite his being ostensibly a China Hand, there was some sense in Crow's move as America lacked experience and on-the-ground knowledge about what was an area that had mostly been under British, French or Dutch control. Crow knew something of Burma and Indo-China, but as these were both crucial supply routes to China they largely controlled by Lattimore's China section. Crow was significantly less knowledgeable regarding Thailand, the Dutch East Indies, Singapore and Malaya and had commented only sporadically on the Philippines since his book on the country had been published in 1914. Still South East Asia briefly became his territory. During the time he spent at the OWI, two men were to have the most impact on him and both were controversial figures: the aforementioned Lattimore and the enigmatic Paul Linebarger.

Lattimore was the more complex of the two characters and remained controversial. Born in Washington DC in 1900, he spent most of his youth with his missionary family in China, only leaving them to study abroad in Swiss and British boarding schools before returning to America in 1919. Later he became the editor of *Pacific Affairs*, published by the New York-based think tank the Institute of Pacific Relations (IPR), and in 1941 acted as a political advisor to Chiang Kai-shek. The chain-smoking, bespectacled and pencil-moustached Lattimore had a clear influence on the thinking of the OWI in particular and the American government on China and Asia. He was to publish *America and Asia: Problems of Today's War and the Peace of Tomorrow* in 1943 which predicted many of the post-war problems in the region.[16]

Lattimore's wife, Eleanor Holgate Lattimore, was also a noted East Asia expert who had been Secretary of the Peking Institute of Art History. The two spent their honeymoon in 1925 traveling across Mongolia and Chinese Turkestan.[17] Lattimore's route to academic Sinology was as unconventional as his upbringing. In 1928 he returned to the US and applied for a grant from the Social Science Research Council, despite the fact that he had never undertaken any formal academic work. Isiah Bowman, the head of the American Geographical Society and later President of Johns Hopkins University, was impressed with Lattimore and his knowledge of Inner Asia, and persuaded Harvard University's Division of Anthropology to give him a grant for a year's research in China. In 1935 Lattimore was persuaded to join the Johns Hopkins' faculty as a Lecturer in the School of International Relations. A year later, he was appointed Director of the School where he was considered a charismatic leader. In 1939, based on the depth of his scholarship, Lattimore was granted indefinite tenure despite his lack of a PhD. Despite this rapid and unconventional rise, academia was not for Lattimore and he took a leave of absence to advise the Generalissimo in 1941. Chiang gave Lattimore the job on the advice of no lesser a personage than President Roosevelt.

After the war Lattimore would become a key plank in Republican Senator Joe McCarthy's anti-communist witch-hunts. He was accused of being a "Red" in the pay of Moscow, of having "lost China" and of being a spy. Lattimore fought the charges and is credited with having coined the term "McCarthyism." Despite the eventual dropping of all charges against Lattimore and the fact that the FBI's omnipotent boss J. Edgar Hoover personally cleared him, the taint of McCarthy's accusations would follow the China Hand to his death in 1989.[18]

In many respects Crow and Lattimore were similar enough to have got along – indeed Crow was familiar with Lattimore's writings on China and cited him in his book on the Tanaka Memorial published in 1942.[19] Both were cantankerous and pernickety; both believed in capitalism over communism; both had strong views on China and Japan; and both knew that being a China Hand was akin to a competitive sport and full of rivalry. Both men were also intrepid travelers in China and Asia – Crow as a newspaper and advertising man, Lattimore at first when he briefly worked for Arnhold and Company, a European import-export firm in Guangzhou. Both were also fascinated by and knowledgeable about Asia though they had unconventional and broken higher education. David Harvey, a Johns Hopkins Professor, stated, "If Lattimore is guilty of anything, I suspect it was simply that he knew the realities of China too well."[20] Given Crow's run-ins with the American diplomatic service in China for his own pro-Chinese leanings and long stance against Japanese expansionism, this was a charge that could be leveled at him too. Both men spoke of China from first-hand knowledge, and had actively backed the KMT and Chiang, but both had reservations about the Generalissimo's competence and conduct.

Despite the similarities, the contemporary divisions of the time separated the two men. Even before the end of the war and the resumed clashes between the Communists and Nationalists in China, America's China Hands were starting to split between those who supported Chiang (again usually with reservations) and those who openly challenged his leadership abilities. Two camps began to emerge with Chiang vociferously supported by a combination of Americans on the right such as the financier Henry Morgenthau, big business associated with the Soongs and H. H. Kung as well as Henry Luce's magazine empire – generically lumped together as the "China lobby." Though the arguments about "who lost China?" and the vicious red-baiting were in the future, as early as 1942 the splits were starting to appear though on more ideological, and less public, grounds. The splits became more obvious following the Teheran Conference between Roosevelt, Churchill and Stalin in November–December

1943 when the question of whether Washington could deal with Mao while remaining allied to Chiang became a serious debate. As Germany's defeat came closer, Washington's strategy prioritized the war in Europe while advancing to Japan occupied thinking in the Pacific theater. With "Vinegar Joe" Stilwell recalled from China after numerous clashes with Chiang, America's policy towards China was drifting, leading to renewed arguments among the China Hands back in the States.

Lattimore was critical of Chiang despite advising him; Crow was too, despite generally urging support to defeat the Japanese. Even before the Communist victory, questions about Lattimore's politics had been asked. At *Pacific Affairs* he had published articles by Marxist writers who were pro-Soviet in what Lattimore claimed was an attempt to balance the journal's content. He had also made comments about the possible benefits limited socialism could bring to underdeveloped countries such as Mongolia. With hindsight these appear relatively innocent remarks, but in the later climate of McCarthy's House Un-American Activities Committee (HUAC) they would be used against him and appear damning to many.

The arguments between the conflicting personalities of men like Lattimore, Crow and others at the OWI China desk were not like the battles that Lattimore later faced against McCarthy. Though heated, hard-fought, passionate and with no intellectual prisoners taken, the internal rows were between men who knew China – they were fierce debates among seasoned China Hands. The American China Hands of the inter-war years were a mixed bunch ideologically, certainly more varied than their French or British counterparts who had imperial interests to maintain. Men such as Crow, Lattimore, Hallet Abend of the *New York Times*, the diplomats Paul Reinsch, Jacob Schurman and Nelson Trusler Johnson, Roy Anderson, J. B. Powell and Edgar Snow – as well as women like the novelist Pearl S. Buck and Agnes Smedley – were far from uniform in their opinions. They ranged from the far left to the far right; and they disagreed on the role of America and other powers in China, the success or failure of the Nationalist government, Japan's ultimate aims, on China's future and pretty much everything else. Yet, in the claustrophobic world of the foreign community of the China coast, they could not avoid coming into contact, debating with each other, and collaborating at times, while all held their views firmly from long and close study.

The East and West Association was formed during the Second World War with the aim of aiding the Allied war effort in Asia and better educating American children about the continent by helping them understand the culture and concerns of the people of China and India. There was little in the ideals of groups like this that a Crow or a Lattimore would have found to disagree with.

Yet the left-wing writer and political activist Pearl S. Buck, whose book *The Good Earth* Crow had enjoyed, led the Association. At a later time when the debate succumbed to political vindictiveness under McCarthyism, merely knowing people like Buck, Smedley or Snow, as well as Lattimore, could be proof to HUAC of being a Red. The tables could potentially have turned as easily on Crow as they did on Lattimore. A search of the Dies Committee indices conducted by the FBI's Washington Bureau in 1942 found that Crow was a member of the Committee for a Boycott Against Japanese Aggression and a sponsor of the American Committee for Non-Participation in Japanese Aggression and had, in 1938, signed an appeal against Japanese aggression in China organized by the American Communist Party's newspaper the *Daily Worker*.[21]

Perhaps an even clearer example of how Americans, and others, of different backgrounds and political shades came together was the INDUSCO movement. In 1942 Crow was one of a number of high-profile Americans with connections to China who urged the government to devote US$500,000 in Lend Lease to promote the work of the Chinese Industrial Co-operatives (INDUSCO). The INDUSCO plan had been spawned by many people, including John Alexander, the Secretary to the British Ambassador in Chongqing (Sir Archibald Clark Kerr); Edgar Snow and his wife Helen; and the leftist New Zealander Rewi Alley.[22] The basic idea was to create a system of more long-lasting use than simply feeding China's internally displaced refugees with aid. The aim was to mobilize them into thousands of semi-mobile co-operatives scattered across the Chinese hinterland, making use of available resources, salvaged tools and machinery. Lend Lease and Chongqing government money would fund the co-ops. This was the essence of what became known as the INDUSCO plan. The idea might have gone nowhere but it was championed by Clark Kerr[23] in Chongqing who put the idea to the Generalissimo, Madame Chiang and H. H. Kung. They agreed to try it.

Kung pledged $5 million in government money and became President of INDUSCO, while Madame Chiang became an adviser and T. V. Soong joined the committee, as did Madame Sun in Hong Kong. It sought money from supporters worldwide in fund-raising initiatives led by Alley and Ida Pruitt[24] which paved the way for the creation of INDUSCO Inc. in the USA with the backing of leading personalities such as Eleanor Roosevelt and Henry Luce. By mid-1941, the amount of money being raised for INDUSCO took a quantum leap when United China Relief, one of the most powerful fund-raising organizations in America, added its weight to INDUSCO. However, later the involvement of many in the movement was to be questioned as it brought together the likes of Luce and Roosevelt, as well as Crow, with several people who became known for their pro-Communist sympathies, such as Alley and Pruitt.

Crow's other major contact at the OWI was Paul Linebarger who acted as a close confidant, though from a distance. Linebarger supplied Crow with feedback on the broadcasts and coverage he created for the OWI concerning South East Asia and also supplied intelligence to Crow on everything from steel demand in Java to the believability of intelligence supplied to the OWI from Japanese-occupied Jakarta and Kuala Lumpur. Very quickly Crow used Linebarger as his editor and fact-checker, sending him copies of proposed OWI propaganda directives for comment. Linebarger replied with detailed comments.[25]

Paul Myron Anthony Linebarger had been born in 1913, in Milwaukee, Wisconsin. He had a good knowledge of South East Asia and China – his father had been a lawyer and a judge in the American-controlled Philippines and also yet another advisor to Sun Yat-sen, as well as a legal advisor to the Chinese Republic. Linebarger had been surrounded by myths since he was a child. Periods of his life in Japan and China were exaggerated. It was said that Sun was his godfather and that he had grown up in the Dr.'s retinue when in fact his father had only spent several weeks in Sun's company. What was true was that Linebarger knew his way around Asia and was, from an early age, an operative with American intelligence. He had a PhD in Asiatic Studies from Johns Hopkins and specialized in propaganda techniques and psychological warfare. Unsurprisingly, the OWI snapped him up immediately and put him to work in the Operation Planning and Intelligence Board's Asian divisions. He also helped organize the Army's first psychological warfare section. After supplying Crow and others with information from around Asia, he was sent to China and put in charge of psychological warfare. By 1945 he had risen to the rank of major. After the war, due to his close association with the intelligence services, Linebarger avoided any of the McCarthyite charges that were directed at Lattimore and became a Professor of Asiatic Politics at Johns Hopkins.[26]

In January 1943 Crow applied for leave of absence from the OWI to write his book *The Great American Customer*. He sent an outline of the contents to Lattimore who granted Crow four months' leave and wished him good luck with the project. This was essentially the end of Crow's time with the OWI. He never returned to full-time employment with them, concentrating on books while also continuing to comment on Asian affairs. In fact he had wanted to return in June 1943 after he had finished work on *The Great American Customer*. However, he lost out for a senior China position in the OWI against Lattimore and decided to stay outside the organization but still agitating in the press and through his books. Ultimately, this was perhaps how he was most useful. In July 1943 he wrote a long piece for *The Nation* in which he responded to an official Tokyo radio broadcast which described how Filipinos were rejecting American customs such as shaking hands and now preferred to bow from the waist Japanese-style instead. Japanese radio saw this as conclusive evidence that the "Japanning" of the Philippines was a success. Crow debunked the reports arguing that any bowing that was occurring was at the point of a bayonet wielded by veterans of the Rape of Nanking.[27]

For better of worse, ultimately Crow did not become further engaged in the debates either over supporting INDUSCO or the schisms within the OWI. His health was fading and his ability to be actively involved in the struggle for China against Japan and for America's war effort was becoming limited; not that that stopped him trying.

22

The Final Prolific Years

A War of Words

Throughout Crow's journalism and writing a constant theme was the successful industrialization of America and the wealthy society and thriving democracy that had been created. Though away from America for a significant portion of his life, Crow always remained a patriotic and enthusiastic American. He had started out before the First World War reporting on America's changing industrial and agricultural society from the heartlands; and while in China, he had always found time to promote America and its values, be it through working at Compub, preparing papers on China for the State Department, as a long-standing Chairman of the American Club in Shanghai, traveling up the Burma Road in 1939, and down the coast of Latin America in 1940 or at the OWI when war was declared once again.

In late 1943 he published many of his thoughts on the origins and uniqueness of the American experiment in a book *The Great American Customer*,[1] sub-titled *The Story of Invention, Mass Production and Our Prosperity*, which traced the development of manufacturing and marketing in the United States from independence to the production and sale of cameras by George Eastman. The first editions of the book published during the war were printed on rough paper in order to conform to government regulations for conserving paper. Crow felt that the book could help remind war-weary Americans that their commercial history had provided them with both a freedom and a degree of luxury and comfort that had never been known anywhere else before and were worth fighting for. He had long believed that American methods of scientific management were responsible for many of the country's achievements, from its growing industrial base to its success on the athletics track, and in *The Great American Customer* he fleshed out this argument.[2]

By now living in Manhattan in a fifth-floor apartment on Washington Place, Crow remained an advocate of greater American support for China in the fight against Japan. In 1942, while still at the OWI, Crow had published *Japan's Dream of World Empire – The Tanaka Memorial*. This small book was essentially composed of the text of a memorial presented to the Emperor of Japan in July 1927 by the then Premier Baron Tanaka which outlined Japan's goals in Manchuria, and attempted to rationalize Japanese expansionism and the eventual conquest of all China. Crow added a foreword explaining the events leading up to the Tanaka Memorial and Tanaka's role as "the leader of the aggressive military party"[3] or faction in Japan. Tanaka had supposedly prepared the document following a conference in Shenyang that had brought together all Japan's military officials in Manchuria and Mongolia. The memorial was published at the time, though the Japanese government denied its authenticity. By republishing it in 1942, Crow was hoping to show that Japan's intentions towards China had been clear at least 15 years earlier. He had some success as the book was widely commended and well reviewed in America. Maxwell Stewart, a left-wing journalist, writing in *The Nation* called the Memorial "Japan's *Mein Kampf*."[4]

He had plans to write additional books on American history including a biography of William Wheelwright, the son of a Lincolnshire master mariner who was born in Massachusetts and eventually founded the Pacific Steam Navigation Company, as well as a history of the American magazine. He also had more overtly propagandist works in the pipeline, such as a history of the resistance of ordinary Chinese in the face of Japanese aggression, including a book to be entitled *Sons of Han* and another to be called either *China, After Forty Centuries* or *China – Forty Centuries Young*. He was also planning to continue to try to raise American consciousness of China's plight with a range of articles that remained unfinished at the time of his death, including *China's Homeless Millions Find a Home* and *Can China Fight for a Hundred Years?* In addition, he was intending to continue his analysis of Japan with draft chapters of several books that were never published. These included a history of Japan for American readers of which he completed two chapters – "Foundations of

Japan" and "The Forty-Seven," as well as another projected book to be called *You Can't Make Friends with Japan*. Finally, Crow had been making notes and keeping accounts of the opium traffic in Japanese-occupied parts of China, a trade he had witnessed when traveling through Tianjin in mid-1930s when he had started collecting data.[5]

In 1944 he did publish *China Takes Her Place*, a book that sought to explain to the American people, with some reservations, how progressive the Chinese Nationalist government had been. It was propaganda in many senses. While many would agree with the London *Times* correspondent of the 1930s, Peter Fleming, that "to read a propagandist, a man with vested intellectual interests, is as dull as dining with a vegetarian,"[6] Crow typically managed to remain eminently readable. In the book, which formed part of the OWI's effort to maintain support for Nationalist China against Japan and to engender American public support for that fight, he largely praised the Nationalists including Sun and Chiang. He backed the uneasy alliance between the KMT and the Communists in order to defeat the primary enemy – Japan. However, as the Second World War drew to a close in Europe and the American government started to prepare for a renewal of the Cold War with the Soviet Union, Crow realized that China would be one of the key battlefields. Chiang, Madame Chiang, Zhou En-lai and others had all told him as much personally.

Though he had worked hard to promote the KMT-Communist alliance publicly, personally he seems to have been more skeptical. He had discussed communism in China both with its leaders and its most vociferous opponents. He had witnessed the brutal suppression of the communist movement in Shanghai and other cities in the 1920s and during the Northern Expedition and had also handled the coins minted with the hammer and sickle that were produced by the short-lived soviet established in Jiangxi province by various communist groups driven out of other parts of China. He became interested in this historical phenomenon but was realistic enough in his understanding to judge that the Jiangxi Soviet was probably much more ad hoc than most of the English language press in China, then in the thrall (or the pay) of anti-communism, would have its readers believe. Most foreigners living in Shanghai in the inter-war years saw Communists, at least in Crow's view, "as White Russians bent on assassinating anyone with a top hat." The Jiangxi Soviet appeared to be independent of any other government in China and was reported to be confiscating private property and redistributing land to share-croppers. Later, during the war, many American officials felt they could do business with Mao and the Red Army as, from a distance, the communist policy of land distribution seemed far more progressive and reasonable to them than the continuing corruption of the Chongqing regime.

While admiring the bravery of the Communist forces in the war against Japan, Crow had felt that their role was overstated and that those, mostly Americans such as Edgar Snow, who had made their way to Yanan and come back to write laudatory books and articles were probably wrong. He felt that their descriptions of life, politics and the leaders in Yanan were "too perfectly perfect to be wholly convincing."[7] He also believed that the pro-Communist writers and those who criticized the government in Chongqing were providing gossip that the Washington cocktail circuit enjoyed but that this wasn't necessarily going to bring China's freedom from the yoke of Japanese aggression any closer.

Relations between the KMT and the Communists certainly weren't improving. Writing in 1944, Crow considered that some sort of eventual showdown between the two forces was likely, though cautioning that "If a civil war is fought over these issues [*the position of the KMT and the Communists*] it will be quite different from any of those that have been fought in the past."[8] He was right: he never lived to see the final outcome, but he did make some predictions. He felt that China's conduct and resolve during the war had earned the country the position of "spiritual leadership" in East Asia and declared that the only conclusion possible was that "Neither in its political nor industrial organization will China be like any other country … China will be unique and independent in thought".[9]

Crow also believed that, while China might fall to communism temporarily, it would eventually become a democracy; indeed he thought that China had for centuries been a democracy in everything but its form of government and that all China's great thinkers – primarily Confucius and Mencius – had upheld the right of the common man to overthrow unjust rulers and revoke the Mandate of Heaven. He also saw various symbols of nascent democracy: the universal civil service examinations that had been open to anyone since the Han Dynasty (though abolished towards the end of the Qing Dynasty); what Crow believed to be the effective abolition of feudalism in the second century BC; the long-established tradition of semi-autonomous local or village government; and the teahouses of China that doubled as town-hall meeting venues for the discussion of anything and everything. Crow finished his last book dealing with China – *China Takes Her Place* – on an upbeat note:

> China is confident of her future and so are most of the foreigners who, like myself, have witnessed the progress of the past thirty years. There may be troubled days ahead, but nothing can gainsay the fact that China is a continent and a civilization – a self-respecting and industrious people who are moving forward.[10]

A Final Battle Lost

By early 1945 it was clear that medical problems were impinging on Crow's work-rate. The Office of Strategic Services (OSS)[11] in New York wanted to meet with him to see his collection of photographs with reference to "our activities in the China Theater," but he never replied.[12] He had already shared his photographic archive with the military and the navy to see what use they could make of it. In April 1945 he wrote to his editor Frank MacGregor at Harper & Brothers that the publisher should go ahead and make revisions to his final book, *The City of Flint Grows Up*, that he had completed in early 1945. The book had been commissioned by his old advertising client Buick to tell the story of how the car-maker had switched from civilian to military production and was supporting the war effort. Sub-titled *The Success Story of an American Community*, Crow dedicated the book to "The men and women of Flint who provided the tools of war for the men who fought overseas."[13] For his labors, Buick paid him the princely sum of US$10,000 (in US$200 weekly instalments).

Crow now knew that he had a growth on the upper part of his oesophagus that was probably cancerous; it had been causing him stomach trouble for some time. After completing the book on Flint, he had moved for a while to rest and finish a revision of *Four Hundred Million Customers* in Harrison, New York. He was heading back to Manhattan for a biopsy and expected to be "out of circulation for some time," whatever the result. In his letter to Frank MacGregor, he was characteristically matter-of-fact about the surgery and the seriousness of his condition.[14] The last few years had been lonely ones – a widower who had never really fully recovered from Helen's death, working hard and living alone at Washington Place with only a black manservant who looked after him and prepared his meals.

The condition was indeed serious. Carl Crow died of cancer at his apartment in Washington Place on June 8, 1945. Such was his fame as a writer at the time that his obituary appeared prominently in the *New York Times*. He left two sisters – Roma Crow-Walters of Washington DC and Laura Crow-Beck of Webster Grove, Missouri. Both sisters had moved around, with Crow mentioning them variously living in Pittsburgh and St. Louis, but they had all kept in close touch by mail. He had also remained close to his aged mother who also died in 1945, aged 81, after a long illness. He had maintained constant contact by letter with her throughout his years in China and regularly sent gifts back to her in Missouri.

His body was interred at the Walter B. Cooke Funeral Home on West 72nd Street, Manhattan, for final internment at the Odd Fellows Cemetery on Main Street, Fredericktown, Missouri, where he was eventually buried next to his mother and father. His final instructions were that there should be no flowers

266 CARL CROW – A TOUGH OLD CHINA HAND

and all contributions should be sent to the American Society for the Control of Cancer. In his detailed last will and testament, he apportioned his belongings in a typically highly detailed way. Most of his money, property and copyrights were left to his two sisters. His nieces got an oriental rug apiece and his nephews a range of items, including his father's desk which he had somehow kept hold of, a globe, a Litchfield clock in a traditional papier-mâché case and a Howard watch; and his collection of books was divided up among his sisters, his nephew Thomas Walters and the Fredericktown Public Library. His papers were sent to the University of Missouri, along with a collection of his published works. His garden tools and his wine cellar were left to two friends. Finally, he donated US$100 to the John Drew Fund of the Players' Club and US$50 to the Ed McNamara Fund of the Players. Neither his first wife Mildred nor his daughter Betty was mentioned.

On the day Crow died, the war against Japan that he had foreseen and written about so passionately and extensively continued. The *New York Times* carried his obituary on Sunday June 10, along with news that between 150 and 200 American B29 Super Fortresses had bombed Kobe, Yokohama and Tokyo, hitting the Japan Aircraft Company's Tomioka plant near Yokohama and an army air depot close to Tokyo. American forces were advancing slowly in Okinawa and meeting stiff Japanese resistance, and American and Australian forces successfully landed on Labuan Island, near Brunei. Meanwhile, Chinese forces under General Chang Fah-kwei had captured the Sino-Indian border town of Chungching, forcing the Japanese army back into Indo-China to join the estimated 200,000 other Japanese troops trapped and defeated in South East Asia. The war in Europe was effectively over despite Russia's Marshal Zhukoff still refusing to declare Hitler officially dead without a body. Winston Churchill and Clement Atlee were hitting the stump across Britain contesting the historic 1945 general election, and debates over the formation of the United Nations continued slowly in San Francisco. At home, 65,000 people bet a total of $776,408 and watched the colt Hoop Jnr. win the 71st Kentucky Derby in Louisville. In Shanghai it was a year since American bombers had first appeared in the skies over the city and by June 1945 the Japanese were starting to withdraw.

Crow had once written that he would like to be buried "… in the hills of Soochow, near the Nine Arch Bridge." He further elaborated: "I hope my Chinese friends will, on appropriate occasions, burn a modest lot of ghostly money and furniture over my grave. And if they want to, my foreign friends are welcome to use the gravestone as a place to open the bottles of beer which are always so welcome after a hike over the Hills of the Seven Brothers."[15] At the time Crow died, Suzhou remained in the hands of the Japanese and a war was raging to free the country and the city of Shanghai. He never made it back to a liberated Shanghai or a free and united China but he will always be intimately linked with that city and that country. As a fitting epitaph shortly after his death, when US soldiers arrived in Shanghai later in 1945, the American army's Armed Services Editions Division that issued books to troops overseas published a "cargo pocket" sized edition of *Four Hundred Million Customers* to be distributed to the GIs as a guide to explaining the city they had pitched up in. What better introduction to their new posting?

EPILOGUE

Gone but Not Forgotten

After the 1949 revolution, Carl Crow was forgotten in China … almost.

In 1974 Dennis George Crow, the grandson of Carl's younger brother Leslie Ray and the son of Carl's favorite nephew George, who had run the passenger division of the Dollar Line in Shanghai and Hong Kong for many years, visited Beijing with his mother Olga. Visas were hard to come by in the last tumultuous years of the Cultural Revolution, especially for American citizens like Dennis and Olga. When Americans did manage to make it to China, their trip was highly orchestrated and planned and their movements heavily controlled and monitored.

The Crows stayed at the prestigious Peking Hotel and toured the capital. One day they were informed that they would be allowed to visit the famous seaside resort of Beidaihe. This was a rare privilege at the time and they were among the first foreigners to see the resort since 1949. The next morning a limousine arrived to take them to Beidaihe along with a group of high-profile visitors that totaled nine people. The Crows had to wonder why there was such luxurious treatment for two Americans with little more to recommend them than a curiosity about China and a tenuous connection to the country's now politically incorrect past.

At Beidaihe the curious group of foreigners were shown around and then interviewed by an elderly man working as a journalist for the Chinese propaganda magazine *China Reconstructs*. Olga was asked by the journalist in excellent English how she liked Beidaihe and what she thought of China – of course only positively glowing comments would ever see print. The journalist asked for her name for the record. After the interview the old man lingered around and eventually asked Olga if by any chance she was related to the great Carl Crow who had once lived in Shanghai? She said she was. The old man became very excited. How wonderful, he exclaimed; as a young man his first job in Shanghai had been as Carl Crow's copyboy and he remembered Carl with much affection. Whatever had become of his old boss?

Carl's infamous network of friends, acquaintances, colleagues and associates stretched further and lasted longer than he could have ever known.

Notes

Introduction

1   *All About Shanghai and Environs: A Standard Guidebook, 1934–1935* (1935), Shanghai: University Press.
2   Carl Crow (1940) *Foreign Devils in the Flowery Kingdom*, New York: Harper & Brothers, p. 223.
3   Crow, *Foreign Devils in the Flowery Kingdom*, pp. 234–5.
4   Carl Crow (1937) *Four Hundred Million Customers*, New York: Harper & Brothers, p. 12.
5   Crow, *Four Hundred Million Customers*, p. 304.

Chapter 1

1   Carl Crow (1939) *He Opened the Door of Japan*, New York: Harper & Brothers, p. 3.
2   Carl Crow (1943) *The Chinese Are Like That*, Cleveland: World Publishing Company, p. 132.
3   Carl Crow (1943) *The Great American Customer*, New York: Harper & Brothers, p. 97.
4   Crow, *The Chinese Are Like That*, p. 86.
5   Crow, *The Chinese Are Like That*, pp. 186–7.
6   *Lead Belt News*, "Carl Crow writes editor of LB news," undated copy in the Crow Archive.
7   Walter Williams (1914) *The World's Journalism* and W. Williams and F. L. Martin, *The Practise of Journalism* (1917), both published by E. W. Stephens, Columbia, Missouri.
8   See S. L. Williams (1929) *Twenty Years of Education for Journalism: A History of the School of Journalism of the University of Missouri*, Columbia, Missouri: E. W. Stephens, p. 31.
9   Report from Kansas City Office of the FBI to the New York Office of the FBI concerning Crow's education, March 19, 1942.
10 Carl Crow (1916) *Japan and America*, New York: Robert M. McBride & Co., p. 5.
11 Crow's articles for the *Saturday Evening Post* included "The business of town building" (April 30, 1910); "Towns built to order" (July 2, 1910); "Cutting up the

big ranches" (August 6, 1910); "Team work in town building" (3 September, 1910); "Old farms for new" (October 8, 1910); "The fee system" (dealing with rising court costs, November 19, 1910); "Building a railroad" (December 10, 1910); and "Selling to cities" (March 4, 1911). Crow also contributed an article to *Pearson's Magazine*, "What the tenant farmer is doing to the South" (June 19, 1911).

12   Carl Crow (1940) *Foreign Devils in the Flowery Kingdom*, New York: Harper & Brothers, p. 224.

13   "Fort Worth editor to join staff of new Chinese daily", *Fort Worth Star-Telegram*, June 8, 1911.

14   "Man in the street", *Houston Chronicle*, undated, 1911.

Chapter 2

1   Carl Crow (1944) *China Takes Her Place*, New York: Harper & Brothers, p. 4.

2   Crow, *China Takes Her Place*, p. 4.

3   Crow, *China Takes Her Place*, p. 4.

4   Carl Crow (1940) *Foreign Devils in the Flowery Kingdom*, New York: Harper & Brothers, p. 224.

5   Stella Dong (2001) *Shanghai: The Rise and Fall of a Decadent City*, New York: Perennial, p. 176.

6   Peter Rand (1995) *China Hands: The Adventures and Ordeals of the American Journalists Who Joined Forces with the Great Chinese Revolution*, New York: Simon and Schuster, p. 24, quoted in Jonathan Mirsky (2002) "Getting the story in China: American reporters since 1972," *Harvard Asia Quarterly*, vol. VI, no. 1, winter.

Chapter 3

1   Carl Crow (1944) *China Takes Her Place*, New York: Harper & Brothers, p. 7.

2   P. Thompson and R. Macklin (2004) *The Man Who Died Twice: The Life and Adventures of Morrison of Peking*, Sydney: Allen & Unwin, pp. 248–9.

3   For a more detailed overview, see B. Goodman (2004) "Semi-colonialism, transnational networks and news flows in early republican Shanghai", *The China Review*, vol. 4, no. 1, spring.

4   John Keay (1997) *Last Post: The End of Empire in the Far East*, London: John Murray, p. 141.

5   Malcolm Rosholt (1994) *The Press Corps of Old Shanghai*, Rosholt, Wisconsin: Rosholt House, p. 9.

6   The building is now the offices of American International Assurance (AIA), the successor to American Asiatic Underwriters which originally shared the building with the *North-China Daily News* and other tenants.

7   Ralph Shaw (1973) *Sin City*, London: Everest Books, pp. 50–1.

8   Now the Ruijin Guest House and grounds at 118 Ruijin Number Two Road.

9   Later to become the Jingwen Flower Market on Shaanxi Road South and demolished for redevelopment in 2005.

10 Even those who worked for Nottingham found the pro-Japanese line excessive, including one Japanese-American, Bill Hosokawa, who worked on the paper in the early 1940s. See B. Hosokawa and T. Noel (1988) *Out of the Frying Pan: Reflections of a Japanese American*, Boulder: University of Colorado Press. In 1941, the paper officially became the English language mouthpiece for the Japanese in Shanghai, and was widely rumored to be financially supported by the Yokohama Specie Bank.

11 Shaw, *Sin City*, p. 50.

12 Technically, the *China Press* was originally funded by a bond issue supported by American and German financiers and planned a Chinese language issue too – at least according to the *Fort Worth Star-Telegram*, "Fort Worth editor to join staff at new Chinese daily," June 8, 1911. However, if there were German investors, they appear never to have taken much interest in the paper and a Chinese language version never appeared.

13 After campaigning hard for President Wilson's election in 1912, Crane (1858–1939) went on to serve as a member of the Root Commission to the Soviet Union, attended the Versailles Conference with Wilson in 1918 and organized the King-Crane Commission to the Middle East in 1919. Crane later helped finance the first explorations for oil in Saudi Arabia and Yemen, as well as serving as US Minister to China in 1920–21.

14 Crow started to file the first reports from China to UP in the autumn of 1911. UP had only been established in 1907 by E. W. Scripps. The work probably wasn't too arduous as in the early years of the wire services in China it was common to transmit only a few words or sentences about the events of the day. Newspaper editors would then elaborate and expand on the stories they received. The downside was that wage rates were very low – between $5 and $20 per article in the mid-1920s, with no guarantees that all articles sent would be used. Crow was listed by UP as a "string correspondent."

15 John Benjamin Powell (1945) *My Twenty-Five Years in China*, New York: Macmillan, p. 7.

16 Powell, *My Twenty-Five Years in China*, p. 11.

17 Sara Lockwood Williams (1929) *Twenty Years of Education for Journalism: A History of the School of Journalism of the University of Missouri Columbia*, Columbia, Missouri: E. W. Stephens, p. 146. Williams (1864–1935) created the School of Journalism in 1908 and served as Dean until 1930. He was named University President in 1930 and served until 1934, when he retired. Born and raised in Boonville, Missouri, he dreamed of being a printer. As a boy, he refused to write any of his homework, preferring to print everything.

18 Williams, *Twenty Years of Education for Journalism*, p. 146.

19 Francis H. Misselwitz (1941) *The Dragon Stirs: An Intimate Sketch-book of China's Kuomintang Revolution, 1927–29*, New York: Harbinger House.

20 Hugo de Burgh (2003) "The journalist in China: looking to the past for inspiration," *Media History*, vol. 9, no. 3, December, pp. 195–207.

21 De Burgh, "The journalist in China," pp. 195–207.

22 Also known as Dong Xiangguang.

23 Wu was awarded the Missouri Press Association Honor Medal in 1948. Also, in 1986, he published *A Historical Analysis of Selected Speeches of Generalissimo Chiang Kai-shek During the War of Resistance Against Japanese Aggression*, Oxford, Ohio: Ohio University Press.

24 British-American Tobacco (BAT) was the largest single advertiser in Shanghai and formed its own modern film studio which produced slides and promotional films for free distribution to cinemas. It was considered one of the most advanced and technically equipped film studios outside America at the time.

25 Williams, *Twenty Years of Education for Journalism*, p. 146.

26 *China Weekly Review*, special edition, October 10, 1928.

27 Hallett Abend (1943) *My Life in China 1926–1941*, New York: Harcourt, Brace & Co., p. 200.

Chapter 4

1 Carl Crow (1984) *Handbook for China*, Oxford: Oxford University Press, p. 222.

2 This became known as the "Double Ten" in the Nationalist calendar.

3 Carl Crow (1944) *China Takes Her Place*, New York: Harper & Brothers, p. 13.

4 Crow, *China Takes Her Place*, p. 14.

5 Wu Ting-fang (1914) *America Through the Spectacles of an Oriental Diplomat*, New York: Stokes; M. M. Dawson (1915) *The Ethics of Confucius*, introduction by Wu Ting-fang, New York: G. P. Putnam & Sons.

6 Hume quoted in J. Spence (1980) *To Change China: Western Advisers in China*, New York: Penguin, p. 168.

7 Crow, *China Takes Her Place*, p. 26.

8 Crow, *China Takes Her Place*, p. 31.

9 Quotation reprinted in *The China Weekly Review*, special new China edition, October 10, 1928.

10 Crow's relationship with Chen was short-lived as his popularity sank due to rising corruption and high taxation and he was soon ousted from his post in Shanghai. He went on to stage several uprisings, including the failed Second Revolution against Yuan Shih-kai in 1912 with Chiang Kai-shek and was then assassinated on Yuan's orders in 1916, a month before Yuan himself died.

11 Crow noted that Webb "got very handsomely paid" for this work: *China Takes Her Place*, p. 35.

12 Crow, *China Takes Her Place*, p. 36.

13 ———— p. 37.

14 ———— p. 37.

15 ———— p. 40.

16 The New Army was created in the wake of China's stunning defeat by the Japanese in 1895.

17 After Yuan's death, Duan fought a half-hearted power struggle and eventually retired in 1926 to concentrate on his Buddhist studies and mahjong skills.

18 David Bonavia (1995) *China's Warlords*, Oxford: Oxford University Press, p. 2.

19 Crow, *China Takes Her Place*, p. 47.

20 Crow, *China Takes Her Place*, p. 50.

21 ———— p. 48.

22 The Chinese term for the official headquarters or residence of a mandarin.

23 Carl Crow (1940) *Foreign Devils in the Flowery Kingdom*, New York: Harper & Brothers, p. 133.

24 Crow, *China Takes Her Place*, p. 96.

25 Foreign Office, FO228 3214, *Shanghai Intelligence 1918–20*, Meeting of December 12, 1918. This registration with the Japanese was later to cause many newspapers acute embarrassment as relations with Tokyo started to deteriorate.

26 Bronson Rea, G. (1935) *The Case for Manchoukuo*, New York: Appleton-Century.

Chapter 5

1 Quote from H. J. Lethbridge, Introduction, Carl Crow (1984) *Handbook for China*, Oxford: Oxford University Press. Lethbridge was formerly Professor of Sociology at the University of Hong Kong.

2 Sowerby was well known as having been a member of American millionaire Robert Sterling Clark's expedition to Northern China in 1908–09. Under Clark's leadership, an expedition of 36 men carried out zoological and ethnological research. The expedition came to an abrupt end, however, when Chinese bandits killed the party's Indian surveyor and interpreter, Hazrat Ali. Clark personally funded several major research trips around the world due to his being an heir to the Singer sewing machine fortune.

3 Carl Crow (1914) *America and the Philippines*, Garden City, New York: Doubleday, Page & Co.

4 "Writer plans to stay in city: Carl Crow visits Manila en route to New York", *Manila Times*, January 10, 1913.

5 At that time, a round-the-world cruise could actually work out cheaper than sailing from point to point.

6 Ray was never heard from again and no trace of his whereabouts was ever discovered. His wife, Mabel, eventually remarried. In the 1930s, Mabel and Ray's son George lived in Shanghai where he ran the passenger division of the Robert Dollar steamship line. Naturally they were close to Carl who treated George as a favored nephew.

7 "Philippines no burden says editor Carl Crow," *St. Louis Times*, November 3, 1913.

8 Living by the imperial palace and the Hie Shrine must have given Crow a fairly immediate sense of traditional Japan. The Hie Shrine (built in 1644–48) is located atop a little hill at the edge of Akasaka and is reached by a steep flight of stairs under a tunnel of orange torii. The shrine grounds are considered an oasis of tranquility in the middle of Tokyo.

9   Carl Crow (1916) *Japan and America*, New York: Robert M. McBride & Co, p. 46.

10   Sometimes called the *Japan Advertiser and Trans-Pacific*.

11   Carl Crow (1944) *China Takes Her Place*, New York: Harper & Brothers, p. 151. The study was eventually published as Carl Crow (1942) *Japan's Dream of World Empire – The Tanaka Memorial*, New York: Harper & Brothers.

12   Crow, *China Takes Her Place*, p. 153.

13   Crow, *Japan and America*, p. 4.

14   Carl Crow (1937) *I Speak for the Chinese*, New York: Harper & Brothers, pp. 2–3.

15   It was also the case that Japan had fought with the British and others to suppress the Boxers in 1900 and this clouded the thinking of many British diplomats and China Hands.

16   Crow, *Japan and America*, p. 299.

17   The Bank of Japan, later renamed the Bank of Tokyo.

18   Crow, *I Speak for the Chinese*, p. 7.

19   Crow, *I Speak for the Chinese*, p. 11.

20   Crow, *Japan's Dream of World Empire*.

21   Crow, *Japan and America*, p. 142.

22   Carl Crow (1943) *The Chinese Are Like That*, Cleveland: World Publishing Company p. 36.

23   Carl Crow (1939) *He Opened the Door of Japan*, New York: Harper & Brothers, p. 123.

24   Samuel George Blythe was a veteran correspondent with the *Saturday Evening Post* and stayed in London to cover the war after crossing Siberia with Crow. He later returned to China in 1917 to interview several prominent warlords.

25   Crow, *The Chinese Are Like That*, p. 216.

26   *Japan Advertiser*, July 19, 1945.

27   Which, of course, he would have: Hallett Abend (1943) *My Life in China 1926–1941*, New York: Harcourt, Brace & Co., p. 60.

28   Earl A. Selle (1948) *Donald of China*, New York: Harper & Brothers, pp. 153–69. Donald was famously tight-lipped about his experiences in China. Selle, a journalist, claimed that the details in his overtly pro-Donald biography were told to him by the man himself in 1946 on his deathbed.

Chapter 6

1   Crow did not write a great deal about his experiences or rationale for becoming a fruit farmer in California. Even if it was to settle briefly while his daughter was born, the choice of fruit farming in California is far from an obvious one and his agricultural skills are unknown. There are few references in his books, personal papers, diaries or later articles to this time. Most of the details of his time in Santa Clara are derived from an essay he wrote – "Silhouette: The Great War on the China Front" – which remained unpublished and is part of the Carl Crow Archive at Missouri University, folder 48A.

2   *Japan Advertiser*, July 19, 1915.

3   *Japan Advertiser*, July 19, 1915.

4   Actually at 53 Washington Square and adjacent to the Judson Memorial Church. The hotel had been established to provide income for the church.

5   "Dining where the adventurers eat in a South Washington Square hotel," *New York World*, September 21, 1915.

6   Steffanson also became known for existing largely on a "raw diet" of unprocessed foods, including raw meats, animal organs and fats. He advocated this dietary regime in three books: *Cancer: Disease of Civilization?*, *Not by Bread Alone* and *The Fat of the Land*. Steffanson stuck to this diet for much of his adult life, changing to a more refined and processed diet only after he married later in life. He is also famous for his wry quote: "False modesty is better than no modesty at all." He was later accused by McCarthy of being a Communist and a spy for Red China, along with Owen Lattimore.

7   Mason led a number of expeditions to South America, including the 1926 Mason-Spinden Expedition to search for Mayan ruins in Mexico. He was also the author of a briefly popular utopian novel published in 1956, *The Golden Archer: A Satirical Novel of 1975*, which imagines the threat of religious war following a stalemate in World War III.

8   Croy was credited as being a member of the first graduating class of the Missouri School of Journalism (though he never actually graduated and dropped out before the course finished). He later gained fame as a writer with books such as *Jesse James was My Neighbor* and *He Hanged Them High: An Account of the Fanatical Judge Who Hanged Eighty Eight Men*. He also wrote several books about the Hollywood film industry, including a biography of D. W. Griffith.

9   Carl Crow (1914) *America and the Philippines*, Garden City, New York: Doubleday, Page & Co.

10   Crow, *America and the Philippines*.

11   Crow never revealed the name of this man but it was most likely Harry Steptoe. For many years, Steptoe was head of the British Secret Intelligence Service in Shanghai attached to the British Consulate and, as well as its own shadowy activities, also undertook the role of collating reports from Special Branch in Shanghai as well as the reports of the British Colonial Police in Singapore and Hong Kong.

12   Now Yanan Road.

13   Crow, "Silhouette – The Great War on the China Front," Crow Archive, folder F48.

14   Crow, "Silhouette – The Great War on the China Front."

15   Carl Crow (1937) *I Speak for the Chinese*, New York: Harper & Brothers, p. 19.

16   Later to be promoted to American Ambassador to China.

17   Crow, "Silhouette – The Great War on the China Front."

18   Carl Crow (1940) *Foreign Devils in the Flowery Kingdom*, New York: Harper & Brothers, p. 219.

19   Crow, *Foreign Devils in the Flowery Kingdom*, p. 220.

20   The existence of these secret treaties signed between Japan, Britain, France, Belgium,

Russia and Italy only came to light after the 1917 Russian Revolution when the Bolsheviks made them public.

21 Also known as Feng Yuxiang (see also endnote 7, chapter 20).

22 Carl Crow (1944) *China Takes Her Place*, New York: Harper & Brothers, p. 117.

23 The author is indebted to Ellen Johnston Laing of the University of Michigan for information on Mildred Crow and her business ventures.

Chapter 7

1 Named after the seventeenth-century French author and now 7 Xianshan Road.

2 To be fair to Sun, this appears to have stopped after his marriage to Soong Ching-Ling.

3 Now Fuxing Park – originally laid out in 1909.

4 The house that is now the official Soong Qingling Residence and Museum at 1843 Huai Hai Middle Road.

5 Cohen eventually became a general in the Nationalist army as well as a property tycoon and arms-dealer. He moved to Hong Kong in 1937, surviving on a pension arranged for him by Madame Sun, and then was interned in the British colony by the Japanese. In 1945 he returned to Canada briefly, only to eventually settle in London's East End.

6 Carl Crow (1943) *The Chinese Are Like That*, Cleveland: World Publishing Company, pp. 196–7.

7 Carl Crow (1944) *China Takes Her Place*, New York: Harper & Brothers, p. 63.

8 Crow recalled his English conversations with Sun in his unpublished essay describing his meeting with Zhou En-lai later in 1938 – "The puzzle of Communism", Crow Archive, folder 36A.

9 Regarded by the British as one of China's ablest soldiers, Chen gained his sobriquet after settling his forces in the Hakka area of southern China. He was originally from Guangdong and had been Vice-Governor of the province in 1911 until ousted in the 1913 Second Revolution. He was considered generally more enlightened than most warlords at the time.

10 Crow himself admitted to following developments in Italy and the rise of Mussolini with interest and an open mind at first before becoming an avowed anti-fascist.

11 Carl Crow (1940) *Foreign Devils in the Flowery Kingdom*, New York: Harper & Brothers, p. 123.

12 Crow, *China Takes Her Place*, p. 75. This friendship appears to have been based more on Crow's reading William's work rather than actually knowing him.

13 The ABMAC was an august body at the time, with Madame Chiang Kai-shek as honorary chairman and prominent supporters included Pearl Buck, Wendell Willkie, Fiorello LaGuardia and a number of film stars. In the period 1937–45, the ABMAC donated more than $10 million in aid to China. The UCCRC was the largest and most important organization of its type at the time with an equally august roster of committee members.

Chapter 8

1   Jonathan Fenby (2003) *Generalissimo Chiang Kai-shek and the China He Lost*, London: Free Press, p. 31.

2   Gunther (1939) *Inside Asia*, London: Hamilton. See also Vincent Sheean (1934) *Personal History*, Garden City, New York: Doubleday, Doran and Co., Inc.

3   Sincere was opened in 1917, Wing On in 1918 and Sun Sun in 1926.

4   Or *Ka Loo Guanggao Gongsi* (Carl Crow Advertising Company) in modern pinyin.

5   Gibb, Livingston & Co. were general merchants in Shanghai and Hong Kong and eventually became part of the Inchcape Group. Jinkee Road is now Dianchi Road.

6   Carl Crow (1926) "Advertising and merchandising" in J. Arnold *China: A Commercial and Industrial Handbook*, US Department of Commerce Washington DC: Government Printing Office, p. 199.

7   Crow, "Advertising and merchandising," p. 200.

8   Crow, "Advertising and merchandising," p. 200.

9   Xie stayed on in Shanghai during the war and later re-emerged after 1949 to create art that supported Mao and his policies. In 1954 Xie and his nephew Xie Mulian were both assigned to the government-run Shanghai Picture Press. Xie was later moved to the Shanghai Painting Academy. He was forced to walk a thin political line and suffered public criticism. He did produce a number of socialist realist works, including "Warmly love Chairman Mao" as well as portraits of the imaginary revolutionary hero and everyman, Lei Feng. Even this did not protect him during the Cultural Revolution when he was personally attacked by Jiang Qing (Madame Mao). He died in Shanghai in 1976.

10   Pearl S. Buck (1944) *The Dragon Fish*, New York: The John Day Company.

11   Ralph Shaw (1973) *Sin City*, London: Everest Books, p. 52.

12   D. de Martel, and L. De Hoyer (1926) *Silhouettes of Peking*, Peking: China Booksellers Ltd.

13   Quoted in John Keay (1997) *Last Post: The End of Empire in the Far East*, London: John Murray, p. 61.

14   Carl Crow (1943) *The Chinese Are Like That*, Cleveland: World Publishing Company, p. 52.

15   Crow, *The Chinese Are Like That*, p. 52.

16   ———— p. 56.

17   Between the wars the cenotaph was one of the most imposing structures on the Bund.

18   Comment by Starr contained in "Letter from New York Office of the FBI to the Coordinator of Information, FBI," April 19, 1942.

19   Carl Van Doren (1885–1950) was an American author and teacher whose writings ranged through surveys of literature to novels, biography to criticism.

20   Carl Crow (1937) *Four Hundred Million Customers*, New York: Harper & Brothers, p. 304.

21   Alice Tisdale Hobart (1933) *Oil for the Lamps of China*, New York: Grosset & Dunlap.

Chapter 9

1 Also known as Feng Yuxiang. Fengtian is now Liaoning province.
2 Carl Crow (1944) *China Takes Her Place*, New York: Harper & Brothers, p. 46.
3 Though the warlords have largely been written out of official Chinese history, Feng appeared to undergo a partial rehabilitation in the early 1990s when the official *People's Daily* referred to him as a "patriotic general" – *Renmin Ribao*, February 21, 1993, p. 5.
4 Later to be denounced as a Trotskyite and purged by Stalin.
5 Or alternatively *dujun* or *junfa*.
6 Peter Fleming (2004) *One's Company – A Journey to China in 1933*, London: Pimlico, p. 131.
7 David Bonavia (1995) *China's Warlords*, Oxford: Oxford University Press, p. 6.
8 When talking about this period, Crow always referred to the bandit leader as Swen Miao, although he is more commonly known by the names Sun Mei-yao or Suen Mei-yao, or even Mao-yao.
9 Carl Crow (1943) *The Chinese Are Like That*, Cleveland: World Publishing Company, p. 313.
10 John Benjamin Powell, "The bandits' 'golden eggs' depart," *Asia*, December 1923.
11 Crow, *The Chinese Are Like That*, p. 314.
12 Crow, *The Chinese Are Like That*, p. 315.
13 Crow referred to Swen's organization as the Shantung People's Liberation Society while J. B. Powell called it the "People's Self Deliverance Army"; and in letters Swen wrote during the crisis he used the term "Self Governed Army for the Establishment of the Country". In yet another version, it was sometimes called the "National Reconstruction and Autonomy Army."
14 Lehrbas had been on the train accompanying J. B. Powell to see damming work on the Yellow River. An Idaho native, he had been a cadet in the First World War and went on to work for AP, reporting on the German invasion of Poland, and was MacArthur's personal aide-de-camp throughout the Second World War.
15 J. Gunther (1939) *Inside Asia*, London: Hamilton, p. 146.
16 Carl Crow (1943) *The Chinese Are Like That*, p. 117.
17 The full story is told in R. Bickers (2003) *Empire Made Me: An Englishman Adrift in Shanghai*, London: Penguin, pp. 189–91.
18 Sometimes spelt Paotzuku or Pao Tse Ku and now the Baodugu National Forest Park and mountain in Shandong.
19 John Benjamin Powell, *North China Herald*, May 19, 1923.
20 The Red Cross often used prominent people on missions such as this – although it also maintained a full-time staff in China. In 1923 the latter included a World War 1 veteran and US army language student (who had been born in the same year as Crow) called Joseph B. Stilwell who later was to become the well-known General Joseph "Vinegar Joe" Stilwell. He was based in Beijing as a Military Attaché but was active in constructing roads and providing famine relief in Shanxi and Shandong, as well as sending reports to the American legation on opium consumption in Shanxi.

21 Crow used the spelling Tsaochwang though Tsaochuang was also common.

22 Crow, *The Chinese Are Like That*, p. 319.

23 John Benjamin Powell (1945) *My Twenty-Five Years in China*, New York: Macmillan, p. 108.

24 A stamp collector sold one of Crow's Bandit Mail Stamps, which are extremely rare and sought after, on a small envelope for a sum in excess of US$5,000 recently.

25 Norwood Francis Allman (1893–1987) prided himself on his consular record, having served at the US Legation in Beijing as well as at Antung in Manchuria, Tianjin, Jinan, Qingdao, Chongqing, and Shanghai. In a later twist of fate, Allman was to resign from the consular service and move into the newspaper business after a period as a successful lawyer in China. After being interned in Hong Kong during the war, he went on to be the Chief of Far East Section of America's Secret Intelligence Branch in the later war years before returning to Shanghai to become the editor and publisher of the *China Press* in 1948. He is also known for his book *Shanghai Lawyer* (1943) New York: McGraw-Hill.

26 Carl Crow, "The most interesting character I ever knew," Crow Archive, folder 107A.

27 Crow, "The most interesting character I ever knew."

28 Carl Crow (1940) *Foreign Devils in the Flowery Kingdom*, New York: Harper & Brothers, pp. 318–9.

29 Anderson sadly died prematurely of pneumonia in 1925 at the point when President Coolidge was reportedly considering appointing him Minister to Beijing.

30 *North China Herald*, June 16, 1923.

31 Crow, *Foreign Devils in the Flowery Kingdom*, pp. 324–5.

32 J. O. P. Bland (1921) *China, Japan and Korea*, London: Heinemann, p. 93.

33 Crow, *Foreign Devils in the Flowery Kingdom*, p. 246.

34 Maurice Tinkler, the subject of Robert Bickers' book *Empire Made Me*, met Crow at the Liuhe battlefield and later thought his version of events inaccurate. R. Bickers, *Empire Made Me*, London: Allen Lane, p. 225.

35 David Bonavia (1995) *China's Warlords*, Oxford: Oxford University Press, p. 33.

36 Crow, *Foreign Devils in the Flowery Kingdom*, pp. 225–6.

Chapter 10

1 Carl Crow (1940) *Foreign Devils in the Flowery Kingdom*, New York: Harper & Brothers, p. 286.

2 Carl Crow (1939) *He Opened the Door of Japan*, New York: Harper & Brothers, p. 124. In making this comment, Crow seems to have omitted the fact that he had already been married for over a decade. The subject of his divorce from Mildred was one Crow did not care to discuss.

3 Crow, *Foreign Devils in the Flowery Kingdom*, p. 275.

4 Crow, *Foreign Devils in the Flowery Kingdom*, p. 275.

5 Hallett Abend (1943) *My Life in China 1926–1941*, New York: Harcourt, Brace & Co., pp. 64–5.

6 Stella Dong (2001) *Shanghai: The Rise and Fall of a Decadent City*, New York: Perennial, p. 124. When Chang died, his concubines looted his safe and fled.
7 Also Wang Jingwei.
8 Also Liao Zhong-kai.
9 Also known as Zhang Jingjiang or Zhang Renjie, or, to the French Concession police, "Quasimodo" due to his spinal deformity.
10 Crow, *Foreign Devils in the Flowery Kingdom*, p. 246.
11 Chiang's old adversary, Chen Chiung-ming, was never to bother him again and went into exile in Hong Kong, eventually dying of typhus in 1933.

Chapter 11

1 Connaught Road is now Kanding Road. Crow's house at 883 is now demolished and a small supermarket stands in its place.
2 John Benjamin Powell (1945) *My Twenty-Five Years in China*, New York: Macmillan.
3 The Japanese tore down the statue of Parkes for scrap in 1941. Now a statue of Chen Yi, the first post-liberation Mayor of Shanghai, stands on the original plinth.
4 Carl Crow (1941) *Meet The South Americans*, New York: Harper & Brothers, p. 11.
5 Crow, *Meet The South Americans*, pp. 11–2.
6 Carl Crow (1943) *The Chinese Are Like That*, Cleveland: World Publishing Company, p. 99.
7 Crow, *The Chinese Are Like That*, p. 100.
8 ——— pp. 260–1.
9 ——— p. 283.
10 Crow, *Meet The South Americans*, p. 15.
11 *The China Journal*, vol XXIV, no. 5, May 1936.
12 The story is retold in *Meet The South Americans*, pp. 129–30.
13 Crow, *The Chinese Are Like That*, p. 39.
14 Crow, *The Chinese Are Like That*, p. 47.
15 The site of the British golf course is now the Shanghai Zoo on Hongqiao Road near Hami Road, quote from *Fortune* magazine, January 1935.
16 Crow, *The Chinese Are Like That*, p. 208.
17 Crow, *The Chinese Are Like That*, p. 25.
18 ——— p. 217.
19 ——— p. 270.
20 ——— p. 271.
21 Stella Dong (2001) *Shanghai: The Rise and Fall of a Decadent City*, New York: Perennial, pp. 202–3. According to Dong, "Light in the Head" was a famous beggar who would drive a nail into the top of his shaven head and then attach a lighted candle to it while the "Weeping Beggar Woman" would cry so copiously that she was always surrounded by a large crowd of onlookers.
22 Crow, *The Chinese Are Like That*, p. 275.
23 Interestingly, as well as Crow's generally well-heeled American friends who

24   Emily Hahn (2000) *No Hurry to Get Home*, Emeryville, California: Seal Press, p. 221.

considered rickshaws exploitative, the other group of foreigners who did not like using their services were the clique of Soviet advisers in Shanghai.

25   Blood Alley was off what is now Jingling Road, while the Badlands area was adjacent to Jessfield Park and the old St. John's University, which is now the Zhongshan Park area. Blood Alley was officially Rue Chu Pao San, off Avenue Edward VII, ironically named after a noted local councillor and philanthropist – and close to the British non-conformist St. Joseph's Church.

26   Carl Crow (1939) *He Opened the Door of Japan*, New York: Harper & Brothers, p. 20.

27   Enid Saunders Candlin (1987) *The Breach in the Wall: A Memoir of Old China*, New York: Paragon House, p. 39.

28   Carl Crow (1940) *Foreign Devils in the Flowery Kingdom*, New York: Harper & Brothers, p. 186.

29   Now the corner of Fuzhou Road and Henan Middle Road and until late 2005 home to the Shanghai High People's Court.

30   The Park Hotel remains in Nanjing West Road; the Moore Memorial Church is now a Protestant church renamed the Mo-En Church at 316 Xizhang Middle Road; the China United Apartments are now the Pacific Hotel at 104 Nanjing West Road; and the Green House is now a nightclub on the corner of 333 Tongren Road and Beijing Road.

31   *Fortune* magazine, January 1935.

32   Ralph Shaw (1973) *Sin City*, London: Everest Books, p. 141.

33   So called after the bubbling well in the Jingan Temple along the street – now Nanjing West Road.

34   Crow, *Meet the South Americans*, p. 57.

35   Crow, *The Chinese Are Like That*, p. 34.

36   Crow, *Foreign Devils in the Flowery Kingdom*, p. 261.

37   Hahn, *No Hurry to Get Home*, p. 255.

38   *Fortune* magazine, January 1935.

39   Crow, *The Chinese Are Like That*, p. 89.

40   Hardoon (1846–1931) was born in Baghdad to a Jewish family. He had worked for the Sassoons, another Baghdadi Jewish family. He married a Chinese woman named Luo "Lisa" Jialing (1864–1941). Property speculation along Nanking Road made him wealthy; he established the Hardoon Trading Company in 1901 and was the largest property owner on Nanking Road by 1916.

41   *Chota peg* was China coast slang for any small drink and derived from Hindustani.

42   The anonymous comments were part of a recommendation for Crow's employment by the American government in 1942. The name of the referee who made the remark has been deleted from the records, Letter from New York Office of the FBI to the Coordinator of Information, FBI, April 19, 1942.

43   Crow, *The Chinese Are Like That*, p. 127.

44   The Lyceum is still at the junction of Maoming Road and Changle Road and is now

a theatre again. Perhaps the most famous graduate from the amateur dramatics at the Lyceum was Margaret "Peggy" Hookham, the daughter of a British-American Tobacco executive in Shanghai. She eventually left to study ballet in London and became better known as Dame Margot Fonteyn.

45 Crow, *The Chinese Are Like That*, p. 146.
46 *Shanghai Municipal Gazette*, February 2, 1935.
47 Crow, *The Chinese Are Like That*, p. 91.

Chapter 12

1 Carl Crow (1944) *China Takes Her Place*, New York: Harper & Brothers, p. 80. Chiang, though, was born only 100 miles south of Shanghai in Zhejiang province.
2 Crow, *China Takes Her Place*, p. 83.
3 ——— p. 83.
4 Officially Mikhail Markovich Grunzeberg. He had taken the name of a Russian composer as a pseudonym to confuse the police.
5 Gould's comments on Borodin were originally in a 1927 article for *The Trans-Pacific* newspaper and were quoted in J. Spence (1980) *To Change China: Western Advisers in China*, New York: Penguin, p. 188.
6 Crow, *China Takes Her Place*, p. 85.
7 The SMC building was located at the junction of Jiangxi and Fuzhou Roads. It was also home to both Special Branch and British Secret Intelligence in Shanghai.
8 For details of Fessenden and Du's connections and agreement in 1927, see John Benjamin Powell (1945) *My Twenty-Five Years in China*, New York: Macmillan, p. 158.
9 John Keay (1997) *Last Post: The End of Empire in the Far East*, London: John Murray, p. 149.

Chapter 13

1 The *Shanghai Mercury* had been a much earlier newspaper that had for a time been taken under Japanese ownership and control before being absorbed by the *Shanghai Evening Post*.
2 Asiatic Underwriters Federal became American International Underwriters (AIU), and then AIG, the first foreign company to move back into its former HQ on the Bund in the 1990s.
3 *Fortune* magazine, January 1935.
4 Ezra was extremely rich and lived in considerable style in the Ezra mansion with Louis XV furniture throughout and a ballroom for 150 dancers, a music room that could seat 80 people, and 25 acres of garden. In 1926, Ezra wrote the book *Chinese Jews*.
5 *Israel's Messenger* was published from 1904 to 1941 – first as a fortnightly, then a

monthly. It was strongly Zionist but also reported on the Jewish community in Shanghai, Jewish communities in other parts of China and world events.

6   Ralph Shaw (1973) *Sin City*, London: Everest Books, p. 53.

7   US Department of State, Document 893.91, June 5, 1919.

8   Carl Crow "Advertising and merchandising" in J. Arnold *China: A Commercial and Industrial Handbook*, US Department of Commerce, Washington DC: Government Printing Office, p. 196.

9   Also known as Chen Youren and Chen Yu-jen. He remained a leftist and eventually broke with the KMT and opposed Chiang Kai-shek.

10 Hallett Abend (1943) *My Life in China 1926–1941*, New York: Harcourt, Brace & Co., p. 19.

11 Starr was later interviewed in 1942 by the FBI as part of Crow's clearance to work for the government. Starr praised Crow as a "brilliant and capable individual" but said that he "had proved to be a rather poor businessman" while at the *Post*, Letter from New York Office of the FBI to the Coordinator of Information, FBI, April 19, 1942.

12 Jinan had a large Japanese population and Tokyo responded violently to Chiang's capture of the city.

13 Peking meaning "northern capital" and Peiping meaning "northern peace."

Chapter 14

1   Carl Crow (1944) *China Takes Her Place*, New York, Harper & Brothers, p. 118.

2   Crow, *China Takes Her Place*, p.118.

3   —— p. 149.

4   —— p. 137.

5   —— p. 139.

6   —— p. 149.

7   Hallett Abend (1943) *My Life in China 1926–1941*, New York: Harcourt, Brace & Co., p.117.

8   Jonathan Fenby (2003) "The extraordinary secret of Madame Chiang Kai-shek," *Guardian Newspapers*, April 11.

9   Mei-ling minored in philosophy and, upon her graduation in 1917, was named a Durant Scholar, Wellesley's highest academic honor.

10 American Lucy Randolph Mason (1882–1959), invariably known as "Miss Lucy," was the daughter of an Episcopal clergyman and scion of a distinguished southern family. She championed the cause of the YWCA and women's suffrage, the Union Labor League and the Virginia Equal Suffrage League. She worked later for the Congress of Industrial Organizations (CIO).

11 Crow, *China Takes Her Place*, p. 143.

12 S. Seagrave (1996) *The Soong Dynasty*, London: Corgi, pp. 136–7.

13 Crow, *China Takes Her Place*, p. 140.

14 Mao Fu-mei was the mother of Chiang Ching-kuo who succeeded Chiang Kai-shek

as President of Taiwan in 1978. After Chiang divorced her, Mao lived in Guangzhou and Shanghai. She was killed in a Japanese air raid on Chiang's home village in Zhejiang in 1939.

15 Seagrave, p.165.

16 Crow, *China Takes Her Place*, p. 136.

17 Crow, *China Takes Her Place*, p. 149.

18 Crow, *China Takes Her Place*, p. 150.

Chapter 15

1 Manchukuo means "Country of the Manchus" and is often referred to as Manchuguo in pinyin.

2 Also known as Wu Tiesheng and referred to as Wu Te-elen by Crow in his notes on the incident. Wu was a former police chief in Guangzhou. After 1937 he escaped to Hong Kong where he organized famously long poker games with Morris "Two Gun" Cohen and then moved on to Chongqing after the fall of Hong Kong.

3 Carl Crow (1937) *I Speak for the Chinese*, New York: Harper & Brothers, p. 55.

4 Arguably the Japanese ruse was even more transparent. W. H. Donald remembered that he phoned the mayor at 11:05 p.m. from his room in the Astor House Hotel to report shooting.

5 Crow, *I Speak for the Chinese*, p. 56.

6 Named after Bishop Boone who had founded the American Settlement in Shanghai.

7 Or alternatively the First Shanghai War – the Second being in 1937.

8 Casualty figures from D. A. Jordan (2001) *China's Trial by Fire: The Shanghai War of 1932*, Ann Arbor: University of Michigan Press. Crow's estimates are from *I Speak for the Chinese*.

9 Soong was back in office within a month, having used his resignation as a tactic to get Chiang to see sense on his expenditure plans. The 1932 Shanghai War did Japan little good economically either as stock prices fell along with the value of the yen.

10 Though Du Yuesheng did organize some sniper squads to target Japanese-held areas. However, this was counterbalanced by the fact that the Green Gang pretty soon started co-operating with the Japanese to keep their illicit businesses running in Japanese-controlled Shanghai.

11 Crow, *I Speak for the Chinese*, p. 58.

12 Crow, *I Speak for the Chinese*, pp. 61–2.

13 ——— p. 62.

14 L. Lee Ou-fan (1999) *Shanghai Modern: The Flowering of New Urban Culture in China, 1930–45*, Cambridge, Massachusetts: Harvard University Press.

Chapter 16

1   Carl Crow (1944) *China Takes Her Place*, New York: Harper & Brothers, p. 163.
2   Then Ichang and now part of the area around the site of the Three Gorges Dam project.
3   Then Chinkiang.
4   Wuhu is in Anhui province. Now Kiukiang is Jiujiang and Anking is Anqing.
5   The Yangtze white dolphin is now almost extinct while the Yangtze alligator – *Alligator sinensis* – is thought to be extinct through a combination of pollution and slaughter for its hide.
6   Meyrick Hewlett (1943) *Forty Years in China*, London: Macmillan.
7   P. Thompson and R. Macklin (2004) *The Man Who Died Twice: The Life and Adventures of Morrison of Peking*, Sydney: Allen & Unwin, pp. 88–9.
8   Crow, *China Takes Her Place*, p. 170.
9   Jehol (also known as Rehe) no longer exists as a separate province in China. In 1955, Jehol was divided between Inner Mongolia and the provinces of Hebei and Liaoning.
10 Crow, *China Takes Her Place*, pp. 183–4. Kalgan being Zhangjiakou; Hepei being Hebei; Tientsin being Tianjin; and the Gulf of Pechili being the Bohai Gulf.
11 Korea at the time was a Japanese colony.
12 Crow Archive, folder 67.
13 Named after the masterless Samurai swordsman of Japan.
14 Crow, *China Takes Her Place*, p. 54.
15 The notes and draft chapters by Crow on the Japanese-sponsored opium trade are to be found in the Crow Archive at the University of Missouri.
16 Carl Crow (1943) *The Chinese Are Like That*, Cleveland, World Publishing Company, p. 246.
17 Crow, *The Chinese Are Like That*, pp. 246–7.
18 ———— p. 249.
19 Also known as Zhang Xueliang.
20 E. Hahn (1944) *China To Me*, New York: Doubleday, Doran & Co., p. 44.
21 Carl Crow (1937) *I Speak for the Chinese*, New York: Harper & Brothers, p. 75. Things did not turn out so well for Chang Hsueh-Liang who, after releasing Chiang, surrendered and was tried and sentenced for his part in the affair. He was pardoned but kept in custody until 1962 when he was taken to Taiwan where he became a committed Christian. He died in Hawaii in 2001 after having moved there in 1995. In 1991, in his first interview on his life, Chang said of the Xian Incident, "It was a rebellion and I had to take responsibility for it."
22 Hahn, *China To Me*, p. 44.
23 The Young Marshall's, and his wife's, cure for drug addiction and hospital treatment were all arranged by Donald while he was his adviser.
24 Carl Crow (1937) *Four Hundred Million Customers*, New York: Harper & Brothers, p. 155.
25 Crow, *Four Hundred Million Customers*, p. 156.

Chapter 17

1 See the letter of January 15, 1937, to Crow in Crow Archive, folder 133. Another journalist, Hallett Abend of the *New York Times*, reported large Japanese troop build-ups in Korea and Manchuria and was chastised by the American Ambassador to China as being alarmist.

2 Carl Crow (1940) *Foreign Devils in the Flowery Kingdom*, New York: Harper & Brothers, p. 251.

3 Carl Crow (1943) *The Chinese Are Like That*, Cleveland: World Publishing Company, p. vii.

4 Christopher Isherwood and Wystan Hugh Auden (1938) *Journey to a War*, London: Faber & Faber.

5 Carl Crow (1944) *China Takes Her Place*, New York: Harper & Brothers, p. 192.

6 Crow, *China Takes Her Place*, p. 192.

7 "Chinese will wear down foe, believes Shanghai man, here," *Seattle Daily Times*, September 16, 1937.

8 Crow, *China Takes Her Place*, p. 193.

9 "Chinese will wear down foe," *Seattle Daily Times*.

10 Crow, *Foreign Devils in the Flowery Kingdom*, pp. 161–2.

11 Now Xizang Road.

12 Crow, *China Takes Her Place*, p. 198.

13 For the best and most thorough account of the events in Nanjing, see Iris Chang (1997) *The Rape of Nanking*, London: Penguin.

14 James Graham Ballard (1984) *Empire of the Sun*, London: Simon & Schuster.

15 Stella Dong (2001) *Shanghai: The Rise and Fall of a Decadent City*, New York: Perennial, p. 255.

16 Crow, *China Takes Her Place*, p. 193.

17 Crow, *Foreign Devils in the Flowery Kingdom*, p. 330.

18 "Chinese will wear down foe," *Seattle Daily Times*.

Chapter 18

1 The grenade, wrapped in newspaper, hit Powell on the shoulder. He picked it up and was left holding the bomb with the firing-pin hanging half out while his bodyguard looked for the assailant. Powell replaced the grenade on the ground until a policeman came along, picked it up and walked off with it to the nearest station: John Benjamin Powell (1945) *My Twenty-Five Years in China*, New York: Macmillan.

2 Ralph Shaw (1973) *Sin City*, London: Everest Books, p. 127.

3 Bill Hosokawa notes that the Japanese found the *Shanghai Evening Post* particularly "irksome": Bill Hosokawa and Tom Noel (1988) *Out of the Frying Pan: Reflections of a Japanese American*, Boulder: University of Colorado Press.

4 Carl Crow (1984) *Handbook for China*, Oxford: Oxford University Press, p. vii.

5   Comments contained in Starr's reference for Crow, Letter from New York Office of the FBI to the Coordinator of Information, FBI, April 19, 1942.

6   Gould got out safely in 1941 and then returned to Shanghai to resume publication of the *Shanghai Evening Post* in 1949. However, things didn't work out between the Communists and Gould and he left Shanghai again, working briefly on the *Denver Post* in America before his death.

7   Alcott got out of Shanghai safely with Gould in 1941 and worked briefly in radio in Cincinnati before moving to Los Angeles where his radio show "Today in Los Angeles" became a hit. He died in Pasadena in 1965.

8   This description of Allman is from R. Elegant, *Shanghai: Crucible of Modern China*, unpublished manuscript.

9   Carl Crow (1940) *Foreign Devils in the Flowery Kingdom*, New York: Harper & Brothers, p. 9.

10 Crow, *Foreign Devils in the Flowery Kingdom*, p. 332.

11 ———— p. 332.

12 ———— p. 335.

13 Bill Wells, Shanghai 1937, web posting: http://www.lakeontariosailing.com/Shanghai.htm

14 Crow, *Foreign Devils in the Flowery Kingdom*, p. 337.

15 Quentin was Teddy Roosevelt's grandson. His father, also Theodore, was the first Westerner to hunt and kill a panda on an expedition sponsored by Chicago's Field Museum. The specimen was subsequently stuffed and exhibited in Chicago. Quentin later returned to Shanghai and in 1948 was killed in a plane crash while flying to Hong Kong in heavy fog. Earle Looker was the author of the 1929 book *The White House Gang* that immortalized their adventures as boys.

16 Crow, *Foreign Devils in the Flowery Kingdom*, p. 337.

17 Crow, *Foreign Devils in the Flowery Kingdom*, p. 337.

18 "A moving incident in Japan's uncivilised conduct," *Sandalwood Herald* (undated copy in Crow Archive).

19 "Chinese will wear down foe, believes Shanghai man, here," *Seattle Daily Times*, September 16, 1937.

20 "Chinese will wear down foe," *Seattle Daily Times*.

21 Crow, *Foreign Devils in the Flowery Kingdom*, p. vii.

22 "Carl Crow, visiting Cape Cod, does first life on Confucius," *Cape Cod Colonial*, undated, 1937.

23 Crow, *Foreign Devils in the Flowery Kingdom*, p. viii.

24 Carl Crow (1937) *I Speak for the Chinese*, New York: Harper & Brothers, p. 78.

25 "Have the Japanese fooled themselves?", *Liberty*, August 10, 1938.

26 Crow, *I Speak for the Chinese*, p. 82.

27 Crow commented "I will say that after living several years in New England it was a relief to travel all about South America without seeing a single girl trying to look like Katherine Hepburn.": Carl Crow (1941) *Meet the South Americans*, New York: Harper & Brothers, p. 31.

28   Carl Crow (1943) *The Chinese Are Like That*, Cleveland: World Publishing Company, p. viii.

29   Carl Crow (1939) *He Opened the Door of Japan*, New York: Harper & Brothers, p. 33.

30   Crow, *He Opened the Door of Japan*, p. 44.

31   Crow, *Foreign Devils in the Flowery Kingdom*, p. 255.

32   Crow, *Foreign Devils in the Flowery Kingdom*, p. 235.

33   ——— p. 237.

34   Anna Chennault was the Chinese-born wife of General Claire Lee Chennault (1893–1958), the head of the Flying Tigers volunteer air force in China.

35   Crow, *Foreign Devils in the Flowery Kingdom*, p. 9.

36   Including "How Japan slams the door", *Saturday Evening Post*, May 7, 1938.

Chapter 19

1   Carl Crow (1940) *Foreign Devils in the Flowery Kingdom*, New York: Harper & Brothers, p. 245.

2   Charles Fulton Oursler Senior (1893–1953) also wrote a number of murder mystery novels under the pseudonym Anthony Abbot, and a narrative life of Jesus Christ – *The Greatest Story Ever Told*. After editing *Liberty*, he moved on to be a senior editor at the *Reader's Digest*.

3   Quote from Crow, *On The Long Road Back to China*, Crow Archive, folder 39A.

4   Oursler's detailed instructions to Crow are contained in his office memo to Crow, "Article He is to do on his trip to China," March 5, 1939, Crow Archive.

5   Carl Crow, *On the Long Road Back to China*.

6   Crow, *On the Long Road Back to China*. The Kialong is better known as the Jialing River.

7   A Chinese saying about Rangoon that Crow noted in his *Burma Road Diaries*, Crow Archive, folder 70A.

8   Carl Crow (1941) *Meet The South Americans*, New York: Harper & Brothers, p. 10.

9   Approximately US50 cents at the time.

10   Crow's experiences in and impressions of Rangoon are taken from *On the Road to Mandalay*, Crow Archive, folder 55A.

11   Carl Crow, *Burma Road Diaries*, Crow Archive, folder 70A.

12   Carl Crow (1944) *China Takes Her Place*, New York: Harper & Brothers, p. 225.

13   Crow, *China Takes Her Place*, p. 226.

14   Crow, *Burma Road Diaries,* Crow Archive, folder 56A.

15   The Lolos are better known today as China's Yi minority and are renowned for their high-bridged noses and Tibeto-Burman language. Lolo is now considered a somewhat derogatory term.

16   "Lolo chiefs interested in General Chiang," *China Press*, August 18, 1936.

17   Then known as Chifon. It is now in China's Yunnan province.

18   Then known as Paoshan, now in Yunnan province.

19 Officially the *Sawbwa* of Manshih.
20 J. Stilwell (2003) *The Stilwell Papers*, Beijing: Foreign Languages Press, p. 199.
21 Crow, *China Takes Her Place*, p. 237.
22 Crow, *On the Long Road Back to China.*
23 Crow, *China Takes Her Place*, p. 238.

Chapter 20

1 Luce was a missionary's son and born in the treaty port of Tengchow (now Penglai).
2 The *Yuan* being the Nationalist's parliament for China.
3 Eugene F. Saxton was a long-serving editor with Harper & Brothers and enjoyed fame in the 1930s and 1940s with a string of popular books, including Crow's *Four Hundred Million Customers* and Betty Smith's *A Tree Grows In Brooklyn*. He was renowned for driving a hard bargain.
4 If he was (and he maintained till the end of his life that he wasn't), he never published them or released them to anyone.
5 Carl Crow, *Burma Road Diaries* Crow Archive, folder 60A.
6 Christopher Isherwood and Wystan Hugh Auden (1938) *Journey to a War*, London: Faber & Faber.
7 Feng Yu-hsiang (1882–1948) held various military positions under the Qing dynasty. His 1914 conversion to Methodism gained him the sobriquet the "Christian General." Between 1920 and 1926 he struggled with various warlords for control of Manchuria before supporting the KMT. He became Minister of War and Vice Chairman of the Executive *Yuan* at Nanjing in 1928. In 1930, he broke with Chiang and launched an unsuccessful military campaign against him. From 1931 he held various offices in the KMT government, but he never again wielded significant power. In 1947, while in the US on an official mission, he denounced Chiang's government. Feng died in a fire aboard a Russian ship while en route to Odessa. For more, see James E. Sheridan (1996) *Chinese Warlord: The career of Feng Yü-hsiang*, Stanford University, California: Stanford University Press.
8 In full, Willys Ruggles Peck (1882–1952) who served as an American diplomatic and consular official in China in 1906–26 and then again in 1931–40. He later became US Minister to Thailand in 1941–42.
9 The mysterious Irishman Crow encountered was probably John Macausland, an Oxford graduate who was originally from Cork. The six-feet Macausland broadcast on Nationalist radio in English, and did wear Chinese clothes and claimed to know 15,000 Chinese characters. He did also accept Chinese citizenship in 1941. Though undoubtedly a character, Ma, or Macausland, was perhaps not as mysterious as Crow remembered. According to Emily Hahn, in her memoir *China To Me*, Ma fell desperately in love with her but was eccentric, dirty and had rotten teeth.
10 Eskelund went on to write a number of books, several of which dealt with his later travels in Africa. He also published *The Red Mandarins: Travels in Red China* (1959), London: Alvin Redman.

11 Cassin (1887–1976) was a First World War veteran who went on to become a law professor at several prestigious French universities. During the Second World War he sided with the Resistance. With the liberation of France in 1945, he became President of the Council of the National School of Administration. He later went on to serve as the President of the Court of Arbitration at the Hague (1950–59) and was a member (1959–65) and President (1965–68) of the European Court of Human Rights in Strasbourg. In 1968, he was made a Nobel Peace Prize Laureate.

12 After working at the Chinese Embassy in Washington in the 1950s, Tong was later to move to Taiwan with the Generalissimo. In 1938, he published his decidedly flattering and one-sided biography of Chiang – *Chiang Kai-shek* (1938), London: Hurst and Blackett.

13 More formally known as James L. Shen and also a graduate of Yenching University in Beijing. He survived three summers of aerial bombing by the Japanese in Chongqing before moving with Chiang to Taiwan and later becoming the Taiwanese Ambassador in Washington.

14 Emily Hahn (1944) *China To Me: A Partial Autobiography*, Philadelphia: Blakiston, pp. 84 and 91.

15 Crow contributed at least one article to *China at War* entitled "Japanese lust for atrocities", published in December 1937.

16 When meeting journalists, the couple's usual routine was for Madame to enter first and then the Generalissimo to "stop by" for a while with Madame interpreting. Exactly the same scenario occurred to a number of journalists, including Hallett Abend and Emily Hahn, who were promised audiences with Madame and the possible sparing of some time by Chiang who would invariably join them as if by accident.

17 See Carl Crow, *Burma Road diaries*, Crow Archive, folder 64A.

18 Chennault quoted in Spence, J. (1980) *To Change China: Western Advisers in China*, New York: Penguin, p. 229. After the war, Chennault's services were retained again by the Nationalist government to set up a civil airline for them.

19 T. V. Soong returned to China in 1944, becoming Prime Minister. However, he eventually fell out with the Generalissimo, became a private businessman and was reportedly for a while the richest man in the world.

20 Crow, *Burma Road Diaries*, Crow Archive, folder 64A.

21 Crow, *Burma Road Diaries*, Crow Archive, folder 70R.

22 ——— Crow Archive, folder 70A.

23 Carl Crow, *The Puzzle of Chinese Communism*, Crow Archive, Folder 36A.

24 Crow, *The Puzzle of Chinese Communism.*

25 Crow, *The Puzzle of Chinese Communism.*

26 Crow, *The Puzzle of Chinese Communism.*

27 Roy, an Indian Brahmin and Comintern operative, was sent to China in the dwindling days of Borodin's influence. He argued that rural revolution was the way forward as opposed to Borodin's emphasis on the industrial proletariat. Roy argued that the peasants should be armed, that revolution should come from below, and that soviets should be set up in the countryside.

28 Jonathan Mirsky (2002) "Getting the story in China: American reporters since 1972," *Harvard Asia Quarterly*, vol. VI, no.1, winter.

29 Crow, *The Puzzle of Chinese Communism*.

30 Crow, *The Puzzle of Chinese Communism*.

31 Mirsky, "Getting the story in China."

32 *The Puzzle of Chinese Communism*. Crow also later elaborated on this theme in a letter to the editor of the *Berkshire Evening Eagle* after he took exception to the report of a lecture given by Mrs. Carveth Wells (the wife of the explorer, author and radio personality of the time) in an address to the Pittsfield College Club. See Letter to the editor, "Chinese communism," *Berkshire Evening Eagle*, February 13, 1940.

33 Carl Crow (1941) *Meet The South Americans*, New York: Harper & Brothers, p. 167.

34 Crow, *The Puzzle of Chinese Communism*.

35 Crow, *The Puzzle of Chinese Communism*.

36 Crow, *Burma Road Diaries*, Crow Archive, folder 64A.

37 This second 'lifeline' to Chongqing was cut after the Fall of France and the Japanese occupation of Indo-China.

38 The Metropole Hotel in Hanoi still stands and has now been renovated by a French hotel chain, while the French Club building is now part of the Hanoi Young Pioneer Palace.

39 As the French translation of *The Chinese Are Like That* (which was called *My Friends the Chinese* when published in England) was titled.

Chapter 21

1 "At bowl of rice party," *Worcester Daily Telegram*, October 26, 1939.

2 Carl Crow (1941) *Meet The South Americans*, New York: Harper & Brothers, p. 1.

3 Crow, *Meet The South Americans*, p. 269. The *Daily Worker* was the newspaper of the American Communist Party at the time.

4 Lord Haw Haw was the nom-de-plume of William Joyce who had been a fascist before the war and close to the British Blackshirt leader Oswald Mosley before escaping internment and reaching Berlin. His broadcasts throughout the war were widely listened to across the UK, mostly with scorn, and he became the butt of many music hall comedians' jokes. After the war, the British hanged him as a traitor.

5 Crow, *Meet The South Americans*, p. 271.

6 Crow, *Meet The South Americans*, p. 284.

7 Carl Crow, letter to the Editor of the *New York Times*, September 1, 1941, Crow Archive, folder 187A.

8 Thomas (1892–1981) began a daily newscast on NBC in 1930. He had been the first reporter to enter Germany following the First World War, bringing back eye-witness accounts. During the Second World War, Thomas broadcast detailed accounts of the war's progress, often from a mobile truck just behind the front lines. His well-known catchphrase was "So long until tomorrow."

9   See Letter from Lowell Thomas to Carl Crow, September 10, 1941, Crow Archive, folder 187C. Also Letter from Carl Crow to Carl Van Doren, April 4, 1938 and Copy of Letter from Carl Crow to H. W. Fowler, Oxford University Press, March 10, 1938 – both contained in the Carl Van Doren Archive at Princeton University Library's Department of Rare Books and Special Collections.

10   Macfadden had three resorts at the time – the first being the former Jackson Sanatorium in Dansville, New York, which Macfadden had refurbished and renamed the Physical Culture Hotel; the Arrowhead Springs Hotel and Spa near Los Angeles; and the Hotel Deauville in Miami Beach.

11   Cosmotarianism taught that the way people got to heaven was to take good care of their physical health. It was a short-lived flop.

12   Crow did indeed provide affidavits for Polzer and his wife Annie to the American Consulate in Vienna. See letter from Viktor Polzer to Crow, August 1, 1941, Crow Archive, folder 149A.

13   Though a reply from Hoover thanking Crow for his information is contained in Crow's archive, the original letter detailing who exactly Crow thought was an enemy agent is not available.

14   Letter from J. Edgar Hoover, Director FBI, to Special Agent in Charge, New York FBI, March 19, 1942.

15   Frederick Vanderbilt Field (1905–2000) was an activist in the American communist movement. He was arrested during the McCarthy witch-hunts for refusing to name names. He was a direct descendant of Cornelius Vanderbilt, the early American tycoon, and his mother was Lila Vanderbilt Sloane Field, a wealthy heiress.

16   Owen Lattimore (1943) *America and Asia: Problems of Today's War and the Peace of Tomorrow*, California: Claremount Colleges.

17   Now Xinjiang Uygur Autonomous Region.

18   Lattimore and his wife eventually left America and moved to England where he was instrumental in establishing the Department of East Asian Studies at Leeds University.

19   See Carl Crow (1942) *Japan's Dream of World Empire – The Tanaka Memorial*, New York: Harper & Brothers.

20   Quoted in J. Simpson, "Seeing Red," *Antipode – Johns Hopkins Magazine*, September 2000.

21   Letter from Washington DC Office of the FBI to the Office for Emergency Management, May 14, 1942. The *Daily Worker* appeal was published on February 25, 1938.

22   Rewi Alley (1897–1987) was a New Zealand writer and social worker who went to China in 1927 and stayed there throughout the Long March, the Revolution, the periods of agricultural reform and the Cultural Revolution. He lived in China for 60 years, from 1927 to 1987.

23   In full, Inverchapel of Loch Eck, Archibald John Clark Kerr, 1st Baron (1882–1951) entered the diplomatic service in 1906 and became Ambassador to China in 1938. He was Ambassador to the USSR in 1942–46 and then special British envoy to

Indonesia in an effort to end the Dutch-Indonesian conflict. He was made a baron in 1946 and served (1946–48) as Ambassador to the United States.

24 Ida Pruitt (1888–1985) was from a family of American missionaries and was raised in a small Chinese village. She lived in China for 50 years and was an early advocate for American diplomatic recognition of the People's Republic of China. She was the author of *A Daughter of Han: The Autobiography of a Chinese Working Woman* (1945) New Haven: Yale University Press.

25 The Linebarger Papers are held at the Hitotsubashi University Library in Tokyo.

26 Despite living the life of a Professor, Linebarger remained interested in psychological warfare and acted as an advisor to the British forces in Malaya during the "Emergency," as well as to the US Eighth Army during the Korean War. However, he refused to advise the US army during the Vietnam War as he considered American military involvement in Indo-China a mistake. To many, Linebarger was better known as the popular science fiction writer Cordwainer Smith. He died in 1966.

27 Carl Crow (1943) "Japanning the Philippines," *The Nation*, vol. 157, issue 5, July 31, 1943.

Chapter 22

1 Carl Crow (1943) *The Great American Customer*, New York: Harper & Brothers.

2 Carl Crow, "America's first in athletics," *World's Work*, December 27, 1913.

3 Carl Crow (1942) *Japan's Dream of World Empire – The Tanaka Memorial*, New York: Harper & Brothers.

4 Maxwell Stewart, "Japan's Mein Kampf," *The Nation*, vol. 154, issue 0010, March 7, 1942. Tanaka (1863–1929) had been Minister of War in 1918–21 and 1923–24. He pushed an aggressive foreign policy and briefly intervened against Chiang Kai-shek's efforts to unify China. He was unable to ameliorate Japan's banking crisis and lost the support of the army when he sought to punish officers for the 1928 assassination of the Manchurian warlord Chang Tso-lin. The Tanaka Memorial is considered by many Japanese scholars to have been a forgery.

5 Details, notes and draft chapters of these works in preparation comprise part of the Crow Archive at Missouri University.

6 Peter Fleming (1936) *News From Tartary: A Journey from Peking to Kashmir*, London: Jonathan Cape.

7 Carl Crow (1944) *China Takes Her Place*, New York: Harper & Brothers, p. 250.

8 Crow, *China Takes Her Place*, p. 258.

9 ———— p. 262.

10 ———— p. 276.

11 The forerunner of the CIA established by order of President Roosevelt in 1942.

12 See letters from Winifred Halstead, Central Information Division, Pictorial Records Section, Office of Strategic Services to Crow, January 30, 1945; letter from Halstead to Crow, February 26, 1945 and letter from Major Duncan Lee, Office of Strategic Services, March 26, 1945. All of these are contained in the Crow Archive.

13   Carl Crow (1945) *The City of Flint Grows Up*, New York: Harper & Brothers.

14   Carl Crow, letter to editor regarding his illness, Crow Archive, folder 210A.

15   Carl Crow (1943) *The Chinese Are Like That*, Cleveland:World Publishing Company, p. 241.

Select Bibliography and Further Reading

Carl Crow Bibliography

1913 – *The Travelers' Handbook for China*, Shanghai: Hwa-Mei Book Concern.
1914 – *America and the Philippines*, Garden City, New York: Doubleday, Page & Company.
1916 – *Japan and America: A Contrast*, New York: Robert M. McBride & Company.
1937 – *I Speak for the Chinese*, New York: Harper & Brothers.
1937 – *Four Hundred Million Customers*, New York: Harper & Brothers.
1938 – *The Chinese Are Like That*, New York: Harper & Brothers. (Also published as *My Friends the Chinese*, London: Hamish Hamilton, 1938)
1939 – *He Opened the Door of Japan*, New York: Harper & Brothers.
1940 – *Foreign Devils in the Flowery Kingdom*, New York: Harper & Brothers.
1940 – *Meet the South Americans*, New York: Harper & Brothers.
1940 – *Master Kung: The Story of Confucius*, New York: Harper & Brothers.
1940 – *America in Stamps,* New York: Harper & Brothers.
1942 – *Japan's Dream of World Empire: The Tanaka Memorial*, New York: Harper & Brothers.
1943 – *The Great American Customer*, New York: Harper & Brothers.
1944 – *China Takes Her Place*, New York: Harper & Brothers.
1945 – *The City of Flint Grows Up*, New York: Harper & Brothers.

Further Reading

Histories of Shanghai are many and varied. Among the best recent histories of the city are Harriet Sergeant's *Shanghai* (London: John Murray, London, 1998) and Stella Dong's *Shanghai: The Rise and Fall of a Decadent City 1842–1949* (Perennial, New York, 2001). In addition, Tess Johnston and Deke Erh's *A Last Look – Revisited – Western Architecture in Old Shanghai* (Old China Hand Press, Hong Kong, 2004) has pictures of many of the buildings and locations mentioned in the text. There are also several more in-depth analyses of the social and cultural changes that occurred in inter-war Shanghai, including Leo Ou-Fan Lee's *Shanghai Modern: The Flowering of a New Urban Culture in China, 1930–1945* (Harvard University Press, Massachusetts, 1999) and Hanchao Lu's *Beyond the Neon Lights: Everyday Shanghai in the Early Twentieth Century* (University of California Press, Los Angeles, 1999). Ellen Johnston Laing's *Selling Happiness: Calendar*

Posters and Visual Culture in Early Twentieth Century Shanghai (University of Hawaii Press, Honolulu, 2004) is a useful study of the wider trends and practices in Shanghai's unique advertising culture.

Related Contemporary Bibliography

Abend, H. E. (1930) *Tortured China*, New York: Ives Washburn.

Abend, H. E. (1943) *My Life in China, 1926–1941*, New York: Harcourt, Brace & Co.

Arnold, J. (ed.) (1926) *China: A Commercial and Industrial Handbook*, US Department of Commerce, Washington DC: Government Printing Office.

Auden, W. H. and Isherwood, C. (1938) *Journey to a War*, London: Faber & Faber.

Barber, N. (1979) *The Fall of Shanghai*, New York: Coward McCann.

Bashford, J. W. (1916) *China: An Interpretation*, New York: Abingdon Press.

Bland, J. O. P. (1921) *China, Japan and Korea*, London: Heinemann.

Bland, J. O. P. and Backhouse, E. (1910) *China Under the Empress Dowager*, London: Heineman.

Chennault, C. L. (1949) *Way of a Fighter: The Memoirs of Claire Lee Chennault*, New York: G. P. Putman & Sons.

Couling, S. (1917) *Encyclopedia Sinica*, Shanghai: Kelly & Walsh.

Fleming, P. (1936) *News From Tartary: A Journey from Peking to Kashmir*, London: Jonathan Cape.

Fleming, P. (1933) *One's Company: A Journey to China in 1933*, London: Penguin.

Foster, J. (1930) *Chinese Realities*, London: Edinburgh House Press.

Geil, W. E. (1904) *A Yankee on the Yangtze*, New York: A. C. Armstrong & Son.

Gunther, J. (1939) *Inside Asia*, New York: Harper & Brothers.

Hahn, E. (1941) *The Soong Sisters*, New York: Garden City Publishing.

Hahn, E. (1944) *China to Me*, New York: Doubleday, Doran & Co.

Hahn, E. (2000) *No Hurry to Get Home*, Emeryville, California: Seal Press.

Hahn, E. (1963) *China Only Yesterday, 1850–1950: A Century of Change*, London: Weidenfeld & Nicolson.

Hawks Pott, F. L. (1913) *The Emergency in China*, New York: Missionary Education Movement of the United States and Canada.

Hedges, F. H. (1946) *In Far Japan: Glimpses and Sketches*, Tokyo: Hokuseido Press.

Hornbeck, S. K. (1916) *Contemporary Politics in the Far East*, New York: D. Appleton.

Hsia, Ching-Lin (1929) *The Status of Shanghai – A Historical Review of the International Settlement*, Shanghai: Kelly & Walsh.

Lattimore, O. (1943) *America and Asia: Problems of Today's War and the Peace of Tomorrow*, California: Claremount Colleges.

Lattimore, O. (1990) *China Memoirs: Chiang Kai-Shek and the War Against Japan*, Tokyo: University of Tokyo Press.

Latourette, K. S. (1917) *The Development of China*, New York: Houghton Mifflin.

Millard, T. F. (1919) *Democracy and the Eastern Question*, New York: The Century Company.

Millard, T. F. (1931) *The End of Exterritoriality in China*, Shanghai: The ABC Press.

Misselwitz, H. F. (1941) *The Dragon Stirs: An Intimate Sketch-book of China's Kuomintang Revolution, 1927–29*, New York: Harbinger House.

Misselwitz, H. F. (1946) *The Melting Pot Boils Over: A Report on America at War*, Boston: The Christopher Publishing House.

Morse, H. B. (1908) *The Trade and Administration of the Chinese Empire*, New York: Longmans, Green & Co.

Morse, H. B. (1909) *The Guilds of China*, London: Longmans, Green & Co.

North-China Daily News & Herald (1917) *The New Atlas and Commercial Gazeteer of China*, Shanghai.

Peyton-Griffin, R. T. and Sapajou (1938) "Shanghai's Schemozzle," *North-China Daily News*.

Powell, J. B. (1945) *My Twenty Five Years in China*, New York: Macmillan.

Putnam-Weale, B. L. (1917) *The Fight for the Republic in China*, New York: Dodd, Mead & Co.

Reinsch, P. S. (1911) *Intellectual and Political Currents in the Far East*, Boston: Houghton Mifflin.

Reinsch, P. S. (1922) *An American Diplomat in China*, New York: Doubleday, Page & Co.

Ross, E. A. (1922) *The Changing Chinese: The Conflict of Oriental and Western Cultures in China*, New York: Century.

Selle, E. A. (1948) *Donald of China*, New York: Harper & Brothers.

Shaw, R. (1973) *Sin City*, London: Everest Books.

Sheridan, J. (1920) *Sun Yat Sen and the Awakening of China*, London: Jarrold & Sons.

Sheean, V. (1934) *Personal History*, New York: Houghton Mifflin.

Tietjens, E. (1917) *Profiles from China*, Chicago: Ralph Fletcher Seymour.

Tisdale, H. A. (1933) *Oil for the Lamps of China*, New York: Grosset & Dunlap.

Tong, H. (1933) *Problems and Personalities in the Far East*, Shanghai: The China Press.

Tong, H. (1938) *Chiang Kai-shek*, London: Hurst and Blackett.

Tong, H. (ed.-in-chief) (1947) *China Handbook 1937 to 1945: A Comprehensive Survey of Major Developments in China in Eight Years of War*: Chinese Ministry of Information.

Tong, H. (1950) *Dateline: China, the Beginning of China's Press Relations with the World*, New York: Rockport Press.

Viles, J. (1939) *The University of Missouri: A Centennial History*, Columbia: University of Missouri Press.

Wu Ting-fang (1914) *America Through the Spectacles of an Oriental Diplomat*, New York: Frederick A. Stokes Company.

Appendix

Chinese Provinces

Then	Now	Then	Now
Anhwei	Anhui	Kiangsu	Jiangsu
Chekiang	Zhejiang	Kirin	Jilin
Fengtiang	Liaoning	Kwangsi	Guangxi
Formosa	Taiwan	Kwangtung	Guangdong
Fukien	Fujian	Shantung	Shandong
Honan	Henan	Shensi	Shaanxi
Hopei	Hebei	Sinkiang	Xinjiang
Hupei	Hubei	Szechuen	Sichuan
Kansu	Gansu	Thibet	Tibet
Kiangsi	Jiangxi		

Chinese Cities

Then	Now	Then	Now
Amoy	Xiamen	Ningpo	Ningbo
Anking	Hefei	Peitaiho	Beidaihe
Canton	Guangzhou	Peking	Beijing
Chefoo	Yantai	Port Arthur	Lushan
Chengchow	Zhengzhou	Shasi	Jinsha
Chengtu	Chengdu	Sian	Xian
Chinkiang	Zhenjiang	Soochow	Suzhou
Chungking	Chongqing	Swatow	Shantou
Dairen	Dalian	Tientsin	Tianjin
Foochow	Fuzhou	Tsinanfu	Jinan
Hangchow	Hangzhou	Tsingtao	Qingdao
Hankow	Hankou	Yunnanfu	Kunming
Kalgan	Zhangjiakou	Wenchow	Wenzhou
Mukden	Shenyang	Wusih	Wuxi
Nanking	Nanjing		

Areas of Shanghai

Then	*Now*	*Then*	*Now*
Chapei	Zhabei	Paoshan	Baoshan
Hongkew	Hongkou	Putong/Pootung	Pudong
Hungjao	Hongqiao	Siccawei	Xujiahui
Kiating	Jiading	Whangpoo River	Huang Pu River
Nantao	Nanshi (the old Chinese City)	Yangtzepoo	Yangshupu

Index

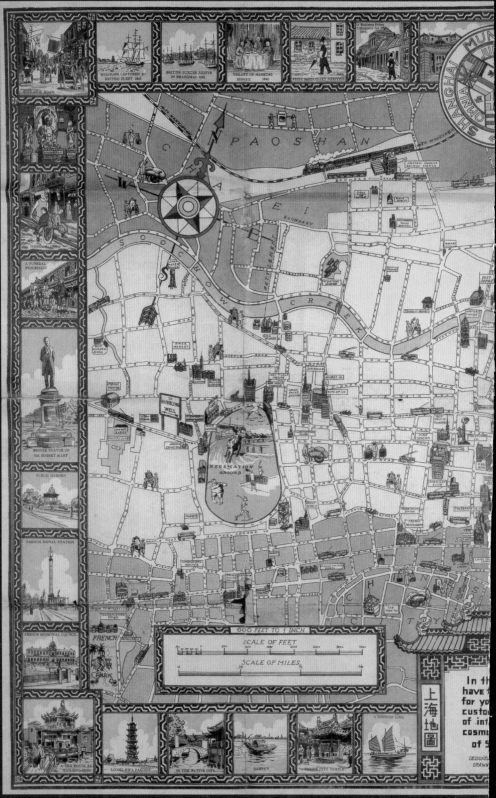

Shanghai 1935 – as seen by Carl Crow